CW00540917

Finding the Words

I wish either my father or my mother,
or indeed both of them, had minded what
they were about when they begot me.

LAURENCE STERNE
Tristram Shandy

This world is a comedy to those that think,
a tragedy to those that feel.

HORACE WALPOLE
to Anne, Countess of Upper Ossory, 1776

The love will have been enough.
All those impulses of love return to the love
that made them. Even memory is not necessary
for love. There is a land of the living and a
land of the dead. And the bridge is love.
The only survival. The only meaning.

The Marquesa de Montemayor's
last letter to her daughter
from THORNTON WILDER'S
The Bridge of San Luis Rey

Finding the Words

A Publishing Life

JON WYNNE-TYSON

MICHAEL RUSSELL

First published in Great Britain 2004
by Michael Russell (Publishing) Ltd
Wilby Hall, Wilby, Norwich NR16 2JP

Typeset in Sabon by Waveney Typesetters
Wymondham, Norfolk
Printed and bound in Great Britain
by Biddles Ltd, King's Lynn, Norfolk

ISBN 0 85955 287 X

As it has taken five years of my uncertain ration
of remaining time to research and write this fourteenth book,
I dedicate it to *all* my long-suffering family
with apologies and love.

Contents

Acknowledgements

I am indebted to John Fowles, William Rees-Mogg, Michael Sissons, and Barry Turner, also to the estates of Alan Clark, Noël Coward, John Gawsworth, Geoffrey Grigson and M. P. Shiel, for use of material evident to any who read further; to my diaries whose daily blank pages have challenged me to record religiously if too often inadequately each day's events since 1 January 1939; to the Centaur Press archive (all twenty or so battered boxes); to Keith Thomas whose helpfulness exceeded his kindness in providing the foreword; to *The London Magazine* who have published 'Go Carefully with Words'; and by no means lastly to my length-sensitive publisher Michael Russell whose ruthless banishment of even some of my better bits was conducted with such elegance and wit that the surgery was almost painless; should the patient die, his share in the blame must be the greater.

Go carefully with words;
   they are the stuff
      of dreams and evil,
         hope and change.
Creators and destroyers,
   words set us up
      and put us down.
Empires have fallen
   on the tinctured tip
      of a syllable;
history has U-turned
   for a phrase.
Minds know the harm in words,
   hearts sense their power.
Words clamped between covers
   make a book; imprisoned,
      hid from the light,
         pages close-paired
            prove our distrust
               of crowds.
Go sparingly with words;
   they can bring joy
      or uttermost despair.
Words can wear wings
   and yet be shod in clay.
Cherish and tame them,
   teach them and learn from them,
      make them your friends –
they can home back on you
   or fly free
      into the pale thin air,
         unpredictable as doves.
Words can bring peace; as casually, wars.
Do not release them lightly to the stars.

                                                J W - T

Foreword

Anyone who bought books in the 1960s and 1970s or who haunts the second-hand bookshops today will know the publications of the Centaur Press. If you are fortunate enough to possess the five volumes of John Leland's *Itinerary in England and Wales* or the three volumes of Richard Ford's *Handbook for Travellers in Spain*, it is ten to one that you have them in the Centaur Classics edition. The role of that series was to reprint books of real merit which had become unobtainable. These minor masterpieces, undeservedly forgotten, included the Diary of the Irish poet, William Allingham, a vivid record of Victorian literary life, and Richard Gough's *Human Nature Displayed in the History of Myddle*, the absorbing contemporary account of a Shropshire village at the end of the seventeenth century. There were also the great Elizabethan and early Stuart translations of Ovid, Pliny, Plutarch, Camoens, Ariosto and Tasso; there were minor poets, like John Oldham, W. S. Landor and William Barnes (the latter in a new and definitive edition); and there were unclassifiable treasures, such as Reginald Scot's *Discoverie of Witchcraft* and Joseph Spence's *Anecdotes*.

What these titles had in common was that they were all pleasurable books which were out of copyright and thus available to be reprinted; at the same time, they were too recherché to be of interest to the big commercial publishers, but had not yet received the attention of the university presses. The Centaur Classics were not cheap, but they were handsomely produced, they were usually edited or introduced by contemporary scholars, and they met a real need.

The Centaur Press was the single-handed creation of Jon Wynne-Tyson. In this, his autobiography, he gives a distinctly uninhibited account of the problems which faced a small, independent publisher in the second half of the twentieth century. We learn the history of the Centaur Press, from its founding in 1954 to its eventual sale in 1998. The independent publisher can publish good books for their own sake and is under no pressure to maximise profit. Jon Wynne-Tyson was able to commission delightful monographs on chimney pots and Post Office letter boxes. But his was a precarious freedom; and a delicate balance had to be struck if the enterprise was to remain both small and solvent. The Centaur Press managed to survive, by adding a few new titles each year and maintaining a long back list, keeping books in print far longer than do most 'commercial' publishers. But the problems of warehousing, marketing and distribution were acute, as was that of finding a satisfactory outlet in the USA. In J. M. Cohen and Geoffrey Grigson, Jon Wynne-Tyson had two superb advisers; and their discriminating signature is very apparent on the Centaur Classics list. I suspect that the series would have done even better if it had avoided abridgements, selections and inferior editions. The success of Leland's *Itinerary* and Ford's *Handbook* was due to their being reprinted in full; by contrast, Philemon Holland's translation of Pliny's *Natural History* and John Nichols's *Literary Anecdotes* were doomed from the start, because they were merely abridgements. People who want books like that tend to want the whole thing. And all the time there was the knowledge that the best titles might be taken up by Oxford University Press or Penguin and reissued in superior editions.

After twenty years of the Centaur Press, Jon Wynne-Tyson began a deliberate shift in its direction, culminating in the foundation of the Kinship Library. As his memoir makes clear, he is a man of independent and strongly-held opinions. In particular, he has a deep concern for the sufferings of all sentient beings, animals as well as humans. He shares Albert Schweitzer's view that 'until he extends the circle of his compassion to all living things, man will not himself find peace'. He has set his views out eloquently in his own books, *The Civilised Alternative*, *Food for a Future* and *The Extended Circle*; and he introduced the Kinship Library to the Centaur list to be a vehicle for reprints of classical works on animal rights and welfare, like Humphrey Primatt's *A Dissertation on the Duty of Mercy and Sin of Cruelty to Brute Animals* and J. Howard Moore's *The Universal Kinship*. This has been a valuable service to scholarship, for the original editions of some of these books are now very rare. It also has a serious moral purpose, in extending awareness of animal suffering and intensifying the determination to reduce it.

Whether Jon Wynne-Tyson is right in seeing an intimate connection between the cruelty of human beings to each other and the human exploitation of non-human species is a matter on which there is room for argument. What is indisputable is his own role in alerting public opinion to the issue. His autobiography is thus an important document in the history of changing sensibilities. It is also a reminder that, in a world of vast publishing conglomerates, dominated by philistine accountants and greedy shareholders, and concerned with sales rather than quality, the need for the independent publisher has never been greater.

With an actress-turned-writer for his mother, and with Dodie Smith and Noël Coward as virtually his adopted aunt and uncle, Jon Wynne-Tyson has never been short of colourful acquaintance. He gives a graphic account of the people he met on his travels in the United States and in the West Indies. His narrative abounds in picaresque encounters with predatory and unscrupulous publishing rivals and with well-meaning but disorganised authors. There are memorable anecdotes of Muriel Spark, seen here in litigious mood; of John Gawsworth, the alcoholic poet and 'King of Redonda'; and of Stephen Potter, the inventor of one-upmanship, whose own life seems to have been one of unrelieved chaos. There are also vivid depictions of the practicalities of being a one-man publisher, whose warehouse was an agricultural barn, open to the weather and passing animals, and whose marketing department consisted of a converted perambulator in which bulk mailings of new catalogues were carried to the post office.

The author himself emerges as a restless workaholic and perfectionist, perpetually subject to psychosomatic symptoms, and a burning idealist who agonises about the fallen world in which he finds himself but has the courage to live by his convictions. Publisher, novelist, dramatist and moral reformer, he has found time for his family as well as for serious causes and he has an unexpected taste for sailing and fast cars. Jon Wynne-Tyson is, in the best sense of the word, an eccentric. He defies the categories and he deserves to be read.

All Souls College   KEITH THOMAS
Oxford

I
Finding the Words

Finding the Words is a book about books, about those who write and publish them, and about why and how a born-to-books loner started, ran, made a living by, and disposed of his small firm in the second half of the twentieth century.

My reprehensibly unplanned drift into publishing was preceded not by university, but by several years' work of little apparent relevance to a bookish role. I spent the brief postwar period in Quaker relief teams; running a residential club in Camden Town for young people as unqualified as myself for finding their peacetime niche; 'enumerating' for the Royal Commission on Population; compiling surveys of listeners' responses for the BBC and other corporate evaluators of social change and tastes; skivvying as a ward orderly in London's University College Hospital until promoted to theatre dogsbody in charge of anaesthetic equipment and the subsequent trolleying of patients to ward or post-mortem room; and as a freelance salesman of children's toys. Then in February 1947 I found my first, if similarly short-lived, 'proper' job in the book trade. This was as assistant in the prestigious art bookshop Zwemmer's in Charing Cross Road, under the stressed but tolerant eye of Anton Zwemmer's manager Mr Beeson. My neophytic help can have done little to lighten his burden, but he bore up well for three months. Then, in need of more income – for I had no assets, private means, or prospects – I was tempted by the chance to sell American fashion magazines to the London gown trade. This paid quite well, gave me experience of dealing with some of the toughest traders to be found (mostly) east of Broadcasting House, but had 'dead end' written all over it. Having reached the age of twenty-three with little to show for it, and judging that it might be pride rather than integrity to decline an introduction to my mother's publisher, I made an appointment to see Katherine Webb, the power behind the throne of the legendary Walter Hutchinson, sad and deranged tyrant over what was then the largest book publishing consortium in the British Isles. Eight months later, having been rocketed into the suicidal role of advertising manager for the entire group, I was dismissed by Walter who seemed to have got over his phase of believing I could do no wrong. During this phase he had once fired everyone except for myself and Mrs Webb and ironically it was I who had made the case for their reinstatement. Now I had to move on to a further multiplicity of jobs, the most enjoyable being that of 'literary adviser' to the under-directed and long-absorbed publishers Williams and Norgate. On a monthly retainer basis, this lasted from June 1949 until April 1951.

By then I had married and had moved from the two rooms I had rented for four years in Hilda Spencer's delightful Georgian house in Pond Street, Hampstead – a huge improvement on previous digs, and a time of happy memories. Her brother Richard Carline shared it with Hilda, who was Stanley Spencer's first wife. As everyone in the Carline and Spencer families seemed to paint, the house had no need of wallpaper, not even in the smallest room. Between the tall shuttered windows of my first-floor sitting-room was a self-portrait by Stanley. One day Richard said I could have it 'for a tenner'. The equivalent of a month's rent was beyond serious contemplation, so a bargain was missed.

For reasons clearly unconnected with my earning capacity, Hilda had indicated that neither she nor Stanley would have opposed any honourable inclination I might feel toward their daughters Unity and Shireen. I think my mother must have been a suitability reference – she had known the family when we lived in a top flat in the High Street in 1930–33. What Unity and Shireen thought of such an idea is not on record, but such are the hormone-driven priorities of youth that I never put their feelings to the test. Instead, I married in idiotic haste a talented but deeply unstable girl, Joan Stanton, whom I had met through Richard when she was taking part in a Hampstead festival; and on 1 January 1951, with Joan pregnant, we moved to the lesser charms of a gloomy ground-floor flat in East Finchley, where our daughter Caroline was born two months later. One of the few better memories of our two-year stay there was an enormously tall pear tree from which, in our second autumn, I picked and sold to the local greengrocers literally hundredweights of pears. Perhaps a vestige of commercial acumen was beginning to appear ...

The marriage was a disaster from the start. Joan had real artistic, musical and literary talent, but she preferred to rely, more indolently, on her natural allure of pathos and pulchritude, in my case a deadly mix. We had married in May 1950, and I should have read the signs. As I emerged from the Heath Street florists that day, carrying a bunch of red roses, there was a sudden snowstorm. Omens are less helpful in retrospect.

By 1950 the pointers were favourable for being able to make my way in publishing, or perhaps writing. The books I had brought to Williams and Norgate were well received on publication, and by December the firm's turnover had increased by over 400% in six months. More to the point, I was later told that only one of the titles I had added to their list had made a loss. On the writing side, there were good portents too. The *Observer*'s Jim Rose accepted a poem; the editors at Methuen, offered my first book, provisionally called *Use of Bath*, a short and light-hearted guide to surviving digs, rooted for it unanimously. But the managing director wanted some facetiousness toned down here and there, and I was seduced by the unqualified and cash-up-front enthusiasm of a new and far smaller publisher who brought it out under a different title before going to the wall (a demise delayed, not provoked, I must hastily add, by my first appearance between covers). For these and other reasons I might have been forgiven for supposing that at last – for I was twenty-six in July – my feet were on a ladder that could lead somewhere. But a faltering marriage was not the ideal platform for sensible decisions. As it was, good times were not yet around the corner.

It is possible – if only just – that my perceptions would have been clearer had I not, in September 1948, caught a bug that put me into Hampstead's New End Hospital as an interesting and potentially terminal case. The bachelor years of inadequate and unbalanced self-catering were suspected of having laid me open to infection, and to recurrent 'anxiety states', as they were then called. These may have been warning signs, but youth feels immortal. I had worked that summer for a ship-broking uncle in the blitz-battered Tilbury and London docks, and the assumption was that I had picked up anthrax, or some other unusually virulent bug, from imported hides or some other disease-prone consignment. Perhaps it was all connected with the chronic fatigue syndrome that developed a few years later after a mismatch of drugs prescribed for influenza. In any event neither my judgement nor experience had been able to cope with Joan's profoundly maladjusted state, for which I was to learn – contrary to professional advice received before our marriage – there could be no cure. By then it was small comfort to discover that older and supposedly wiser people than myself, including several psychiatrists, had been equally unsuccessful in understanding her complex sociopathic condition, or in making an accurate prognosis.

The decree absolute, granted in May 1955, was a formality of small importance compared with the outcome of the custody proceedings a year earlier. The lawyers seemed more concerned with professional confrontation than with what might be best for our daughter. Thankfully, Mr Justice Sachs cut through their irrelevancies and granted me 'care and control' (an uncommon concession to fathers in that era). Considering the modest material security I could offer her, this showed a percipience for which I am lastingly grateful. I wish he were still alive to learn how wonderfully she was to vindicate his judgement.

But the toll of these frittered years of marriage had been financial as well as nervous. In March 1953, on the eve of Caroline's second birthday (her delight in Edward Lear's 'Calico Pie' had prompted the nickname 'Tilly-loo'), I had already accepted that occasional journalism was leading nowhere, that the brevity of the necessarily part-time and short-term jobs was telling me something, and that solid lasting employment was – in Wodehousian jargon – of the essence.

The main victim of this overdue realisation, and of the demands on time and nervous health made by the stressful months of the custody proceedings, was an excellent and long-assimilated firm of paper merchants in the City. During 1953 and 1954 I spent nineteen months trying to convince Spicer's and myself that I could become an ambitious underling in a large organisation. They hoped, and at that stage I felt I could assure them, that my connections would enable me to sell book papers to publishers. An ethically-run firm of good reputation, they were fair and patient, and I did my best, despite spending some of my training period playing cricket in the basement sample room with a strawboard roll and scrunched-up 'quad crown offset cartridge'.

Although moderately successful when I hit the road, I had a pit-of-the-stomach feeling that it could never be for a lifetime. I learned about the product and understood my mission, but selling a brand-new commodity, be it a book or a new idea for drawing corks, is one thing; selling sheets or rolls of paper that a handful of mills have supplied to numerous competing merchants, who then sell it on to printers and publishers under different 'house' names, is quite another. The merchant's salesman is faced by two choices: to woo the satisfied customer away from his present supplier; or merely to locate the dissatisfied customer and secure his business with promises of superior service and longer credit. After a while, and understandably, Spicer's became restive about my inclination to opt for the latter way in, rather than for both. Our parting, marked by a three-months' salary send-off, was amicable, but inevitable.

By then convinced that I was an unlikely candidate for industry's prize for Corporate Man of the Year, and unsatisfactory material for any firm seeking long-term commitment, I knew I must settle for self-employment, regardless of the small snag that I had no capital and virtually no expectations. However, I had at least decided that my future lay in books, and probably in publishing, bolstered by Williams and Norgate's gratifying approval of my editorial judgement.

It was one thing to identify the goal, another to reach it. From October 1954 I went back to free-lancing: reviewing books for newspapers and magazines; condensing books for *Reader's Digest*; selling for printers' blockmakers; even holding the writer Louis Golding's Hamilton Terrace fort while he worked on a book in the Greek islands and married his long-suffering Annie. There was a small additional perk in selling review copies to the Fleet Street library suppliers, who lived fatly off literary editors and their ill-paid hacks. I would only manage three or four at a time but I recall the editor Peter Quennell, whose office in the early 1950s was in Coleman Street, staggering in with two bulging suitcases. The total proceeds must have been well into three figures, and his journey was doubtless a weekly occurrence.

All this was not an adequate answer to such problems as paying the rent, far less the salary and keep of au pairs before and after Joan had moved on to pastures new. She was to die comparatively young of a brain tumour, though this was said to have no connection with her unstable personality. It was sad to follow, and where possible to try to ease, her bleak and rootless progress, but the truly psychopathic personality is mesmerised by its self-destructive star.

John Kings was the small publisher who had set up shop under the somewhat grandiose imprint of Britannicus Liber and was so keen to publish *Use of Bath*. He brought it out under his preferred title of *Accommodation Wanted* in 1951. It was delightfully illustrated by Joan under her maiden name, and received some good reviews. I even caught a sailor manifestly enjoying it on a bus. I couldn't resist mentioning, modestly, that he had met the author. He didn't believe me.

Pleased by the little book's reception, John wanted us to produce a follow-up, so Joan and I collaborated on an even shorter 'funny', *Grin and Bear It*, an irreverent take-off of Marie Stopes's lyrical portrayal of the joys of motherhood. But John's tiny business was already in trouble, so time was lost and the project was shelved. This proved to be a blessing in disguise for my own career, if not for John's, for while working in University College Hospital I had made friends with a fellow floor polisher, lavatory cleaner, and conscientious objector, Graham Farmer, whose father owned a cooperatively-run printing firm in Paddington. Following a chance meeting, I showed Graham the typescript and Joan's draft drawings for *Grin and Bear It*. His enthusiasm prompted his father to underwrite the production costs of an initial four titles, on a pay-when-sold basis, if I could meet all other costs in setting up as a publisher. So Centaur Press Ltd came into being in the autumn of 1954, with no resources other than the loan of £1,000 from a friendly publisher who had faith in my ability to make a go of it. Most of the money went on overheads, including an essential car, but I was able to repay the insistently anonymous backer in fairly regular instalments.

Graham became a director of Centaur, but in 1956 his Christian Socialist ideals took him and his wife to Madagascar, where he spread the word not only as a missionary, but by starting a printing business run on similar cooperative principles to those of his family firm. This major move must have influenced his father to restrict our agreement to the four starting titles, and Graham gave up his Centaur directorship. The dismal failure of the most costly of these titles was doubtless the deciding factor. Unfortunately, the failure was the last of the titles to be published, by which time modest receipts from its rather more successful predecessors had been absorbed by overheads. Our parting was amicable and regretful, but as Farmer's were repaid on a when-sold footing, they did not lose disastrously. But three years were to pass before I could make Centaur my more-than-full-time occupation.

The headaches of starting a small publishing business on a shoestring have nothing on the difficulties of disposing of it in a climate where money is for most the sole consideration and the only true god; but that, and the years between, may be gathered in due course. Those years have not lacked their crises, but on balance the advantages of independence – at least for someone of my temperament and lack of material ambition – have far exceeded the drawbacks, thanks in part to my having been spared any more serious illness than a mix of imperfectly labelled psychosomatic symptoms. I had no formal training; rudimentary business acumen; minimal commercial nous; nil independent means; a woozy conviction that small, if not always beautiful, was at least more workable; and a disinclination to cultivate those literary and media moguls who can be helpful on life's ladders. I would come to moan at being faced by a daily desk load that in small firms of comparable size might be shared among two or three people, but those moans have been stifled by great gratitude that bills could be paid, a family raised, and that I have had the good fortune to enjoy, or at worst find tolerable, the varied chores that truly solo publishing entails. Had I – as in recent years seemed more than likely when no satisfactory home for Centaur was offered – died in harness, I would at least have been able to thank the dimming stars that I had not only survived being a mini-entrepreneur, but had known job satisfaction through most of a working life-time. Which is a lot to be grateful for.

Human language – according to those who see our species as superior to all others – is the major difference between *Homo sapiens* and the rest of the animal kingdom. But are our deepest levels of communication improving? Leaving aside the curious but not yet buried assumption that, for some reason unknown to God or nature, non-human creatures necessarily lack the means for inter-communication – patent nonsense to those who have studied them objectively in their natural habitat, rather than in laboratories and those prisons we call zoos – it is clear that our ability to remember, evaluate, and use words is vital to making and sustaining relationships, and therefore to self-advancement and recognition from those around us. Words make our human society go round, as, for their world, do the linguistic and more subtle communicatory skills of other life forms if left to live the lives they were designed for.

In publishing, the ability to find the words – others' words as much as our own – is a constant concern and satisfaction. This had a bearing on my setting up as a publisher, seeing that my foremost ambition to make my way as a writer was unlikely to be realised without serious prostitution, or risking the health and happiness of my family. A bourgeois decision, no doubt, but 'art is all' is a more inspiring slogan for the footloose young than for those on the sharp end of life's grittier realities.

For myself, one of those realities was that although I had shown some aptitude for putting words on to paper, I lacked confidence in my oral proficiency. Although reasonably articulate and at ease with family and close friends, I have never been comfortable in large groups. Perhaps much of a lifetime spent alone at my desk for most of every day has not helped. Humanity en masse may be a reassuring prospect from a politician's rostrum, or a balcony in the Vatican, but in myself it has always stirred a certain unease. I came to realise that I was not suited to a working life within a corporate business structure; and even running my own business, I would feel more at home at home, rather than staffing an outside office. I was brought up solely by a watchfully religious mother. I saw little of my father until the last few years of his life, when he came to live with us after his third wife opted for her own 'space'. My formal education ended on the outbreak of the Second World War, and anything of value that I had learned by the summer of 1939, when I became fifteen, had been from my mother's ever-questioning and diligent mind, and from merciful access to books. Via a paternal gene, no doubt, I was far from idle physically, enjoying then and to this day almost any non-team game, especially if it involves hitting a moving ball. Nonetheless, I am well aware of the huge slice of life that has been frittered on such elusive pursuits as perfecting the unreturnable serve in squash, the cross-court backhand slice at lawn tennis, or the languidly laid 'less-than-half-a-yard' chase in its ludicrous but glorious precursor, royal (aka court, aka real) tennis. I cannot argue with those wholly intellectual friends who despise such trivial pursuits when they delight in pointing out that in the time squandered I could have written or published many more books. Only fellow idiots will understand the compulsion to achieve mastery over a small, bounce-able sphere.

My mother's direction, though well-meaning, to question acceptances, and to value empathic and creative goals, took small account of the problems facing an idealistic youth obliged to make his way in a far from idealistic world. Mary Baker Eddy's *Science and Health with Key to the Scriptures* was a poor substitute for *Boy's Own Paper* and the hands-on doings of Harry Wharton at Greyfriars School, and somewhat inadequate preparation for a wartime teenager with few street-wise skills apart from experience at identifying which of the planes above were likely to drop bombs.

In the harshly competitive postwar world of Fleet Street, publishing, and what we now call the media, I was an innocent about the store set on cronyism, the cultural brotherhood centred on school, university, regiment and club. Being more at ease with women, and with men older than myself, I was constitutionally incapable of making up to useful contacts whom I could not envisage as friends. It was not prissiness or puritanism that from an early age made me diffident of seeking favours, but a naive assumption that – independent of my contemporaries' goodwill – ability would be recognised, and opportunities would come for reasons of merit. This to some extent proved to be so, but during the period in which I met life's relentless bills not only by journalism, but by such freelance work as reading publishers' slush piles, and sub-editing papers for the Royal Society of Arts, all I was doing was persuading established editors that I was deserving of modest rewards for adequately performed chores. This was encouraging, but not exactly the acceleration of a career.

As Centaur gradually replaced the more ephemeral sources of income, my lack of cronyist tendencies became less of a brake on progress. By the time it was finding its hooves, I had reviewed several hundred books for a fairly wide range of publications, including *Apollo*, *Country Life*, *John o' London's Weekly*, *New Statesman*, *Observer*, *Poetry Review*, *Spectator*, *Sunday Times*, *Time and Tide*, *Times Literary Supplement*, *Tribune*, and *Truth*. By such mild networking – mostly during the years 1949 to 1953 – my switch from journalism to publishing ensured that I was at least known to literary editors and others who might feel an interest in my change of horses. This was an advantage to me in the early years of publishing, less so when they eventually moved on. Some of their youthful replacements were apt to ask 'Who?' if I had to ring them, for working seven days a week in the sticks meant I very seldom attended London functions.

Grateful though I am for having been enabled to make an adequate living by such a pleasant occupation as publishing books, when asked if I regret having passed on Centaur into younger hands, I can truthfully answer 'No.' It is a different world, one that has changed more quickly and fundamentally than in perhaps any previous half-century. I hope that by writing this book I shall have helped to depict a period when the printed word was the product of a more hands-on technology; when a book was a prized and proudly conceived artefact; and the obsession with maximising profit was constrained by the feeling that one's priority was to contribute to readers' enlightenment. This may sound a touch highfalutin, but it was of genuine concern to at least some of my contemporaries.

There are still, no doubt, opportunities for small publishers to set up and survive. Certainly they will need more familiarity and liking than I have felt for the present state and promise of technology. Yet despite declining values, they will still meet many more interesting, pleasant, amusing, and (though I hate the term) genuine people than they might find in most commercial spheres. That bonus, and having at the end of the day created a few shelves of books whose contents do not belie their challenging but tasteful exteriors, must be worth more than a row of genetically modified beans.

2

A Room with a View

There was nothing pretentious about the beginnings of Centaur Press. Before I started work for Spicer's, Joan, Tilly and I had moved, early in 1953, to a small flat at the bottom of Highgate West Hill. No. 9 St Anne's Close had been converted from the stables of a big Georgian farmhouse by its owner George Fairweather, a tiny but distinguished Scottish architect under the control of a large wife and a brace of severe daughters.

Since Tilly's birth in March 1951, my freelance writing and other work was paying the household bills, but nothing more. Space was tight, and nearly everything had to happen in the living room. While it was fitting that the odd article or poem should be dashed off when sharing the one-bar electric fire with the slowly drying nappies of my first-born, the publishing ambience fell a little short of John Murray's premises in Albemarle Street.

However, I was already sceptical of the implication in Sir Stanley Unwin's landmark book *The Truth About Publishing*, that minimum set-up requirements included a Bloomsbury office, the odd million pounds, and a sprinkling of aristocrats' daughters in vaguely secretarial capacities. Stanley was only trying to frighten off the opposition, and his own employees were so emaciated that they could hide behind lamp-posts; so I had no qualms about starting at the other end of the entrepreneurial spectrum, though mindful of his warning that 'It is easy to become a publisher, but difficult to remain one; the mortality in infancy is higher than in any other trade or profession.'

In June 1954 the solicitor who was handling my divorce found a moribund business that cost me all of fifteen pounds. The Granta Publishing Company had been producing the magazine of that name, so its articles of association fitted my intentions for Centaur fairly closely. The change of name was a trifling technicality.

I then had to create enough working space for building a modest empire. My chippy skills were just up to erecting shelving at the far end of the living room, so I was able, with the addition of three sliding doors made by a firm across the Heath in Hampstead, to obtain filing and limited storage space at one bound. Most of the remaining area was taken up with two chairs, a radiogram, a sagging divan, and a hefty Victorian sideboard (for which I had had to pay 'key-money' to get the Finchley flat), later replaced by a wall-length modern cupboard made out of solid afromosia planking that I had to cut with a handsaw. The only item that might slightly have impressed the visiting author, had one thought of calling at that stage, was also ex-Finchley – a substantial roll-top desk that I positioned to overlook our small garden and the not-much-larger paddock beyond. From there, as she grew, I could keep an eye on Tilly as she played on her swing or chatted up the male talent from the houses across the paddock.

By the end of May 1954 Joan had left and I engaged a live-out nanny-au pair who, on the other side of Hampstead Heath, had been housekeeping for Cyril Joad of Brains Trust fame. With the divorce pending, and it being too soon to judge how Tilly might react to the separation, a resident au pair seemed unwise. As publishing, initially, could only be part-time, when I needed to make business calls I usually left Tilly in Hampstead with Hilda Brook, a remarkable woman who was Joan's mother's oldest friend and was later to marry, and literally be the saving of, Laurence Hills, co-founder with her of the Henry Doubleday Research Association. But sometimes I took Tilly with me, and once left her with the receptionist when calling on a literary editor.

Centaur's first four titles were a mixed bag. *Grin and Bear It* was the first, published in November 1954. The next three – *Harlequin's Revenge*, *The Best Years of Their Lives*, and *Victor Silvester's Album* – came between May and November the following year. *Harlequin's Revenge*, four plays for puppets, was the work of Margaret Stanley-Wrench, a Newdigate prize-winning poet whose work was deservedly anthologised. She was a writer who genuinely 'reached and delighted all ages', a term of praise in those days. Peter de Morny's *The Best Years of Their Lives* was a collection of potted biographies written under a pen-name by my mother, whose early talent for journalism had not yet been eclipsed by her later more scholarly output. The twenty-nine digests of famous women who did their best work, and often began new lives, after the age of forty, was well reviewed, sold out, and brought in useful funds from serialisation and other sales of subsidiary rights. Both my mother's book and *Harlequin's Revenge* deserved reissue by more suitable imprints, and although *Grin and Bear It* went into a new and revised edition in 1960, just when the dark clouds of penury were starting to show a silver lining, it too failed to find a later life with a publisher with a more suitable list.

Victor Silvester's Album was a frankly cynical throw-together of articles by or about dancers, producers, and the shows and ballrooms in which they performed, all compiled with 'lavish illustrations' drawn from the files of such trendy magazines of the period as *Dancing Star*, *Heiress*, *Teen and Twenty*, and *Music at Home*. As it was Peter Craig-Raymond's idea, he did the scissors and paste work and wrote some of the text. It was perhaps the sorest thumb in Centaur's corpus, not least because its poor sales repaid Farmer's support with a loss, creating a damaging hiatus.

In 1956 no new Centaur title appeared. Income from the first four, supplemented by work for Louis Golding, and by continued journalism, allowed a period of somewhat rapid breathing space in which to review my haphazard thirty-two years, to consider how to make better use of the next thirty-two, to marry in July Jennifer Tyson (stet, but no known relation) whom I had met in February 1955, and to work out how to keep Centaur's flag twitching while seeking the opportunity to plant it conspicuously on some more commercially hopeful project.

In 1957 another four titles were published, three of them slim volumes by good minor poets, the fourth a curious exercise in breast-baring: *Judge Not* by Aymer Roberts. Sub-titled 'An autobiographical confession of man's spiritual, secular and sexual nature, which every adult should read', this was, I suppose, my first and only flirtation with the steamy world of 'adult' literature. The blurb on the front flap, where less discretion seemed permissible, announced that 'The main purpose of this unusual autobiography is to promote a greater understanding of the problem of homosexuality'.

Well, even in the days when that great bookseller Sir Basil Blackwell – whose wonderful Oxford establishment was to become Centaur's best customer by far – found his soul tarnished by a reading of *Lady Chatterley's Lover*, you could have fooled us. Jennifer and I each read the typescript once, and then we read it again. It failed miserably to strike us as likely to put either the author or ourselves into court for corruption of the nation's morals. Any contrary conclusion was not helped by the fact that Aymer Roberts was the pseudonym of a scholarly, religiously-minded, happily married, and rather elderly barrister, with three impeccable daughters and a son, all of them well educated, well spoken, well mannered, as only the cream of what used to be called the upper classes can effortlessly be. Moreover, 'Aymer's' family could hardly have been older or more distinguished, liberally laced with military, naval and ecclesiastical connections, and a JP ancestor said to have prosecuted Shakespeare for poaching deer in his ancestral parklands. Of his charming wife's background, little was revealed in the book, but she handled with great dignity and fortitude the occasions when it was necessary to exchange visits for the furthering of her husband's revelations.

But perhaps I had founded Centaur in the twilight days of Britain's love of understatement, for to our surprise *Judge Not* was made an *Observer* Book of the Year, and the *Medical Review* found it 'full of enlightenment for those living at times when moral sense and justice are conspicuously absent'. Dear Stevie Smith – she lived near us in Highgate, and we consoled each other with coffee and sympathy when we both worked for Newnes in Covent Garden – wrote in the *Spectator*:

> The book shows, in the most fascinating, absurd way possible, how an eccentric English gentleman – soldier, barrister and theological student – a gay, friendly creature with homosexual leanings, enormous intellectual appetite, and some brave and hilarious adventuring, notably in India, can square being at every moment every inch his own not always edifying but most honest self with Christ, faith and fondness. Incidentally, what he says about homosexuality is very sensible.

One could only admire Stevie's perspicacity for deriving such pleasure from a book so oozing discretion and obliquity. Before the subtitle and blurb had even been drafted, we had only dimly grasped – so restrained was the writing – that the text was hinting at a homosexual preoccupation. True, there was a teasing mention of his childhood visits below stairs in the family mansion, and of how one of the footmen, changing his trousers before football in the park, was noticeably 'polite' in young Aymer's presence. Later, as an Army officer staying in a Normandy château, he made friends with a young man who, on their parting, pecked him on the cheek; but he himself 'experienced no physical attraction, only a sympathy and love which knows no lust'. Things looked more promising for the prurient by the middle of the book when Aymer met the fourteen-year-old son of German friends, noting the lad to be 'well built and strong, with a ruddy complexion, blue eyes and flaxen hair … a perfect Nordic specimen'. However, after some idyllic walks with rucksacks and a guitar in the Rhineland, they parted for two or three years. When, after a brief reunion in Frankfurt, Aymer learned that the boy had joined the Hitler Youth Movement, becoming 'engulfed in the frenzied fight for Freiheit', the bond was severed. Only one line in the book might today be seen as proof of sexual orientation: 'For as my readers will perhaps have gleaned, I was essentially gay at heart with laughter on my lips, even though it often masked a heavy heart.' Alas ... Nonetheless – and I feel slightly mean to mock it – *Judge Not* went into a second edition after three months, and was followed in 1960 by the same author's *Forbidden Freedom*. That, however, confined itself to castigating the Government for not implementing the Wolfenden Report, and, being even less racy, sank without trace, hardly qualifying as 'adult' in the naughtier sense of that word.

For the books published in 1957, and for some later titles, I used the imprint of Linden Press, for no better reason than that Linden is my middle Christian name, for which I have had no other use. Most were printed by a friend since early childhood, John Villiers Sankey. With 'a fairly typical philistine middle-class English background', an indulgent and musical Christian Science mother, and a Rudolph Steiner education, John had been 'wildly excited' by his early discovery of Braque, Modigliani, Matisse, James Joyce, D. H. Lawrence, Henry Green, Ezra Pound, Dylan Thomas, David Gascoyne, and other such innovators of gentler days. He started to write verse – in our teens we co-edited, by post, an incestuous typed 'magazine', imaginatively entitled the *Tyson Times*, with a contributor and readership base of two – but he became depressed by the competition from more keenly-honed egos, and decided that if he could not write poetry, then he 'should at least be handmaiden to the arts and *must not profit by it*'. Flirting with anarcho-syndicalism at the time, he found this idealistic resolution not too difficult to realise. He set up a hand-printer in his bedroom in the family home and launched a small magazine called *The Window*. This he edited from 1950, first publishing Harold Pinter, Michael Hastings, Patricia Beer, Margaret Crosland, Vernon Scannell, Alan Brownjohn, and other candidates for the postwar poetic firmament.

John's dedication attracted the attention of contemporaries in the field, notably American magazine publishers wanting to save on printing costs. Thus encouraged, he installed a proper press in a corner of a jobbing printer's in Islington, later moving to his own premises in Tufnell Park. From there he played an empathetic part in establishing the Beat poets, gaining a modest but transatlantic reputation for printing the work of such luminaries as Charles Olson, Robert Duncan, Denise Leverton, Robert Creeley, and Gary Snyder. From printing *Origin* (Boston) he went on to handle mostly Californian magazines, including the *San Francisco Review*. Ginsberg's *Howl* was followed by all the Pocket Poets published by Lawrence Ferlinghetti, and the latter's own work at the City Lights Bookshop. By the mid 1950s, sixty per cent of his turnover lay in the USA. Numerous poetry and general literary magazines followed. Notable Villiers Publications productions (for that was his imprint both as printer and publisher) were the entire run of Marvell Press (Hull), from Larkin's *The Less Deceived*, through Snodgrass, Enright and others. From about 1958 to 1962, Villiers's work included the journal *Listen* and the whole run of Scorpion Press (Peter Porter, George MacBeth, and Bernard Stone's limited signed editions of the work of Christopher Logue and others). From then on, his work centred increasingly on trade journals, and academic and short-run book printing. In my case, with poetry figuring strongly in the Linden Press's early output, it made sense to put work in the hands of an old friend who was also extremely local.

Publication of 1957's titles had highlighted a gap between full-scale commercial publishing and the meretricious products of the 'vanity' publishers. That gap, at its most distinguished level, has long been filled by university presses able to subsidise theses and other works of minority concern that hold too little profit to interest the commercial houses. Few publishers, however, have not published work subsidised by the author, the author's friends or relations, or by an institution or special-interest group. The main difference between such publishing and that of the vanity firms (leaving aside qualitative considerations) is that the latter will usually take on almost anything if their own profit is ensured.

The Linden Press offered, to work of an adequate standard, the benefit of reasonable (and often shared) printing costs, Villiers's short-run bias helping to keep these to a minimum; distribution by the firm that sold Centaur titles to the bookshops; production; cataloguing; despatch of review copies; warehousing and the meeting of orders; return to the author or backer of the major proportion of all sales receipts, or less if costs had been shared. It was not a bad package, but for Centaur it was more a means of showing output than making fast bucks. In a few cases, where the work was suitable only for private publication – in other words, either arcane or frightful (or both) – I took the role of farmer-printer, passing it on to Villiers with printing instructions if asked, but not supplying the Linden Press imprint or attempting to market it. John kept an imprint of his own for private-consumption material, such as family histories and autobiographies.

Today the division between trade and vanity publishing has been further muddied by the now quite common practice of self-publishing. This can achieve good results if done properly, but a number of firms have been set up to offer self-publishing services – a concept which is at best something of an oxymoron. 'Self-publishing' means you do it your-self, employing the printer, designing (or at least collaborating over) the lay-out, the style, and the jacket, handling the publicity and despatch of review copies, calling on the bookshops, invoicing and sending off orders from your warehouse under the stairs or your bed. In short, learning and applying all you can of the publishing process. Between handing over such chores to someone offering 'self-publishing' services, and going to a vanity firm, there can be a very hazy distinction. In 1989 Centaur was to publish the first edition of my booklet *Publishing Your Own Book* in which, *inter alia*, the fine lines between these specialist activities are briefly drawn.

To have published the young poet Patrick Galvin's first book, *Heart of Grace*, without some form of subsidy would have been impossible in 1957. Fortunately, Paddy was not without female admirers. In fact, despite becoming known as the foremost Marxist Irish poet, he married a beautiful deb of impeccable breeding. One such devotee, with Christ-mas pending, undertook to bear the brunt of the production cost of the 300 copies. Our mutual agreement that a selection of Paddy's poems should be between covers was endorsed by the subsequent reviews, the best coming from Robin Skelton in the *Manchester Guardian*, from Edwin Muir in the *New Statesman and Nation* (his identification of 'a rude but authentic poet' was nicely on target), and by A. Alvarez's assur-ance in the *Observer* that his 'poetry is the real thing'. The influence of Lorca was noted, but seen as not yet getting out of hand. A few months later, again under the Linden imprint, I published the tenth book of the older poet, and friend of Galvin, Ewart Milne, whose shared politics and nationality ensured a satisfactory Irish press, and that both selections were not overlooked by the *Daily Worker*. But Ewart had meagre reviews for *Once More to Tourney* in the English press, apart from seri-ous attention in *Time and Tide* by James Reeves; not surprisingly, per-haps, for his very Irish humour lacked the universal appeal he thought his right. My ten years' correspondence with him may hold interest for historians of Irish poetry, but when he learned that his overly support-ive wife Thelma, who enjoyed some 'means', had extended her largesse to subsidising another poet's work, and that that poet was his friend Paddy Galvin, his responses became so consumed by hurt and passion that the letters may have turned to ashes. Certainly I have been unable to trace a single sheet on the relevant file. But he was devastated by Thelma's later death, and unlike the laid-back Paddy was a sad case of the ageing poet out of kilter with a world slow to recognise the extent of his talent. His acute sensitivity to any comment on his work made difficulties for the author/publisher relationship. Every word written to him had to be weighed with infinite care, for the tendency to detect, in the most innocuous or even flattering term or passage, a double meaning, a deep-seated antipathy, or a woeful lack of comprehension, imposed a severe burden on the sender. Even to chance a comment on the weather was to stray toward perilously thin ice.

A more quietly endearing man, light years away from any recognised Movement and at his best a superior poet to Ewart, was Eric Knight, whose *Beyond Words* was the second Linden Press poetry selection. Editor, actor, cricketer, businessman, organist, theatre manager, and equally catholic as a man of letters (to use a term of his day), Eric was little known outside his Birmingham world, and happy enough in the shadows. His sometimes faith-impelled work was not in tune with postwar 'realism', but enough poems justified their publication. However, coming from a poet unknown in the south, under a new and untried imprint, the selection brought nothing but a cautious nod from a handful of provincial papers, none of which acknowledged the best he had to offer.

The more successful of the other 1958 and 1959 titles included Robert McCurdy's *Smoking, Lung Cancer and You*, an informed and powerful little edge-cutter written by a medical officer of health in a climate still saturated by wishful thinking. It received responsible attention in the *Daily Telegraph*; nothing in the *Times* group other than a brief attempt by the *TLS* to kill such regrettable subversion at source; and firm endorsements from the *Lancet, Nursing Mirror, Royal Society of Health Journal, Chest and Heart Bulletin*, and all the other medical and nursing journals who had received copies. It was, I believe, the first book on the subject to be addressed to the general public. Helped by an advertisement in the *Manchester Guardian*, quoting strong recommendations from the Director of the Central Middlesex Hospital, and the Chairman of the National Society for Cancer Relief, it finally sold out by 1964.

Making their mark, if in less challenging fields, were Armin Arnold's *D. H. Lawrence and America*, surprisingly overlooked by university presses, and tachist painter Frank Avray Wilson's *Art into Life*, a difficult but important work that paved the way for Routledge and Kegan Paul to publish its follow-up, *Art as Understanding*, five years later with a foreword by Herbert Read commending both books as a 'comprehensive and profound analysis of the social significance of the art of our time'. *A Tale for the Fall of the Year* was a selection of Margaret Stanley-Wrench's poetry. Its title poem, like the also included 'An Old Woman Remembering', was repeatedly broadcast on the Third Programme.

The author of another admirable work was Cyril Upton, who had responded to an entry in *The Writers' and Artists' Yearbook*. His letter from the 'Villa l'Horizon, Boulevard du Jardin Exotique, Principality of Monaco', was intriguing, the seductive address seeming out of keeping with the letter's opening:

> I have put into book form a thesis on eclectical mysticism which has had much success in lecture form in the French universities and academies. It is, in effect, an attempt to find a middle way between the extreme materialism of the scientific humanists and the obsolete superstition of the dogmatic religions, in the light of contemporary scientific progress. It is not, of course, a 'popular' subject, but controversial articles and correspondence are perpetually boiling up in the press – particularly the *Sunday Times* and the *Observer* – which go to prove that this eternal question still interests a great number of people despite the current popular taste for the superficial. My book has been written after a lifetime of travel in India, China, Tibet, and, of course, Europe.

Panaceas for the world's ills were then, as now, the bane of publishers; not because solutions are not desperately needed, but because the vast majority of submissions are either well-meant but uninspired restatements of moribund dogmas, passionate interpretations of esoteric theories rooted in obscure reaches of astrology, or highly subjective visions supported by bewildering charts, symbols, and other paraphernalia from the darker corners of the occult and off-beat.

Upton's letter and synopsis raised no fear that his book would be in these categories, though I had reservations about its title, *What IS Wisdom?* I suspected that the stress and the question mark would not help it to reach first base with literary editors; and if an author's work is not reviewed, it is virtually impossible, in the majority of cases, to let the public know of its existence, let alone its content and quality. As it is, editors have space to grant reviews to only a fraction of new books.

But Upton was wedded to his title, so I drew comfort from the likelihood that a widely travelled, highly educated, fluent writer, who lectured at the universities of Grenoble and Aix-en-Provence, was a Member of the Aix Academy, an officer of the Légion d'Honneur and of French Public Instruction, and a holder of the golden Palmes Académiques, would be granted enough press attention to get his book moving. Although it was obviously not going to be a serious earner, its subject matter was in line with the direction I hoped my list would take, and this touched on the very *raison d'être* for starting my own firm.

I replied almost immediately to Upton's realistic and businesslike letter, and in his equally prompt response he stressed his need of advance copies for a USA lecture tour planned for the autumn. His friend Dr Victor Purcell, a distinguished Cambridge lecturer in Far Eastern History, had already chosen the route of private publication for a book in which his publishers had seen inadequate reward. This strengthened Upton's determination.

It was already May (1959), so rather than waste time awaiting his typescript, I obeyed gut instinct and rang him to say I would come to Monaco and read the script there. If it fulfilled my expectations we could save weeks by discussing editorial, production and promotional matters on the spot. Armed with some of the books I had already published, I took the train from Victoria to Paris. It was not a journey to prepare one for a discussion of matters practical, philosophical and spiritual with a sophisticated elderly man I knew from two letters and a three-minute telephone call.

A sad and loquacious Polish lady shared my compartment, and there was no getting away from her. She barraged me with ideas for the books I could commission her to write, and her qualifications for writing them. 'Sex! My God! What I could write about that!' I didn't doubt her. At the Gare du Nord the steam engine was exchanged for a diesel, and I was able to book a couchette for the night to come. For the remaining daylight hours, however, she kept on at me without pause, and would have continued through the night had the other berths not been filled by raucous matelots returning to Toulon. I have never slept well, and my allergic rhinitis responds hysterically to a single cigarette across an aircraft hangar, let alone to five sailors dragging on Gauloises in the closeness of a couchette.

At 10 a.m. Upton met me on the sunlit platform at Monaco, and took me to the Monte Carlo Palace Hotel. There he left me to recover some semblance of human form before joining him and Madeleine, his solicitous French second wife, for lunch in the Villa l'Horizon apartment she had taken over from her parents in 1936. She was clearly devoted to him, expressing her feelings volubly, although they had been married for nine years.

The flat had a stupendous view over the Condamine and across the shimmering sea. The books, photographs and figurines in Cyril's study testified to his concern with concepts more Eastern than Western. I learned that after being at St Paul's School with Bernard Montgomery, a man of similar physical stature but of distinctly different mental mould, he had first been a medical student. After the First World War he became a director of physical education at RAF Cranwell, then served during the Second World War as an intelligence officer with the Resistance in south-east France. This progression from a largely physical and active life to one governed by preoccupation with the philosophical and spiritual did not surprise me. My parents had several friends in the Services and the arts who, disillusioned by conventional 'remedies' for the tragic consequences of human inadequacy, particularly the inability to link cause and effect, had tried to address more hopeful, if longer-term, solutions that focused on values and realities neglected in most educational systems. It was one such friend, Air Marshal Sir Victor Goddard, admiring my mother's dedication to the thinly shared task of civilising the civilisers, who recommended the editors of *Who's Who* to send her an entry form. They did so, but by the time I had retrieved it from the drawer to which she relegated secondary matters, and completed the form on her behalf, she was terminally ill. Her biography appeared in *Who Was Who 1971–1980*, posthumously.

The following days in Monaco confirmed numerous shared perceptions and priorities that are discovered all too seldom between strangers. Not that 'strangers' is the appropriate term, because it is possible for two people meeting for the first time to feel as if close friendship is merely being resumed after long separation. Where, as with Cyril, there is the bonus of a compatible sense of humour to support an almost telepathic awareness of the other's thoughts, age differences disappear, and friendship, as distinct from acquaintanceship, can be slipped into almost instantaneously.

Although cautiously reviewed by a handful of national and provincial papers, *What IS Wisdom?* inevitably met the incomprehension of those incapable of understanding a mind dissatisfied with both materialism and dogmatic religion. However the second half of the twentieth century comes to be defined by the historical pigeon-holers, it will not be seen as the era of the mystic. Nevertheless, the book sold out in time, for there is a widely scattered hunger now as then for concepts that challenge what some see as the abysmal values of the present. But the causes of spiritual evolution and humane education tend to be restricted to word-of-mouth within the ranks of those seeking a more workable pattern. Censorship resides in silence and neglect, not in fairly conducted examination of new concepts. The British understand this form of mind control better than most.

The titles for which Linden Press offered a subsidy basis, with the back-up of Centaur distribution, helped to make the imprint known as I marked time pending some more positive sense of direction. On the whole, I think I avoided any temptation to sacrifice quality for much-needed income, and no author complained that his experience had not matched my expectation. As the financial basis was the reverse of the normal royalty contract, where the publisher takes the sales receipts and pays the author a (usually) 10% royalty, the arrangement made more friends than profits.

Another disappointment in this period, if less deep-seated than the poor response to the Upton book, was my inability to do more for Centaur's first work of fiction, Laurence Clark's *Kingdom Come*, a satirical novel that in 1958 brought good reviews from the papers that mattered. John Metcalf, in the *Sunday Times*, found 'Mr Clark has done an Anglo-Indian Kafka on us ... under the firm control of a caustic and original mind'. Simon Raven in the *Spectator* welcomed a 'triumph ... that will have enormous appeal not only to professional soldiers but to anyone blessed with a glimmer of imagination'. But despite the *Observer*'s 'exquisitely funny', the *TLS*'s 'delightfully absurd, almost Firbankian day-dream on the tribulations of the Anglo-Indian military man', and other favourable notices, there was no interest in paperback or other rights. In the hands of a larger publisher with the time, know-how, and those damned 'connections', *Kingdom Come* could have set Laurence on course for recognition as a major fiction talent. It was a sobering early lesson on the dangers of a small firm, its imprint unknown for fiction, sticking a novel into its list with all the relevance of a cook hiding an unshelled walnut in a plum pie. *Kingdom Come* also provided my first major experience of most booksellers' indifference to new small publishers, and the *Bookseller* gave me my head on the subject in a letter they published on 7 February 1959.

However, I stuck my neck out again a few months later by publishing *Behind the Smiling Moon* by Michel Fourest. It was a parody of the humourless, moody, transient, sensual self-centredness for which the fiction of such writers as Françoise Sagan was admired, complete with a T. S. Eliot quotation and a rather vague French tag to lend that touch of authenticity. The blurb's warning that 'The raw details of this powerful first novel will not shock the open-minded reader', and its Paris setting, may have helped, but I was surprised when it was taken by a paperback publisher following reviews that, failing to sense the tongue in the cheek, were largely and rightly critical of the central character's callous self-obsession. About the kindest comments were 'splendidly written' (*Manchester Evening News*), and a rave notice in the *Shetland Times*, possibly indebted to the clear air of those islands, or more probably to a literate sheep. Oswell Blakestone in *Time and Tide* came nearest to suspecting it should not be taken straight, but he doubtless guessed I had written it during a slack weekend after fulminating to him about the quality of so much fiction that was gushingly welcomed by those determined to be seen as in touch. I was probably wise not to have offered it to another publisher under my own name, and I was quite pleased by the *TLS*'s verdict that it was distasteful. It was a kind of vindication. The only review that made me feel slightly ashamed was quite long, quite serious, admiring of a 'fine study of introspection', and of the 'commendable economy of words', and appeared in *The Times of India*. If, as may well be the case, the reviewer was young enough to be still alive today, I hope he will forgive the spoof.

These skirmishings and experiments were all very well as time-markers and list-fillers while I felt my way, but the wagon needed hitching to a star. In the strange way that these things can happen, it was a long-deceased second-hand bookseller in Charing Cross Road who watered the scarcely sprouted seed of an idea that was to provide Centaur's backbone in the decade ahead.

3
'But westward, look, ...'

Even today, London's Charing Cross Road is associated in the literate public's mind with books. In the 1950s it was still the hub of the second-hand side of the trade, though most of the more rarefied anti-quarian dealers were housed then, as now, in grander premises west of Regent Street. CCR's retail outlets were less in evidence, Foyle's and Better Books being the main meccas for those able to afford publishers' latest products.

On the east side of the road, south of Cambridge Circus, between Litchfield and Great Newport Streets, was the main cluster of second-hand shops. Zwemmer's, handling both new and second-hand art books, occupied the north-west corner of the block. The south-west corner, no. 48a, was the domain of E. Joseph. Enjoying west- and south-facing windows, Joseph had a commanding view of all three exits from Leicester Square underground station, at least when the customary murkiness of his plate glass had received the infrequent attentions of a duster. The Arts Theatre Club was a few yards to the east, the Hippodrome Theatre less than a stone's toss away, and bang opposite on the west side of the road was – and still is – Little Newport Street, a popular passageway to the fruitier temptations of Soho. Joseph, it could be said, had it made.

And it showed a little. Some found him a grumpy old skinflint, and he could afford to be impatient with time-wasting callers. The London antiquarian book trade suffered Joseph as one of its 'characters'. At a Sotheby sale in the mid-1950s I watched him bidding, by a mere wrin-kle of his unmissable nose, then going on to disparage others' would-be acquisitions by raising his bids in shillings rather than pounds. The ploy was ignored by Maggs, Quaritch, Marks, Thorpe, and his other competitors, who restored the status quo immediately and without apparent irritation.

Grumpy and sly he may have been, but I knew from my Zwemmer days that he was a mine of knowledge.

'I've started a publishing business,' I told him.

He nodded. 'Going for the real money, are you?'

'Well, it's not coming my way unless I can find some decent backlist titles. I'm thinking of a series. Classic stuff, preferably.'

'Like Johnson and AMS, you mean?' Johnson and AMS were two of several North American firms who put out stark offset reprints of anything that would sell a few hundred copies to world libraries, with nothing added and nothing taken away from whatever past edition they had chosen to photograph. No editing, no updating introduction, no apparatus (notes, appendices, etc.), often not even a dust-jacket.

I shuddered appropriately at this coarse suggestion. 'No,' I said, 'I want to publish new editions, even if some have only a new introduction or just a foreword.'

He pointed at his south window. 'That's what you're after.'

'That' was a three-volume set of Thayer's *Life of Beethoven*, sunbathing as best it could behind the grubby glass, and standing slightly apart from its fellows, as if conscious of its better breeding. The set had a lean on it, its tops were grimy, and the spines a faded blue. It looked as if it had been seeking a friend for some time.

'It looks ...' I began.

'You couldn't fail,' he said. 'Everyone's after it. It's the *great* life.'

He was so positive, and I was still young. Well ... ish.

'It would cost a pretty penny to kick off with a three-volume work,' I said dubiously. 'I don't have capital, and you know what printing costs are.'

'Well, that's your problem,' he replied, beginning to look bored. 'But if you raise any, that's the book you've been looking for. I'll knock five bob off, just to get you started.' He retreated into his dingy cave, a spider on the lookout for fatter flies than young publishers *manqués*.

I cannot recall whether I later told him the outcome of his recommendation. But I did let him know that I had reprinted the Thayer as the first title in the Centaur Classic series, albeit by offset with only a four-page additional introduction, and that I was very grateful for his suggestion. Although the gestation period was horrendous, at the end of the day Joseph's tip vindicated his judgement. Profits from the subsequent reprint went a long way toward covering the cost of our later home in Sussex.

Alexander Wheelock Thayer, an American, wrote *The Life of Ludwig van Beethoven* in English, but had not finished it when he died. Translated into German by Hermann Dieters, three volumes were published by Schneider of Berlin in 1866, 1872, and 1879. Dieters himself died before the fourth volume could be completed and the whole work revised from Thayer's notes. This was eventually tackled by Hugo Riemann, who added volumes four and five in 1907 and 1908. The five volumes were later translated after further revision by Henry Edward Krehbiel and published in three volumes by the Beethoven Association of New York in 1921. The set in Joseph's window had some excuse for looking a little weary.

Its new life as a Centaur Classic, with an introduction by Alan Pryce-Jones, then editor of the *TLS*, began in 1960. Pryce-Jones did not over-state the case by writing that the work was 'one of the most exhaustive and judicious biographies ever attempted; the central document upon which our knowledge of Beethoven must rest'. Most of the serious papers that mattered were to review it with praise and pleasure. But although the best things in life are often free and simple, neither – as will be seen – was the case with Thayer. The Centaur Classics series became the backbone of the Centaur Press through the 1960s, and the major part of the backlist thereafter, but its success was ensured only by a degree of application and stress debatably incommensurate with the financial return, welcome and needed though that was.

Although the early 1960s were to be the turning-point in Centaur's fortunes, much of the second half of the 1950s had been absorbed in laying the basis. Distribution was one of the biggest headaches for very small firms setting up with minimal capital, as doubtless it is today. In essence, distribution means the warehousing of the books, and their invoicing and despatch to meet customers' orders. Those orders – at least for general rather than academic or educational titles – were largely obtained from and through booksellers, for whom the award of the local library budget could mean the difference between decline and survival. The biggest publishers produce enough titles in sufficiently large editions to pay their sales people to call on most trade and institutional buyers. This vital part of the exercise is usually assumed to be an inseparable part of the distribution process. Few small publishers, however, can afford to keep their own salaried sales teams on the road, their turnover being inadequate to cover the costs. Their best hope, such as it is, is of being carried by the sales force of a bigger publisher, whose own wares are understandably likely to be first out of the rep's bag, and more persuasively sold.

One alternative for the smaller publisher is to employ freelance representatives on a straight commission basis, which may or may not include a percentage toward travel costs. But under this arrangement the 'bag' is being shared not with one large publisher, but sometimes numerous small ones, from whose combined revenue the rep hopes to earn enough to cover his on-the-road overheads. All sorts of problems can arise from following this route.

Further down the scale, though not necessarily less effective, is reliance upon in-house selling to selected outlets by the small publisher himself. At this level the publisher's turnover, and the number and frequency of new titles, are likely to be too small to be of interest to another firm's sales team or to the majority of warehousing and despatching businesses. To the small publisher trying to give his all to the crucial search for new books and then their manufacture and promotion, the headaches of distribution can be an onerous additional chore, though if he happens to have ample storage space under his own roof, or in outbuildings, he can sometimes get by with occasional personal calls on key bookshops.

For the first four titles in 1954 and 1955 I was able to get the Rockcliff Publishing Corporation to act as sole selling agents and distributors. They held enough stock to meet six months' estimated needs, most of the balance being held by Farmer's in Paddington. As Rockcliff used their own invoice forms and listed the titles in their catalogue, I was spared investment in those areas, and did not publish our first catalogue until 1958. Rockcliff also sent out review copies at the princely cost of three and a half old pence per copy, plus postage, and circulated advance dust-jackets to the library suppliers. Their sales figures were not staggering, but all that might reasonably be expected by a new firm needing to create enough of an image to impinge on the fickle goodwill of stressed booksellers. I was later to realise what a good deal Rockcliff had in fact offered.

My being lent a pre-war Rolls-Royce, outwardly showing no sign of having covered the 200,000 miles on the clock, probably helped in the early struggle to find both distribution and credit-flexible printers and binders. Prior to Rockcliff taking us on, I had called on a firm in South Audley Street, parking the Rolls a short distance from their entrance (this before the days of parking meters). It seemed appropriate therefore, when invited into the managing director's office, to go to the window and murmur, pointing: 'Do you think the banger should be all right down there for a little while?' I left the building as an apparently acceptable client, but for forgotten reasons they seemed not quite right for Centaur.

A week later I had a less uplifting interview with Peter Guttmann, owner of Hammond, Hammond and Co. Ltd, a publisher with an

advertised interest in humour, though on that occasion there was little
to amuse. He told me, with some justice, that my list was too nebulous
to tempt his highly-honed distribution skills, and doubted my admission that I lacked the capital to guarantee a more tempting output
unless turnover could be perked up. I should leave publishing to savants
such as himself. At first I thought he was being self-mocking, then that
he was perhaps genuinely trying to save me from the pitfalls of my
youthful idealism. When, however, I confirmed my determination to
make a go of publishing, he said he would introduce me to someone
who might change my mind. He pressed his desk bell, the door opened
and in came John Kings, the sheepishness on his face vying with an
attempt to smile. On Guttmann's shelves I had noticed a copy of
Accommodation Wanted.

'There you are,' Guttmann said triumphantly, waving a hand toward
John as though he had been a hatstand, '*this* fellow thought he could
start his own firm, and now he's glad to be working for *me*.' John, I
gathered, was in the throes of divorce and other problems, which must
have made his embarrassment more painful than mine. I left that
Bloomsbury Street office more determined than ever to show the
Guttmanns of this world that somehow or other I would confound
their knavish tricks and, if unsuccessful, go back to cleaning lavatories
in the nearby University College Hospital rather than seek employment
by Hammond, Hammond. Guttmann died eleven years later and his
firm disappeared into the mist of mergerland, as that beavering bookseller Ian Norrie prettily put it in his last (1982) editing of Mumby's
great work, *Publishing and Bookselling.*

The arrangement with Rockcliff – who, as it happened, took over
Hammond, Hammond after its own merger with James Barrie – could
not survive the crisis produced by the failure of the Silvester book, as
distributors quite reasonably expect continuity and expansion from
their clients. With no new titles on the immediate horizon, Rockcliff's
turnover, along with Centaur's, was clearly set to decline.

This was no shock to the system, as I had never felt that the distribution arrangements were satisfactory. In 1955 I approached numerous
printers and publishers, most of my suggestions seeking from them
more than distribution at its most basic. I gave to each what I felt was a
quite interesting, if somewhat eclectic, list of the titles I had lined up for
publication. These included a biography of Sheila Kaye-Smith by G. B.
Stern, both family friends; *Pillar and Post*, a monograph on public
lighting; a book by Havelock Ellis's fond companion Françoise Delisle

on her continued communication with her dead lover; a vegetarian cookery book by Roy Walker's wife Janet, which I passed on to Neville Armstrong's company Neville Spearman, feeling that the ever-underfunded Walkers would enjoy more royalties if the book was under Neville's imprint rather than mine; a biography of Sir Henry Lunn; memories of the 1920s by W. Macqueen Pope; a feminist guide on how to escape male dominance by creating your own space on a houseboat; and the life story of the founder of a chain of old folk's homes for whom I had worked until it was evident that his personal gender problems might get out of hand. Also cited were promises from mainly family friends such as D. L. Murray (one of my mother's unrequited suitors of her middle years); B. L. Jacot (a First World War flame who lit no candle for her with his more-macho-than-Hemingway approach); Gerard Hopkins (with whose guidance I was offered the opportunity to build up a sound line in translations); and Eleanor Farjeon, who claimed baby Susan as her 'spiritual goddaughter'. (Obediently, Sue took on Eleanor's same caring and looking-after nature that her godmother immortalised in her poem 'Mrs Malone'.) In the event, all but one of these proposals had to be dropped in favour of the more certain returns from concentrating on the Centaur Classics series.

Among the most helpful and kindly responses to this list of boyish enthusiasms were those from Mark Goulden of W. H. Allen, Robert Hale, A. S. Frere of Heinemann, John Boon, Max Reinhardt, and the ever-courteous J. Alan White of Methuen. It was White who had been willing to take on *Accommodation Wanted* under its earlier title, had I accepted some suggested alterations, and I regretted later that financial straits and impatience tempted me to fall for the unqualified enthusiasm of John Kings, delightful man though he was.

Even before accepting that I must publish under my own steam, I had considered the possibility of small independent publishers (the species was officially recognised in 1974 by capital initials in Ian Norrie's first revision of Mumby) combining to solve, at the least, their selling and distribution problems. In 1954 I had discussed this major small-publisher dilemma with Christine Campbell-Thomson, the literary agent, who had known my mother (then Esmé Wynne) and Noël Coward when their youthful friendship was at its peak. Christine mentioned her recent meeting with Lord Darwen, who had set up as a publisher a few months earlier, but seemed uncertain what should happen next. On 6 July (irrelevantly, my thirtieth birthday) I called on him at Darwen Finlayson's offices in Bloomsbury Street. Cedric's lack of experience soon came through, and he seemed grateful for such modest pearls as I was able to drop in the hours we then spent in his office and in the nearest Oxford Street branch of Lyons. In both locations I noted his addiction to strong Indian tea. This, I was to learn, all too often replaced the square meal his poor constitution doubtless needed. He was interested in my SIP plans, and suggested we join forces, but a close working collaboration was not at that stage my aim with anyone knowing even less than I did; though we became and remained friends until his death in 1988.

In February 1956 Cedric and I had a meeting with John Calder, who in 1949 had started his firm of John Calder (Publishers) Ltd, later Calder Publications Ltd. Depicted by his fellow publisher Anthony Blond in his 2004 memoir as a 'small, neat, huffy, puffy walrus of a Scot' who 'had always been a braver man than I', John was and still is best known for his focus on avant-garde European literature and censor-testing raunchiness. John was also interested in some kind of SIP merger, but more concerned at that stage with taking other firms' distribution under his rather too flighty wing. Except that he was then married to the wildly extravagant and glamorous Christya Myling, a minor actress of Swedish/Brooklyn origins, John's enthusiasm for the peanuts that were likely from handling other SIPs' humble goodies was not easy to understand. In 1955, the year in which he sold his shares in the Calder family's commercial empire, and attended no fewer than fifty-two operas, he lived in a large flat with sexy bathrooms in London's Wilton Terrace. That his creditors were finding it increasingly difficult to reach him was unsurprising, for he spent much time touring Europe in a newly-bought Rolls-Royce, in search of suitable locations for a film in which Christya was to appear, and having steamy nights in expensive hotels when not fending off the constant stream of lusting males with similar designs on his difficult but friendly wife. He subsequently (2001) wrote of these and many other matters in his mammoth autobiography *Pursuit*, billed as unexpurgated, which was as true as that it was un- (or very little) edited. Nudging a quarter of a million words, it is in parts an informative and entertaining read, perhaps especially for small publishers, opera buffs, voyeurs, and those prone to malevolence.

Although, in the still bleak postwar years, new publishers were coming, and some as quickly going, most of them, including Cedric, to judge by his office address, showed signs of being in thrall to Stanley Unwin's awful warnings and the priorities spelled out in *The Truth about Publishing*. The ups and downs of these here-today-gone-tomorrow minnows in the publishing pond were a staple of the two leading trade papers, *Publishers' Circular* (the doyen by twenty-one years, having been founded in 1837), and the *Bookseller* (1858). The latter was gaining supremacy under the civilised if quirkily individualistic control of Edmond Segrave and Philothea Thompson, while *Publishers' Circular* was destined to enter the 1960s – though not for long – as a monthly under the new name of *British Books*.

By now well aware that finding ideas and authors was child's play compared to selling the end product, and only too conscious of how easily the un- or under-capitalised SIP could flounder, I sent a letter to the *Publishers' Circular* which they published on 9 June 1956:

Sir,

Once upon a time there were a lot of little fish called 'S.I.Ps'. One by one they were tempted to swim in Deep Waters, wherein sailed some Enormous Creatures called 'B.I.Ps'. And if they but once plunged recklessly beyond the shallows, they had undoubtedly had it.

As one of these live-bait, reluctant to be swallowed book, line and sinker, I feel a compulsion to get into a shoal, and I invite others of equivalent fishiness to discuss whether we could not avoid our apparently certain fates by making a combined effort to solve, at least, our problems of making efficient and economic arrangements for travelling and distribution.

I believe we need not feel that the only alternatives are to be last out of the bags of the representatives already carrying several lists, or to rely upon a bigger publisher who can only consider handling us at a prohibitive commission.

I feel it should be possible under (for trading purposes – invoicing, statements, etc.) some heading such as 'The Bloomsbury Group', to combine our distribution and selling activities. A closer form of amalgamation may even be desirable, such as sharing of premises, collaboration in production, joint ownership of a van, and the employment of a packer-driver. There would seem to be many possibilities – and problems. No harm can be done if we remove our independent heads from the rock-holes and meet on common sand.

While a new concept of the Bloomsbury Group was still a long way from being realised, the responses were favourable. No one, however, offered to take on the thankless chore of coordinating the vague enthusiasms of sometimes awkward individualists into serious collaboration. With Centaur as yet contributing little to our essential income, I was equally short of time and energy to follow up my letter with more than occasional discussions.

But I had written the letter with less hope than its style might have suggested. Although, from 1958, I was to send the yearly Centaur catalogue to all the publishers approached about a SIP merger, only two of them returned the compliment before joining the non-responsive majority who apparently considered this a too costly way of keeping in touch. I had also, much earlier, when trying to get Centaur on to its hooves, done a lot of market research, offering to pass on to other SIPs the identities of jobbing printers whom I had trained up to produce adequate book work at a competitive price. One might have supposed I was trying to plant a bomb in their basements. The trouble, I concluded, was that too few SIPs had learned their trade before starting their own firms, and there is nothing more cautious and suspicious than an untrained business man. Those who know their stuff, and also that the learning curve is infinite, are grateful for a little cooperation and a good tip.

Eventually a backlog of frustration prompted an article, 'Home Distribution and the S.I.P.' The *Bookseller* published it on 25 January 1958. This time the responses were more positive, and after a meeting of small publishers convened in the offices of Imago Publishing at the invitation of Marianna Rodker, who published in the field of psycho-analysis from the end of the Second World War until the early 1960s, there were faint signs that the revolutionary suggestion that SIPs should, in some areas, consider the possible superiority of cooperation over isolation might at last take off.

It did, in the end, but not until 1962, by when our home and office had moved out of London, and Centaur's still modest but growing stock had been long held and distributed by Trade Counter Ltd, who operated from crumbling hay-loft premises in Stanhope Mews West, off Kensington's Gloucester Road. Trade Counter's working director was Ivor Davies, a kindly but maddeningly relaxed man who could usually be found trudging over the scattered contents of broken packets of his publishers' livelihood that carpeted the aisle between the book stacks, puffing contentedly at his pipe. He was also a director of Christopher

Johnson Ltd, whose owner Donald McI. Johnson MP ran his small publishing firm from the same address. As Ivor, wearing his Trade Counter hat, was in touch with so many small publishers, I had quite often spoken to him about possible SIP cooperation, and when the penny finally dropped he prompted Johnson to invite some SIPs to get together for a discussion at a cocktail party in the House of Commons on 5 March. I stressed Cedric's interest, for if anyone was fitted for the role of chairman in those rank-respectful days, it was a small publishing lord. And that is what came about. Besides Johnson and Centaur, the other firms to attend the first meeting were J. A. Allen, Blackwoods, John Calder, Geoffrey Chapman, Cohen & West, Crosby Lockwood, Darton, Longman & Todd, Darwen Finlayson, Hugh Evelyn, Kenneth Mason, Merlin Press, Peter Owen, Phaidon Press, Polonica, Scorpion Press, Sidgwick & Jackson, Charles Skilton, Vincent Stuart, and Thomas Yoseloff. William Kimber, Pall Mall Press, George Ronald, and Vision had responded with interest but were unable to attend.

By July the working name of 'Small Independent Publishers' had been replaced by 'Independent Publishers' Group', and four years later, after numerous meetings held in Bloomsbury and Soho pubs, and several three-day conferences in country hotels, the image was lifted a notch by being retitled Independent Publishers' Guild, with Sir Stanley Unwin as honorary president. I attended the first two conferences, several pub meetings, and Christmas parties, but the sixties were Centaur's busiest decade, collaboration from outside London had its logistical drawbacks, and with the feeling that I had served my purpose, and that my contributions and benefits did not justify the time needed, I resigned in December 1965. The IPG went from strength to strength, the independence of some new members becoming less apparent than their smallness, which somewhat fuzzed the original concept. Today the Guild is open not only to independent publishers, but to professionals in allied fields such as packaging and paper-selling, with a subscription approaching the three-figure mark. Smallness may be beautiful, but bigness usually takes over. But to return to the humbler scale of the mid-fifties ...

In September 1956 I asked Rockcliff to pass the Centaur stock on to John Calder, by then operating from his accountant's Leicester Square address, and distributing his handful of other small publisher clients under the imprint of Skyline Press. I was also able to shed most of what was being held in the Highgate flat. It had occupied about sixty per cent of Tilly's small bedroom, though to judge by the number of books that her own children were to keep in their rooms in years to come, the experience had not put her off the printed word.

However, in going over to Calder I had not taken into account the extent to which those with pecuniary priorities may regard others' money as something from which to make more for themselves, this being accomplished by the simple device of hanging on to it as long as possible, thereby reducing their overdrafts and adding to the return on their investments. By March 1957, with a modest programme aimed at getting Centaur airborne again, and owing sums to printers to whom I had promised instalment payments on a monthly basis, I had received neither a statement of sales nor a penny of payment from John's accountants. His family fortune derived largely from timber, and as a good Scot he would see it, I suspect, as a deserved compliment to be labelled as tighter than bark on a tree. The trade representation that was offered as part of the Calder package was clearly going to do little for a list whose only commercial hope for that year was *Judge Not*. So it was up-sticks once more.

As John and his clutch of hopeful publishers were warehoused and despatched by Trade Counter Ltd, I fell in readily with their director Oliver Moxon's suggestion that they continue to hold and despatch the Centaur stock, accounting directly to me instead of to Skyline. This helped the cashflow a little because booksellers paid Centaur direct and I received regular batches of invoices from Trade Counter's only and stalwart typist and ever-available trouble-fielder, Kay Sladden. This enabled me to keep a check on every title's progress, and to deal with errors, booksellers' inquiries, and the sending of statements to slow payers. Abandoning the Calder connection left it to me to make alternative arrangements for representation to the trade, as Trade Counter were not equipped to offer this service. For several years I employed a succession of freelance reps, a full account of which would make a volume in itself, as would my own role in selling Centaur's list to the shops. It all helped to implant certainty that personal involvement with every aspect of small-scale publishing was essential to survival.

For better and worse, Centaur remained with Trade Counter for many years. Like most distributors, however, they could hold only a working stock for clients whose turnover was rapid or who could afford to pay the warehousing cost for the entire edition of each book – a mighty item in the case of slow-moving titles. But Trade Counter had a chronic and worsening space problem in any case, and the day loomed when the bulk of Centaur's stock would have to be stored at minimal cost elsewhere. There was no hope of that elsewhere being in London. Given my determination, even need, to stay solo, a London house large enough to store all the stock surplus to the distributor's need was not an option. A sometime move out of London possibly was.

But if anything is as important to a new publisher as finding a workable distribution arrangement in the early years, it is having something for the distributor to distribute. The Thayer seemed a hopeful beginning for a series, but it was not until the middle of 1959 that the name, nature and feasibility of the Centaur Classics – as the series was to be called – firmed up sufficiently for me to seek the participation of others in getting the ball rolling.

In July 1958 I had met E. J. Carter, a director of the National Book League, at a friend's house in Hampstead. He showed interest in the problems of SIPs, and when I said I needed advice on starting a series of high quality reissues and selections of classic texts to give a backbone to a list that was so far a bit of this and a bit of that, he suggested I contact J. M. Cohen, the translator, biographer, editor and critic. Having previously been in touch with Jack Cohen over a Penguin anthology, and finding him a kindly, patient and thoughtful man of wide scholarship and with a delightful sense of humour, I lost no time in sounding him out.

At this stage I also had my eye on the possibility of publishing translations of European novelists. Jack came up with Juan Rulfo's *Pedro Paramo*, Perez Galdos's *Miau*, or 'maybe something by Enrique Amorim', but soon sensing that my lack of resources was a fact of life rather than the usual publisher's poverty ploy, he emphasised gently that not only would the translators' fees add a lot to my budget, but that I might have difficulty in selling across the pond – the fact that a novel had already been published abroad did not in itself persuade American publishers that it was a work of genius. I was disinclined to argue with him on either count. 'Why not', he asked, 'go for something needed and recognisable, such as the poems of Oldham, or if you must do a translation, then a reprint of Fëdor Sologub's *The Little Demon*?' Given my pitiful grasp of foreign languages, the Oldham sounded more like something I could get my head round, and should team with old Joseph's recommendation of Thayer's *Life of Beethoven*.

Jack, a wartime schoolmaster with a concern for detail and precision, seemed just what was needed by a new publisher of resisted formal

education and little time for the editorial research demanded by a
would-be list in the humanities. In my day I have looked a good few gift
horses in the mouth, but not that one.

By the end of 1958 only about ten of the books published could have
been called serious titles. That is, they had been reviewed where it
mattered, and had made a little money. I even sold an edition of one of
them, Armin Arnold's *D. H. Lawrence and America*, to a New York
publisher, shipping them to him as finished books with his imprint on
the jacket, cover and title-page. But it was all pretty small beer, and
Centaur's first two catalogues, showing titles to come in 1958 and
1959, did not set the book world a-quiver with anticipation.

If the learning curve had hardly left the ground, the few good
reviews had been encouraging. Like an inexperienced angler, however,
I wasn't good at winding my catches on to the bank. A book by
Michael Byrom was a case in point. A painfully sensitive young man,
with an appalled vision of human society and its values, Michael submitted a typescript entitled *Evolution for Beginners*. It was the era of
the 'outsider' and the Angry Young Man. Had his book been taken up
by a more experienced publisher with financial strength and promotional flair, many AYMs of the day might have been eclipsed, their
anger often being little more than petulant adolescent railing against
parental influences, the idiocies of officialdom, and their understandable inability to find a place in a society whose sense of direction and
priorities had been deeply damaged by the Second World War and its
prolonged aftermath.

After resisting the education offered by his English public school
(1939–40), American private school (1940–42), and American high
school (1942–43), Michael was inducted into the Royal Navy in 1944,
hastily transferred to the Infantry, equally quickly switched into the
RAMC, and then spent 1945–46 as a reluctant member of the British
Raj, where he was rapidly passed from one unit to another before being
designated as unfit either to slaughter or heal his fellow men, and
granted a medical discharge. His social record thereon was one of
nervous collapse, voluntary solitude, and meditation. He would have it
that 'the perceived status of the original artist and thinker is little
removed from that of the criminal'. His only published book by the
time we met was *Thus Spake Zumperkinck*, a comic satire published by
Andrew Melrose in 1953.

Evolution for Beginners was a book of seven essays loosely based on
the philosophical concept of Creative Evolution. It was intelligent, not

without humour, clearly 'young', but a readable and idealistic attack on materialism, apathy and complacency. The underlying impetus, however, was moralistic and ascetic, which probably did no more to commend his views to a public gearing up for the hedonism of the sixties than did his focus on the neglected teachings of Jesus Christ, and on the evolutionary understanding of Schopenhauer.

By comparison, Angry Young Men such as John Osborne (who, to his credit, dismissed the overworked label) and Colin Wilson (who drew media attention by sleeping rough on Hampstead Heath, and in picturesquely squalid digs when the weather closed in) paled into insignificance so far as the content of their unease was concerned. Nevertheless, Colin was one of the few critics generous and fair enough to give the praise due to someone who not only suffered more than he did from the state of the world, but stuck his neck out by daring to suggest the remedies:

> Michael Byrom's writing has a Shavian clarity and brilliance that held my attention until I had finished the last page. His incisiveness and the range of his ideas entitle him to be called an 'Angry Young Man' far more than most of the writers who are lumped under that heading.

Colin's commendation came in a 1958 issue of *Books of the Month*, in his review of Kenneth Allsop's *The Angry Decade*. He expressed surprise that Kenneth had not acknowledged Correlli Barnett or Michael Byrom, 'two writers of immense promise who deserved space far more than many whom Ken has analysed'. But Michael did not whinge at the lack of press attention for his book. Unlike most tyro authors, his saving grace was a strain of realism, and he had not expected it to be welcomed by any but a few of what was later to be known as 'the fringe'. Unsurprisingly, however, he seemed to retreat even further into his solitary shell, living precariously on a small private income. Although convinced that he was surrounded by hostility and incomprehension – which, in the heart of Devon, he possibly was – he had too much fibre and certainty to lapse into the self-pitying nihilism of many neurotics. He came to terms with his sociophobia by setting up as a Punch and Judy man in Worthing in 1964, moving to the West Pier at Brighton from 1965 to 1969, and to Paignton sands from 1970 to 1989. As good an artist as a writer, he deployed his philosophy behind the anonymity of a thin sheet of painted cloth, working his hand-made puppets not merely to delight the children, but – sometimes at indoor functions – to belabour the somewhat startled adults. In 1972 he published the first edition of his historical study, *Punch and Judy: Its Origin and Evolution*, now recognised as a standard work, and Centaur Press published its sequel, *Punch in the Italian Puppet Theatre*, in 1983. This was deservedly well received and is still – like himself, so to speak – happily in print.

I shared Colin's regret that Kenneth Allsop had not responded to Michael's less orthodox environmental concern, but Ken was years ahead of his time, his labours reaching a splendid culmination in such trenchant television series as 'Do You Dig Our National Parks', and 'Down To Earth'. The perceptions of deep ecology had not yet struck root. Ken was a friend of whom I wish I could write at appropriate length, for I understand so well the conflict he felt between the journalism needed to earn a living and the books by which he would have preferred to be remembered. His ambition was to be a novelist in the style of Graham Greene, and a nature-writer whom his friend and literary idol Henry Williamson might have acknowledged as a near equal. It was cruel that the frustration of so talented a man should be compounded by three decades of nagging physical suffering that ended only when he took his life in his Dorset mill house when his wife Betty was in London for the Chelsea Flower Show. The letter he left for her, a copy of which she sent to me with permission to make use of it one day, shows how much his despair was deepened by the way the world was going, and by the seeming impossibility of arresting its insane progress. I wept at its beauty, sadness, and resignation, made bearable only by its confirmation of the deep affection that, after the ups and downs of their marriage, and many a mood of black despair, had finally triumphed over the less tranquil times.

Ken had known, of course, such minor satisfactions as being remembered as 'the best Rector Edinburgh ever had', and the fame and rewards of a major journalist, but more valued than that were his rare opportunities to study the ornithology of the countryside as far away as possible from the urban jungle. It would doubly have pleased him to know that the creation of the Kenneth Allsop Memorial Trust to honour his conservation work was to benefit, only three months after his death, from a gala performance of the film of *Jesus Christ Superstar*, for his musical interests were nothing if not eclectic.

He never let up, as evidenced in his farewell letter to Betty, eventually published in his daughter Amanda's *Letters from My Father*. Ken's PS was unambiguous:

You know my feelings about cremation, love: please, if you can, save me from that sickly charade. If it can be done I'd like to go decently into the ground: one's chemicals might be nutrients for a tree.

I hope he might find appropriate the few lines I dedicated to him:

ECOTRIP
(for Kenneth Allsop)

As scattered ash beneath this beech
I'd bid farewell, content
to be within a tree trunk's reach
of final firmament;
then drawn, transmuted, sap in May,
through root and branch and leaf ...
Ah! what an ecostatic way
to mock at passing's grief –
free-borne upon spring's knowing breeze,
bound for what unknown bliss,
symbiotic with the trees
in photosynthesis.

If Centaur's first catalogues cried out for a more positive sense of direction, so did my family. Jennifer had produced our baby, Susan, in November 1957, and both showed a modest interest in being fed, clothed and kept warm. Tilly seemed happy at a small school a few yards up West Hill. But it was a penniless and uncertain period, and I had all too little time to be more than a background presence. Tilly, besotted by her baby half-sister, mothered Sue devotedly, and to this day is not unknown to slip back into a solicitous and at times admonitory role.

On Easter Monday, 1959, I drove to Whitehall Place early in the morning with Tilly, who had just turned eight. We took the tube to Turnham Green and walked to the assembly point in Chiswick to join the second and most publicised Aldermaston March. It was led by Canon Collins, Donald Soper, Jacquetta Hawkes, Victor Gollancz, Michael Foot, and numerous 'names' from the arts, theatre, sciences and other creative and intellectual levels. Tilly, big-eyed, was not keen to let go of my hand. All identifiable groups, professions, political parties, religions, and nations, seemed to be carrying banners. SWEDEN and DENMARK, waving above the walking heads, were fiercely supported by FINCHLEY SAYS 'NO'. Back-up was given by a steel band that encouraged feet already wearied by the previous days' trudging; and numerous guitars, a brass band, and a drummer competed with the singing of songs that were on sale in penny broadsheets. 'Ban the Bomb' was the dominant slogan to be shouted by hundreds of young voices, switching with varying synchronism to 'Ashes to ashes, dust to dust, if the bomb don't get you, the fall-out must'. When we stopped near the Albert Hall to eat our sandwiches, Tilly and I sat on the steps of the Albert Memorial with Donald Soper, and I suggested he write a follow-up to Dick Sheppard's *We Say 'No'*, whose influence on me I mention in a later chapter. But like so many powerful orators, Donald was less at ease with a pen, and the suggestion came to nothing. By the time we reached Big Ben at 2.45, the march was a slow amble, and Whitehall was so congested that we shuffled into Trafalgar Square at 3.10. Jennifer had brought Sue by bus in her push-chair to meet us, and they were standing on the edge of the pavement near the Whitehall Theatre, enjoying baby-buggy privilege. The whole route had been lined with spectators, many clapping, and our reception at the finish was certainly not confined to the Communist element that some tried to make out were responsible for the whole thing. At 3.35 Collins announced that the tail of the march had only just reached Knightsbridge, and the hoarse and foot-sore began to disperse, we to the car that someone had damaged in, perhaps, the mood that makes peace marches necessary.

In May 1959 I could write to Jack Cohen with the news that I had managed to get a West Country printer's agreement to 'absorb their spare capacity' after their acquisition of a new photolitho camera. Wheaton's of Exeter were an old and ethically-run firm who seemed to be finding difficulty in keeping up with the postwar recovery in the industry. They had responded with enthusiasm to my outline of the Centaur Classics series, although at that stage I could only hold out hope of finding the American connection that should make all the difference. As three of the provisional titles could be manufactured almost entirely by the photographic process, Wheaton were happy to start with the Thayer; *The Poems of John Oldham*, introduced by Bonamy Dobrée; and *Letters of Edward FitzGerald*, which was introduced by Jack himself. Needless to say, they looked for a return on their outlay, and the necessity to find a collaborative American publisher for the series glowed like a beacon in the western sky. But it was first necessary to ask Jack if he would be general editor for the Centaur Classics, and after a year of bouncing ideas off each other, he seemed happy to settle into a named role. He even produced a professional jacket designer who translated my crude roughs into a workable scheme for movable blocks that could be used for any format the book might be given. Delightful to work with, Jack was always helpful, modest, and appreciative. I was able to maximise his fees by paying him in crates of wine. Formal invoices would have been unthinkably coarse. 'Another dozen Meursault '57 would be welcome before Christmas', scribbled at the foot of card or letter, was all the hint needed.

But before I could put up a tempting package to an American publisher, the plans were threatened. A six-week printers' strike hit Wheaton as badly as it did the rest of the country. In July I was told by the New York Public Library that Dr Elliot Forbes, an American academic, was editing a revision of the Thayer, although this was held up pending the publication of a new collection of Beethoven's letters. The NYPL indicated that with all this afoot they saw no case for our reissuing the original edition. This was only the start of a nightmare scenario in which the mighty Princeton University Press came on heavily against the very idea of the Elliot Forbes being upstaged by a Thayer that took no account of subsequent scholarship. Almost overnight the fledgling series was plunged into the kind of crisis that only the marriage of academia and commerce can produce. The full horror of what was to follow would need a book to itself, but is not going to get it.

Nor was the torment confined to copyright dispute, to the intervention (on Centaur's behalf) of Rubinstein Nash and Co., the Gray's Inn solicitors famous for handling major lawsuits in the field of publishing and authorship, and to the involvement of unsuspected past players on the Thayer stage. Shattering production problems were to arise at Wheaton's, filling our tiny flat with hundreds of seriously imperfect sets. Nonetheless, Centaur's slightly larger 1960 catalogue, suitably coloured green, proudly announced the Centaur Classics series under the General Editorship of J. M. Cohen. 'Whatever the manner of revival,' it said proudly if rashly, 'only books of first-rate importance will be included in the series.' With several thousand copies of a sixteen-page catalogue already mailed to booksellers and libraries world-wide, there could be no turning back. As well as four Centaur Classics, eleven other titles were announced, press opinions were shown of a further nine 'recently published', and a page of 'other books in print' listed twenty-five more, half a dozen of which, plus two by G. B. Stern published in association with another small firm, Coram

Ltd, had brought favourable attention in the national press. The slim volumes of poetry by Patrick Galvin, Ewart Milne, Susan Miles, Eric Knight, and Marc Alexander, among others, had been suitably and on the whole pleasantly received. The Centaur and Linden Presses may not have arrived, but they were knocking on the door.

The fourth Centaur Classic to be announced for 1960 was J. A. Stewart's *The Myths of Plato*. Professor Stewart's work was the first to assemble the *Myths* from the various Platonic dialogues, and to treat them as so many aspects of a consistent system of thought. His viewpoint was primarily poetic. Jack had asked G. R. Levy, the archaeologist and authority on ancient religions, to edit the Stewart, and in her introduction she stressed the religious-philosophical side of the *Myths*, tracing parallels with Hindu, Tibetan, and Orphic scriptures unobserved by Stewart. It was one of the most important Centaur Classics and had to be reprinted ten years later, when Barnes and Noble took part of the reissue for the USA.

However, by the middle of 1959 I had not tracked down originals of the two most prominent works with which the Centaur Classics were to be launched. Before I got round to forking out the fiver required for Mr Joseph's fading Thayer it had found a more solvent buyer.

That June I took an early train to Oxford. There I found not only the Plato, but a set of the 1921 Thayer in Blackwell's music department in Holywell Street. By then it was rather easier to spare the twelve guineas involved than it had been to lay out Joseph's humbler sum. I bore my trophies down the High to Magdalen Bridge and took a punt up the Cherwell. It was a poet's spring day. Tying up under a willow, I removed my shirt and gave the sun a chance to tinge my winter-white skin. Undoing the soft tape that held the Beethoven volumes reverently together, I began to discover just how right old Joseph had been. After tea at McKay's in the High, and calling at the porter's lodge at Balliol for the address of a school-friend not seen since 1941, I caught the 5.32 train back to London. It had been one of those better days.

But the last and most important player had still not been found: that New World seeker of culture, with a feeling for the products of the Old. Not surprisingly, it turned out to be a university publisher for whom, at least in the early days, the maximising of profit was secondary to the quality of content and presentation. The interest came not from a Boston or other East Coast press, but from the deep south of the Middle Western state of Illinois, some 100 miles south of St Louis. My letter of 3 November 1959 was the opener:

Mr Vernon Sternberg
Southern Illinois University Press
Carbondale, Illinois

Dear Mr Sternberg

I have been given the tip that you may be very interested in a new series of books which we are starting to publish this year – the Centaur Classics, with J. M. Cohen as our General Editor.

The 1960 catalogue for spring and summer is in the press, so I can only send you the enclosed 1959 list, but, briefly, Centaur Classics aims to reprint, with or without revisions to the text, and invariably edited and/or introduced by leading authorities, books long unobtainable but already classics in their own right. We are kicking off with:

Thayer's *Life of Beethoven* with an Introduction by Alan Pryce-Jones.

Stewart's *Myths of Plato*, revised, with the Greek translated and introduced by G. R. Levy.

Letters of Edward FitzGerald edited by J. M. Cohen (with intro.).

Poems of John Oldham, introduced by Bonamy Dobrée.

The Beethoven presents some problems because the copyright is rather tenuously held by a publisher in the States, and while we could probably sell a small edition to an American publisher without causing real trouble or ill-feeling, I am not one for inviting such headaches.

The FitzGerald and Oldham speak for themselves, but for prestige value the Plato is of course on the same level as the Beethoven. A first-rate and much sought-after classic, of real worth and now excellently re-presented by Rachel Levy. It is making a medium octavo volume which will sell at three guineas here.

If these initial details interest you, will you let me know if you would like first option? In view of the standing of the works and their editors you may feel able to give your answer quite soon, and as my agent in America hasn't yet got cracking (no proofs or jackets are available yet) I should like to cut out the time-wastage of third-party submissions. It would obviously be very pleasant if we could get together on all C.C. titles available for America, but I have been advised that the Plato may be particularly 'you'.

Yours sincerely,
JON WYNNE-TYSON

Sternberg responded with enthusiasm, expressing 'our strong interest in your Centaur Classics series'. The preliminaries were agreed before Christmas, by which time I had received SIUP's order for 500 copies of *The Myths of Plato*, 500 of the Oldham, and 750 of the FitzGerald. We were off, and the first Centaur Classic to be published was the Plato, on 2 May 1960 in the UK. The *Times Educational Supplement* spread the welcome news that it was 'a work of the first importance to all who are interested in the scholarly exposition of some of the most deeply imaginative writing in any literature', and although the *TES*'s 'all' did not amount to a horde, even back in 1960, at least the sales merited a further edition on both sides of the Atlantic. The 1960s had started well.

Ironically, although the *Myths* involved expensive translation and typesetting, it was the fifth Centaur Classic to be published, an untypically 'bare' offset reprint of *Shakespeare's Ovid*, with no additional apparatus other than a publisher's foreword, that became one of the most sought-after titles. Shakespeare scholars' need for Arthur Golding's translation of the *Metamorphoses*, edited by W. H. D. Rouse for the de la More Press who published it in 1904, had for too many years been inexplicably overlooked by the Oxbridge presses. Although it was agreed that Southern Illinois would take 750 copies of revised and newly typeset titles (the *Myths* order had underestimated SIUP's need), and 500 of those printed by offset, in the case of the *Ovid* we were unwise to make it a limited edition of 1,500, half of which went to the States. With nine-tenths of Shakespeare's classical mythology having come from the *Metamorphoses*, it was a text that had been badly missed for many years. Although the Centaur edition was a handsome book (the original typesetting had been sharp and well designed, the mould-made laid paper of the highest quality available, and the binding in the series' Oxford blue cloth prettified with coloured tops and headbands), it would have found its buyers if it had been manufactured to a much lower specification. But from the start the plan had been to set a good standard of production, and this intention was never deliberately abandoned, though not always realised. Any temptation to flout the *Ovid*'s limited edition status having been resisted, second-hand copies brought good rewards to knowing antiquarian booksellers for some years after, until the demand was sopped up by a less outwardly attractive reprint from another publisher.

Between publication of the first four Centaur Classics and, in 1961, the *Ovid*, there was a gap of eighteen months. SIUP needed time to test the first four titles in the US market, and to reconcile their accountants to signing largish cheques in expectation of a slow return on outlay. While production costs swallowed most of their payments to Centaur, what was left over helped not only to meet our domestic overheads, but to lessen the risks in filling the gap with such less academic titles as might give Centaur a rather trendier image. With further Centaur Classics agreed for the future, it was at last possible to budget for an ongoing programme for both the academic and general sides of the list.

It seemed a sensible moment to make my first (and last) visit to the Frankfurt Book Fair. Although it had yet to reach its peak as the major European book-promotion event, it lost much of its charm and focus in the years to come. The British Council had a large stand at the Fair, which gave small publishers the chance to exhibit their wares without incurring the trouble and expense of taking their own stands. Twelve Centaur titles were displayed that year. I may have done a little good by circulating catalogues to other publishers, meeting friends and new faces, and calling on Frankfurt bookshops; but being committed to the solo path, and believing there were enough ideas in the pipeline and on the back-burner to keep me busy without scanning American and European stands with an eye to buying rights in others' finds, I flew on after three nights to see booksellers in Berlin and Hamburg. The contrasts were remarkable, both between the eastern and western zones in pre-Wall Berlin, and in the quality of the hotels I stayed in. Berlin's Kempinski was dire, while Hamburg's Four Seasons vindicated Ian Fleming's assertion that it was still one of the few remaining great hotels of Europe. But Berlin gave me the most evocative experience of that crowded week – not of beerhouses, brothels, Hitler's bunker, or even of suspecting my shoulder to be dislocated by the friendly slap of a transvestite in the Eldorado night-club where I was sipping a drink, but of walking into the eastern zone's Unter den Linden and finding in the cavernous remains of the huge Adlon Hotel a cellar full of wine racks half buried in the rubble of crockery, tiles, and washstands that had fallen from the blitzed floors above. It was perhaps the feeling that it could all have happened yesterday that was so poignant and sobering.

As the Centaur Classics consisted of new editions or selections of distinguished names seldom read beyond Academe and major libraries, my growing list needed the balance of a few titles written by real living people. These included *From Stalin to Khrushchev* by Goronwy J. Jones, acknowledged by the *Daily Telegraph* as 'a concise and instructive account of Soviet foreign policy over the last thirty years', which in time paid its way; Dr Henry Speedby's *The 20th Century and Your Heart*, whose enthusiastic reviewers reflected the insatiable British appetite for anticipating the hazards awaiting the corporeal man (the corporeal woman, by and large, lives longer and more healthily); *The Last Victorian*, an engaging study of R. D. Blackmore, the author of *Lorna Doone*, by Kenneth Budd; Patrick Galvin's second book of poems, *Christ in London*, which was not only panned by the laid-back Alvarez, but coincided with Ewart Milne discovering that – unknown to me at the time – Thelma had been the benefactor who bought 150 copies of Paddy's book to reduce the Linden Press's likely loss; a rather emotional study, *Tchehov, the Man*, by Beatrice Saunders, whose earlier book, *The Age of Candlelight*, was a 1959 Centaur title that did well after favourable notices in major newspapers. Beatrice was a resilient woman: bubbly, as they like to say today.

Although I had published some twenty titles in the eighteen months before publication of the *Ovid* launched the major phase of the Centaur Classics series, the secure feeling prompted by the SIUP's friendliness tempted me to write another novel – despite the muscle pain, depression, poor sleep, and other symptoms of mild chronic fatigue syndrome that teamed joyfully with allergic rhinitis for many years to discourage my energy levels. It was called *Square Peg* and I published it myself under the pen-name of Jeremy Pitt.

The late *Reynolds' News* found it a 'cheeky little satire of the kind of people who bay like hounds after the vogue trends in art and life' (which is what it was), while Isabel Quigly in the *Guardian* hated it (for just that reason). Not that *Square Peg* pretended to be much more than gentle social satire, and in 1961 there were some who could still recognise that mode without confusing it with any of the other forms of humour spelled out in *Modern English Usage* by the late lamented H. W. Fowler. At least there were positive aspects to the book's anonymity. When the *Evening Standard*'s readers were told that the book could be their credo, and *Books of the Month* welcomed the laying bare of several aspects of the current culture, I could be sure they were not being kind to a friend, or to a friend of a friend. The most welcome reaction was from the *Sunday Times* who, in addition to employing adjectives dear to an author's heart, gave it the leading fiction review and predicted that 'this book may prove to be the contribution of the 1960s to that long tradition, from *Candide* to *Juan in America*, of the innocent and humourless hero meticulously examining contemporary society'.

But if the chosen anonymity was not a mistake, giving in to my urge to test the water with my first serious attempt to write a satirical novel probably was. If I was to consolidate the publishing, make up for errors and omissions of the past, and put the family first, I could not also find the time to work at becoming a full-time writer. My nerve failed at the crossroads, perhaps, but at the time I felt I had taken the right turn in the circumstances. Apart from a shorter and even gentler novel, *Don't Look and You'll Find Her*, published under the same pen-name six years later, again to keep my hand in, the publishing slog kept the lid on my fiction-writing ambitions for more than twenty years.

One of the most attractive minor titles before the Centaur Classics got into their stride in 1962 was Marjorie Broughall's *Pastel for Eliza*, welcomed by *The Times* as a 'delicious little cameo'. At the same time, I published Laurence Clark's second novel, *More than Moon*, a slightly more 'clever' satire than his *Kingdom Come*; and completing the trio published that October of 1961 was *Kashmir*, a workmanlike introduction to its heritage and history by J. P. Ferguson, a college teacher in India, fluent in Hindi and Urdu, who loved the beautiful country and knew it well.

Selling out quickly in hardback, and reissued several times as a paperback, was R. L. Bowley's *Teaching Without Tears*; his later (1976) *Readings for Assembly* met a proven need. Another book for which 'workmanlike' was possibly the best term it could expect, was Bryan Bevan's *The Real Francis Bacon*. A large number of mostly provincial reviews helped it to sell, if slowly, more than did the *TLS*'s faint praise for its sobriety, and regret at its failure to produce many new facts.

So far I could not claim that Centaur Press was showing a clear sense of direction. To present a front, I was accepting almost any general book that seemed of adequate quality and was not actually baneful. The welcome given to the Centaur Classics, however, showed editors' and reviewers' approval of the series, and it was going to keep me too busy to worry in the short term about a stronger image for the rest of the list. We were paying our way, and in March 1961, with the comfortable feeling that the SIUP agreement had created a lasting symbiosis between East and West, I bought my first bit of real estate – a bungalow of timber and asbestos construction at Selsey in Sussex, where children could still enjoy the nearby sea and the sense of freedom I knew there in my own school holidays; properties could be left unlocked in the daytime without fear of intruders.

The new decade had a hopeful feel, but I was not yet seriously counting chickens.

4
Breakfast at the Vanderbilt

The 1961 catalogue – printed, of course, in 1960 – had been nothing if not eclectic. It announced the coming of five more Centaur Classics, quoted approving reviews of their four predecessors, and promised twenty-three new general titles ranging from an unpublished work by D. H. Lawrence and a study of William Beckford by Boyd Alexander, to 'Some Books for Beatniks' by such as Kerouac, Olson, Snyder, Creeley, Bob Brown, Philip Whalen, Frank O'Hara, and others. I had imported the latter after my first visit to New York in April 1960, when I made a reciprocal arrangement with the Eighth Street Bookshop in Greenwich Village. Most of the titles published under the subsidiary imprint of the Linden Press had turned out to be modern poetry, but the imprint was also used for work peripheral to my still hazy notions of how the general side of the list should develop. With hindsight, there were several Linden titles that should have taken the Centaur imprint. There was also a third imprint – Winterson Company – kept for fillers for which I could offer only printing services through Villiers, and the handling of usually unsolicited orders. It took on few titles and died an early death.

The 1961 catalogue listed a further nineteen 'Recently Published' general titles with approving press quotes (the disapproving are seldom immortalised by publishers), and a page of thirty-two 'Other Books in Print', mostly Linden and Winterson. Compared with 1959's small-format twelve-page list, 1960's and 1961's larger sixteen-pagers had more of a 'We've arrived' feel about them.

Arrival – if that is what it was – also spelled, in August 1961, our move from the Highgate flat to the Selsey bungalow, from where we sought, and soon found, a permanent home and a temporary office. The new home was a fairly primitive pair of woodmen's cottages that had been knocked into one and were sandwiched between the peaceful beauty of the National Trust's Slindon Park beech woods and the ever less tranquil Fontwell Park racecourse. Centaur's only away-from-home office was in the spacious cellar of 5 West Pallant, a double-fronted Queen Anne house in Chichester. I was the sub-tenant of the splendidly formidable 'Billie' Longe-Schreiber, still remembered as one of Chichester's 'characters'. A member of the Vernon family of Hanbury Hall, Billie was well into stately homes, and after her husband's death she kept her mind and artistry exercised by buying small houses in good situations, then selling them after she had worked over their interiors on the lines of the country seats she had known from her childhood. Potential purchasers, viewing small rooms rigged out in damask, tapestry, and thick braided curtain pulls with tassels and imposing ornamental knobs, seldom questioned the price asked. She claimed to have done over some seventy-five such properties, never once employing a professional surveyor. As my much-beamed and timbered office was tastefully embellished by some of her fabrics and antiques, the ambience suited the growing shelf of Centaur Classics to a tee.

But not for long. On 27 October we moved home and office to Fontwell, a month before publication of the last three titles to be published in 1961. These were a translation by A. E. Watts of *The Poems of Sextus Propertius*, the paperback of which was later issued by Penguin; the *Ovid*; and the sixth Centaur Classic, the *Memoir of Thomas Bewick*, long a rarity in the second-hand market. Edmund Blunden, introduced by Jack Cohen, but not met until a delightful day spent with him in Long Melford seven years later, responded enthusiastically to the suggestion that he write the introduction. He remarked therein:

> Bewick himself, perhaps, would go so far as to wish his name to be ultimately and principally connected with the *Memoir*. It was his testament of beauty; his advice to the twentieth century (on its increasing practical problems); his opening treatise on the nature of things. There is a greatness here and there in the later chapters which possibly he never exhibited even in such a masterpiece of art and feeling as that last print 'Waiting for Death'.

Courteous, charming, and obliging Edmund, always anxious to please, placate, and focus on the positive. His affinities with Bewick made him the man for the job. Unfortunately, the Cresset Press, started by Dennis Cohen in 1927 and run by him until it was swallowed by Barrie in the mid-1960s, reissued the *Memoir* simultaneously (if less lavishly) at a third of the price, and introduced by Montague Weekley. Weekley, however, omitted seven chapters that were retained in the

Centaur edition, and each text supplemented, or improved in some way on, the other. Both books, consequently, were reviewed in the papers that mattered. Moreover, both editions were criticised for the quality of their reproductions of Bewick's wood engravings. The main exception was *The Times*, whose reviewer cited the Centaur illustrations as 'admirable examples of the great artist's craft', and criticised the Cresset edition for omitting Bewick's religious views, deemed essential to evaluating him in the round. Raymond Mortimer, in the *Sunday Times*, giving both editions the lead review, compared their illustrations unfavourably with both the King Penguin and Reynolds Stone's edition of the engravings as published by Rupert Hart-Davis. Raymond Williams, in the *New Statesman*, thought the illustrations were 'marvellous' in both editions.

Such honeyed if conflicting endorsements were a red rag to Geoffrey Grigson, the Great Leveller of the literary world, feared since editor in the 1930s of his legendary *New Verse* magazine. Reviewing both books in the *Observer*, the Readers' Rottweiler was having no truck with established reputations and the wishy-washy susceptibilities of editors and publishers. While savaging the reproductions and the editors of both editions, his incisors sank deepest into the Centaur version, damning it as irresponsible and expensive.

Buoyed up by the generally welcoming reviews that appeared mostly in November and December, I was cut to the quick by the Grigson lambast, published on New Year's Eve. Indignation prompted me to do what I don't recall doing before or since – I wrote to the reviewer and treated him to a piece of my mind. Not, as a rule, a very wise indulgence from a small and scarcely established publisher to a leading and generally dreaded reviewer.

1st January 1962

Dear Mr Grigson,

A good few years ago, unknown to you, I saved you from a 'roughing up' at the hands of Roy Campbell by detaining that knuckle-happy poet in a pub while I attempted – with how little success! – to convince him of the superior powers of non-violence and the pen.

Reading your review of the Thomas Bewick in yesterday's *Observer* almost makes me wish I had cheered him on his way. I don't think I have ever written to a reviewer to castigate him for irresponsible dealing, but your destructive and carping criticism of the Centaur (*and* the Cresset) Bewicks compels me to break a very good rule.

In heaven's name, what is 'irresponsible' about reprinting the original *Memoir* as edited by his daughter Jane and thought worthy of reprinting by the Bodley Head in 1924? Rightly or wrongly, reviewers who know the subject have criticised Weekley for his omissions, but short of having gone back to Bewick's own manuscript (and by golly you'd have objected if we had reprinted *that* without a lot of editing) it would be interesting to know what constructive alternative you would have suggested. Expensive the Centaur edition is, compared with the Cresset, but unlike more fair-minded reviewers you carefully fail to tell the readers that the Centaur edition is far more <u>expensively</u> produced and with quite a large number of full-page illustrations; quite apart from being the complete 'Jane' edition. It is this sort of 'damning by omission' that is such a very unpleasant aspect of your reviewing activities.

I think I agree with you that Bewick as an engraver has been somewhat over-praised, but when I read your second criticism – that both editions fail to reproduce Bewick's 'fastidious black to silver effects' – I begin to wonder just how much you can possibly know of such matters as publishing costs, price-to-sales ratios, and, more importantly, the technical limitations which printers and publishers have to accept. Your eye apparently failed to notice that our edition was a photo-litho reproduction, but I am sure that the Cresset Press would agree with me that 'silvery' effects are not easily come by even in letterpress printing.

All right, I am in a paddy because of a bad review, but I assure you that I normally take such things fairly calmly. In this case, I hope, the more balanced and responsible notices that the book has had in leading papers already will soften the effects of your own one-sided efforts to find something nasty to say at any cost (a habit in very young reviewers, I know, but unworthy of someone of your status). The fact that I have written as I have is, in my mind, some measure of your fall from generally accepted standards; but I don't expect you to agree with this.

Yours sincerely,
JON WYNNE-TYSON

P.S. In my determination to be fair until given good cause to be intolerant, I had intended, having seen your article in the *Observer* of March 5th ('Good Books Cost Too Much'), to send you a complimentary set of *The Poems of William Barnes* (to be published in May). As the two volumes, comprising over 1,000 medium 8vo pages, will necessarily be brought out at the Oxfordish price of 8 guineas, this would obviously be enough to blow several valves and would presumably be unwelcome. Anyway, while you continue to be the sort of reviewer whom publishers hope to God editors won't think of, such an act on my part would be pure masochism.

Grigson's suave handwritten reply came by return of post:

January 3rd, 1962

Dear Sir,

You must excuse me if I find your letter of January 1st a faintly comic beginning to a New Year. You start by announcing that you conferred an unknown benefit on me in the past, you end by announcing that you had intended to confer a benefit on me in the future. The inference seems to be that I should have been properly grateful for these benefits, though ignorant of them, and given you in return a good review for a bad book.

A bad book. Of course it is irresponsible, when the manuscript of a book is known to exist (but did you know it existed?) and is accessible, to reprint an inferior version; just as it is irresponsible to reproduce Bewick engravings, by whatever method, in a travestied form; just as it is also irresponsible to preface this poor reprint into [with?] a correspondingly poor piece of writing which might just have passed in the hey-day of E. V. Lucas. Expensive production – your underlining – doesn't excuse anything. At the cost of scratching my own back, I shall affirm that your 'more balanced and responsible', i.e. less critical reviewers, who measure, alas, to the 'generally accepted standards', did not know much about Bewick, or care much about him, didn't bother to compare the three versions, and seem never to have looked without a dull eye at a Bewick original.

Of course it isn't impossible to make at any rate tolerable reproductions of Bewick. Compare yours with the King Penguin or the Art and Technics books of 1949.

Someone – J. M. Cohen? On your behalf? – wrote and asked me

to introduce a reprint of the *Memoir*. I said I didn't think it worth reprinting. I am not sure it was, even if the edition had been final and definitive. There you are: you had back luck in the coincidence of another reprint from the Cresset Press, and the additional bad luck that this other edition was better, cheaper, and more useful, if by no means perfect.

In return for your restraints on the veldt baboonishness of the late Roy (though I could well have defended myself against his paranoiac advances, and should both have regretted and enjoyed the opportunity of bashing him), I shall offer you an unwanted list of several books worth reviving: Dasent's *Norse Fairy Tales*, Henry James's *Partial Portraits*, William Allingham's *Diary*, not reprinted since the original edition of 1907. Also Allingham's *Laurence Bloomfield in Ireland*. Also an English edition, complete, of the New Zealand poet Mary Bethell (1874–1945). Also a proper selection from Landor.

A good list for insolvency, I daresay.

Yours truly,
GEOFFREY GRIGSON

As intended, this left me suitably abashed, and after a slightly longer reaction interval I sent my conciliatory, if not abject, response:

11th January 1962

Dear Mr Grigson,

Thank you for your letter. Yes, I agree that to start and end such a letter with favours lavished and intended *was* faintly comic – indeed, very comic. But I was very cross when I wrote it, I am afraid, and sent it off before I knew I would change my mind. It's the only way.

I won't go on at you about the Bewick any more except to say that it is clearly a matter of opinion rather than of fact that stands between us, as regards both the 'Jane' edition and Blunden's Preface. A life-time association with authors, critics and publishers has been a pretty disillusioning experience – which just goes to show how much your attack got under the toughened skin.

I had forgotten, or didn't know, that Cohen had written to you about the *Memoir*. I shall pass on your suggestions for further Classics to him, and will let you know if any seem possible (because of the small margin on most Classics, we have to avoid copyright material wherever possible). Any idea that is adopted automatically entitles its originator to a ten guinea fee, whether or not they have been saved from massacre by publishers' argumentativeness or know the technique for dealing with veldt baboons (I may say I found Roy's personality quite odious, so would have been extremely glad to cheat him of *any* prey). It is good of you to fling me ideas after I was so cross with you, and it seems to indicate that you may be better at presenting the other cheek than I am.

Had my intention been bribery and corruption, would I not have appeared in shining armour before now, in the early days when Centaur could most have done with good reviews, claiming your loyalty for services rendered!

With, I hope, no hard feelings,

Yours sincerely,

JON WYNNE-TYSON

In early April I wrote again to confirm the reactions of Jack and Vernon to Grigson's suggestions. Although only two of the first batch were taken up – *William Allingham's Diary*, for which he supplied the introduction, and *Poems* by Walter Savage Landor, which he selected and introduced with predictable professionalism, and for both of which he was paid, after a brief struggle, by flat fees rather than by royalties – over the life of the series he put up some sixty further ideas. Fifteen of these were adopted, and a further two we published in Centaur's short-lived Travellers' Classics series. By then Geoffrey's preferred remuneration was cases of claret or burgundy from Robert James of Grape Street. He also gave some helpful advice, was understanding about the problems of small publishers, and on several occasions reviewed titles in the series in his column in *Country Life*. His necessarily workaholic condition, and a tiresome habit of disappearing for months on end to work an enlarged cave in Loir-et-Cher, made him often infuriatingly slow in his responses. But as his supportive and protective wife Jane (of later fame) wrote after receiving – and here I am shooting way ahead of the intended chronology of this chapter – one of my tether-end notes of appeal in September 1968:

Dear Jon,

I'm so sorry. The trouble is that he's writing a book and is not really with us at all at the moment. But anyway he feels he can't write the introductions [for Smollett's *Travels Through France and Italy* and William Morris's *Icelandic Journals*] himself. Nor can he think of anyone else. Which is not much help. In fact no help at all. He doesn't know anything about the gentlemen whose names you mentioned. Auden seemed so perfect for Morris. What about William Sansom for the Smollett? That is the only (anguished) squeak I can get out of the boss. No, Lawrence Durrell he says. Shouts from above ... As a matter of fact ... I like organising things in a haphazard manner ... Geoffrey ... never knows whether we've got +6d in the bank, or −6d. And doesn't much care. It's all very exhilarating.   Best wishes, JANE

Nearly twenty years Geoffrey's junior, I knew then as I know today even more acutely, the frustration of never clearing one's desk or mind of things clamouring to be done. How often have I wished that I was one of those laid-back, unmotivated, world-accepting bon vivants, happy to earn my crust in a field demanding minimum effort or comeback, content in my usual pub corner, puffing at my foul pipe, indifferent to the probability that I would end up in the had-it ward with blackened lungs fifteen or more years before my time. But I wasn't and am not, any more than was Geoffrey, so while my demands for his responses did not ease over the years, offence was taken on neither side. We were both enslaved by the work ethic, and resigned to submitting to the even more tyrannous creative urge which compels its victims to go on churning out books, music, or art, until the last marble is relinquished or the final perch has given way.

I did not meet the Grigsons until a few days before Christmas 1965, when I drove to Bristol to collect the 1966 Centaur catalogue from its printers. Jane had invited me to lunch, but wanting to make an early start I had opted for breakfast instead. My two-hour drive to Broad Town Farmhouse on the Marlborough Downs was delayed, so I restricted myself to a coffee while Jane, Geoffrey, and six-year-old Sophie tucked into their postponed breakfast in the charming flagged kitchen already hung about with the pots, pans, ladles, and fierce steel knives of the serious cook. (Jane's first cookery book was to appear two years later.)

Although it would be absurd to claim Geoffrey as a long-standing and intimate friend – of which, I suspect, he had not very many – my visit confirmed the impression that he was a much nicer man than his critical persona so often suggested. Our correspondence and telephone conversations had revealed what I might have expected from what I knew of his Cornish background: a straightforward, uncomplicated man, less happy with humankind than with nature, and stubborn in the convictions that mattered to him. But I had underestimated the vein of kindliness, and was able to empathise particularly with his loathing for his schooldays, and his conviction of the importance of children being happy if they are to adjust to the world and contribute anything of value to it. He admitted ruefully, however, that one of his daughters by an earlier marriage had been expelled from Dartington Hall 'for sleeping with a millionaire'. This rather dented the progressive image I had of Dartington, but I had never heard that the place came cheap, so could better understand why, despite the energy and professionalism that had gone into Geoffrey's prodigious literary output, the mortgage had only recently been paid off. Idealism fills few coffers.

That last sentence may produce snorts from those still around who felt the lash of his wit and waspishness. But even then it was a pardonable form of idealism to set standards for oneself. But in describing, say, John Hayward as 'that Grey Eminence of bad poetry writing', or castigating the Kipling estate for charging for the quoting of a poem 'as if it were a piece cut out of the Leonardo cartoon', Hayward's wheelchaired condition, and the likely pressures on Kipling's trustees by the writer's beneficiaries, did not, I imagine, come into his mind. The individual perpetrator was irrelevant. His wrath was directed not so much at what he saw as the incompetent or opportunistic 'personality', as at the generally worsening climate of short-sighted laziness and greed, and their effect on the literary and artistic standards he valued. But his impatience had a sound base, and when many years later Derwent May published his formidable history of the *Times Literary Supplement*, *Critical Times*, I was pleased by the fair and interesting assessment of Geoffrey's little ways.

I recall no more meetings with Geoffrey after my visit at Christmas 1965, though I would have liked to have taken up invitations to Trôo and Wiltshire. There was a gap of three years in our correspondence, but he was still in the picture when in 1972 I published John Aubrey's *Three Prose Works*, edited by John Buchanan-Brown. It was to be the last title in the Centaur Classics series, but we kept in touch until Geoffrey's death in 1985. If his period in the literary annals is ever granted attention, there should be a selection of his letters. I could contribute, at the least, a rather appropriate photograph taken at the end of my 1965 visit to the rambling farmhouse. The back door was the one usually used, and my shot was of Geoffrey standing beside the four dustbins that testified to the Grigsons' already established interest in culinary exploration. As a reminder of Griggers's long crusade against trash, the backdrop seemed just right.

But I have jumped some years, for when the Bewick was published in November 1961 nearly a year was to pass before Southern Illinois signed a formal agreement with Centaur Press. Everything seemed so positive and congratulatory that I had no worry about using friendly letters from Vernon to reassure the printers. The vibes seemed wholly favourable. Vernon's letter two years earlier had confirmed SIUP's 'strong interest in your Centaur Classics series'. Hot on its heels came the assurance that 'my board of governors has given me permission to negotiate with you for the American rights to your very fine series'. They sought the exclusive right to the whole series, and permission to reprint any of the titles by offset if they should go out of print. SIUP's responses boded well.

Nor were most critics anything but welcoming. One reviewer described Centaur Press as 'a little Oxford [University Press]'. In that the Centaur Classics published work that OUP might well have taken on themselves, had they had the idea or had not been put off by the modest financial return that was likely, I saw no reason to quarrel with this flattering comparison.

I was less justified in taking for granted the likely longevity of the Centaur/SIUP marriage. After six years of feeling my way into a pattern for serious and profitable publishing, Vernon's letter probably went to my head, prompting casual attention to a later sentence: 'However, I cannot commit the Press for an indefinite period in the future.' As no one can commit themselves to anything for an indefinite period, except perhaps death, my reply was confined to intelligible specifics. It must have pleased him, as a response a week before Christmas thanked me for my 'most generous letter', and by the end of January (1960), on receiving an advance dust-jacket for *The Myths of Plato*, he wrote 'I am perfectly delighted with your plan and execution. If you will forgive me for saying so, you seem to be American in your thinking about these matters.' I forgave him.

By February 1960 his letter endings glowed 'warmest personal regards'. These were entirely reciprocated, if differently phrased. Vernon came across – as I am sure he still would – as a thoroughly regular guy. On 9 March he wrote that he could only salute you again for the daring and imaginativeness of the Centaur Classics series. We are of course honored – and quite exhilarated – to be in on the project, and we will do everything we can to cover the market for the books in the United States. As you no doubt have perceived, the series suits us perfectly. Among other things, we are building a backlist. Everything you are doing here is just right.

In April a long letter from him confirmed a list of the starting titles that SIUP were happy to receive. It seemed the right moment to cross the pond and press the flesh. On 24 April, after flying a kite with Tilly, who was tearful at our parting, I left for London Airport to board the Eagle Airways DC6 for Bermuda.

I flew via Bermuda for two reasons. Eagle was owned by my second best man, Harold Bamberg, in whose Keats Grove house I had met E. J. Carter in 1958. Three years before that I had travelled in Harold's ex-Berlin Airlift planes to various parts of Europe and the Balkans as supernumerary crew, and now that we were both more established he allowed me a serious discount for the first stage of my trip to the States. Covering 3,350 miles at a ground speed average of 257 m.p.h. might not have been the speediest route, but I had three seats to myself and solicitous attention from Harold's air hostesses.

The second reason was one of the Linden Press's lady poets, Agnes C. Tucker, whose undertaker husband Dickie was a member of one of Bermuda's best-known families, with a fitting and caustic sense of humour. Had I been able to persuade him to write his memoirs I would have done far better, I regret to say, than with Agnes's poems.

I was invited to stay at the Tuckers' bungalow home at East Paget. They were most hospitable and helped me to take in the Bermuda Book Store and library, in addition to the botanical gardens and other attractive spots. They were ruled by eleven cats and a dachshund, who lived – to the full – as family. This included use of all linen, china, glass, cutlery, and kitchen utensils. I was and have always been fond of animals, tame or feral, particularly in the sense of acknowledging their right to be spared human exploitation. The Tuckers certainly lived that ethic without reservation. When, on the third day, they put me on a DC7 to fly BOAC to New York, I must confess that parting from the family's quadrupedal members was consolation for leaving the quiet attractions of Bermuda for the mad maelstrom of Manhattan. My lowest-fare seat was in the front cabin next to the crew, and again I had ample room to spread out papers and books and plan for the days ahead.

I had not been to the United States before; nor, come to that, to anywhere else so far from England. In the bus ride from Idlewild Airport I had my first sight of the Manhattan skyline in the dusk: darkening grey silhouettes of skyscrapers against a smoked-salmon pink sunset – beautiful, but with more than a hint of the inferno. It looked impregnable, far too sure of itself to be impressed by my lowly ambitions.

My room at the now long-demolished Vanderbilt Hotel on Park Avenue at 34th Street was on the sixteenth floor and looked into an uninspiring courtyard. It was not up to much by today's standards, but the neurotic air-conditioning unit was at least useful in prompting some of the 'business' in a play I was to write many years later. (It made Boston, but was not brash enough for Broadway.)

Unpacked, I took a bus uptown to see Howard Moorepark, who worked from his apartment at 440 East 79th Street. Howard represented a number of small British publishers. He was a tiny, melancholy, nervous man, permanently sedated by any social or medical drug that could get him through the stresses of making his living as a freelance agent. He had various manuscripts to show me, all from small American publishers hopeful of finding a home for projects they knew would not make the grade with the Collinses, Methuens and Routledges of London. I was short of sleep and jet-lagged, and beyond making palatable to Howard the truth that Centaur was not the right home for his offerings. He also handed me a clutch of letters, mostly from people I hoped to see while over there. One was from Neville Armstrong, who in 1999, at eighty-five, was to publish his 'part-autobiography', describing how Neville Spearman came into being shortly after I started Centaur Press. Spearman grew big in UFOs and erotica, which made a lot of money and was for some a good excuse for taking offence at Neville's bumptiousness and lack of tact. Unfortunately, and perhaps to save a stamp, he had enclosed the letter to me with one addressed to Howard. It confirmed that he was chucking Howard as his agent. Surrounded by the unappealing typescripts Howard had offered me, I found it difficult to be suitably diplomatic.

The next morning, true to type, I woke at six and tried to nod off again to a television lecture on cosmic ray particles. At least it was some proof that American television was not unrelievedly low-brow. I had

hardly got back from a drug-store breakfast when my room phone rang
and a strained English voice said 'Thank God you've arrived. When can
we meet?' It was Neville. With my diary full of appointments with
publishers and authors, I said it was going to be difficult for the
moment.

'I tried to get back to London yesterday,' Neville said, 'but there
wasn't a seat to be had.'

'You'd only just arrived,' I pointed out.

'This bloody place.' He grumbled on about the police sirens, the fire
engines, the traffic, the noise the buses made, the speed and ugliness of
it all; the 'ghastly canyons' they called streets. Couldn't I spare half an
hour?

This wasn't the tough, self-assured Neville I knew.

'Let's keep in touch while you're here', I said, 'and meet in a few
days' time if you'd still like to.'

We met only once, five days later, when he came to breakfast at the
Vanderbilt. He seemed to have come to terms with Manhattan and to
be back in commercial trim. More in line with the man who, when I
had rejected the devious Maurice Girodias's offer of J. P. Donleavy's
The Ginger Man, and passed the copy on to Neville, got the author to
delete the naughtier bits, reprinted five times, and made a packet before
selling the paperback rights to Corgi Books.

New to the place, I found Manhattan a mega-whirlpool, dragging
the newcomer into its dizzying centre at ever-increasing speed. Apart
from some sixty office meetings with publishers, and countless get-
togethers in restaurants, authors' homes, at the Player's Club, and at
parties in such overworked rendezvous as Madison Square and Hotel
Pierre, there were booksellers to call on, from the mighty Brentano's
and Gotham, where collectors' dreams could come true, to Greenwich
Village's fashionable Eighth Street Bookshop where I had agreed with
Eli Wilentz to distribute some of the Beat writers whose poetry he was
publishing, in exchange for which he took some Linden Press poetry
titles.

On business in Manhattan, it proved difficult to eat alone, but I
slowed the frenzied itinerary by occasional snacking in my hotel room
or at Stauffer's luncheonette counter in Grand Central Station, so well
geared to those on the hoof and in a hurry. The meal that mattered
most, of course, was the 7 a.m. breakfast I gave Vernon at the Vanderbilt. I cannot recall what we ate, nor whether a word of negotiation
passed our lips. I suspect we exchanged the usual details of our careers

and families. We had, in fact, met briefly in another's office a few days earlier. But it was, I suppose – at least on Vernon's side – the finalising ritual, the one-to-one, face-to-face deal clincher, where each would judge whether all was likely to be as well as the encouraging transatlantic exchange had suggested. I think we parted without any reservations. It was my last full business day in New York. It had been a stimulating and encouraging trip, and I had been met with great hospitality and courtesy, and given the feeling that I was thought to be on the way up.

I left Manhattan on a Friday afternoon for Westport to spend a recuperative weekend in an early Federal farmhouse between Wilton and Ridgefield in Connecticut. In delightful New England style, it was attached to a nineteen-acre smallholding run by friends of my host, Henry Bailey Stevens. Author, playwright, agriculturalist, and a professor at New Hampshire University, Henry was a distinguished environmentalist long before that term – in its sense as one concerned with the necessity and implications for ecological balance – had come into use. Indeed, he was in some respects far in advance of both his students and his contemporaries, having contributed to the debate well beyond the narrow confines of anthropocentric conservation. Although better known for his *Johnny Appleseed and Paul Bunyan*, it was in *The Recovery of Culture* (1949) that he brought together strands of biology, anthropology, horticulture, philology, sociology, and religion, to form what Toynbee called the only true record of the past – Synoptic History. Although the book was still selling when Henry died at eighty-four in 1976, I could sense from our long talk by the farmhouse log fire – provisioned, laid and lit by him at 5 a.m. while I slept off Manhattan – his deep frustration at society's growing resistance to the eclectical mind in favour of the tunnel vision of the specialist. Fine when it comes to repairing boilers or broken chair legs, specialism is the curse of academia.

It had been a busier weekend than I have recorded, but I felt a lot fitter on the train back to New York. Known locally as the psychiatrists' special, it took stressed writers, media men, declining entrepreneurs, and the hopelessly ill-matched, to consult their shrinks. As I studied the faces and the body language on the 8.10, I suspected that the 9.13 could scarcely be more indicative of what it took to wrest bucks and satisfaction from Neville's 'ghastly canyons'.

Lockering my luggage in Grand Central, I spent a tourist's few hours doing the Museum of Modern Art, the Whitney, the New York Public

Library, the Empire State Building (then, and now again, the tallest), Yankee-style, and would have sampled the Guggenheim, Metropolitan and Frick museums, had they been open on a Monday. Instead, I walked in Central Park, unwisely entering its awful zoo that was enough to make a sadist weep at the inhumanity of man. What is it with our aberrant species that in the centre of such brutal and brutalising sky-high monuments to our inordinate material prosperity and spiritual emptiness, we can derive some spark of perverse satisfaction from penning up a few heaps of moth-eaten old coats that should be bisons and bears? I realised – though perhaps it came to me later – that at the end of a journey to seek a share in that prosperity, I had stumbled on an emotive symbol of the underlying sickness of the Western ethos.

5
Not Swinging, but Drowning

Economy class on a BOAC Comet in 1960 seemed as cramped as its equivalent forty years later, and with so much now lined up for Centaur's future I was impatient to reach home, family, and desk. A boy in the next seat was returning to his school in Surrey, still sniffing back the tears after being put on the plane by his father. He told me he had no mother. I did my best to cheer him up, and before parting he gave me a fearsome American comic, doubtless sensing I was a little out of touch with the real world. I gave 'Dennis the Menace' my best shot, but realised I had progressed little beyond the mindset of pre-war Beano and the feasible adventures of Harry Wharton at Greyfriars. I feigned sleep as an excuse for thinking over the immediate past and the seemingly promising future. Had I developed any skill with a crystal ball, I might have been sobered by just how much I was letting myself in for.

Leaving aside slim volumes of poetry and miscellaneous ephemera, I published about 150 titles between 1954 and 1994. Eighty of these appeared in the 1960s decade, many of them substantial and scholarly works, some in sets of between two and five volumes. These may be figures to prompt amusement or commiseration from today's conglomerate publishers, but for an uncapitalised loner tackling every aspect bar hands-on printing, working within a budget that made employment of in-house staff impossible without a dreaded expansion, it meant little relief for many years from seven-day working weeks with few evenings to call one's own or one's family's. I could only justify this proximity to the grindstone by the feeling that, for all my failings as a fun-providing and attentive father, I was at least nearly always on hand – in the house until 1972, and thereon in a purpose-built office suite across the drive.

The reader, surveying his own shelf of books, may not see why eighty of them should take a grown man a whole decade to plan and put between covers. But books, as already mentioned, are not identical cans of beans which, once tinned, shelved and consumed, are transmuted and forgotten and have no mentionable afterlife. Every book, with the exception of much poetry, most novels, and a few other evanescent categories, has its hereafter, for all that its author may be long dead, buried, and (in the publisher's eyes) thankfully out of copyright. This is the more so with a long-lived serious backlist, the storage of whose stock over many years is a formidable challenge. So, in terms of time and nervous energies, can be the backlist's authors if – and one would want no less – they stay, alive, kicking, producing ever better books, and anxious to be loved. The bulk of the Centaur Classics (thirty-two titles) was published in the 1960s, as were most of the general titles that made any money.

If the sixties were starting to swing, I was not much aware of the fact except through the eyes of Tilly. Her passion for the Beatles had been instant, immoderate, and sustained. Even today, the mother of teenagers, and well aware of the pop-and-drug culture's threat to her own chicks, she becomes tetchy at an incautious reference to that mindlessly permissive era that frightened the wits out of my generation of parents, fearful of what it was all too likely to lead to – and did.

Although the decade gave little time for paternal anxiety about such matters to bear literary fruit, the subconscious must have been mulling things over, as in 1972 I was to publish my first serious non-fiction book, *The Civilised Alternative*. An early plea that IQ be seen as no more important than EQ (emotional intelligence) and the more recent concept of SQ (spiritual intelligence), it suggested a 'pattern for protest' to those increasingly drawn to the negative gesture of merely 'dropping out' of the directionless society that two generations of their elders had bequeathed them. Not that Tilly dropped out. She contributed substantially to a chapter of the book, and by the time it was in print she was on course for a career as an exemplary and much valued teacher. Nearly seven years her junior, Sue was more interested in dropping into life than dropping out. Gentle and kind-hearted, she worked during her school holidays in a home for handicapped babies, surprising no one by going on to make nursing her career, in which to this day her caring nature gives her as much opportunity to work as her lone parental role allows.

Until then, my 'swinging' was confined to the ponderous and sometimes frustrating process of producing books of enough worth to make libraries, universities, and other institutions feel obliged to buy them in adequate quantity to fund Centaur's speculative future. With an exchange of letters the only tangible evidence of SIUP's collaboration in the Centaur Classics series, I was perhaps showing too ready a trust in Southern Illinois's continued dazzlement at the prospect of receiving such prestigious goodies as Bernard Jones's painstaking two-volume

1962 definitive edition of William Barnes's *Poems* (in the dialect, with somewhat simplified phonetic notation); in 1963, Anne Ridler's *Poems and some Letters of James Thomson* (no admirer of James 'B.V.', Grigson nevertheless gave the book nine inches of such compulsive prose in the *New Statesman* that he must have helped considerably to send it out of print); Paul Turner's crown quarto selection of Sir Thomas North's translation of Plutarch's *Lives* (weighing in at over two and a half kilograms, Centaur's heaviest two-volume production!); and a massive reissue, edited and introduced by Graham Hough, of Sir John Harington's translation of Lodovico Ariosto's *Orlando Furioso*, a medium quarto whose 592 arm-breaking pages put it only an ounce or two below the Plutarch. (These physical comparisons may slightly offend sensitive ears, but to small publishers who have to heave packets of books from place to place, such considerations are unfortunately relevant.) Like the others, the Ariosto was well received, and in due course all stock was cleared.

I had sometimes wondered, though with no way of finding out, what proportion of Centaur titles of a high production standard was being bought by collectors. I suspected that libraries – public and institutional – were the main buyers by far, which would indicate a much larger market in the States. But there was no future in speculating, any more than in working up a worry about SIUP's willingness to stay the course, though I was not unaware that North American publishers shared their country's tendency for quick and short-lived enthusiasms. It was an irreversible in-for-a-penny-in-for-a-pound situation. Horrendous sums were pledged on the strength of a smile across the pond, and there could be no thought or wish to turn back.

Between return from the USA in May 1960 and our move from London to West Sussex in August 1961, followed by the further double shift to our permanent home/office in Fontwell in October, the seventeen months brought a workload that may have precipitated a breakdown in health. Almost my only physical counterbalance before we left London had been squash, played several times a week in Whitehall Court, whose comfortably equipped court was beyond the energies of ninety-nine per cent of the other members of the National Liberal and Authors' Clubs. It was as much a reason for joining as was the former club's excellent library – the main consideration when my grandfather put me up for it in 1944. However, the 'straw' may have been my rushed tour of the Caribbean in January 1961 to research the response for a thinking traveller's guide to the West Indies (of which more later), following which I was smitten by what was given the handy label of 'flu, for which an earlier-mentioned and over-zealous GP prescribed a number of powerful drugs that I was later told were probably incompatible. Whether these, overwork, and inadequate rest finally overtaxed the system I shall never know, but for many years it was a daily struggle to cope with symptoms variously attributed to, or named as, neurasthenia, ME, anxiety states, depression, neuralgia, cardiac arrhythmia, and a host of other convenient terms for 'don't really know'. The only one to remain a serious companion to this day was allergic rhinitis, though except in the months of blossom and moulds it has shown – like myself, maybe – less stridency with age. But enough of that. Possibly a West Indian bug triggered the whole thing. Certainly the seven years it took to find the right author, and to produce and market the two-volume guide, were anything but a time of recuperation.

The other Centaur Classics to be published in 1962 were a selection by Paul Turner of Pliny's *Natural History*, taken from the Elizabethan version of Philemon Holland, the so-called 'translator-general' of his age, and said to be one of Shakespeare's sources; and Edward Fairfax's translation of Tasso's 'final masterpiece', *Jerusalem Delivered*, introduced by Roberto Weiss, Professor of Italian at the University of London. Little seems to be known about Fairfax except that he died in 1635 and was praised by Dryden.

Outside the series, the title of most general interest was Boyd Alexander's study of the writer, collector, eccentric and Grand Tourer *par excellence*, William Beckford, *England's Wealthiest Son*. Alexander, who took first class honours in history at Oxford, and shared Beckford's interest in Old Masters, gardens and finance, was intrigued by him from childhood. His great-grandmother, sister of the first Duke of Westminster, had inherited the ruins of Fonthill, which was a fine playground for any youngster with a tendency to romanticism, and the potential financial acumen needed to indulge it. Entrusted by the Duke of Hamilton with the Beckford papers, Alexander had earlier edited Beckford's *Journal in Portugal and Spain* in 1954, and translated his French and Italian letters under the title *Life at Fonthill*. At his request I gladly produced *England's Wealthiest Son* in a format and style virtually identical to that of *Life at Fonthill*, a handsome volume published by Rupert Hart-Davis in 1957. All three books were received enthusiastically by critics such as Rose Macaulay, Cyril Connolly, V. S. Pritchett, Harold Nicolson, and (yes) Geoffrey Grigson.

Less exotic than the Beckford, though setting a similar style of production, the other quite important general title that year was *The Symbolic Meaning*, hopefully but not inaccurately announced as an unpublished work by D. H. Lawrence. It consisted of the first versions of Lawrence's unpublished essays, *The Transcendental Element in American Literature*, written in 1917–18 before Lawrence's sympathy toward America had turned into bitter hatred. The inferior 1923 versions, published as *Studies in Classic American Literature* in 1923 (New York) and 1924 (London), were not well received. *The Symbolic Meaning* went into a second impression in 1975, but sold only a little over 300 copies in the next twenty years, hardly justifying the further investment. Armin Arnold had edited *The Symbolic Meaning*, and it was blessed and prefaced by the American author, translator and Lawrence authority, Harry T. Moore. It was the third time Armin had put his name to a Centaur title – in 1959 we published his bibliography of Heinrich Heine, largely on my side for the rather frivolous reason that I had fond early-life memories of some Margaret Armour translations of Heine's poetry.

In June 1960 Harry Moore had thrown a Lawrence party in the Burnsall Street house of Sir Richard Rees, painter, writer and pre-war editor of the *Adelphi*. The most startling guest present was Fredric Warburg's wife Pamela de Bayou, whom neither Jennifer nor I had met before. The vast flower on the front of her hat had the seeking air of a miner's lamp, and the equally overstated gold 'DE B' on her massive handbag removed any vestige of uncertainty of her identity. Fred's splendidly, if ironically, entitled story of his publishing career, *An Occupation for Gentlemen*, confirms that their marriage held together, and I doubt if he would have got far without Pamela's shrewd, caustic and relentless control. Every publisher should have one.

It was, I think, Warren Roberts, Professor of English in the library of the University of Texas, who looked round at the misleadingly sober-suited throng who had written, were writing, or were intending to write yet another book about Lawrence, and remarked drily and unarguably: 'If the Bomb fell on this house tonight, Lawrence would die.'

But in that era Lawrence lived, and Graham Hough, D. J. Enright and Bernard Bergonzi were among those who, in addition to the *TLS* and other literary heavies, gave *The Symbolic Meaning* serious, and on the whole favourable, attention. Considering that few writers have aroused more passionate disagreement, we were lucky that on balance the feeling was that Armin had done a service to literature in ensuring that both versions of the essays were at last available.

I have mentioned three of the Centaur Classics that were published in 1963. The rest for that year were:

1 Francisco de Quevedo's *Visions*, which in Sir Roger L'Estrange's translation is seen as one of the few exemplary examples of Restoration prose. In his introduction, J. M. Cohen gives pride of place to the translator rather than to the author – not because there was nothing that could be said about Quevedo's racy life and savage responses to the many targets of his venom, but as acknowledgement of L'Estrange's rendering which, while taking undoubted liberties with Quevedo's actual words and syntax, keeps close to the spirit of his work. Of the inevitably few reviews, one was by Bonamy Dobrée in *Books of the Month*, and there was an expansive welcome in the *TLS*, then a good friend of most things Centaur.

2 Anicius Manlius Severinus Boethius's *The Consolation of Philosophy*. This had had translators as various as Alfred the Great, Elizabeth I and Geoffrey Chaucer. But the Centaur edition's editor William Anderson, with Jack Cohen's approval, felt the 1609 translation by the anonymous 'I.T.' (possibly John Thorpe, *fl.*1570–1610, architect to Thomas Sackville, Earl of Dorset) to be the most suitable for the present day.

Bill did a good job, as the reviews made plain; but in the 1960s revivals of classical philosophy were hard put to it to ignite the Thames. Boethius was executed in 524 for attempting to leaven the corruption of his day with the civilising influence of philosophy and poetry. Although he wrote *De Consolatione Philosophiae* when imprisoned prior to his death, the beauty of his last work, as Anderson remarked, is that it soars to a region far beyond the squabbles of sects and intellectual animosities. The Centaur edition sold out after twenty years, if largely to scholars whose involvement was intellectual rather than spiritual.

3 Luis Vaz de Camoes's *The Lusiads (The Portuguese)*, the supreme work of one of the greatest epic poets of sixteenth-century Europe. In Sir Richard Fanshawe's translation, edited and introduced by Geoffrey Bullough, this received above-average attention, not only from the *TLS* but from a good swathe of the middling-to-highbrow papers. Sales were steady and satisfactory, spreading the return of investment until ownership of Centaur was transferred. A perfect backlist title for the small firm. However, there is always the danger with long-life titles that

a rival edition may appear, seriously damaging the health of your sales chart. This did not happen with the Camoes, but competing editions of a few other titles were published, some of them by 'big Oxford' (OUP).

4 Jean Froissart's *Chronicles*, the last Classic for 1963. In Lord Berners's translation, the selection was edited and introduced by Gillian and William Anderson. The all-important *TLS* review was a tad carping, but with the help of other Friends of the Classics (as we had begun to see papers such as the *Scotsman*, *New Statesman*, *Guardian-Journal* (Nottingham), *Church Times*, and *TES*), over 600 of the UK edition of 700 copies sold in thirty-five years. One could not reasonably have wished for more.

As may by now be obvious, new editions of works of such academic appeal, at a time when short printing runs necessitated a dangerously high selling price, were only possible if the UK publisher could find an overseas market (mainly in the USA), preferably by exporting a bulk quantity bearing the importing publisher's imprint on title-page, cover and dust-jacket, rather than by the sale of rights. By printing, say, 1,500 copies and shipping (usually) half to the SIUP, the lower unit cost of production made possible a 'consumer-friendly' selling price in both markets. Even so, as the originating publisher Centaur would not have ended up in profit had I taken on the luxury of a secretary, or an outside office and the overheads that this would bring.

Although, by the mid-1960s, Centaur seemed to be standing on its four legs and to have earned approval from those that mattered, its list lacked the predictability of an OUP or even a Macmillan. But the small publisher can indulge the odd whim without censure or surprise. One such minor fancy was to reissue *Peter's Pencil*, a tale for the five-to-elevens that had been published by John Lane in 1920. Its author, Phyllis Morris, whose friendship with my mother, Esmé, dated from the First World War, was one of my favourite 'aunts'. Caustic, combative, and very funny, she was a joyous source of the morally and politically incorrect to a child whose mother and nanny had closed implacable ranks to save him body and soul from the world's contamination. Her first play, done by the Repertory Players in 1926, had five offers for a West End production before the final curtain, but having a private income sadly weakened her incentive to develop her skills to the full. Nevertheless *Peter's Pencil* was a triumph remembered fondly from my constrained childhood, and if Tilly's reaction to it was anything to go by, juvenile taste had not much changed by the autumn of 1963 when, with minimal updating and in a smaller format, the Centaur edition appeared. About a boy, passionate to draw everything around him, whose magic pencil invented a world in which he preferred to live, and which could be changed by merely rubbing out its nastier aspects, it cantered out of print with little media help and almost no representation to the bookshops.

Phyllis was an equally old friend of another of my surrogate aunts, the playwright Dodie Smith, in whose *Call It a Day* Phyllis's role as a charwoman established her as a character actress of the first rank. The play's run of fifteen months was the longest ever hitherto for a woman dramatist, but it was Dodie's *Dear Octopus*, written three years later, that made her name and is still being performed. I found her, however, a less satisfactory aunt in my early years – she lacked Phyllis's seditious humour and easy empathy with the child mind. Phyllis's entrenched passion for dispute was fortunately not my problem. Dodie certainly found it a disruptive downside to their friendship, but for all that they saw more of each other than of Esmé who was preoccupied with her plays, novels, and journalism through the 1920s, and anyway preferred correspondence to more time-consuming meetings with her friends and relations.

In the earlier years of their friendship Dodie had found Esmé supportive and helpful. My mother had enjoyed success on the stage and was an established writer with good critical judgement. Moreover, Dodie (whose mother had introduced her to Christian Science in childhood) discovered in Esmé a convincing interpreter of the not always crystal clear wisdom of Mary Baker Eddy and was much helped by her friend's ability to bring 'Science' to bear on several aspects of her increasingly fraught life. These ranged from problems with the writing of *Autumn Crocus*, her first produced play, to coping with the joint birthday gift from her future husband, Alec Beesley, and Phyllis of a dalmatian puppy, Pongo. A professional Christian Science practitioner had to be called in when the now grown-up Pongo was reputedly in a poor state of health. Valerie Grove, who in her biography of Dodie writes delightfully of her subject's love/hate relationship with Phyllis, records that this bowler-hatted gentleman, a Mr Waddington, 'merely gazed on' the seemingly moribund Pongo, who 'at once took a turn for the better, and within weeks was his own self'.

Phyllis and Dodie, like many stage people, but unlike Esmé, whose sense of loyalty was as strong toward ideology as to her fellows, were distinctly fair-weather Scientists. Dodie, in particular, put her work before everything with a sometimes understandable ruthlessness that

NOT SWINGING, BUT DROWNING

could cut across even her deepest friendships. As for the Deity, he was there to serve Dodie. Only from correspondence little drawn upon by Valerie Grove could a more in-depth study of her be written, and that seems an unlikely prospect. But the story of her inner turmoils, especially those induced by leaving England to live in the USA from 1940 to 1953, deserves to be more seriously recorded. For the rest of her life Dodie regretted that the geographical and cultural hiatus had greatly diminished her ability to write convincingly of that society she had so well understood and brilliantly portrayed in her pre-war plays. Spending most of the gap years on the west coast of America, writing and working for Hollywood, she was desperate to understand, to feel, the atmosphere of England in the war years – a desire heightened by snide reactions of 'friends' who were happy with their own interpretations of her motives for staying in the States.

Her husband Alec was equally keen to keep in touch with life in the UK, and a proportion of my own correspondence with them, spanning 1940 to Dodie's death in 1990, was prompted by his interest in my uncomplicated observations of, and reactions to, wartime England. Indeed, so revealing was the surviving correspondence that in 1976 I put to Dodie the case for Centaur publishing an edited selection of her correspondence with Esmé, perhaps including exchanges with friends of both parties. *Inter alia*, I suggested, it would explain in her own words the wartime period that caused her and Alec so much soul-searching, fear and regret. By then the first volume of her autobiography had been published, and it was perhaps clearer to some of her friends than to Dodie herself that as a novelist she was unlikely to find a public as appreciative as that for her plays.

Dodie's negative reaction was surprising and rather sad. Her strong desire to be seen through her writing as still 'with it', and part of the 'real world', prompted excuses and statements that her own correspondence contradicted. But she was nearing eighty, and as I had put up the idea more out of long friendship and as a return for many kindnesses rather than with any certainty that the book would be a commercial success, her refusal was not difficult to accept. Later, aware that she was having great difficulty placing the fourth volume of her autobiography, I said I thought it might be acceptable to Anthony Blond. It was. It was published that same year (1985), then reprinted, but by then the Beesleys had reached the end of the line, and *Look Back with Gratitude*, in the light of despairing messages I received from them, proved a rather inappropriate title for Dodie's last book.

With the help of Pongo and his successors, it was I who planted a thought in Dodie's mind that was to reward her materially more than all her plays and novels put together. In 1954, remembering the many letters about, and photographs of, their dogs that the Beesleys had sent from their numerous homes in the States, I suggested to Dodie (with very little hope of my squeaky-new Centaur Press being considered a suitable home) that she write a book about her beloved dalmatians.

> Dearest Jon [she wrote on 15 November], Bless you, I could no more write a little book on dogs than an epic poem – I just can't write to order. And I don't like reading about dogs, let alone writing about them. I just like dogs in the flesh. As for anything more 'substantial,' my two publishers, English and American, have never ceased to encourage me to do another novel, and heaven knows I want to, as 'Castle' made far more than any of my plays. But get going I cannot ...

Get going she did, however, waking at midnight four days before that Christmas, when 'the whole plot of *The Hundred and One Dalmatians* unfolded itself in my imagination'. After letting it simmer, she began the writing of her first children's book in March 1955, seeing it published by Heinemann in 1956, in America in 1957, and filmed by Disney in 1961.

I can take no credit for the storyline that unfolded for Dodie in the night watches, but I sometimes wonder whether I might have done better materially as a literary agent rather than as a publisher.

It was then, when nice things were being said about Centaur, when 'How I ...' talks were being invited, when the sun was shining and the path ahead seemed broad and welcoming, that in November 1963 a letter came from Vernon to say he had taken a long hard look at SIUP's costings of, and receipts from, the fourteen Classics they had received. The punch-line was explicit: 'I must terminate our agreement for the Classics as of this day.'

He enclosed an analysis. This showed gross receipts for only nine of the fourteen titles. The first four (the Beethoven, Plato, Oldham and FitzGerald) had cost SIUP a total of $7,518. Their gross receipts had so far been $10,421. These figures struck me, after so short a shelf-life, as a cause for celebration rather than precipitation, since all further sales of those titles had to be clear gross profit. On the other five titles for which he had up-to-date details, SIUP's expenditure had been $25,185, and receipts $10,102. As there had been an eighteen-month gap between the birth of the first four titles and the first of the later clutch, both sets of figures seemed satisfactory – it had, after all, been agreed from the start that we were collaborating on building a scholarly and inevitably slow-moving backlist. We both knew that reviews take time to appear in the scholarly journals – some of them quarterly or even yearly. Our own sales had done no better in so short a time, nor had I expected or dared to hope that they would.

But there was no mileage in argument or hurt. It seemed clear than an accountancy decision had been made from on high. Forty years on, I have surprised myself by re-reading my restrained response to Vernon's unexpected and shattering letter. Nerves are stronger in middle age, no doubt, and hope springs eternal in the younger breast – and needs to if books are being dealt with in any shape or form. But although I suggested, and repeated, such obvious solutions as that SIUP took smaller editions of the series, it was clear from the lack of reasoned response, and unconvincing calculations, that a policy switch was behind the decision to 'want out'. Two months later Vernon wrote:

> I meant to make clear that our small publishing program cannot support larger editions [publishing bigger editions, perhaps in paperback, at a smaller per-copy price, had also been mooted] because of the additional capital involved. We now have a good deal of 'automatic' publishing going on, which ties up a lot of money. If it were not for this fact, I would be inclined to plump for larger editions. All of us here are very sorry. In fact, one of the University Vice Presidents was almost inclined to find some money for me to continue the series.

Almost! I am sure Vernon had not intended knife-twisting commiseration, but his closing confirmation that 'Our experience with the Classics has been very good, and I continue to be grateful to you for them' was as comforting as closing one's teeth on a lemon mistaken for a peach. It had to be faced that the US product now took priority, the euphemism 'automatic publishing' suggesting that the University's alumni were pressuring for funds to be put into theses on gender features among middle-western water beetles, and preceptive and visceral significance in the middle period of Grandma Moses.

Vernon had assured me that SIUP would honour their agreement for the remaining titles, and I am sure he meant it. The next few years, however, were far from plain sailing. Vernon was doubtless under increasing pressure from accountants and faculties unable or unwilling to be flexible. In March 1964 I was able to tell him that Sir Edward Hulton's wife (of whom more later) wished to buy Centaur Press; that Secker and Warburg were going to represent Centaur in the home market to fill the gap left by the departed Hart-Davis; and that this meant we should be able to sell more of the Classics in the UK and overseas markets, expanding into paperback editions. By these means we could get by with selling smaller editions to SIUP, and I asked if on that basis they would stay with the series beyond the programme agreed. Two and a half months later he replied that he had 'agonised' over the matter, but could see no possibility of continuing even on a limited basis, and had to look forward to as early a termination of our agreement as possible, while hoping he would be able to fulfil SIUP's commitments in the meantime.

I had tried, in vain, to let SIUP off the hook altogether by reaching an agreement with some other American publisher, two of those approached being Alfred Knopf and the University of Chicago Press. The latter's director had written: 'I have long envied Vernon Sternberg the prestige and variety that your Centaur Classics added to his very fine list', but in the end his colleagues preferred an alternative, larger, and homespun project that had been put up to them. None of the firms approached felt happy, I suspect, about taking over a fellow US publisher's reject.

SIUP's decision reduced the advantage to Secker in taking on the Centaur list, and weakened my hand in negotiating with the Hultons' money-men. There seemed nothing for it but to carry on producing the agreed titles for SIUP, which I did until 1972. Even so, the ensuing years were a bumpy ride. SIUP ducked, weaved, cajoled, threatened, seemingly hoping by the attrition of long silences and inadequate responses to wear me down to submission and worse. I am sure that was not Vernon's own considered intention, but sensitivities are not heightened by distance between actions and their effect, whether in so-called peace or war. Had I not gently wrested from SIUP a formal agreement in September 1962, I doubt if Centaur could have survived. By 1965, attempts to deny that several titles had been agreed at all were sullying the correspondence with Vernon, who I suspect to this day was but the helpless mouthpiece of a faceless Admin. Nevertheless, that April, with thousands of pounds tied up in irreversible fees, paper and printing, I had to write to him in no uncertain terms, spelling out the facts – Centaur and personal. He seemed to take on board at last that a small publisher is bound to have cash flow problems if he is financing expensive ventures that have to be paid for long before the product begins to return the investment. From then on, with some worrying hiccups, amiability reigned for a few years.

In August 1970 Vernon sent me an inventory of the twenty-eight Classics they had so far received and sold. I checked on our own editions and reported that of only four titles had Centaur sold more than SIUP. Of some titles, SIUP had sold more than double. In the month following, with only a few agreed titles still in the pipeline, Vernon wrote that 'the American universities are in such great danger I personally doubt anyone can do anything for them'. Assuming that so doom-laden a statement meant that his masters' priorities were putting him through a mangle of mega proportions, I sent, far from the first time, suggestions that I hoped would ease his problems. They were fair, reasonable, and with mutual goodwill, workable; but they were ignored. We had reached a point where, I imagined, he was under such pressure to allocate his funds to other projects that no reasonable response could be expected. The growing ruthlessness of scholarly publishing (forget the gentle groves of Academe) was clearly calling the shots. In fairness, whatever my private views about SIUP's accountants, they were always prompt and considerate about payments.

To try to end the affair on a friendly note, I said I would not press SIUP to accept several of the agreed titles, and I bought back some of their slower-moving stock. I was, and remain, grateful to SIUP for enabling me to build a solid core of worthwhile texts into my early publishing, and I realised I had been at fault in failing to investigate their funding and publishing policies from the start – though how I could have done this, I am not sure. The series had not deserved to be axed, and others lamented the phasing out that commonsense collaboration and adjustment could have avoided. But an older and wiser head than mine might not have been dizzied by SIUP's initial enthusiasm. In those days it had still meant something to American universities to acquire a prestigious share in Britain's academic output for their publishing arms. Their rhapsodic responses to the ideas and scholarly names that were proposed for the selections and editings were obviously genuine, and at that stage financial limitations had not seriously been raised. Vernon and I had shown more youthful enthusiasm than caution, but there is nothing new in that.

I have skimmed the 'politics' of the early Centaur Classics years only briefly, as an illustration of one of the major perils that lie in wait for the small-scale and unsubsidised publisher. It can be just as devastating if he finds himself coping with an unexpected best-seller that tempts immediate expansion, for which he finds he needs more capital than his successful title brings in. As in other aspects of life, the trick is in getting the balance right.

On the general side in 1963, the least commercial title published (with the help of a subsidy) was L. L. Johnson's translation, in the metre of the original, of Lucretius's *De Rerum Natura*. The *TLS*, though approving, was not alone in its amazement that anyone should attempt to render Lucretius's *On the Nature of Things* into English hexameters (the *Humanist* reviewer actually praised the impertinence). But more is needed than reviews. Even today, a printed catalogue or web-sent announcement of one's forthcoming titles and backlist responses is as important as not losing one's head over an incipient best-seller. Centaur's 1958 and 1959 lists had been eight and twelve-page crown octavos (7½" x 5"); for 1960 the format jumped to 8¼" x 5¼", a heavily trimmed demy octavo of sixteen pages. That size was held until 1968, when the page total rose to a heady twenty, only to return in 1969 to sixteen pages in the small format of 4⅜" x 6¾", and set in a smaller typesize as evidence that the lack of new titles in the Centaur Classics was hitting turnover. That format was kept for 1970 and for the two biennial catalogues of 1971–72, and 1973–74. Thereafter we got by with full lists for 1979, 1983, and 1992, interspersed with occasional checklists for pricing updates and confirming details of the few new titles until the final publication in 1994. After several decades of continual publishing, the imprint was well established, reducing the necessity for yearly catalogues.

Even with the help of a wife and two daughters to address, collate, fill, and stamp envelopes, usually at that time of the year when the job could be done by a log fire in the sitting room, the catalogue mailing was a major chore. In the early years in Sussex our nearest post office was the 10 ft x 6 ft front room of a tiny eighteenth-century cottage at the top of a bank on the further side of the then easily negotiated A27 road, almost opposite the long garden to the south of this house. In those days our farming neighbour could still herd her cows daily across this now lethal dual-carriageway, to pasture on the other side of the A29: a double-risk venture not to be taken lightly today.

The catalogue mailing was too vital a task to be assigned to anything but in-house family care. When the 4,000–5,000 lists were ready to go – mostly in singles, but some in bulk – they were put into the Centaur 'van' for taking down the hill to the post office. This unique vehicle was a long timber box that I had knocked up in the workshop, bolted to the supporting frame and wheels of Tilly's coach-finished Silver Cross perambulator, bought second hand in the lean year of 1951 from a family in Kensington's Edwardes Square.

Possibly because, after the encouraging reception for Centaur Press, I had returned subconsciously to a state of guileless innocence, I took on a biography of (and entitled) *Muriel Spark*, written by the poet and critic Derek Stanford. It was published in September 1963, two months before Vernon Sternberg's unsettling letter.

Stanford, as followers of literary history of that period will know, was an old friend of Muriel Spark who, in the time she could spare from her writing, and after working in the sparse surroundings provided by the publisher Peter Owen, whose furniture consisted largely of packing cases, helped him to determine his amatory orientation. They had collaborated intensively, and there was evident rapport, though for Derek, or for that matter anyone else, to have been part of Muriel's life and output in the days when her reputation was beginning to blossom was bound to prompt somewhat seismic emotional crises and intellectual tensions. Writers tend to mix better together when they live apart. Not that I was near the centre of their often stormy relationship, nor sought to be, having enough problems of my own. Muriel and Derek were part of the postwar London set of 'Soho' writers and bohemians, generally rather older than myself, of whom I saw little after we came to live in Sussex, for my bohemianism had for the most part tended to be voyeuristic rather than flaunted. *Square Peg* was not entirely free of autobiographical content.

Two of Derek's poems, written when their association still held some semblance of friendship, spoke of and defined their essential separation. His 'Idyll', its first line 'Between the chestnut boughs at Camberwell', finished:

> No continuity
> attends our stubborn lot; and when I speak
> I praise not things that are nor things that were,
> but life that might have been – a liar's feast.

Another, from a published selection of his 1946–79 work, spoke,

apropos vacating an 'uncongenial flat', of 'rooms which knew our
poverty and doubt'. But it might be more fair to his muse to quote one
poem in its entirety – 'Leasehold', an aptly chosen title for a time-
limited relationship:

> A black umbrella in among the boughs,
> and at their feet a blaze of brittle stalks.
> Tinder and fern and touchwood for a couch;
> such was the transitory pleasure-house
> in which these wanderers heard the rain discourse.
>
> Think not their thorny lodge was less than snug,
> or unappointed with domestic ease;
> he, furnishing the flame with deft intent,
> while she, upon the escritoire of her knees,
> bent to indite, in speech of choicest blend,
> news of their sojourning to ingenious friends.
>
> And now, about this domicile of twigs,
> rain falters; and the country-agent sun,
> retiring, serves an urgent note to quit
> before his master's properties grow dun
> with sylvan shadows unplacatable:
>
> he treads the fire; she puts away her pen;
> they sigh, rise up, look back, and ramble on.

Since publication of *Muriel Spark*, I have realised how few references
have been made in print to their friendship. In *The Fitzrovians*, Hugh
David mentions Derek, but not Muriel. In *War Like a Wasp*, Andrew
Sinclair refers to them both, but in just as sparse detail. Robert
Greacen, in *The Sash My Father Wore*, expresses surprise that they did
not marry, but neither as an item, nor singly, do they appear in
Memoirs of the Forties; but Julian Maclaren-Ross's sudden death
accounted for numerous Notable Omissions. In *The Answer to Life Is
No*, however, the anonymous author Charles Wrey Gardiner referred
generously to them both, but under false names – as he did with equal
and wise caution in mentioning other literati of the period. It was the
final volume of his intriguing life story, and I was left the revealingly
annotated copy he inscribed for his 'oldest friend', the poet, editor and
biographer John Gawsworth. Wrey was a bohemian by any definition
of that state, but he was also a quietly observant, kindly, and – by

intention, at least – truthful man. To those aware of the code, his book tells much that has not been disclosed in print elsewhere, but was generally known at the time in most of the pubs and drinking clubs of Soho. There are not many of us left ...

When, in March 1962, Derek offered me his 'biographical portrait', it was only some 22,000 words in length. Muriel had soared to fame and was a Book Club choice both here and in the States. I was moving away from the short book, and I knew Americans were resistant to potted biographies and etiolated 'studies'. So Derek doubled the wordage of his very restrained, respectful, and respectable little book, which was scarcely more than a rather breathless and whispered essay in the style of a Victorian vignette. It still made a short book that had to be printed with lots of space between the lines, and generous margins.

If Derek could have been judged, by the company he kept, as a bohemian, he was the mildest example I knew. He wrote of Muriel as if she had been dead some fifty years and entombed in Westminster Abbey. He referred to her as 'Miss Spark'. Even forty years ago, this was a trifle quaint. I don't think he was all that happy with my mild attempts to achieve, at the least, a little stylistic and terminological updating, as there was a gap in our correspondence, broken after two months when he wrote that 'arrangements over the Muriel monograph with Dobson [Dennis Dobson, the publisher who had contemplated issuing the book as it stood] were not satisfactory'. Derek now offered greater length and 'to bear in mind what you have already suggested, and add matter of a biographical nature a good deal more "relaxed" in tone'. My hope that 'Miss Spark' could be changed to 'Muriel' (in the circumstances) was rather more than he could stomach, but when he sent the finished book in September he had done his best: 'Muriel Spark' was a frequent compromise. His earlier wish to call it a recollection had been abandoned for the 'alliterative advantages' of 'a medallion'. After a hint that this seemed a somewhat atavistic improvement, he settled for the subtitle of 'A biographical and critical study'.

In no way had these minimal adjustments brought *Muriel Spark* within a million miles of being judged as a work of racy reminiscence or raunchy revelation. If one had tried to place it in a 'stable', it would have stood, in its primeval innocence, in the next stall to Aymer Roberts's *Judge Not*. Nevertheless, life being what it is, and authors being what they are, as a precaution and a courtesy I wrote to Muriel to tell her I had agreed to publish Derek's critical and biographical study. The main paragraph read:

Derek's life has got somewhat complicated of late, and I am frankly having all hell getting the book out of him ... I anticipate some difficulty in keeping to my intention to publish it this autumn. I would – in view of having known the Derek/John Bayliss/Robert Greacen gang for a good many years – be rather glad if you could spare the time to have a look at the book before I get it under way, and in fact what I would very much like to do, if you are agreeable, is to see you when I have received the TS and have been able to glance through it myself. We could then go over any points that might seem to you to need attention. As you will probably guess from knowing Derek, it is no 'stark revelation', but nevertheless I should like to feel you were quite happy about it.

Five days later, the phone rang and a sepulchral voice, choked with rage, said without preamble, in tones reminiscent of Edith Evans's handbag line, 'You are a *disreputable* publisher!' A great deal followed, in an unstoppable stream.

The tirade was so blistering that it seemed only sensible to write at once to Michael Rubinstein of Rubinstein, Nash and Co. Falling in with Derek's precautionary mode of address, I also wrote to Muriel, enclosing a copy of my letter to Michael.

14 February 1963

Dear Miss Spark,

While making every allowance for the fact that you have, you say, had a lot of trouble with Derek Stanford, and were therefore more than necessarily disturbed to receive a letter from me saying that I was publishing his study of you, I was more surprised than I can say to receive the allegations – extremely libellous allegations – that you levelled at me on the telephone this morning. It is perhaps fortunate that a witness overheard the entire conversation.

In view of the fact that you threatened me with court proceedings (not to mention with an 'appeal to the public' this very afternoon), I must restate my position quite clearly and will notify my solicitors accordingly.

Among your accusations was that I am a 'disreputable publisher', and you implied that I was 'one of his (Derek Stanford's) associates'. You further asked me: 'Are you trying to get money out of me to suppress publication?' The implication about being one of Derek's associates is unimportant, perhaps, because this could mean merely that I was his publisher, although I sensed you meant the statement to stand in a different light. But I must regard your other two remarks far more seriously.

I see that when I wrote to you on the 9th of this month, to which your phone call has been the only reply, I sent you my current catalogue. If you had troubled to go through this (and one of your remarks was that you haven't the time to bother with anything to do with Derek Stanford or his writings), you would have noticed that I am not precisely a specialist in the publication of saucy revelations. Nor do I think you will find that I have any reputation for publishing irresponsible books.

Please don't think I am unsympathetic to your position. People who attain a certain reputation in the field of writing, the stage, etc., can often be worried by the publicity that follows. But as I made perfectly clear in my letter of 9th February, Derek Stanford's study is (I quote from my own words) 'no "stark revelation"'. At least, it certainly wasn't when I passed it back to him for further attention, and I have no reason to suppose it will be when it is back in my hands. I am not interested in that sort of publishing.

You will appreciate that I was under no obligation whatsoever to write to you and offer to spare some of my extremely occupied time in going over the typescript in order to ensure that there was nothing in it that would worry you or that was inaccurate in any important detail. You seemed to accuse me on the phone of not having approached you before, but when Derek offered me the book it was already completed, so surely it was for him to extend you that courtesy originally, not for me. Until the final version was in my hands, there would have been no point in writing to you, and I only did so ahead of receiving the final version because Derek has been so long in turning it in that I was afraid I could not bring the book out in the autumn as intended. Your remarks on this aspect were also most unnecessary and ill-mannered, and entirely uncalled for.

The position now, then, is that you have absolutely refused to see the typescript or to have anything to do with Derek Stanford or me. I think and believe that you have behaved in an impetuous and short-sighted manner, but whether or not you are willing to offer me some apology for your extremely offensive response to my quite genuine and friendly approach, I am still quite willing to discuss Derek's book with you before it is published.

If I do not hear from you again I shall assume that you do not wish to take advantage of my offer to show you the book and discuss it with you.   Yours sincerely,

JON WYNNE-TYSON

Half an hour after the letters caught the afternoon post, Michael Rubinstein rang and said: 'I have Muriel Spark with me.' My mother had known Michael's father, the lawyer and playwright Harold Rubinstein, since the 1920s. Michael was already, and remained until his death in 2001, a valued and supportive friend. Muriel, not knowing of the connection, any more than I knew of hers, could hardly have gone to a more suitable solicitor. He saw the typescript subsequently, so was able to assure her how far it was from the realms of lubricity and exposure. From Muriel, however, I received only an unsigned typed note from her Camberwell address, dated 15 February 1963:

Mrs Spark acknowledges receipt of Mr Wynne-Tyson's letter of the 14th February.

Mrs Spark regrets that she has nothing to add to her decision, communicated by telephone, not to authorise, and to dissociate herself from, any writings by Mr Derek Stanford that touch upon her personal life.

It was far short of an apology, so I made do with noting that the address was in copper-plate blush-pink lettering.

But the matter was not allowed to rest in peace. On 4 October, a few days after *Muriel Spark* was published, the *TLS* printed a letter from the book's subject. The gist was that if Derek had consulted Muriel before his biography had been written, she would have 'advised against this undertaking, on the grounds that my work is only begun, it is not yet ready to be assessed, I have not covered anything like the novels that I have in mind if I am spared ... it is a pity to dignify, as it were, a small group of minor sketches by subjecting them to a whole work of criticism'.

These were not the objections that had got through to me during Muriel's vituperative phone call, and it was interesting to note that at that time her 'small group of minor sketches' included *Memento Mori*, *The Ballad of Peckham Rye*, *The Bachelors*, and *The Prime of Miss Jean Brodie*. Muriel ended her letter with the assertion that I had 'applied to (her) to supply biographical material' which she 'emphatically' refused to do, and 'also declined to read any portion of the book lest it be supposed that I was in any way authorising the project as such'.

On 11 October the *TLS* joyfully published letters from Derek and myself. With rare waspishness Derek suggested that if Muriel's corpus to date was a small group of minor sketches, 'it would seem that, with so modest an artist, her writing needs rescuing from the insignificance to which she relegates it'. Feeling that to maintain a dignified silence could be counter-productive, I wrote:

> Sir, I hope you may allow me to correct certain inaccuracies in Mrs Spark's letter in your last issue.
>
> It was February 9 this year that I wrote to Mrs Spark to say that I had received the typescript of Derek Stanford's biographical and critical study which I proposed to publish under the title *Muriel Spark*, and to ask if she would care to read it in case there was any inaccuracy she would like to see repaired. At no time, then or since, have I asked Mrs Spark to supply biographical material. My letter to her was purely a courtesy, and it took care to stress the restraint of the study.
>
> Had Mrs Spark accepted my offer to show her the typescript, she would not have had to spend these months in fear and trepidation of whatever it was she apparently supposed the book would contain. I confess that to this day I cannot see what the fuss was about, for as a study of her work it is, and attempts to be, no more than an examination of her progress to date, and contains in addition a fifty-five-page 'Recollection' by an old and frankly admiring friend who had known her well at an early period in her career. No one is suggesting that we have here a definitive study of her Life and Works!
>
> I feel that if Mrs Spark had not so emphatically declined the opportunity to read the book before publication – and it appears that she has still not seen it, though active in her campaign against its circulation – she might have spared herself and others a good deal of trouble. JON WYNNE-TYSON

Publication was greeted by Frank Kermode with over forty column inches in the *New Statesman*. However, it was less a review than Kermode's own critical study of Muriel's main novels to date. Prophetically headed 'The Prime of Miss Muriel Spark', which may or may not have pleased her, its general tone was favourable to her work while hardly mentioning the biography other than to give author, publisher and price.

The *TLS* reviewer's response to Derek's regret at the unsympathetic light that Muriel cast on her novels' Catholic heroines prompted a further letter from Derek to the editor, denying the reviewer's seeming assumption that he was biased against Catholicism, but confirming his dislike of 'the author's misanthropy and lack of charity which she seeks to present in Catholic dressing'. Other reviews took a similar line. But in general the notices, most of them minor, were cautiously non-committal. Burnett James was fair and sensible in *Books of the Month*, but the best review by far was written in the *Poetry Review* by John Bayliss, an old friend of both Muriel and Derek. John received an OBE for his work on the British Government's Low-Priced Books Scheme, which made textbooks available to students in developing countries. He would have deserved it equally for his fine work as a poet, and certainly for his diplomacy, fairness, and a kindliness that in this instance could have caused no justifiable offence to either warring party, yet said what had to be said and conveyed the facts accurately and percipiently.

The book sold poorly and is still in print, Muriel may be glad to know. By 1990 her file on *Muriel Spark*/Derek Stanford had yet to be stamped RIP. In the *Independent on Sunday*, Lynn Barber reported her as still seething. If Barber's interview is to be believed, her references to Derek, though not named in the article, were still mean-spirited toward a one-time friend and writer far less materially successful than herself, and infinitely less aware of those varied talents needed to master the art of getting hyped. A 'premature' biography would not have aroused her anger, I suspect, had it been written by an eminent man of letters.

When Muriel published her autobiography, *Curriculum Vitae*, two years later, things had got no better. 'Her principal target', wrote the *Daily Telegraph*'s 'Peterborough' in May, 'is her biographer and some-time companion Derek Stanford, whose 1977 book, *Inside the Forties*, claimed that Mrs Spark believed T. S. Eliot was raiding her larder and sending her coded messages through the blurbs of Faber books.' Compared with what Muriel found in *Inside the Forties*, the sins of *Muriel Spark* had become very small beer. I suppose it was at least an olive branch, if only to myself, when she admitted as much after I responded to her published request for letters or reminiscence about the 1947–49 period at The Poetry Society. Having known many of the

Society's poets, staff, and major feudings of those days, I wrote offering help, adding a little friendly 'update'. Perhaps mellowed by age and
the Italian sun, she replied in amiable terms, confirming she had not
seen Derek since the early 1960s. I told her what I knew of his unhappy
circumstances, and offered to print, for insertion in all remaining
copies of *Muriel Spark*, a sheet of her corrections of the alleged inac-
curacies. In two letters that month she admitted that 'Stanford's more
outrageous claims were in fact in a book not published by yourself,
called *Inside the Forties* ...', and acknowledged that 'It is nice of you
to want to put in an erratum sheet, but in fact there are too many distortions, etc., to be worth anyone's time, but thanks all the same.' I
thought better of assuring her of how few erratum slips were likely to
be needed, for all that it would have held a cheering element, but I had
made the offer largely in the hope of the sun not setting in Toscana on
any remnants of grievance. For Derek – the *pisseur de copie* Hector
Bartlett in *A Far Cry from Kensington* – the sun is getting low in his
terminal old folks' home in Brighton, and it would be nice if he were
to receive an olive twig from Toscana before there is only a headstone
to receive it.

   This résumé of the *Muriel Spark* controversy will not, I hope, open
old wounds. But apart from the amusing aspects, and the insight it gives
into the problems that can arise for the small publisher when writers
clash, this seems the obvious opportunity for an all (we hope) passion-
spent recounting of a literary anecdote that will otherwise be lost to the
annals.

Although in workload and worry terms the first three years of the
1960s had been pretty horrendous, and it was going to be a long time
before they let up, a rhythm had been set, and a pattern had begun to
appear. The general reception for most titles had been gratifying, we
were paying our bills (D – and SIUP – V), and there was no lack of ideas
for the list ahead. The serious backlist was beginning to overshadow, if
not outnumber, the slighter and more ephemeral titles with which my
lack of capital had forced me to launch Centaur. If there was a major
concern at the back of my mind, apart from what might be brought by
the west wind, it was whether I could continue to cope single-handed
with the sheer volume of work ahead. While Tilly dreamed dreams of a
world that was swinging, her father fought fears of the rising tide.

6
Cabbages and Things

The cloud that hung hereon over the future of the Centaur Classics did not seriously affect the choice and order of the forthcoming titles, as these had already been agreed with SIUP. Jack Cohen had been kept in touch with the situation, and had been as supportive as his brief and experience allowed. We both hoped, without much encouragement from Illinois, that they would see the sense in modifying their lethal decision. Meanwhile we could only plug on with the programme.

The first Classic to be published in 1964 was William Cobbett's *Journal of a Year's Residence in the United States of America*. It had been suggested by Grigson when some fourteen months into putting forward his proposals. Had the Cobbett been among his first ideas, I might have suspected a subtle plan for steering Centaur on to the rocks. Although Cobbett had lived in the United States from 1792 to 1800, *A Year's Residence*, full of technicalities and statistics, was written while he was living on a rented farm at North Hempstead, Long Island, between 1817 and 1819. Partly about rural mores, land values, and politics, it is heavily into livestock, potatoes, cabbages, and above all, ruta baga culture. Ruta baga, as the agricultural highbrow needs no telling, is also known as the Russian – or sometimes the Swedish – turnip. Or was, when anybody last thought about it. I shall not risk prompting the reader to switch to his bedside airport-bookstall blockbuster by going into further detail, but as J. E. Morpurgo pretty well admitted in his introduction, ruta baga and most of Cobbett's worthy study seemed likely to strike its British audience as just about the dullest thing since the invention of tapioca pudding. Jack, sending me his comments on the list of possible titles I had received from Geoffrey, had somehow missed the Cobbett, but grudgingly admitted on the phone subsequently that it might be all right if it had been forgotten for long enough.

Vernon, however, did not demur. Seventy-five percent of the state of Illinois – admitted as the twenty-first of the Union in 1818 – is, after all, given over to farming, and Cobbett's connection was agreeable to the New World in the postwar days when their cultural focus took more account of the products of the Old. The sales experience of the UK edition, however, gave me some credit for my doubts about the likely reception from the British, for whom *Rural Rides* was the beginning and the end of Cobbett's literary fame. Where, by August 1970, the SIUP had sold 312 of their 750 copies, Centaur's edition had struggled up to 153, coming almost to a halt twenty-five years later, by when another sixty copies had found a home. If all the Centaur Classics had done as badly, Centaur would have met the fate of D. H. Lawrence as forecast at Richard Rees's party in Chelsea.

The next two Classics that year (1964) were the Landor *Poems*, already mentioned, and *Anecdotes, Observations and Characters of Books and Men*, edited by the splendidly named Samuel Weller Singer, and 'collected from the conversation of Mr Pope and other eminent persons of his time' by the Reverend Joseph Spence. Again, Geoffrey had suggested it, and Jack gave it his blessing, but it did not do as well as the Landor, whose SIUP edition was nearly exhausted by 1970, while the UK's was welcomed enthusiastically by the Friends of Centaur. Although newly introduced by Bonamy Dobrée, and highly recommended in the *Financial Times* by Peter Quennell, Spence was given a drubbing in the *TLS* that doubtless told on library sales, though the *TES* looked kindly on it, and *Country Life* (yes, Geoffrey again) gave it twenty inches.

It had not been a good year for the Classics. Almost as much of a flopperoo as the Cobbett was 1964's fourth Classic (erroneously dated 1965), William King's *Heathen Gods and Heroes*, introduced by Hugh Ross Williamson. Perhaps too much store had been set on Robert Graves's 1955 assurance in his introduction to *The Greek Myths* that official English literature from the sixteenth to the nineteenth centuries cannot be properly understood except in the light of Greek mythology, for there was no sign of scholars queueing round the block. The best of the very few reviews was in the *TLS*, but while the SIUP's edition did moderately well, it was one of the worst-selling Classics under the Centaur imprint. Most of Geoffrey's recommendations had proved sound, so the King got under my guard despite a warning hint from Jack who, when the choice of an introducer was discussed, wrote: 'As for King, I think Grigson should do this himself, since the book is quite unknown except by him.'

Published in the same month, and again introduced by Williamson, Reginald Scot's *The Discoverie of Witchcraft* found both a scholarly and a niche market. In his 1885 study of insanity, Sir William Tennant,

Hon. Physician in Ordinary to Edward VII and President of the British Medical Association, had written that the *Discoverie* 'stands brightly out amid the darkness of its own and the succeeding age as a perfectly unique example of sagacity amounting to genius'. Whether or not Professor Tennant's recommendation counted for anything eighty years on, SIUP had only thirty-six of their copies left by 1970, and Centaur sold its last in the 1980s. Penelope Mortimer in the *New Statesman*, Chaim Bermant in the *Observer*, and Isobel Murray in the *Scotsman* welcomed both the content and production, but most of the other reviewers were not quite sure what to make of it, the *TLS* hack exercising his anonymous prerogative to damn with faint praise what he had sniffed out to be a facsimile edition – which, in part, it was, though handsome to boot. It was crying out to be turned into a paperback, and in 1990 Dover Publications took the hint.

John Leland's *Itinerary in England and Wales* (or, to be picky, *The Itinerary of John Leland in or about the Years 1535–43*, edited by Lucy Toulmin Smith with a Foreword by Thomas Kendrick) – at just under three kilograms for the five volumes, Centaur's weightiest work – could not have been expected to be reissued as anything *but* a facsimile, for the typesetting cost alone would have been horrendous. An average passage reads:

> Heere was *in hominum memoria* a priory of blake chanons of the Patronage of the Duke of Clarence or York. When this priory was suppresid there were 3. cantuaries erectid in the chirch of Lechelade: and ther remaynid ontylle of late dayes one Undrewoode, decance of Wallingforde, founde meanes that 2. of these cantuaries should be at Wallingford-College, and a third to remaine at Lechelade.

Sir Thomas Kendrick's learned, lucid and entertaining foreword to the reissue was written with the authority to be expected of so considerable an admirer of England's earliest modern antiquary. The *TLS*'s review was short but welcoming; Anthony Powell, giving the work nineteen inches in the *Daily Telegraph*, was as congratulatory to Centaur Press as to Leland's far more deserving editor; and Geoffrey, needless to add, gave it a good splash in *Country Life*. By the end of 1970, over 300 of the Centaur edition had gone, and over the next ten years another fifty-five sets. At a retail price equivalent in today's terms to well over £100, it was useful backlist material. With some unbound sheet stock sitting in the binders, I put the Leland into paperback in

1971, and by the end of 1980 another 260 had been sold. By August 1970, however, SIUP had moved only 196 of the 1,000 sets they had taken, so I could appreciate that by then the Illinois accountants must have been directing some fairly penetrating flak at poor Vernon.

It had also made sense, in 1971, to put the remaining sheet stock of the Landor and King into paperback. This perhaps indicated that the series could have continued profitably if the SIUP had been open to discussing a strategy that took account of the growing student market.

In the first five years of the series, twenty-two titles had been published. In the next eight years, a further eleven Classics would bring it to an end. Two out of these eleven were not taken by SIUP. The middle years of the series had been entered more suddenly than had been expected.

The only general title to be published in 1964 was a quixotic but serviceable 'tour of the castles of the Morea', *In Crusader Greece*, written by Eric Forbes-Boyd with photographs by his wife Aileen. Eric had published several plays and novels. One of the latter, *The General in Retreat*, I had published, with reservations, in 1960. Sadly, the favourable-to-excellent reviews were not enough to rescue *The General* from demise-by-neglect. It suffered the same fate as most of my wilful essays into fiction. I can only say in my defence that I never encouraged an author to set his expectations very high, and none appeared to blame me subsequently.

Yet, for *In Crusader Greece*, there had been a good swatch of reviews, but possibly no one of them was powerful enough to start the snowball down the hill with any oomph. The *Daily Mirror* was enthusiastic, and the best was in *The Lady*, a paper that can be very helpful to authors, but only in certain categories. However, something under 1,300 copies sold in the end, plus remainders, and a USA edition of 2,000 copies sold to W. W. Norton of New York.

This book was a good example of a title whose sales potential was unlikely to hook one of the larger publishers, but might be acceptable to a smaller imprint with lower overheads. As with every book I published, better sales would doubtless have been realised had I had the organisation and quality of representation to command shelf space in the shops. But with Centaur's modest turnover from largely academic and literary works, the cost of supporting the additional staff and structure would greatly have exceeded the income from additional sales.

If the individual's middle years have their difficulties, so also do those of the small publisher intent on staying independent. Independence can be lost not only by being taken over, but by expanding one's list, employing staff, and accepting others' judgements of how best to keep it solvent. Ambition never took me that way. I felt the need to continue to rely on my own judgements, but to be more selective. The Centaur Classics were one thing, for if no other publisher had got round to offering them, Centaur was their best hope for revival; they should find their way for as long as the series lasted. But there were other titles – the best of the fiction, and general 'one-offs' such as *Teaching Without Tears*, *England's Wealthiest Son*, *The Symbolic Meaning*, *Art Into Life*, and even *Muriel Spark* – where it was frustrating, and had begun to seem rather pointless, to add to Centaur's list more books whose potentiality I was not equipped to exploit fully, and for which I often lacked that quiver of enthusiasm that ideally lies at the heart of a publisher's acceptances. Besides which, while survival had compelled me to muster sufficient interest to do my best for such books, I was unhappy that neither they nor their authors were enjoying their just deserts. Now that capital was accumulating, I had the choice between taking on staff and paying their wages and the increased overheads from ever more commercially motivated titles in which I might have little personal interest, or using some of that capital to publish work that, whether or not it made a profit, offered a more satisfying *raison d'être*. It was going to be some years before our circumstances allowed the latter course to bear a little fruit beyond the occasional indulgence, but it was one worth aiming for.

By the time Centaur's 1963 catalogue appeared, it was obvious from a number of quarters that the Press had aroused interest and goodwill. Early that year I had told Michael Rubinstein that with the publishing threatening to run me off my feet, I had been pondering the way ahead and would seriously consider something over £50,000 for the whole caboodle. The figure had not been plucked hopefully from thin air, but was deemed realistic by Calder Marshall, Ibotson and Bound, the City accountants who handled my small affairs, and whose senior partner Richard Davson was an old and good friend.

Michael put his experienced ear to the vine and came up with Victor Gollancz and Anthony Blond. But Centaur's list was probably moving in too academic a direction for the former, while Anthony – something of a butterfly in life's wide meadow – was already toying with the pollen prospects in a 'technical publishing house with a large and solid back-list'. A few days later, Michael rang to set me on course to meet Sir

Edward Hulton's second Russian wife, the glamorous Princess Nika Yourievitch, through the intercession of John Jolliffe of London International Press. Anthony had kindly – or perhaps not so kindly – given Jolliffe the tip.

At the Hyde Park Hotel lunch that followed, Lady Hulton's interest in Centaur was beyond doubt. She would be 'so happy', she assured me, in a voice that could be huskily seductive, if I would supervise the transfer on a 'one-or-two-days-a-week basis'. Michael rang the next day to say Jolliffe had confirmed that Lady Hulton had 'taken' to me. I had meanwhile been told by a friend on the *TLS* that Edmund Penning-Rowsell, journalist and (from 1935 to 1963) publisher, had had a less than happy time working for her, for she was 'a very difficult girl'. Wiser men would have left it at that, maybe, but after an ingratiating call from Chalmers Wade, her accountants, I went to see them in London Wall, and they wondered if I would be interested in £20,000 and fifty per cent of profits. Naive in City matters I might have been, but aware by now of her ladyship's passion for world travel, I confirmed that my interest was in need of tender and more realistic fostering. Undashed, Chalmers Wade sent a young man to Sussex to check that costs and sales figures bore out my assertions. He had to confess that they did. A few weeks later, Richard Davson said the Centaur accounts showed a profit on the year that made clear I should be seeking more than £50,000. A Hulton Publications director then took over negotiations, and after further exchanges it was admitted that Nika wanted my full and indefinite involvement. The prospect of becoming her permanent poodle held less appeal than retaining my autonomy. Even at £50,000 cash down, I was not, I confirmed, interested. In June 1963 a 'New Hulton Publishing Project' was announced. Called Edward Hulton, its projected list bore a close resemblance to Centaur's.

I heard no more until October when Jack mentioned that Bill Anderson, who had edited two Classics for us, had been taken on by Nika to handle the book production for her new imprint. He was having a rugged time, being an amiable young scholar not long down from Oxford, who had done some work for Penguin but knew nothing about book design, printing technology, or of the other practicalities inseparable from converting a raw typescript into a finished book. Doing his best to wrest a living from writing and editing, Bill had presumably come cheap. Nika had swanned off to foreign pastures, leaving him with the uplifting parting shot that she was only employing him 'to keep Sir Edward happy'.

If any book was issued under the new Hulton imprint (not to be confused with Hulton Educational Publishers Ltd, of which Nika lacked sole control), I saw no sign of it, and in March 1964 I was invited to lunch in Hyde Park Gate. I drove to London in the almost mint Aston Martin Mark III DB 2/4 drophead I had bought the previous June on the recommendation of John Sankey ('one of only about twenty made') who, thankfully, has advised me on most car purchases. (Not that I have ever owned a more major motor than that Aston. It had belonged to Bill Turnock, a wealthy entrepreneur who used it only between Belgravia and Rome, flying it to Switzerland when wanted in Italy in connection with his financing of films such as *The Leopard*.)

Bill Anderson, as Nika made brutally clear while the butler shimmied attentively, was of use to her only in an editorial capacity. She was still very keen, she assured me, as my glass was refilled, that I should take charge of the business. For the first time, she herself admitted that her main reason for owning a prestige literary/scholarly list was that it would give her the excuse to travel as much as possible (with, I assumed, the usual tax benefits). Her husband's trade journals, and the educational list, which earned far more than a literary imprint was likely to bring in, simply did not interest her. Sole ownership of a small hunk of culture was her aim. Possibly she saw it even then as part of her après-Edward portfolio, though they were not divorced for two years after this. Anthony, I don't doubt, knew all about what was going on, perhaps even before it happened.

Before the dessert, I was beginning to feel uncomfortable. Nika had emphasised her hope that matters could now be decided without putting me to further trouble, and it was clearer than ever that a mind, body and soul acquisition was intended. I tried to change the conversation by telling her about my flying the Aston to Geneva the previous September in order to do the Grand Tour in the company of a childhood friend, John Foster White, who was then the editorial director of Macdonald and Co. (Publishers) Ltd, and how we had been offered the bridal suite in our Positano hotel because the manager clearly sensed in an instant what I had not realised in a lifetime until, when John came to stay with us in Sussex, he had suddenly 'outed' with a hysterically funny piece of campery in the conducive Lanes of Brighton. But the lady was not for deflection, nor even amused. She was rich, she was single-minded, and she was Russian. With a shared sense of humour, I thought, sipping, much in life can be survived, if not necessarily achieved; but this proposition just wouldn't do. Besides, I had had one omen already that morning. The butler had shown me into the library, and Nika's secretary had invited me to look at the paintings in an adjoining room. They included works by Klee, Degas, Chagall, Rouault, Corot, Monet, Turner, Modigliani, also a Henry Moore and other modern sculptures; and – prophetically, perhaps – a Picasso of two centaurs locked in conflict. I looked through the window at the quiet garden with its tennis court and statuary, a stone's throw from Kensington Gore. It was not enough to suppress the negative vibes.

My discomfort was increased by learning that Nika had only two books in production, one on festivals, and the other a guide to Kensington restaurants. She was obviously uncertain about both. She had a facial twitch I had not seen before, and I felt she was unhappy. Knowing my susceptibility to pathos, especially in pretty women, I made my excuses soon after the coffee, and she came with me to the door. The silver Aston looked rather right in its millionaire cul-de-sac. She gazed at it with seeming alarm. 'My God!' she said, *basso voce*, 'I wouldn't even sit in it!'

The resolve to bring the Hulton flirtation to an end had been strengthened by what seemed to be a more hopeful interest from another, though hardly comparable, quarter. A month before my final tête-à-tête at Cleeve Lodge, the *Bookseller* carried an anonymous publisher's advertisement offering trade representation for an additional imprint. My cautious response brought a prompt reply from George Prior, the sales manager of Martin Secker and Warburg Ltd, suggesting an early meeting and telling me that their sales force in the British Isles consisted of five representatives handling about 100 new books each year. As I had seldom reached a yearly total of more than about one sixth of this, Secker's output sounded just right: big enough to attract experienced salesmen, but not so huge as to ensure that the bookseller would be wanting his lunch by the time he was being offered your own titles from the bottom of the rep's bag.

Formed when Fredric Warburg took over Martin Secker's prestigious literary imprint in 1936, Secker and Warburg had become one of the most highly regarded independent literary – and particularly fiction – publishers of the early postwar years. Until then, they had been carrying the distinguished list of Rupert Hart-Davis Ltd, but the relationship had not worked out. They were keen to fill the gap. An early meeting took place, and on 19 March Secker's director David Farrer, doyen of fiction editors, wrote that Fred Warburg was looking forward to signing a contract, and that they were delighted to welcome a list of such 'high class' into their fold. They felt sure they would at least double Centaur's turnover, and after further correspondence and cordial meetings, Secker's representation began on 6 April.

After the irritating and time-wasting negotiations with Nika and her minions, I had doubts about entering an alternative collaboration, fearing that greater turnover would bring additional commitment over and above the extra editorial work needed to meet Secker's predictable wish to see Centaur's output stepped up. But they appeared keen, prompt, businesslike, and were established and well thought of, so it seemed negative not to take the plunge. What I did not then realise from my rural fastness was that with the passing of Warburg's long-standing fellow-director Roger Senhouse, the management of the business was going through a period of instability that was to lead to takeover by Heinemann – an arrangement that Secker survived well, but that Hart-Davis, who also came in under the Heinemann umbrella, did not; it was bought up shortly afterwards by Harcourt, Brace of the USA, only to be re-swallowed by the Granada empire in the UK, so further losing its identity. By 1971, Fred had handed over control of Secker to Tom Rosenthal, who yet again restructured its much edited management, wisely retaining the indefatigable David Farrer until the early 1980s.

To these future developments I was naturally not privy in 1964, but had been surprised when, at the start, after I had emphasised my wish to finance the Centaur list from income and not by borrowing, Fred had offered to put up £35,000 to hasten its expansion. As the summer passed, the impression mounted that Secker's sales forecasts were not being realised, and when Fred and Pamela asked themselves down to Sussex for a weekend to 'discuss the development of Centaur Press', I agreed readily. Owing to mutual work pressures, however, the venue was switched to London. Fred stressed his enthusiasm for the Centaur list, made clear he would welcome a yearly increase of titles, and again offered financial backing for expansion. His concern seemed solely with growth, our talks having apparently convinced him that I was not lacking ideas for future titles. He wanted Centaur to quadruple its advertising in the TLS, and put out paperback editions alongside the hard-cover originals. I repeated my intention of financing growth at the modest rate that was all I could cope with while remaining a solo operator, and my wish to stay that way. Back in March, I had told him of the Hulton interest and of my disinclination to commute from Sussex, to be involved in matters outside my control and sphere of interest, or to hold a minority share interest in another's operation. He seemed unable to understand that I did not crave the chance of a capitalised director-ship in his undoubtedly respected firm.

At the time, those sharing my ignorance of how things were shaping up for Secker and Warburg might have thought me stupid to turn down such an opportunity. Had I had more ambition, they might well have been right. But at the time there seemed no point in beating about the bush. Instinct resting on modest experience had not suggested that a merger would be beneficial. I had to tell Fred that it was proving to be an expensive short-term luxury to be paying territory commission on the necessarily high-priced Centaur Classics backlist, whose sales had been virtually unaffected by Secker's representation. Territory commis-sion is on all sales, whether or not the orders have been the responsibil-ity of the reps; journey commission is paid only on orders personally solicited by the salesman, and in some cases on all orders emanating from an account that has been opened by the salesman. Fred's reply was: 'Wait and see is the main directive, is it not?'

I understood his interest in increased turnover, and his reluctance to accept my concept of sensible growth. A black crow is a fixture on many publishers' shoulders, and the equation between turnover and overheads is of constant concern to all employers. In the last chapter of *An Occupation for Gentlemen*, Fred quoted the trade adage that a small firm either grows or goes bankrupt, adding: '... and it is true.' It was not true, of course, nor is it today – necessarily. It depends on several factors, especially a realistic sense of balance (in e.g., staff numbers, title numbers, backlist and the transitory, need and show, caution and impulse). When *Occupation* was published, Fritz Schu-macher's *Small Is Beautiful* was still fourteen years away, but I suspect that his lucid sanity would never have been wholly agreeable to some-one of Fred's splashy egotism, civilised and sensible though many of his opinions were. But he also wrote: 'A new imprint can establish itself by its willingness to publish books so unusual or so unpopular that the established houses won't touch them with a barge-pole. It was mainly by this method that Secker came slowly to the front.' Although Centaur kept a lower profile, Fred and I had that in common, at least.

By November I was seriously concerned about Secker's results, in particular where the more saleable back-list titles were involved. In one territorial area our arrangement was apparently being financed almost entirely from provincial sales of *Grin and Bear It* (potentially Centaur's best-seller *par excellence*). Nor was that area East Anglia, then known in the trade as the Booksellers' Graveyard. George Prior promised discussion at a forthcoming policy meeting, and after the sales conference I attended before Christmas, he wrote that my input should have helped the list's promotion. This had not been my impression, and there the matter was clearly going to be allowed to rest, so in the middle of January I sent him a three-page analysis of a sample quarter's results, and suggested we continue on a journey-order basis until things picked up. But his mind was elsewhere. When I gave him lunch in Wardour Street's Chez Victor in early February, he said he was leaving Secker to manage Penguin's home sales. With nothing more to lose, I replied that I had confirmed to Fred that Secker's representation had cost me four times the value of the additional business brought in. The rep covering the East Midlands, East Anglia, the South and the South West, had done well. The two covering the London suburbs, and the North and the West Midlands, had sent in reasonable results. But the other areas had produced very little business, the most worrying being that brought in from Central London, whose rep had been with Secker and Warburg since its inception, and had proved himself invaluable to them. Apart from eliciting a cautious interest in current general titles, he did little but intercept orders that would have come in without his intervention for *The Discoverie of Witchcraft* and one or two other active recent Classics. Reps have to live, but this had to be balanced against consideration of Centaur's own urge for survival.

George was not – or was not allowed to be – moved. Nor was my suggestion that the Classics be excluded on a territory basis from the arrangement acceptable. If a lesson had been learned from the Secker experience, it was the pointlessness of employing reps to subscribe the more academic side of a list, as while they can easily enough bring home the initial orders which are, or were in those days, destined for the libraries, most bookshops were not tempted to invest in repeat, speculative orders once the first fine careless rapture had subsided. And one cannot blame them.

In January I had invited George to tell me if he would feel happier if we called it a day, and in February Fred proposed we did so on 30 April. There seemed no alternative. Turnover had hardly increased, least of all for the Classics. If the reps had been told to treat Centaur on an equal basis with Secker, only two had complied, or Secker's own turnover must have been in a worse state than I had supposed. The London rep, by then elderly, could have achieved more had he wished to, but he had shown a rather niggling attitude at sales meetings, suggesting that even if appropriately briefed, he was going to follow his own agenda. With hindsight, I suspect he was unhappy with the portents at that stage in Secker's history, and had little enthusiasm for selling outside imprints. But this is conjecture. The only certainty is that waylaying orders from the library suppliers, obtained by Centaur in-house through expensive mailing of dust-jackets, formed the bulk of the business sent in by Secker. Our parting was without rancour, though at Secker's wish I had run off thousands of extra unbound sheets for several titles, with later paperbacks in mind. I eventually put them out in that form, but without representation it was at that time very difficult to shift up-market paperbacks. The only sour note – though I did not voice it – was that although it had been understood that Centaur Press would be the only additional list in the reps' bags, I learned that the Alan Ross imprint was being distributed before the Centaur arrangement ended, and 'fully integrated'. But I believe that little came of this, and that Ross – who long and doughtily edited the subsidised *London Magazine* – put out few book titles.

It was annoying that time had been wasted in exploring the possibilities of a merger with the Hultons and Warburg, but the morale was boosted a little when it was later shown that the miserable consideration that Nika's accountants had offered had been hopelessly unrealistic. The end of the Secker collaboration was more disappointing, bringing home to me that without sacrificing autonomy, or taking on a work force for which I would have to pay by publishing material solely to meet salaries, I was fated to continue to reject – or at times pass on to other publishers – some good ideas and the occasional deserving out-of-the-blue submission. But at least my instinct to decline an appointment to the Secker board had been sound. Tom Rosenthal may not have done much to save the sinking ship, except to winch it into the davits of HMS Conglomerate (Diana Athill's *Stet* tells amusingly of the tug-o'-war between Deutsch and Secker over Naipaul's *Guerrillas*), but it would probably have foundered sooner if I had taken over the helm.

Most publishers can look regretfully at the book-that-might-have-been. The serious traveller was the unwitting loser from the failure of the Secker experiment, in that Cyril Upton, who as well as having contributed regularly to *The Times* as their Provence correspondent, and to *Punch* in its heyday, and for numerous other outlets including French literary reviews, for one of which he was co-editor, had in 1963 reacted well to my suggestion that he tackle an up-to-date history of

Provence. His writing was fluent, informed, witty and readable, whether in prose or poetry, and his range of knowledge went well beyond philosophy and religious systems. French and Provençal academicians had long acknowledged him to be the only English-speaking *provençal* qualified to write such a book, and the French government had already commissioned from him a major article on the evolution of Provence and the Riviera for their official review *Urbanisme*. The book was to deal principally with that which was and would continue to be permanent, about a third focusing on the amazing story of Provence – prehistoric, Greek, Roman, medieval, Saracen, papal, King René, Renaissance – up to the Mistralian Renaissance. The remainder would cover the historical treasures and natural beauty of the individual regions. In all, a readable and informed backdrop, to reinforce the general run of guidebooks. It was, I believe, and maybe still is, a much needed text.

Secker's team had been keen on the Provence proposal, and the author's agreement had been sent to Cyril in May 1964, by which time he had already written four chapters, promising completion by November. But his health was failing, and the task proved more demanding than he had anticipated. By the following spring, in his seventy-sixth year, it was clear that he would not finish the book, though we both played the game of pretending otherwise. Our final meeting was in 1969, a month before his eightieth birthday. I had driven the family to St Cézaire, near Grasse, where Aubrey Vernon, Billie Longe-Schreiber's younger brother, had lent us a villa in the hills. We drove over to see the Uptons. Cyril was at the doctor's, Madeleine said. Everything he ate gave him painful hiccups. I had looked forward to showing Jennifer and the children the views from the flat, which seemed darker than I was expecting on a baking day in July. The reason was soon clear. Since my last visit to Villa l'Horizon in 1964, the outlook had deteriorated shamefully. Enormous tower blocks had closed in on all sides, blocking out the yachts in the harbour, allowing only a slit-glimpse of the sea beyond. It was all depressingly symbolic of 'progress' and the Uptons' sad state. We drove Madeleine into the centre to meet Cyril and give them lunch at the Royalty restaurant that looked down the gardens to the casino. Cyril picked at a little fruit, drank some wine and coffee, then lit his pipe. He was clearly terminally ill. He had forgotten about the book on Provence, and Madeleine had to remind him that he had four grandchildren by the daughter of his first wife. For reasons I had never inquired into, he had not seen his daughter or her children for many years. Outside the restaurant we parted with the usual platitudes about meeting sooner next time, all knowing it would never happen. They went off to their car in one direction, we in the other. When I looked back, Madeleine was limping beside Cyril, using her stick in one hand so that she could support him with the other. On 11 November I received the expected telegram: 'Cyril died cancer oesophagus. Heart broken. Madeleine.' I wished, and still wish, I could have been the publisher his talents deserved.

The first title to be published in 1965, Porphyry's classic treatise *On Abstinence from Animal Food*, had contributed much to the direction my mind was taking. My mother, deeply immersed during the second half of her life in comparative religion and philosophy, had drawn on Porphyry when writing what have remained her two best-known books, *Mithras*, and *The Philosophy of Compassion*, both of which I was to take over from their hardback publishers and reissue under the Centaur imprint.

On Abstinence, translated from the Greek by Thomas Taylor (1758–1835), had been allowed to go out of print and was a rarity in the second-hand market by the 1960s. The climate for such a title, however unimpeachable its contents, seemed little better in that decade than when Porphyry's works were publicly burned by Theodosius; but the times were changing. Although the total sales (including an edition taken by Barnes and Noble in the States) are still short, I am told, of 2,000 copies, the sales graph showed one of the slowest declines Centaur had experienced, and demand found a level that amply justified keeping the book in the backlist. Had it been published 'in paper', instead of as a hardback, it should have tapped the student market far more successfully, for scholars of the calibre of Richard Sorabji, Professor of Ancient Philosophy at King's College, London, have 'discovered' the relevance of Porphyry, Plotinus, Origen, Pythagoras, Plutarch, and a host of more recent philosophers, to the current concern over our obligations to other forms of life in our threatened environment. Sorabji's *Animal Minds and Human Morals*, subtitled *The Origins of the Western Debate*, is a powerful contribution at the higher academic end of the spectrum.

Considering the small and grudging press that the Centaur Porphyry received, its adequate sales showed that the market was greater than the defenders of 'establishment' mores wanted to suppose. No major newspaper gave it a line of attention, but had not been expected to, the 'protesting' spirit of that era's young having comparatively recently awakened student interest in 'alternatives'. The two most influential papers at their own level, the *TLS* and *Church Times* (whose circulations today lie between 30,000 and 40,000, and would not have been much different then), grudgingly printed very short Shorter Notices. The former's cautious reviewer did the best he could with his few lines:

> This translation (1823) of one of the few works of the great Neoplatonist to escape destruction by his Christian opponents was worth reprinting. Not only does it contain valuable extracts from earlier writers; it also places in a philosophical and religious context the whole problem of man's relation to the animal kingdom, and discusses vegetarianism from the viewpoint of those who aim at the contemplative life of the ascetic rather than the somnolent hedonism of the materialist.

Sniffily dismissive, the *Church Times* found *On Abstinence* to be merely 'a curious work ... notable for the expression which it gives to the importance of compassion'.

More approval was shown for the other main title of 1965. When I had published, in 1959, Margaret Stanley-Wrench's *A Tale for the Fall of the Year*, it was deservedly well received by Al Alvarez in the *Observer*, Austin Clarke in the *Irish Times*, Leonard Clark in *Time and Tide*, and by an agreeable number of poetry and literary journals. Margaret had won the Newdigate Prize in 1937 after publication of *Newsreel*, her first poetry selection. Her work had been widely broadcast and anthologised. This had slight bearing on the decision to publish her translation into Modern English of Chaucer's *Troilus and Criseyde*. Undertaken to help her own Training College students, the translation was nigglingly reviewed by the *TLS* and *TES*, but – and more importantly – well received by the *Teacher* and *Teacher's World*. It had to be reprinted in 1971 to meet the demand stimulated by its adoption as a set book for London University A-levels. Unfortunately it was then upstaged by a rival translation by Nevill Coghill, published by Penguin, which caused Centaur's hardback sales to drop from a peak of 244 copies in the month of October 1970 to a total for the whole of the succeeding twelve months of 625; after which it faded gracefully to a further 400 copies before becoming a trickle.

But it had not been a bad experience, and Billie (as her friends knew her) was well satisfied. I was also relieved, for Billie – an industrious, kindly, sensitive, romantic woman, with that underlying homeliness that is not always successfully suppressed in the female intelligentsia – was hopelessly in love with the man to whom she dedicated her book. When he backed out of the relationship, she was devastated, and although medical reason might have dismissed the connection, I believe that the rampant rheumatoid arthritis that horribly ended her life was another name for a broken heart.

The two Classics in 1965 were a handsomely turned out crown folio facsimile of the 1938 edition of Robert Burns's first *Commonplace Book*, with an added foreword by David Daiches, which has probably sold as many copies for Burns Night prizes as to the nation's librarians; and a new edition, introduced by Basil Willey, of Thomas Burnet's *The Sacred Theory of the Earth*, a work whose interest and importance Professor Willey had emphasised in his 1940 classic *The Eighteenth-Century Background*. Once again, *TLS* and *TES* paid suitable respects, but the *Church Times* – unsurprisingly – didn't find it in their hearts to laud this 'curiosity of seventeenth-century theology and science' as much more than 'a work which has great period interest'. (I have sometimes wondered why no publisher has got round to commissioning *A Dictionary of Contemporary Euphemisms*.) By 1970 the SIUP had sold twice as many copies as had Centaur, for whom it never really took off.

In 1965 we had to build on to the west end of the house in order to cope with the growth in business and family, and to create a ground-floor study so that the main bedroom could revert to its proper use; above, we were able to add a needed guest bedroom. One wall of the study was taken over by a built-in bookcase with good cupboard space for files below, and for the wall opposite a scarily expensive black settee and chair were delivered by Peter Jones to give printers and authors the comforting feeling that Centaur might be here to stay. It also seemed advisable to replace the side panel of a Victorian wardrobe that had been my main working surface ever since the roll-top desk in Highgate had been given to the Salvation Army; we imported in its place a fairly impressive modern desk to show that life was being taken seriously.

Jennifer, who had not taken very kindly to our move from London, was by now a little more reconciled to living in the country, finding the ever-increasing hum of traffic on the A27 far from disagreeable. But many years were to pass before she admitted, in a rash moment, that she would not want to live in London again. She had lived there virtually her whole life, was educated at the Froebel, and had been trained from the age of six in the Cecchetti method of ballet. After taking professional examinations with the Imperial Society of Teachers of

Dancing, she began a full-time dancing career that included work with two ballet companies, and many engagements in the London West End theatre, on tour, abroad, and on television. With Susan on the way, she had given up dancing, after which she taught it for several years, in both London and Sussex. In 1966 her book *So They Want to Learn Ballet* was published by Darwen Finlayson Ltd.

Luckily for Centaur Press, although a consummate dancer – pretty, graceful, and never out of work – she was an avid reader, had sometimes wished she had been encouraged to take up librarianship, and had wondered in idle moments whether marrying a publisher might kill two birds with one stone. Her mother Enid, however (whose grandfather Charles Patton Keele, a Southampton surgeon, had married the frail Elizabeth Leveson Gower), was herself far from strong, and steered her older daughter toward a dancing career to counter physical weakness and poor survival rates on both sides of the family. Everything comes at a price, and in his novel *Lothair* Disraeli provided a clue to the self-defeating priorities of the Gower line:

> ... a family with charm that always attracted and absorbed heiressess ... beautiful women who generation after generation brought their bright castles and their broad manors to swell the state and rent rolls of the family ... (Stuart, 1982, 30).

Whether or not Jennifer had half an eye on all the reading matter that marriage to a publisher might make available – and her fondness for books, and a talent for quiet assessment of character, are but two of her attributes that helped me to make a go of Centaur – the percentage of titles that most people would see as a light read was not high. This was the case, if in different senses, with the only two books I published in 1966; both Classics, and both suggested by Geoffrey. He had sent a tempting list of possible Classics in early 1963, nine months before Sternberg's fateful letter. The 1966 choices were Richard Ford's *Handbook for Travellers in Spain*; and *Reliquiae Hearnianae*, being extracts from the MS diaries of the great antiquary Thomas Hearne, compiled by Dr Philip Bliss in the late nineteenth century. John Buchanan-Brown was invited to edit and introduce the Centaur edition.

Of the former title, which became a major pillar of the Classics series, Geoffrey wrote only that it was the 'finest travel book of its kind ever written', which endorsed the view of William Keir (later Sir William Stirling-Maxwell) who, in his obituary of Ford in *The Times*, when referring to the first edition published by John Murray in 1845, declared: 'So great a literary achievement has never before been performed under so humble a title.'

Possibly it was a mistake that the Hearne title should follow the Latin by being put out as *The Remains of Thomas Hearne*. I felt this set a rather dismal, if not funereal, note, but my more scholarly advisers were given their head. The grey and black used for printing the jacket was my own choice (by now we were beginning to run out of ideas for suitable colours) and cannot have done much to drop a hint that Centaur was offering a lighter read than the title suggested. Although published in October, the book got most of its reviews in middle to late December. Geoffrey, perhaps hurt by the *TLS*'s friendly but very brief notice, went to town on the Hearne in *Country Life*. But three days before Christmas is not the best time for any book to be reviewed. The few other notices were also welcoming, but I felt in my bones that the *Remains* were destined for little but remaindering, and so it eventually proved. By 1970 the sales had struggled up to 157 copies, and the SIUP had done little better. Maybe a mild moral lies somewhere between these lines.

The Ford was a different kettle of fish altogether. The initial plan had been to reproduce the 1845 two-volume edition in its entirety, 'with the single modification that an improved road map replaces the indifferent maps with which Ford originally provided his volumes', and this was announced in the 1964 Centaur catalogue. On further reflection this was seen to be inadequate treatment of a book thought of as the only guidebook to be also a major work of literature. Although still reproduced in full after being edited, indexed and reset, it was augmented by an improved but contemporary road map, and illustrations supplied by the author's great-grandson Brinsley Ford. Sir John Balfour, British Ambassador to Spain 1951–54, wrote the foreword, and the editing and introduction were entrusted to Ian Robertson.

Robertson was a sound choice. Conscientious, enthusiastic, tireless and perceptive, he was to embark on a twenty-five-year freelance connection with the publishers of the famous Blue Guides, rewriting or compiling, in several cases from scratch, the volumes to Spain, Portugal, Paris and Versailles, Ireland, Cyprus, France, Austria, and Switzerland. With his background in publishing and antiquarian bookselling, he was constantly alive to the gaps and opportunities in the literature of travel. He lived in Spain from 1971 to 1990, then in Provence. At his suggestion, Centaur published a reissue of William Beckford's *Recollections of an Excursion to the Monasteries of Alçobaca and Batalha* in

1972, edited by Boyd Alexander. In 1992 Ian wrote *Portugal, a Traveller's Guide*, published by John Murray, and in 2000 Pallas Athene brought out his editing of Ford's *Gatherings from Spain*, a shorter and so more accessible work that drew heavily on the *Handbook*. He has also revised and originated several entries for the *New Dictionary of National Biography*, including that of Ford (of whom he published a full biography in 2004).

At well over 1,500 pages in three medium octavo volumes, the hardbound *Handbook* cost the earth to produce and could not be put out cheaply. But it was greeted with unreserved joy by the *Daily* and *Sunday Telegraphs*, *The Times* and *TLS*, the *Observer* and *New Statesman*, and by several more academic journals. By August 1970 the SIUP had sold rather more sets than had Centaur, whose copies continue to move steadily. Sets in the original Oxford cloth binding can sell second-hand for prices in excess of the three-figure sum that the remaining sets bring in their later 'cloth-type' binding.

No general title was published in 1966, but the hiatus was filled in 1967. Three Classics were also added to the series. The first, a selection from John Nichols's *Literary Anecdotes of the Eighteenth Century*, was edited by the erudite bibliographer Colin Clair. Nichols (1745–1826), whose haphazardly-thrown-together 6,580 pages ran to nine volumes, each of 700 or more pages, announced his vast work as a 'Mine of literary materials, whence future Biographers and Historians will readily and unsparingly collect what may suit their several purposes'. His prediction was correct, in that shoals of writers drew on his huge hoard, with or without acknowledgement, but it was not until the daunting task of disciplining Nichols's exuberance fell, at Jack Cohen's suggestion, to Colin's lot, that any serious attempt was made to catch the *Anecdotes* between hard covers. His labours were rewarded by only four reviews, that in the *TLS* being distinctly grudging. But in the absence of any other edition, the book did averagely well.

William Tyndale's formidable work *The Pentateuch* (1530) followed, one of Centaur's least frivolous Classics. The Revd J. I. Mombert's standard edition of 1884 was reproduced, supplemented by what the *Jewish Chronicle* acknowledged to be a valuable introduction by F. F. Bruce, Professor of Biblical Criticism and Exegesis in the University of Manchester, to 'a work that will be warmly welcomed by all students of the Bible and of English literature'. The *Church Times* was no less generous in its praise, and the *Catholic Herald* shrugged off Tyndale's anti-papal wit – but then Rome had already wreaked its vengeance.

Lay, but not unfriendly, reception came from the *TLS* and *TES*. Sales, however, were somewhat short of being brilliant. While less than three hundred of the UK edition had sold by 1998, the graph promised an indefinite if uneventful future, about which I had no complaint, for in those days a steadily selling backlist was a cause for celebration rather than for manic measures by neurotic accountants.

The third Classic, for which Grigson wrote the introduction, was the *Diary* of William Allingham. Allingham's great hero was Alfred, Lord Tennyson. On the whole, Tennyson took William's adoration patiently, quite often feeding the lad, but he must have been relieved that some of the burden was shared by those other literary giants whom Allingham devotedly pursued, by post and in person, on both workdays and holidays. Up the airy mountain / down the rushy glen / William's off a-hunting / the bane of famous men.

The *TLS* was kindly toward Allingham, critical of Jack for a technicality as much my fault as his, and ticked off Grigson for not giving details of the original diaries' whereabouts, or what Mrs Allingham chose to omit from the 1907 text. The Belfast and Dublin papers were torn between welcoming the reissue of a neglected Irishman, and complaining that it was not available in a cheaper format. As it has recently (2000) appeared in a paperback from Centaur's new owners, that omission has at least been repaired, and a new generation can learn about Allingham's sad charm and wide-eyed prattle on meeting the 'personalities' of his day.

On the general side, I had high hopes for the first title. A reference work pure and simple, the *Dictionary of Contemporaries* was thought up and compiled by André Launay, an eclectic journalist, novelist, scriptwriter, ex-advertising copy-chief, and author of over twenty books including a graphic account – told with a chilling excess of objectivity – of the obscene cruelties inflicted on sentient creatures to give our unlovely species some transient fillip from 'exotic' food. The purpose of the dictionary was to show the reader, at a glance, the contemporaries of writers, composers, artists, philosophers, historians, and other influential and usually creative people of note. As a guide to the cultural mores of any given period, and the influences exerted and sustained by the subject's predecessors and successors, it seemed a most useful source for students in many areas. The *Teacher's World* commended it wholeheartedly, but the *TES*'s reviewer seemed incapable of 'getting his head round it', focusing so pettily on the book's deficiencies (inevitable with most such first-time-ever ideas) that, in the absence of reviews in the wider press for such a stark reference tool, his strictures must have done much damage. About 1,200 copies sold, but it was clear from the continuing, if modest, sales graph, and from how often the public library copies I have seen have been studied, that it deserved to be put into paperback by one of the bigger publishing houses known for reference books, whose imprint would have carried more weight than Centaur's.

Don't Look and You'll Find Her, 'Jeremy Pitt''s second and last novel, was published in the spring, but while the *Nottingham Evening Post*'s reviewer welcomed its 'refreshingly light-hearted and adventurous literary approach at a time when fashionable emphasis seems to be on heavier themes', he came closer to explaining the general press silence in finding it a 'remarkably accurate cameo of the varied philosophies found in modern life'. The novel was a gentle satire, but even a gentle satire of the priorities of the 1960s was not to the taste of their devotees, or to journalists not wanting to be seen as out of line. The *Daily Telegraph* might have stuck its neck out, one felt, but in the end funked a warmer commendation than 'makes pleasant entertainment'. But it was a lack of judgement on my part to have tackled another novel merely to keep my hand in until such time – as I fondly fooled myself – that I would be able to get down to something more demanding. But I had made the decision to pay life's bills by publishing, rather than expose the family to the likely consequences of trying to wrest a living from a craft whose successful practice demanded more than ideas and an ability to use words. In family terms I was probably right, but the longer I kept publishing, the more difficult it was going to be to break back into writing.

Forty has long been the F-word for hypochondriacs, heralding intimations of mortality and decay by sundry aches and pains foreign to those fortunate enough to be able to mix, penalty free, a sedentary life with sporadic bursts of violent physical activity.

With the World's Classics pocket edition of Tolstoy's *Essays and Letters*, in Aylmer Maude's translation, a well-thumbed text since adolescence, and convinced by that great man's insistence that we should aim for balance between the mental and the physical, I had not by middle life lost my urge to play ball games as often as possible. Admittedly, the thought sometimes occurred that Leo would have been more impressed had I chosen to split logs or trudge for miles through deep snow to alleviate the lot of peasants. But having taken on an acre of garden when we moved to Fontwell, I hoped he would have looked benignly on my less commendable preferences. Our garden's produce was at least organically grown and distributed to family and friends, if seldom through deep snow. Despite my efforts to strike the Tolstoyan equipoise, the hours at my desk were too long, and the times on court or in garden too infrequent, to ensure the optimum balance. While shaving one day in March 1965, I felt a sudden pain in some now forgotten part of the torso. My mind riffled through the possible explanations, none very agreeable.

'Hasn't anyone', I asked Jennifer at breakfast, 'thought of compiling a medical dictionary that leads you from the symptom to the possible cause, instead of the usual idiotic arrangement that describes the disease, but leaves you to plough through heaven knows how many pages on the off-chance of finding the symptom that matches?'

Although of unquestionable femininity in most respects, Jennifer tends to be economical with words. Even when cross. Especially when cross. Her great-uncle Granville Keele, the twin of John Rushworth, and described in *Yacht Racing*, that one-time bible of the sport by B. Heckstall-Smith, as 'one of our greatest ... the most trusty and coolest of steersmen', almost never spoke at all. But although brain-cool, as a foremost helmsman of the metre classes needed to be, he could show warmth of heart as well. Doubtless concerned by her peekishness, for a treat he sailed his niece Enid over to the Isle of Wight in choppy seas, plying her regularly with egg sandwiches, but saying not a word. An already taciturn child, now cold, sprayed, and fighting to keep down her uncle's well-meant provender, too frightened by the wind howling in the rigging to move an inch, Enid survived one of the worst days of her girlhood and was seldom if ever to leave dry land again.

'Well, *you* have,' Jennifer said tersely.

The title *Dictionary of Symptoms* seemed to have flashed so vividly on to the bathroom wall that it only remained to find the best person to write it. So a short classified advertisement appeared on 13 March under Miscellaneous in the *Lancet*:

Publishers seek General Practitioner, possibly retired, to compile medical reference book. Acceptance as a standard work is very likely.

Replies varied. Enough GPs responded to suggest that their work-loads in 1965 could not have been as onerous as they are today.

Surprisingly eager letters came from consultant physicians, surgeons, an MOH, a distinguished FRCS at the Radcliffe Infirmary, a group pathologist, and several medical journalists, including an MD working for a pipeline construction company in Algeria. Some of the applicants were highly qualified, but my short-list consisted of three GPs – from Cricklewood, Richmond and Wimbledon.

Instinct told me that Wimbledon should win. Dr Joan Gomez, the only woman to have written in, was married with family commitments, not the least of these being ten children ranging from two to eighteen years, six of them adopted. She had a nominal NHS list, but her husband was also a GP in a partnership of four with 14,000 patients. George and Joan ran a research and clinical trials group of 170 GPs, and Joan wrote topical medical articles for four magazines and two national dailies. Her style of writing was admirable – fluid, intimate, reassuring, and free of jargon, pomposity, or mystique. In view of her access to the patients in her husband's partnership, coupled with running an old people's club in their home, also a nursery group, and visiting housebound patients on both medical and social missions, it struck me that at forty-four she might have enough on her plate already; but her obvious dedication, energy, and keenness to take on the work, was impressive. When she had submitted her synopsis, which was most encouraging, I drew up the formal agreement early in June.

I felt it only fair to offer the option of a flat fee as an alternative to a royalty agreement. That way, if the book flopped, she would at least have received a few hundred pounds for her trouble. As I had supplied the idea and the title for the book, and had a choice of editors, an outright fee would have been appropriate, and she was agreeable to this, declaring forcibly and believably that financial return was not her main concern. However, feeling in my bones that both the idea and the editor were winners, I stressed that if the book took off she would make a lot more money from a royalty agreement, which carried the usual advance payment on account of royalties. I was quite relieved that she chose that basis, as I could have had it on my conscience later if she had taken the flat fee. Had I but known, I would also have had the consolation of far greater profit for infinitely less stress.

For a long time, however, it was to be honeymoon all the way. A vast file of correspondence testifies to the good feeling that marked our collaboration. Slightly embarrassingly, unsolicited but very acceptable tokens of cordiality arrived, sometimes with warm and I am sure genuine thanks for my having chosen her for the job, from centre court tickets for the finals of the men's singles at Wimbledon, to goodies from Fortnum and Mason and Jackson's of Piccadilly. There were invitations to stay if we were going up to a theatre; Tilly, then training at the Froebel Institute for her teaching career, was told she would be welcome at Gomez parties.

Although collaboration with Joan went smoothly, it was a demanding task. I felt I should not inhibit her reassuring flow of words by too much insistence on the pedantries that govern many books of reference. Some matters of form, consistency, style and emphasis could not be ignored, however, and after amiable exchanges the balance seemed about right. On the medical side, Joan was able to call on several distinguished authorities in various fields, their appearance on a preliminary page helping to give the impression that the dictionary was a serious project; as indeed it was. First in its field, it was to attract many imitators on both sides of the Atlantic, and in terms of the role the book played in sparing the nations' general practitioners needless surgery visits from their neurotic patients, Joan and I deserved a gong apiece.

Some errors at a less important level were inevitable. One howler, which no one appeared to notice until long after publication, and for which I had only myself to blame, was in the last sentence of the jacket blurb, where some brief 'biodata' of the author was given. This read: 'She has ten children ranging from eighteen to two years, her husband being a family doctor in a large London practice of 14,000 patients'. It is strange how often jackets contain clangers more strident than those to be found in the text pages.

Villiers Publications printed the dictionary, and John Sankey brought Joan down to Sussex in September 1966 for one of our proofing sessions. It was a more successful visit than when she had driven down by herself in the previous March. On that occasion, although we had had friendly and pleasant discussion, and Jennifer had gone to particular trouble over preparing lunch, Joan had looked desperately at the inoffensive jug of French dressing that was the only edible substance on the table before we sat down to eat, and said plaintively and out of any related context: 'Really, I'd rather go home', then did so. While no offence was taken, the incident was thought-provoking and probably timely. We had failed to realise until then that the stresses in her own life – which, from her C.V. alone, must have been considerable – might have provoked problems that doubtless helped her find the formula for reassuring her patients and readers.

My main reservation concerned the dietary section of the book. In

February 1967 I sent a tactful letter, suggesting that some of the information was some way behind current nutritional thinking (such as it was). The letter proved to be *too* tactful. The nearest Joan had come to offering a table of prohibitions for those seeking to preserve health was 'You need not have more than you want of white flour, cakes, candies, chocolate, pastries, etc.' She replied to my letter, in her large open handwriting: 'Lovely to hear from you! Don't worry about the diet. I think it's fearful, too. But it is entirely taken from American 1966 sources; also have had a couple of visiting professors to vet it.' I resisted the temptation to reply that some American 1966 sources were exactly what we should be at pains to avoid, but as the Great British Public thirty-seven years ago was even less convinced of any connection between food and health than it is today, I let it go through; but when the first American edition appeared, edited for that market by Dr Marvin J. Gersh in 1968, many Betonesque banalities had been modified or removed, as was the UK edition's Senior Years section, in deference to a culture in which no one must admit to being more than twenty-nine.

The Centaur edition was published as a hardback on 19 June 1967, subtitled 'A medical dictionary to help sufferers, by easier self-diagnosis, to eliminate groundless fears and know when to consult their doctor', a form of words which I felt might reassure the medical profession that we were not trying to put them out of business. The fairly small number of reviews were good to excellent, but they were slow in coming. By the end of June Joan had begun to despair, especially when Cliff Michelmore sent up the book unmercifully and with strange spite on television's '24 Hours'. This prompted several returns from booksellers. Unfortunately, Michelmore was not on good terms with Kenneth Allsop, then on the same programme, and to whom I had sent the press copy. But despite Joan's gloomy forebodings, I replied to her letter by return, and believed most of the soothing things I wrote. I was as convinced as one could be in the uncertain world of publishing and the media that word-of-mouth would be the deciding factor in bringing sales not just of the book, but also of subsequent subsidiary rights.

Seemingly cheered by a few more reviews, a month later Joan, George, their ten children, the dog, and for good measure a marmoset, came for a brief disporting on our fortunately sizeable lawn. After loading them with vegetables from the kitchen garden, we led their mini-bus to Itchenor and introduced them to Dr Alan Stoddard, a leading osteopath and old friend who had proved to be as philoprogenitively inclined as Joan and George. It may have helped to bring about this August get-together that I had also been able to send Joan the good news that the New York publishers Stein and Day were buying the American rights in the *Dictionary*. Howard Moorepark had three publishers interested in it, and had closed the deal with Sol Stein who had 'a good reputation for being aggressive'. Certainly he was wise to bring in Dr Gersh, who had the standing needed to get AMA approval for the book; an important factor in its considerable success in the States.

But the Centaur edition, due largely to the usual problem of getting adequate booksellers' cooperation, and perhaps also to the wearisome British distrust of home-grown new ideas, did poorly. I had printed 5,000, all in hardback, and when it went out of print in 1997, it had sold less than 2,000 copies. The rest were remaindered (prematurely, as it turned out). However, the UK paperback rights were taken by Granada who published it in 1970 under Paladin, one of the success-ful imprints originated by Reg Davis-Poynter when managing director of MacGibbon and Kee. This almost halved our 1971 hardback sales, and caused them to plummet from 1972, but the Paladin edition did so well that this hardly mattered. The book could have had a far longer life had Paladin's interest in preparing an updated reissue for the 1980s not been sabotaged by the unhappy circumstances that arose some years earlier. In June 1970 I had received a letter from Howard that read:

> I think you ought to know that Dr Gomez is over here, and appar-ently saw Sol Stein, who called me up today and said that she was disturbed because she had not received any money beyond the original payment and was under the impression that the book had done badly here.

As Joan had not only been paid her advance, some of it before it was even due, but had received her royalties punctually and in full each year thereafter, and in 1970 the biggest cheque I had ever sent to a Centaur author, I was stunned by this extraordinary assertion. I wrote to her, asking for explanation. She did not reply. Time threw some light on the matter.

In 1969 I had flown over to New York, part of my agenda being to discuss with Sol the ideas for two further books by Joan. One would have set out to unfrock Spock; the other's provisional title was *How to Be All Woman*. Sol and I discussed them over lunch at The Baron, a few doors from Stein and Day's offices on East 48th Street. Sol also told me about Sol: his success as a publisher, novelist and playwright; his seven children; his house on the Hudson. Back in my room at the Algonquin – far from clean, but full of expensive associations with Manhattan literati – I made a note of Sol's clear assurance that although Joan's ideas were too diffuse, he was very keen to 'zero in on another workable proposition'. A year later, I had reason to suspect that the workable proposition had been Joan.

Blame apportionment in these situations can be difficult. That Sol signed Joan up for a further project without my knowledge or agreement is fact. He would have been far from the first publisher to poach a hot property from another firm. From Sol's track record, the only reasonable conclusion was that he had made a direct pitch to break her faith in a publisher who had supplied the idea and the encouragement to write a first book that was destined to be a best seller. She had already shown herself to be a pretty complex mix of intelligence, ambition, unpredictability, and neurosis, and there was nothing slow about Sol's perceptions. Only Sol's office cat might have been able to confirm just what fears Sol may have put into Joan's head, and what words into her mouth. How readily she accepted, or even encouraged, them, and with what forward planning, even the cat could not have known. When authors start to earn real money, the soil is fertile for the sowing of doubt and suspicion.

But it did neither of them much good in the long run. On Christmas Eve 1982 Howard had died, and Perry H. Knowlton, President of the Madison Avenue literary agency Curtis Brown, took over the Gomez file. In 1983 Granada, with the licence expiring the following year, revived their earlier interest in an updated edition of the *Dictionary*. Stein and Day were also courting a new edition. But Perry was having all hell getting several years' back royalties out of Stein and Day, and they went into bankruptcy in 1989. By then other publishers on both sides of the Atlantic were producing numerous rival dictionaries, some under almost identical titles and blatantly plagiarising the Centaur concept. To make the situation even more confused, unpleasant, and self-defeating, Joan, instead of collaborating to meet Granada's entirely sensible wishes, had instructed two solicitors – one in 1970, the other in 1978 – to reawaken her baseless grievances against me. Not until my factual and initial responses had turned into angry accusations that they were extracting fees from a client who, as they must by then have realised, had no justification whatsoever for getting them to threaten me, did both firms stop wasting my time and nervous reserves (by then, few).

It was a textbook example of avarice and over-ambition defeating their ends. At one stage Joan had had to ask me to hold back her royalties because they would only disappear in tax if I paid them to her. Apart from the UK and US hardback, and several paperback editions, plus sales to the three main American book clubs, rights had been bought in several European translations, and others as far away as Japan. Serial and part-work rights in various countries had added to the income.

I saw no point in disturbing the hornets' next that further effort to collaborate over a thorough revision was likely to arouse. It would have certainly not earned Joan's gratitude, and some things are just not worth the money they bring. We shied off the solution of finding an alternative editor. For all her failings, Joan had a stylistic touch that would have been difficult to replicate. I wrote to David Bolt, the literary agent who had interceded in the later stages, to say I was calling it a day so far as the *Dictionary of Symptoms* was concerned. The readiness with which he appeared to approve of my decision strengthened the feeling that I had not been impetuous. It had been my only really bad experience with an author. I heard subsequently that in later life Joan had become a psychiatrist. I was not surprised.

Far less stressful, and closer to the heart, was an undeservedly overlooked translation of German short stories, *Among Animals*. This made available, for the first time in the English language, the complete animal tales of Manfred Kyber, the German mystic, poet, playwright and author of serious philosophical works, as well as of fairy tales. Kyber (1880–1933), a close friend of Dr Rudolf Steiner, suffered intensely in the First World War when he and his wife, German Baltic people, were considered 'civil prisoners' by the Russians. Released through influential connections, they went to Germany where they endured near-starvation. In that period Kyber wrote his fine book of poems, *Genius Astri*, dedicating it to Steiner.

In their language of origin, Kyber's animal stories had long been seen as a classic of German literature. By 1927 over 100,000 copies had been sold, and when the Centaur translation appeared it was still in print in Germany and being widely read. Of a selection published in England in the 1930s, the *TLS* reviewer wrote: 'A modern Aesop outwardly addressed to children, but with satire for grown-ups. May take its place beside Grimm and Andersen.' While this prediction was fulfilled in Germany, the English language *Among Animals* failed to catch on, although sensitively translated by Olive Fishwick.

Much easier to sell, and still doing so from the stable of Centaur's new owner, was *Donkeys: Their Care and Management* by M. R. de Wesselow, the last title to be published in 1967. It began as a hardback, and after ecstatic reviews in everything from the *Sunday Times* to the *Donkey Show Society Newsletter* has been through several paperback editions. Not having needed all that many extra pairs of hands to count Centaur's out-and-out successes, when the *Bookseller* kindly invited me to give my account of Centaur's progress, I included *Donkeys* in my article 'The Centaur in Our Paddock' in their 2 August 1969 issue, recalling that 'after fighting a losing battle with docks and nettles ... we added Dumbo, a donkey, to the existing strength of two children, a cat, and several goldfish. The donkey carefully ate tracks through and around the docks and nettles, then glared angrily at us over the top of them and yelled for something it was apparently not getting. A panic-journey to W. H. Smith disclosed that no one had written a concise handbook about what to do when you find yourself lumbered with a yelling donkey ...'

With a new and revised paperback edition of *Teaching Without Tears*, which in its own quiet way had proved to be a useful little earner, 1967's output had totalled nine titles. This was above the average for the 1960s, but it was falling, and continued to do so. Given my solo inclinations, this was both deliberate and inevitable. While the Centaur Classics sometimes had time-consuming birth pangs, their after-lives were generally quiet, and their sales received little promotion other than to be listed in the yearly catalogues. Trade representation, as the Secker experience finally showed, was just not worth the candle. As new titles were added to the series, the backlist income held up satisfactorily, allowing for increasing speculation with general titles and for channelling what profits were left into such more stable investments as bricks and mortar.

Although the yearly graph of new publications was slowly, if fitfully, falling, few titles went out of print and ceased to have a life. The total workload from one year to the next had eased little, if at all. One way or another, 1967 had been an exhausting year, and the sixteen-page catalogue that was printed each year from 1960 to 1967 was going to need another four pages, plus the inside back cover, partly because two new series were to be announced. Some people never learn.

7
Trade Winds and Chimney Pots

Despite their announcement in the 1968 catalogue, the new series did not start to appear until 1969. Although Centaur's most demanding decade was beginning to ease off, 1968 brought publication of a two-volume title that had been gestating fitfully and frustratingly ever since I first flew to Bermuda in April 1960. There, visits to the Book Store in Hamilton and to the town's public library had suggested the guidebooks to the locality were inadequate. It gradually struck me that what was needed was a guide that would cover not only Bermuda, but also the Caribbean – something more inspiring than tricked up regurgitations of the information packs put out by each area's tourist office. These days, guides such as the Footprint Handbooks (Passport Books in the USA) go to great pains to verify facts while conveying something of the atmosphere, byways, and intriguing esoterica that can lift a holiday out of its rut. Travel unprompted by an awakened imagination can turn out to be a forgettable slog.

Harold Bamberg, still willing to show that being my best man had meant just that, gave me a fifty per cent discount on a second trip to research the matter further. On 6 January 1961 I took an Eagle flight to Miami via Gander and Bermuda; but the Britannia was diverted to New Providence Island (usually referred to by the name of its capital, Nassau), having missed the connection in Bermuda.

The manager of Nassau's Fort Montagu Hotel was as keen on the proposed guidebook as were most of the hoteliers I was to meet on my tour – he endorsed his enthusiasm by making no charge for his most expensive suite. Mr Boon of Moseley's Bookshop was equally encouraging and thought that Captain Kenyon Goode, a local resident, could tackle the writing if my researches decided me to go ahead. If not Goode, Boon said, I should try Sir Victor Sassoon. As Sassoon had not, so far as I knew, written anything much but stiff memos to bank staff, the suggestion was of less value than Boon's third recommendation – that I track down Kenneth Jackson Marshall, the publisher Collins's sales representative in the West Indies, during my island hopping ('Ken's bound to be somewhere in the Caribbean at this time of year').

Goode, as true to his name as Boon, gave us both a meal at the Buena Vista. He was something of a Bahamian Cyril Upton, and author of a cookery book published by Hart-Davis. He might have made a decent job of the book, and he dangled his ability to sell several of its pages for advertisements; but while the redirection of a little of Nassau's inordinate wealth to this worthy end was a tempting prospect, I was uncertain whether Goode's knowledge of islands beyond the Bahamian chain would be adequate. I was sorry I could not promise him a spell of creative relief: he was evidently finding life on a tiny island containing 'eighty-seven multi-millionaires' a cultural and social strain. I felt the more guilty when he had paid the bill, remarking as he did so that Caracas was the only place in North or South America that was more expensive than Nassau.

The next day, a Sunday, I spent swimming, skin-diving, sending cards, calling on more hotels, generally making my number and getting the feel of the island. The gardener in me had reservations about virgin ground that needed dynamite before serious planting could be considered. The following morning, after exploring the hope of reduced inter-island fares, I left in a Viscount for Miami, where the Everglades on Biscayne Avenue let me in at half-price. The manager of the bookshop department at Burdines took a more mainland view of the proposed guide, and stocked few titles of UK origin. For a further glimpse of the Miami hotel scene, I called on the Department of Publicity whose director arranged for me to have dinner with the glamorously sculpted PR director of the Eden Roc in whose restaurant she ate an ounce or so of a two-pound, two-inch thick steak, and I stormed a hillock called Peach Melba, feeling suddenly homesick for apple-crumble or even a decent British biscuit. She then took me to see the Fontainebleau Hotel, whose connection with anything within a thousand miles of Fontainebleau was totally indiscernible. Everything about Miami, but particularly the excessive overstatement, set in stone my suspicion that few of its holidaying visitors would find much of interest in a British guide for the intelligent traveller.

Up at 5 a.m., for a date with an airport limo outside the Columbus Hotel, I was glad to be en route for Jamaica. Leaving the plane at Montego Bay to finalise a visit to Port Maria to stay with Noël Coward, I overstretched my rest stop and saw my luggage leave for the other end of the island. But there was a bookshop called Fourgreys that seemed worth a visit, after which I lunched at Gloucester House, whose surrounding profusion of flowers was a welcome sight after the barrenness of Nassau, and inspected the Doctor's Cave beach before catching a virtually empty Boeing 707 that had come in from New York.

Kingston's airport terminal, in those days wooden shacks not much advanced on grass huts and with basketwork furniture, would have impressed the early aviators. Still, my bag and coat were produced promptly by Customs and the exuberantly-driven taxi held together for long enough to get me into town. There, the Jamaica Tourist Board's Calvin Bowen suggested a room at the Myrtle Bank Hotel, then still regarded as almost a symbol of Kingston, but largely destroyed by fire five years later. After the soullessness of Miami's concrete jungle, however, I opted for the alternative of the out-of-town Manor House Hotel at Constant Spring, where I was offered a cottage apartment in the aggressively verdant garden.

Needing to be back in Kingston the next day, I rang Noël Coward's private number before dinner, as I could see I was not going to reach Port Maria, on the far side of the Blue Mountains via a winding road, much before dusk. The phone was answered by Cole Lesley, one of Noël's immediate on-hand 'family' of four, the others (not then in Jamaica) being Graham Payn and the admirable and indispensable Lorn Loraine, without whose firm ministry over the 'boys' the Master's career might not have reached such dizzying peaks. Noël, Cole said, was having his before-dinner snifter on the verandah of Firefly Hill, his retreat above his first Jamaican home, Blue Harbour. At Firefly he could write in the comparative cool, unplagued by the telephone or any but the most knowing callers.

In the morning the Manor House's bus got me to Kingston by 9.30. I called on Sangster, the main bookseller, who endorsed Boon's recommendation of Ken Marshall ('If you can get him') as the best publishers' sales rep in the Caribbean. As I had never met Ken, a rep prized by one of Britain's largest companies, nor seemed likely to, I put Sangster's commendation on ice. At the Myrtle Bank, overlooking the harbour, Bowen gave me the names of other islands' tourist board managers, and even of the odd prime minister. By the time I had returned to the Manor House, lunched, had a constantly-needed shower, and paid my halved dues, it was three in the afternoon. When the taxi dropped me at Blue Harbour, Noël had given me up for lost and gone up to Firefly, having spent the day in and around the pool with Cole, expecting me to join them. My message had not been adequately relayed. Undeterred, the ever-devoted 'Coley' drove me up the bumpy track to Firefly and left me for a long talk with Noël on the verandah. Backdropped by the now shadowy outline of the Blue Mountains, the bay hundreds of feet below held a seemingly circular island covered thickly in palms. It was all quite ridiculously peaceful, beautiful, and romantic.

'What do they do on that little island?' I asked.

'Copulate, darling. The natives. They paddle over in droves.'

I suppressed further inquiry into the natural history of Jamaica, and we returned to the subject Noël invariably raised whenever we had more than a dressing-room meeting – my mother. The friendship between Noël and my mother dated from 1911 when Dorothy Estelle Esmé Innes-Ripper, who had taken the stage name of Esmé Wynne, took the leading part of Rosamund in the original production of the staggeringly jingoistic children's play *Where the Rainbow Ends*. It rivalled *Peter Pan* for nearly five decades, and it was first produced by Charles Hawtrey at London's Savoy Theatre, with music by Roger Quilter. (Valerie Langfield's biography of the gentle and timid Quilter (2002) gives an entertaining overview of his life, work and times. His *Rainbow* music made a substantial contribution to his popularity.) At the end of the opening run, Hawtrey produced Esmé's children's play, *The Prince's Bride*. Noël, having been given, more by persistence than talent, the bell-boy part of William in the *Rainbow*, was both in awe and intensely jealous of its rather superior leading lady, who was now also a playwright and had received plenty of public and press attention. He never made a secret of the fact that Esmé's star status was a powerful spur to his acting ambitions, and that it was her little play that prompted in him a competitive determination to make his name as a writer. As well as taking and making every opportunity to act together, and to be in each other's company when not working, they collaborated in plays, sketches and lyrics, their rapidly formed friendship becoming closer than that of most siblings, with an intimacy all the more objective and intense because of the absence – needless to record – of anything sexual in their association. No-holds-barred confidants on matters of life, relationships, and their ambitions, they knew more of each other's lives and minds than their own parents. Their names soon came to be linked in the public's mind, and Noël assumed that their collaboration would be for ever. They even discussed whether they should make a platonic marriage, but Esmé's difficult mix of a passionate nature and greater respect for the conventions ruled this out. After playing the role of Faith in the original production of Noël's play *I'll Leave It to You* in 1920, she was to make a decision that meant the abandonment of her stage career and was to upset Noël's expectations deeply. (So many biographies of Coward have been written that a pointer to the more reliable sources may be useful. In my view, the two best full biographies, both entitled *Noël Coward*, are by Clive Fisher (1992) and Philip Hoare (1995). The latter draws on primary source material and is seen as the definitive life of Coward. Cole Lesley's *The Life of Noël Coward* (1976) is affectionate and, unsurprisingly, a little star-struck; Sheridan Morley's *A Talent to Amuse* (1969), written when Noël was still alive, and not agenda-free, has a most useful chronology and other appendices.)

On 22 June 1918 Esmé had married Linden Charles Tyson, a twenty-one-year-old RAF lieutenant who had been through the First World War in the Army, the Royal Flying Corps, and the RAF, with three years' active service in Egypt, Gallipoli and France. A few months after taking part in the first Battle of the Somme, Linden had met Esmé through a fellow officer at the Junior Naval and Military Club. By the time they married he had been taken off flying by the Medical Board and posted at the instigation of Noël's friend General ('Splash') Ashmore to a job in London interviewing applicants from civilian life for commissions in the RAF. In March 1921, with a permanent commission, he was stationed in Scotland as adjutant at Donibristle, where Esmé became friendly with a retired colonel's wife, Maud Watson, twenty-two years her senior, and also with the wife of Linden's commanding officer, Group Captain Burnett. The more perceptive wives of OCs are not unknown to take an interest in the weaknesses of their husbands' juniors, and Mrs Burnett, aware of the strong sexual bond between Linden and Esmé, warned her that if she wanted to make a success of her marriage, it would be foolish to try to follow a stage career in London while her husband was in Scotland, or liable to be sent abroad.

Despite her affection for Noël, which was to last and be reciprocated for the rest of their lives, Esmé had already become dissatisfied by the theatre's constant demand to push one's personality; as a career she felt it was not stretching her intellectual capabilities. More importantly to her, from the age of six she had had a fierce desire to understand the meaning and purpose of life, and her search – implanted by her father's stern emphasis on the God-bestowed penalties to be expected for sin, exacerbated by the two terms she spent in a Belgian Ursuline convent in 1914 – had received little encouragement in the theatre milieu. Mrs Watson, understanding Esmé's eager pursuit of the definitive *raison d'être*, introduced her to Christian Science. Her timing was perfect.

Esmé, feeling she had been 'shown', and wanting to do what should be right for her marriage, decided not to return to the stage.

Her decision was shattering news to Noël, as he made clear on almost every occasion we met or spoke through the rest of his life. He was, at the time of her decision, writing *The Young Idea*, with a role for Esmé, and he found it impossible to understand how she could abandon the seeming certainty of remaining a West End actress when she knew he would always be there to write plays with parts in them for her. It was a huge blow to his ego. He had understood her wish to marry, and was in no way jealous of Linden; he had known him for several years, and they got on well. However, being already familiar with what the distorting lens of sexual passion can do to common-sense and good judgement, he could entertain without malice, but perhaps a little hope, the possibility that Esmé might in time return to acting.

This might have been the case had she not met Maud Watson. Although Esmé's questioning mind was never to be wholly satisfied by the rigid framework of the Mother Church's party-line, she studied the Christian Science textbooks for the rest of her life, maintaining to the last that she owed a great debt to Mary Baker Eddy. Her own later books, however, showed how much further, and more deeply, she had studied philosophy and comparative religion. If that had been all there was to it, Noël could have been reconciled. What alarmed and some-times infuriated him was Esmé's allegiance to the reformatory concerns of Christian Science, with emphasis on the 'unseeing' of Error, the pros-elytising pursuit of Ultimate Truth, and the fearsome prospect for her intended convert of that inner reform she saw as the natural corollary. Her increasing preoccupation with these concepts was depriving their friendship of much of the shared joy of their younger years. Those years had been a period of intense and seldom broken companionship, and Esmé's affection for Noël developed into a deeper attachment than he was ever to know with the kiss-kiss luvvies who could supply only a tinsel veil between himself and the human race he saw to be 'cruel, idiotic, sentimental, predatory, ungrateful, ugly, conceited and egocen-tric to the last ditch ... the occasional exception [being] as deliciously surprising as finding a sudden brazil nut in what you *know* to be five pounds of vanilla creams'.

These lines come from a letter Noël wrote to her in 1936, more than twenty years after the nightmare of the First World War had introduced them to the cruelty and unhappiness of the man-made world. She could be excused, perhaps, for her persistent attempts to dig out some deeply-buried remnant of the old Noël, but the counter-attractions met with on his rise to stardom had proved too strong. There is one consolation: if Esmé's determination that Noël should one day submit his tarnished soul to God's best shots achieved nothing more, it sparked letters to her that he probably never surpassed in wit and irony. Some are now in the keeping of London's Theatre Museum. Frustratingly, many early letters and collaborations were destroyed by fire shortly after the Second World War. Enough remain to throw light on their formative, unusual, and mutually valued friendship, which ran the gamut between furious childhood squabbles and a genuine concern for each other's health and happiness in their terminal years; but most of their collaborations have gone for ever.

In the 1920s and 1930s Esmé's religious and ethical certainties still left room for an exchange of comments on each other's writing, for she was turning out both plays and novels through the 1920s, as well as a great deal of journalism in the national and literary press. But she shot a few reformatory arrows to keep Noël on his spiritual toes. Chastised in 1928 that he was antagonistic to Christian Science, he replied from Ebury Street:

Darling,
Your letter and wire safely to hand – your letter frightfully to hand. What a poop you are, but a very dear poop I must admit. I *doooo* wish that you'd understand that it isn't your Science that ever irritated me, but just certain dear old feminine (ultra) qualities which were always with you and seem lately to have become slightly enhanced. You've always since the Brixton days been awful about other women, but whereas before you frankly called them bitchy, you now profess that you're sorry for them, which is just the same old face under a different hat. But I love you and shall always love you and if you don't come to see me next time you're up I'll come round and slap your always protuberant botsy. All love, Poj. The play's a hit and I'm divine.

The heavier Esmé's spiritual urgings became, the more carefully Noël honed his flippancy. Although increasingly incapable of arguing with her on the philosophical level, his concern and practical help throughout her marital problems in the 1930s proved a loyalty and affection perhaps unknown to luvviedom scribblers focused only on surface impressions, but he knew he could always defuse her evangelistic surges

with his ability to make her laugh. In 1949 Esmé had sent him her first
postwar non-fiction book, *The Unity of Being*, which in his introduction her collaborator, the novelist J. D. Beresford, compared flatteringly
with Aldous Huxley's *The Perennial Philosophy*. It is highly unlikely
that Noël read further than the title of either book, but his reply left all
options open (the nicknames 'Poj' and 'Stoj' had been adopted during
their childhoods).

Darling Stoj,
    It was lovely to hear from you and to know you are still bright
as a button and not lost and gone before.
    I am writing this before reading your book because I am at the
moment in the throes of doing a new musical, which is very cheerful and robust and neither Victorian nor nostalgic, and am also
casting my new comedy and putting finishing touches to the film I
have just done; and as your book does not seem the sort of little
book-stall number that would make an unnecessary journey go in
a flash I shall wait two or three weeks and read it carefully. In the
meantime, do you ever come up to London or are we never to
meet again until I am on my deathbed and you appear with, I
hope, not *extreme* unction?
    You ask me how I am thinking these days; do you know, the
awful thing is I don't believe I am thinking very differently from
the way I have always thought. My philosophy is as simple as ever.
I love smoking, drinking, moderate sexual intercourse on a diminishing scale, reading and writing (not arithmetic). I have a selfless
absorption in the wellbeing and achievements of Noël Coward. I
do not care for any Church (not even the dear old Mother
Church) and I don't believe there is a Universal Truth, and if you
and J. D. have found it you are better men than I am, Gunga Din.
    In spite of my unregenerate spiritual attitude, I am jolly kind to
everybody and still attentive and devoted to my dear old Mother
who is hale and hearty, sharp as a needle and occasionally very
cross indeed.
    I have built myself a little house in Jamaica on the edge of the
sea where I eat bread-fruit, coconuts, yams, bananas and rather
curious fish and where also I lie in the sun to relax and paint a
series of pictures in oils, all of which I consider to be of great
beauty but which, in reality, are amateur, inept and great fun to
do.

I have not yet found Jesus but I am pegging on with my nose to the grindstone and my shoulder to the wheel and also with a great deal of love for my childhood playmate whom I should like to see again if some old Universal Truth would lead her (in an off moment) to 17 Gerald Road, S.W.1.

Love and kisses,

POJ

P.S. Lorn sends her love.
P.P.S. I also drink rum in Jamaica.
P.P.P.S. I am looking very pretty in a chocolate-boxy sort of way.

Noël had once again 'found the words', for after Esmé's admission that she was replying when still 'heaving with laughter' from reading them, she said nothing reformatory other than to remind him that 'in the most clear-sighted period of our close companionship' he had neither smoked nor drunk alcohol, 'thinking it was more original and sensible not to'. She ended: 'Heaps of love, my pretty lamb, and big hugs, Stoj.'

On 6 June 1952, when Esmé was staying in our Finchley flat, Noël asked her to lunch. She told me subsequently that she found him 'smoking his head off, incapable of concentrating for two minutes', and drinking 'three glasses of brown liquid, after which he was incapable of clear thinking'. She also admitted that he had written a 'very funny lyric about Mary Baker Eddy'. Her diary entry read:

Went to lunch with Poj. Saw Lorn. We talked for an hour and a half – very sweet. After lunch his accompanist came and he gave me a pre-view of the programme he was going to do at the Café de Paris at £1000 per week. Terrific thunderstorm. Wore spotted blue dress and white hat.

What might be termed her Christianly Scientific recording of their reunion, which she had clearly intended should be unmarked by any outward sign of 'inharmony', was not similarly immortalised by Noël's own diary entry that night. As well able to sense the unspoken as the spoken sisterly strictures, but lacking the language and logic to defeat in open debate the passionate moral certainties of his oldest, fondest, yet most infuriating friend, he allowed his wit and insight to be eclipsed by raw rage. He ascribed her disapproval to 'failure', to 'envy' of his material success, and to a deeply repressed regret at her own 'denial of life'. All good Freudian stuff, written in a fury intensified by his knowledge that it was total nonsense. Thirty years later the entry was included in *The Noël Coward Diaries*, whose editors claimed in a footnote that the friendship had 'evaporated in the 1920s', and that the entry was prompted by a correspondence 'just before' their 1952 meeting; whereas the correspondence was three years earlier, had been affectionate and amusing, and probably forgotten by both of them. In the *Times Literary Supplement* of 15 October 1982, discussing David Hare's rightly-founded suspicion that what Noël was afraid of was thought, I suggested that the diaries' editors had done him no favours in selecting such an entry, for not only were its statements 'wildly inaccurate on several counts, but they strengthen a view of Coward as a witless, vindictive, pompous, disloyal and spoiled child rather than as a middle-aged man who, for all his failings, was still capable of loyalty, affection, and of acknowledging that others had a right to a preferred design for living and to a different notion of star quality'.

It was true of course that while Esmé wanted to grow ('evolve', as she sometimes put it), Noël wanted nothing to change, least of all himself. One can understand his motive for defending the status quo so passionately. His public looked for the same as before and would not have warmed to some sudden Shavian or Tolstoian makeover. Yet his inability to come to terms with Esmé's 'defection' was revealing. Gertrude Lawrence could replace Esmé as a player of parts – though no more than that – and one could not realistically claim that Noël's career had been seriously harmed by the ending of his and Esmé's professional collaboration. The truth was that he was missing something more fundamental than her presence in his plays. While, right up to the early 1970s, when both were to die, his letters continued to reflect his regret at the ending of their collaboration, his greater hurt was that she wouldn't settle for the sort of frivolous friendship that – without her almost daily and more intelligent influence – he increasingly preferred. Every time she showed her passionate but often exasperatingly expressed concern for his moral and spiritual wellbeing, it was both proof of a more profound and adult affection than he had known from any other woman, and at the same time a knife turning in the wound left by their separation: a deep and subtle form of flattery, even if not seen or intended as such. Although he was to find a degree of mental companionship with friends such as Betty Chester and Gladys Calthrop, and was wonderfully supported by the down-to-earth commonsense and realistic loyalty of Lorn, the early years with Esmé could never be replicated.

In this respect Noël and I had a lot in common. We enjoyed a shared victimhood. As Esmé's only child, and lacking from the age of eight a father to absorb some of the heat, I was far more often the target of her fervent desire to see me make the most of my spiritual potentialities. It was rough going, and it never let up, but I never saw it as other than well meant. While I climbed little beyond the lower slopes of her awesome ambitions for me, my failure was through human weakness and inexperience rather than from being able to fault most of the idealistic goals she had set for me. Like Noël and most of her circle of old friends, I had to grow into an understanding of the sincerity of Esmé's feelings. She could be exasperating, she could provoke her less instinctive recipients to near-homicidal heights, but she *cared*. She really wanted people to be better, for their own and for the world's sake. And she charmed, even in old age. Had she wished to marry again, for material security, she could have taken her pick from successful, interesting and wealthy men, some of whom tried to use me as a go-between; but she wanted none of it. It was all part of the package that Noël could not understand for many a long year, and which exacerbated his urge to 'get back' gently and with humour in books and plays, and even in major roles that he created to mock some aspect of his old friend's unrelenting search for a truth more satisfying than the values of this all too corporeal world. But she enjoyed his mockings, for her sense of humour, like his, stayed life's course; though where, in her case, it could mean digging through innumerable layers of spiritual priorities to find it, in his it seemed at times irrevocably buried beneath a post-*Cavalcade* jingoism that was to deepen into the snobbery revealed by embarrassing name-dropping in one of his later books. Some of their older mutual friends understood. Rebecca West was to touch the nerve-ending of Noël's regret at Esmé's self-inflicted retreat from his world with the realisation that 'your mother is one of the most brilliant women of her generation, Jon, but she *will* sacrifice what is interesting to The Truth'.

While it may be difficult to present a balanced picture of a relationship, especially where differing sexual orientation is a factor, I have attempted it in this instance because Noël's influence on me – indirectly more than directly – was in some respects greater than that of my father. The Coward bandwagon has been subject to much wishful thinking and gender agendas, and I may be a little better equipped than most to make some needed adjustments, at least in respect of Noël's most influential friendship.

Fashionable focus on Noël's sexual targeting, although of little more importance *au fond* than where and how often he obeyed nature or brushed his teeth, has stolen the limelight that should have shone on his creative accomplishments, his wit, his kindliness, and that whole package of qualities, bad as well as good, that make us what we are. Although Esmé hit the nail in saying that the keynote of Noël was his flippancy, even flippancy has its aetiology, which makes it a more interesting subject for study than where Noël chose to put his willy. It is a truism in more than one sense that man is more than the sum of his parts, and before those who dispute this succeed in boiling the Master down to a clutch of half-remembered tunes and a sexual football booted between those who cannot even agree, despite overwhelming evidence, whether he was homo or hetero, I will quote a few more letters that go some way to proving that there as a less trivial side to the man than his detractors – who include some of those most in debt to him – have chosen to suggest.

The 1950s were not an easy decade for either Noël or Esmé, both of whom had work worries as they dealt at their separate levels with a cultural climate that heralded the sixties and all they stood (or failed to stand) for. In Esmé's case, physical self-neglect, prompted by an unwise disregard for the commonsense care of the digestive system, about which Mrs Eddy had nothing specific to say, had exacerbated problems that meant she hardly ever moved from the desk in her primitive Selsey bungalow, from which she refused to be uprooted. If she and Noël corresponded by more than seasonal cards in those ten years, I hold little paperwork to prove it. On 24 February 1960, by which time she had been writing reclusively for thirteen years since the death of J. D. Beresford, she wrote after a long interval, on hearing that he was suffering from phlebitis:

My darling Poj,
    Living – mercifully – without wireless, 'telly' or daily paper, the hermit Stoj gets whatever news she does get very late. However, neighbours eventually brought to my notice that you were apparently 'tied by the leg', so I wrote to Lorn for your address so that I could write to you by air direct. I am most relieved to hear from her note this morning that you are *very much better* – but not surprised, as you have known the power of Mind so long that you are not likely to neglect it in a physical need.
    However, as a little bit of merely human comfort, I wanted you

to know that Boj [their name for her father] suffered considerably from phlebitis on and off from about the age of 45–65, and often had to retire for 'rests', attending to business by telephone from his bed. But after the age of 65 (he [died] at 86) we never heard a word of the complaint, and he was reasonably nimble to the end. I tell you this because I well know that when plunged in a complaint, especially when painful, a distinct depression is apt to occur and it is hard to imagine ever being your normal self again; and yet that is just what you have to 'imagine' quite clearly and persistently (you know I nearly [died] in 1948!). The only time I ever saw Boj in tears was when his legs were in such a state – and certainly looked awful – so I want you to know that any depression you may feel is 'natural' to the complaint. At such times a comforting and true thought to which I have often held is 'all things vanish; good remains'.

And my word how they do vanish! And we have to learn that, finally, our connection with the Good Mind is all we have to help us. Yesterday I heard that your old friend Edwina Mountbatten had departed. But how enviable – in her sleep! No unpleasant illness or suffering, apparently. A shock to those left, but they should be grateful for the sake of one who has escaped so much. What I find much harder to endure is the thought of Teddy Holstius who, as you probably know, has had to have BOTH legs removed, after years of medical experimentation. I have not heard many details, but it is probably connected with his 'tin tummy' which, as you know, he had from the age of twenty. The longer I live the more all prayer seems reduced to the primary one – from Indian sources: 'May all living things be delivered from pain.'

I wonder if you remember us standing in a field during that awful Charley's Aunt tour, realising (as I see it was now) POWER. We admitted to each other that we felt within us the power to achieve anything, and your INTEGRATED wish was to have the world at your feet, theatrically speaking. How surely the wish came true! Yet how far from it you seemed at the time. Mine – just as integrated – was to 'know the truth'. It has taken much longer, but it's happened. What I have learned from eight years of hermit life alone on this beach is incredible, and how often I've wished you could be here to hear the bits that would interest you. If you have read my last book, *Mithras: the Fellow in the Cap*, published by Rider, you would have some idea of what I've discovered about how and why mankind is – heaven help it – as it is. But what I have learnt since has burst forth in a book which only a miracle could get published, as it exposes the whole incredible racket of the thought-manipulation of mankind from the time of Nimrod, and will offend practically everyone who reads it [*The Philosophy of Compassion*, Vincent Stuart, 1962]. Only those who truly pray the Indian prayer referred to over-leaf will love it, and they are such a tiny handful!

YOUR wish has, I know, given you much pleasure in the fulfil-ment. Mine has given me much inward content, but the dreadful irony of mine is that, after finding the Truth which I wanted not only for my sake, but to bring it to the world and particularly to those I was fond of, I discover that it is the very last thing the world wants to hear about or that those nearest to me will accept [a too sweeping statement, as it turned out]. I admit I had never visualised that possibility, mainly because I was so uneducated and knew nothing of the many people throughout the ages who'd shared my wish – and fate. Altogether, Poj darling, there is a fairy tale quality about our two wishes that would make a wonderful book – for the right kind of writer if he could be found in these materialistic days. But then we would have to find someone to read it – and they're all glued to their 'tellies'.

I do hope one day to hear something more of your new Swiss home. But for now, just my very fondest love and hopes for a full and quick recovery.   STOJ

Noël replied on 9 March from Switzerland:

My darling Stoj,

I was so very very pleased to get your sweet letter. And what with telepathy and Annie Besant and one thing and another it arrived just as I was thinking of you. I happened to be having my annual re-read of the E. Nesbits, which I still prefer to any other literature, and there on the fly-leaf of *The Magic City* was the evocative name of Charles Steuart. And I remembered without remorse how we had broken in and stolen it! Out of evil cometh good is what *I* always say and I don't believe a *word* of it. The phlebitis was a grave bore and my monotonously beautiful right leg swelled up like a pink sausage and I had to be carried about like a parcel. Fortunately I have an Italian house boy who is quite square like a biscuit box and *likes* carrying wardrobes up and down stairs, so he placed me on the loo every morning and then placed me back in bed again and the stupid old clot disappeared and the Good Mind sodden with universal truth suddenly decided that this was all too easy and so, in order to teach me a further sharp lesson, gave me congestion of the left lung which was *not* serious but jolly painful for three days because of my stubborn devotion to the frivolous pleasures of life such as breathing! However that has now disappeared too and I am scampering up and down stairs like a 60 year old and waiting eagerly for the first joyous signs of syphilis.

I was very distressed about Edwina's death but, as you say, what an enviable way to go. The sadness, as always, is reserved for those who are left. In any case so many of my friends have upped and died during the last few years that I'm becoming sort of hardened to it. I start practically every letter now quite automatically with 'Words are useless but please accept my deepest etc.' All I ask of my friends who are left is that they should live through dinner.

The thing that horrified me in your letter was the news of poor Teddy Holstius. I *didn't* know. How cruel that such an innocuous, amiably disposed character should have to suffer so much.

I remember I remember so very very well that long ago day in that far away field. I think we both decided then and there (if not before) that we were going to get what we wanted and, both being determined characters to say the least of it, we succeeded. I only know that if I should happen to [die] to-morrow I have no complaints. I have had a very happy and full life with enough sadness here and there to highlight the happiness. I have had, to quote that classic *Bittersweet*, 'a talent to amuse' and, with it, have been able to make many millions of my fellow creatures laugh, which, when all is said and done, is not a bad accolade to retire to the grave with! You have found peace and content in research and solitude. A rare treasure. Whether or not the truths you have discovered are transferable is not the point. The point is that *you* have discovered them. Or It. But don't, dear perrenial* reformer, waste *too* much mental energy trying to impart it because that, my darling, leads to disillusion, irritation, discouragement, a thorough upset of your spiritual acids, and frequently spots on the back. Just be grateful that you are *convinced* and healthy and still have a twinkle in your eye.

I have utilised my convalescence to finish a novel. It has been hanging over me like the sword of whoever it was for ages. It is so light and *un*significant that I think they will have difficulty in getting it between covers. Hurray!

I am really in love with this house. When I first saw it it was hideous beyond belief but now, after spending forty million pounds eighteen and fourpence on it, it is lovely. The views are fabulous, lake and mountains and, at the moment, snow. In the Spring it still looks like snow because of the wild narcissi.

Kindly write again and oblige your ever loving POJ

* I know this word is wrongly spelt but I have an Italian typewriter.

While Esmé thought his letter 'the funniest I have ever had from you in my life, which is saying something when I think how letters from you preserved me from near-suicide at that dreadful convent in 1914', it brought on his head the firm reminder that 'we went to Steu's flat armed with a letter' of authorisation, and she added:

But, darling, aren't you a bit unrealistic in your advice to me not to impart what I know? It is just as though I said: 'Yes, Poj darling, you have indeed a talent to amuse, but don't use it to make other people laugh. Just sit in your bath and have a thoroughly good time with your own jokes.' People don't search for a lifetime to find something for the good of mankind and then sit in a corner of a very stony beach mumbling to themselves about it.

Coping with Parkinson's Disease and other physical problems, Esmé was constantly weeding out her files and destroying letters and other documents she felt she would never need.(I, by contrast, hoard almost everything against a rainy day and 'because you never know'.) A few of Noël's Christmas cards survived, probably because they usually depicted himself. 1964's read:

Oh, dear, I do wish we saw each other more often. Let's have a try when Spring breaks through again! Isn't it peculiar about me being a promising young classic and the pride of the National Theatre? Dame Edie [Edith Evans] is a hundred years too old for the part but most certainly doesn't look it! I suppose our old friend Mary B. E. is at it again! [Edith Evans was a Christian Scientist.] Love, love, love, Poj. Don't be put off by this elegance. It's all a hideous mockery. I *still* pick my nose.

In 1966 Esmé wrote, after hearing he was leaving England, recalling:

… your mummie making the most delicious coffee I have ever tasted over the open fire of Hickery-Dickery when Jon was 'on the way', [and also when] you did your perhaps most marvellous work of raising the (very nearly) dead at Connaught Mansions when Aishie Pharall and I were stricken with that frightful 1918 flu; and you came in without a trace of fear and made me laugh … Fondest love, darling. Bits of us remain just the same as they were fifty years ago, and we're probably right to keep to them, instead of meeting and *dis*agreeing on many issues. All good is always the wish for you of your loving Stoj. Big hugs.

Noël's 1967 Christmas card, showing his right and left half-profiles, and sent after hearing that Esmé's health was making her chosen solitude increasingly difficult to cope with, read: 'Darling Stoj, I hope these two aspects of my lovely little heart-shaped face will jerk you to your feet again. Fond love, Poj.' His 1969 'card' from Esmé was a copy of her book *The Dialectics of Diotima*, published by Centaur Press as part of her Christmas present, as there was no chance of finding a commercial publisher to take what was going to be her last – and anonymous – book. This brought from Noël a card whose handwriting was even more difficult to read than her own:

My darling Stoj,
This can't be a long letter as I am going straight up my favourite apple tree with dear Diotima. I have a feeling that both are above my head. I send you all E.S.P. I have by me at the moment. You *know* how it runs through one's fingers.
All fondest love as always, X X X Sir Poj

A day earlier (19 January 1970), two years before Esmé's death, he had written the last letter she kept:

My darling Stoj,
I have now had two sweet letters from you so here is one sweet letter from me. I am of course delighted to have the knighthood but what moved me most was the manner in which the Queen offered it to me. It was in the middle of a birthday lunch given for me by the beloved Queen Mother. (You know dear old democratic me – lunch with the Queen one day and Norah Howard the next.) She gave me the impression (the Queen, not Norah Howard) that

it was I who was conferring the honour on her instead of the other way round. How's that for Royal Grace? So from now on I shall expect a great deal more deference and respect from you than I have received in the past. You must *never* sit in my presence – unless I happen to have thrown you onto the sofa – and you must *always* address me as Sir Poj. I hope all this is clear in your dizzy mind. All loving love my darling old pal X X X X X (These are ennobled kisses).

                                                    Your devoted old Sir Poj

The era of challenge and reaction had passed. Little time left, all passion spent. Their last exchanges rounded off a sequence of late-life pointers to a nostalgia, affection, and urge to cheer that those who seemed to wish upon Noël an inability to sustain a true friendship have done their best to suppress.

For the record, my own response to what I felt were the least deserved of Esmé's guidelines for my spiritual rebirth had been to give in to childish outbursts that did not – according to Jennifer – diminish with time. More positively, I hope, I published *Marvellous Party* (John Calder, 1989). This 'sophisticated and revealing comedy that supposes a middle-aged reunion in Las Vegas between Noël Coward and Esmé Wynne (-Tyson), his real-life oldest, closest, and most exacting female friend', is the only play to have portrayed Noël and Esmé as they might have spoken and behaved, given the highly improbable setting I chose for Esmé. It was greeted enthusiastically by a large number of actors, writers and producers – only some of them known to me – including Iris Murdoch, John Gielgud, Alec Guinness, Arnold Wesker, Eileen Atkins, and Dorothy Tutin and Stanley Baxter who took the leading roles in the shortened version I made for a BBC radio 'Play of the Week'. But although the play has been produced in the provinces and overseas, nothing has happened in London's West End or in New York. This bewildered us all, especially James Roose-Evans, whose encouragement spurred me to write the play. By now, however, those on the greenery-yallery grapevine of theatre politics have some idea of the reasons. But to return to the Jamaican twilight ...

After reaffirming his 'great debt' to Esmé and his lasting regret that her changed priorities had so much reduced the opportunities for meeting on common ground, Noël suggested that my projected guidebook be written by Esther Chapman – a thought quashed subsequently by several advisers with direct knowledge of her dominating temperament. Maybe Noël felt that my maternal background would have given me the needed strength. Not for the first time, he showed surprise that I seemed to have survived Esmé's powerful personality.

Concerned that the Master should have left for a dinner engagement, Coley ran me back to 'Bluers' where we ate soup, rice, egg, and banana baked in lime and brown sugar, before plunging as nature made us into the sea-fed, velvet-warm pool. One saw why Noël found his Caribbean retreat such a battery-recharging necessity. On the swinging poolside seat, Coley (whom I first met at Gerald Road circa 1937 when he had joined Noël as his valet) entertained me into the small hours with the love lives of, among others, Graham Greene; the splendid gaffes of Clemence Dane; and less repeatable memories of a host of household names. As Noël slept in the cooler night on Firefly's hill, I drifted off in Bluer's comfortable sleigh-bed in the high-ceilinged 'Master'-bedroom.

The necessarily brief visit ended on a mildly sobering note. In 1960, by which time Noël had owned Blue Harbour for several years, I had suggested a coffee-table book depicting himself and friends in and about Port Maria's scenic hideaway. He replied, *inter alia*:

> ... I am going to be completely honest and tell you that the idea does not really appeal to me. There are several reasons for this; to begin with, there are not enough photographs to fill a book and even if there were they would, of necessity, be rather lacking in variety. Page after page of them would become extremely monotonous. Then too, I feel that to expect the public to buy a volume consisting of nothing but photographs of one man is asking rather a lot; and when that one man is depicted as having an apparently endless holiday the reader – or should I say looker – might become slightly irritated.

Just as I was leaving and Coley had gone to the door to answer the taxi-driver's bell, I noticed an album-sized book on the glass table top. I flicked through part of it. It consisted of page after page of Noël and his friends having an apparently endless holiday in the gorgeous surroundings of Blue Harbour. It was just what I had had in mind. I looked at the imprint on the title page, as publishers always do. It was Anthony Blond's. But I couldn't really blame Noël. Centaur's 1960 catalogue may have had a certain restrained panache, but was hardly evidence of a track record for coffee-table ephemera. I never asked Anthony how it had sold. I am not sure I would have wanted to know.

Trinidad was a mild culture shock after Blue Harbour. I put up at Port of Spain's Queen's Park Hotel, and there, in the seminal moment of my tour, I was surprised and pleased to find Ken Jackson Marshall at breakfast the next morning. He seemed to feel I must be serious, if not foolhardy, to have travelled so far in pursuit of a hunch. But he was a mine of information and encouragement, and felt sure that if I got my act together he would be able to arrange for Collins to represent the guide in the West Indies. He wrote off Noël's suggestion of Esther Chapman, as the lady was 'overpowering and a proper trial'. Reg Murray, Educational Adviser to the Ministry of Labour and Social Affairs, he thought, might be glad to write the book for me. Doors seemed to be opening.

British West Indian Airways' Basil Pantin, a Creole as English as Cheltenham, arranged for me to island-hop henceforth at 'one hundred per cent discount'. Trinidad's Deputy Prime Minister, Carl La Corbinière, drove me to the house of Albert Gomes MP, director of Standard Publicity, who promised thirty to forty pages of advertising at £100 or more per page. La Corbinière's Minister without Portfolio also drove me around, and took me to meet Reg Murray. Today it would be seen that Reg's West Indian origins made him a politically sound choice. Then it just seemed commonsense to consider someone who obviously had the requisite local knowledge. After our meeting I was returned to the hotel in the official car, to find my tatty room issued with new tablets of soap, flagons of iced water and clean towels – a telephone had even been placed in the centre of my bed.

In the end, nice guy though he was, Reg Murray was not able to complete the task adequately. Bermuda and the Bahamas were outside his patch; his government was not exactly hastening the process; he wanted more time than he was permitted to allot, and more guidance than could be given to the procedures for getting and checking the material needed. Caribbean politics can be as tricky as any other. Ken did his best to help things along, but by spring 1963 could see no hope of Reg producing the goods. A further year was to pass before we could formally call it off without offence to any party, and Reg was paid for his abortive work. The thought of meeting some of the production and other costs from advertising revenue also fell by the wayside – recommendations influenced by advertisers, hidden or otherwise, were liable to be suspect. In the end, no advertising was accepted for the two-volume work apart from five 'prestige' displays, none of which could hope for direct benefit from a text mention: BWIA, Colonial Insurance, a reproduction furniture company, Grace Travel Department, and Appleton rum. It was an expensive decision, but any other would have nullified the aim of ensuring that 'Editorial recommendations of hotels, etc., are based upon direct, on-the-spot experience, every possible effort having been made to ensure complete accuracy, balance and impartiality'.

Apart from a useful session with the tourist board's manager and his wife at their pleasant out-of-town house, then taking Ken to a well-deserved dinner in the Belvedere restaurant 600 feet above Port of Spain, the Trinidad touchdown was over, though I squeezed in calls on several booksellers, who seemed very happy with what I could tell them.

My next landing was on the grass strip that served Tobago as an airfield. Almost nothing in Tobago seemed to have changed in the previous fifty years. Photographs of the capital, Scarborough, taken in 1910, showed it had been altered hardly a jot. Driving through the Santa Cruz valley in Trinidad, my driver Mahomed had told me a man could keep a family in comfort if he had twenty acres of citrus, nutmeg, bananas, cassavas, and the like. I was surprised that he needed as many acres as that. In those days an acre of land could be bought for 6,000 'bee-wees' (the BWI dollar was worth four shillings and sixpence), and five years earlier for 1,000.

I stayed in the Crown Point Hotel, a solitary start to the development of that beautiful end of the island. The hotel's owner, Maurice Tawil, took me on a tour round Tobago, and for the first time I opened a fallen coconut with a borrowed machete. Its fresh milk was ambrosial. Why do I recall that brief, unexceptional moment with such pleasure?

The next day I had to return to Trinidad in order to fly on to Grenada, a miniature Jamaica, but with a far more attractive airport-to-capital drive of some fifteen miles over forested mountains. By the end of it I was as in love with the Spice Island for its lush beauty as I had been with Tobago for its open simplicity and unspoiled reefs. I booked in at the Silver Sands on Grand Anse Beach, whose rather primitive standards were more in keeping with my impression of the island. The tourist board director took me round and showed the customary keenness for my project, as did a developer who offered half an acre of a glorious headland for £7,000 and took me on a conducted tour. St George's was reminiscent of Portofino, but as a paradise for book lovers it was little better than Tobago, an SPCK bookshop being the only source. It was sad that the two islands to attract me the most should lack a decent bookshop; but what the hell was I doing trying to increase holidaymakers' enthusiasm for places as yet – thank goodness – unruined by the human presence?

The next day, resisting the temptation from Beresford Willcox, who was developing Westerhall Point, to buy a plot with a two-bedroomed house for £4,300, I flew on to Barbados, which I remember best as the island from which I most wanted to fly straight back to Tobago or Grenada. It seemed flat, dull, over-populated and over-exploited, though the beaches, if not the best in the Caribbean, were certainly good. Other islands asked for radio and press interviews as soon as I had been through customs, but Barbados went at it as though I was something special at the Cannes Festival. But at least they drove me to the St Lawrence Hotel for the interview, and I stayed there for the one night I spent on the island. The hotel was run by Peter Morgan, who was deeply into tourist promotion, and the tourist board manager gave me tea there after laying on a taxi to take me into Bridgetown, where I called on several bookshops. The American widow who ran the Cloister Bookshop offered to 'show me a bit of Barbados' and appeared in the evening complete with dancing shoes. It was an expensive and tiring encounter, and I fear that she cannot have remembered me as the most exciting publisher to have visited Barbados. But by comparison with finding Carib and Arawak shards on Westerhall Point, as I had done the day before, tropical nightclubs struck me as a very poor second. There seemed no point in staying around.

Antigua was discovered by Columbus on his second voyage in 1493, and named by him after a church in Seville, Santa Maria la Antigua. The Britannia flight there gave a clear view of St Lucia, Martinique, Dominica, Guadeloupe, and (had I used my binoculars) Redonda. My two nights' stay at the Anchorage Hotel in Dickinson Bay gave me time to meet Vernon Nicholson and his son Desmond. The Nicholsons had sailed into English Harbour in their schooner *Mollihawk* in 1948, intending a new life in Australia. The story of why and how they stayed in Nelson's derelict dockyard is beyond my brief, but it was Desmond and his American wife Lisa who enabled me in 1980 to spend a winter writing much of my novel *So Say Banana Bird* in the picturesque timber officers' quarters, cooled by the on-shore trade winds and enjoying one of the most evocative views in the Caribbean.

After a few swims among dive-bombing pelicans, and finding fish and fossils in Dickinson's Bay, I flew on to Bermuda where friends had found me a room in a yachty guest house. Offered a Sunfish and crew, I declined the responsibility for helming a boat I didn't know in a Force 8, where-upon Eagle rang to say the midnight flight to London had been put for-ward to 6 a.m. the next day. My timeclock seemed disproportionately stressed by the frustration of this eleventh-hour disruption and ... well, I was homesick. Endless meetings, travel, new beds to get used to, come hard to the habitual loner, and time and again I had wished that the better moments could be shared with the family. I was the more impa-tient to get home for having decided to go ahead with the guidebook, though it was not until 1965 that I finalised Ken's suggestion that it be written by John Crocker, who covered the Caribbean for the (London) *Observer*'s foreign news service. Family and desk had become an obses-sive priority, though Jennifer was to say I had not put them in that order of importance. So it was a vast relief to be whizzing along in the Bermuda Aviation Services' bus at 4.30 a.m. on my third day on the island, with a New York singer belting out 'What are the simple joys of maidenhood?'

After seven more years of toil and trouble, February 1968 saw the publication of *Bermuda, the Bahamas, Hispaniola, Puerto Rico, and the Virgin Islands*, and in September came the companion volume, *The Caribbean and El Dorado*. The *Sunday Times*'s reviewer declared that he had 'found no other [guidebook] which goes into such detail, is so entertaining to read, nor is half as balanced and frank'. Other reactions were equally welcoming. The books sold, though not well enough in commercial terms to justify the considerable investment of time and stress. With UK sales limited by inadequate trade representation, the worst blow by far was in 1969, from the sudden death in Rio de Janeiro of Ken Jackson Marshall. This left sizeable bad debts in the Caribbean that only he could have recovered, and the guide's fate in other and now indifferent hands. A law unto himself, Ken had been valuable enough to Collins for them to allow him to befriend another publisher's wares. Without him, Collins's small financial incentive to continue selling the guide in the West Indies was insufficient to retain the bond. They reneged on Ken's assurances, writing off the Centaur connection as a purely personal arrangement. It *had* been, of course, but the Caribbean representation was a vital component. The Crocker guides submerged slowly, leaving me to argue with Collins over the flotsam, and only the books' reputation kept them modestly alive for a few more years. It all added to that damned learning curve, no doubt, the chief lesson being that the really small publisher who pins his hopes on a single individual in a really big publisher's employ is a chump.

Derek Hudson's *Talks with Fuddy and Other Papers* began 1968 with a slim volume in the despised field of *belles lettres*, which made little impact. Another slim volume was *High Dive* by Greenwood Poetry Prizewinner Margaret Rhodes. Of the few poetry selections I have mentioned publishing, this was one I liked more than most. Once 'Evoe' in *Punch*, and often anthologised, she wrote as effectively with prosody and rhyme as in the more fashionable mode. Two hundred and fifty copies of *High Dive* were printed, some thirty of which were sent for review. The production matched, I think, the quality of the book's content, as I aimed to do with all the poetry I felt deserved to be taken seriously. But Richard Church summed up the problems of getting to the market in a letter acknowledging receipt of the book I sent to him personally. 'As you say, poetry of her kind, like my own, has now no platform in the familiar weeklies and Sunday papers. There is nothing we can do about it except to continue working in our own way and leaving the rest to time and posterity.' From what I have seen of posterity, the signs are hardly more encouraging now than they were thirty-six years ago. After eight years, *High Dive* sold out. All 200 or so copies!

The only Centaur Classic to be published in 1968 was Richard Gough's *Human Nature Displayed in the History of Myddle*, originally entitled *Antiquityes and Memoyres of the Parish of Myddle, County of Salop*. W. G. Hoskins, Professor of English Local History in the University of Leicester, introduced this 'enchanting picture of seventeenth-century England', and the reviews were unanimous in their enthusiasm for a long-unobtainable classic of local history. C. V. Wedgwood, in *History Today*, rated this 'uniquely valuable source' as highly as Aubrey and Pepys. Unfortunately, SIUP refused to accept *History of Myddle* because it had not been agreed prior to their decision to drop the series. It was taken for the USA by October House Inc., a New York imprint with whom I had been in discussion over the possibility of their taking on SIUP's backlist stock and honouring their commitment to the titles still to come. October House, however, proved to be in the late autumn of their fairly short days, and the travel-battered copies of *Myddle* that they eventually shipped back to us had to be remaindered. A few years later, another UK publisher, realising *Myddle*'s standing from the reception for our edition, brought out an edited and cheaper edition which seemed to do well. A sad waste of one of the most prestigious ideas that Geoffrey had come up with.

When we arrived at our present house in 1961, the central chimney

stack was topped by two clearly hand-made terracotta pots, each punc-
tured round its top half by intriguingly random holes about the size of
the core of a loo roll, and with obviously thumb-impressed pastry-crust
moulding round the flanged rim. We guessed they must be contemporary with the property, said to have been built about 1720. In time, I
got round to researching this minor domestic mystery. It was a frustrating pursuit, no one seeming to have given a thought to an object which
all capable of raising their eyes above guttering must have noticed
countless times. If there had been recognition that pots still to be seen
on many older houses were a minor craft product, no book appeared to
have explored it. Drawing blank in the libraries of the British, London,
and Victoria and Albert Museums, and even on the usually unfailing
shelves of the wonderful London Library, I wrote in desperation to the
architectural historian Alec Clifton-Taylor. He liked the idea, being
'practically sure that there is no book on chimney pots', but 'a need for
one'. He thought I would find a suitable writer in Charles Dobson ('The
London Library is his spiritual home'), as he might have time in his
retirement and had given Clifton-Taylor much help over the years. He
rang Dobson, who responded enthusiastically, and being a down-to-
earth fellow who wrote hugely informed articles in the technical press
should have been ideal. Sadly, after several meetings and a quite long
correspondence, he fell terminally ill and had to abandon the project.
I then responded to a piece in the *Daily Telegraph* about Dr Francis
Celoria, a Field Officer at the London Museum who had organised a
'chimney patrol' of people devoted to tracing and rescuing pots of
historic and artistic interest. Another correspondence began, and an
agreement was sent to Celoria, but he found increasing difficulty in
making time to build on his slight knowledge of the subject, especially
after shifting his place of employment to the University of Keele. He
warned that the job would take him years, which at the rate at which he
seemed to lose the letters I sent to him, and also those he was despatching, was quite believable. The agreement having never been signed, I
accepted that Celoria was clearly a man happier in the field than at his
desk, so we called it a day.

By the time (early 1967) I had begun to feel that I should abandon
the whole idea, I was put on to an article in *Country Life* of 15 September 1966 encouragingly entitled 'In Praise of Chimney Pots'. Its author,
Valentine Fletcher, turned out to be the vicar of Littlemore, Oxford ('A
deadly dull city for chimney pots,' he wrote, 'but the best place for
libraries and books'), and he was at our door a few days after I had

written to him via *Country Life*. Every fibre of his being exuded the
enthusiasm of the fanatic. When I showed him a pot on a cottage at the
end of our lane – it appeared, for all the world, to be a terracotta jerry
missing its handle – he photographed it from every angle with a trem-
bling joy. So far as dedication went, this was our man.

I cannot say that Valentine produced the best book that might have
been written on the subject, but when *Chimney Pots and Stacks* was
published in 1968 it was received by the press with that joyous recognition it often reserves for a subject that is new, out-of-the-way, eccentric,
English to the core, and carrying no political or moral baggage. The
book caused me, once again, more work than could possibly be justified in terms of financial return, especially as, in 1994, just before he
died, I reprinted it as a paperback, more to bring him pleasure than
with hope of seeing the production costs returned within twenty years.
But at least it is still in print, and so far as I know has no serious rival,
though the typescript exists for a much more comprehensive study,
should another retired cleric be bitten by the bug.

Of the two hand-made pots on our house, one is still on its stack, and
of great rarity. The other took pride of place in Valentine's own collection, housed with his patient wife's blessing in the small garden of their
retirement home in Tollard Royal, Wiltshire. Before his death he
unwisely entrusted this to a rural 'museum' where the pots were left in
an outside concrete yard to take their chance with loose livestock,
looser tractors, and visiting small boys who recognised a climbing challenge when they saw one. The pots came off second best, and investi-
gating archaeologists a millennium hence will have a field day.

No less superstitious than most mortals, publishers can hold strong
opinions as to in what month, or even week, a title should be
announced. While it is pretty obvious which kind of book should do
best on the approach of Christmas, it can be apparent that with certain
categories it really doesn't matter a hoot, if only because book-tolerant
newspapers publish reviews every week of the year. Although I
normally avoided January and December (the former being booksellers' normal stocktaking month) it had become clear that some
titles could come out on Christmas Day, August Bank Holiday, or with
no announced publication day whatsoever, without damaging their
chances. On this rather laid-back basis, the last two titles in 1968 were
published on 16 December. One of them perhaps had a Yuletide
connection, being about food, but it was a reissue of a classic work of

the 'take-two-swans' kind that I could not imagine anyone today savouring beyond the confines of an armchair. As it turned out, brief but enthusiastic reviews appeared in December and January of E. S. Dallas's *Kettner's Book of the Table*, splendidly introduced by Derek Hudson.

A handy little spin-off was that the famous Kettner's Restaurant in Soho took 500 copies. They displayed them in their foyer, reverently encased in a glass-topped cabinet. Having arranged with Monsieur Bonvin, the maître d', that any meals I took in the restaurant could be set against what they currently owed me for the book, it was pleasant when eating there to be greeted by Bonvin's assurances that so-many dozen copies had been sold since my last visit.

When the children had left home, I felt a second-hand bookshop might be a filler for the post-adolescent void. An old friend, the poet and biographer Margaret Crosland, joined forces with Jennifer to run it.

No. 9 St Pancras, Chichester, was a minute hairdressing salon when we bought it in 1976. Not that it seemed quite so small when we were faced with having to erect shelving and fill the place with stock. Before Keele's Bookshop was opened, however, in October 1977, literate friends had rallied to the cause. The West Country, for instance, was a good source of books, and Tim Lumley-Smith, with not much to do but shiver behind the four-foot-thick granite walls of a dank house on Bodmin Moor, became 'our man in Cornwall', alerting us to book auctions requiring journeys of heavy mileage but usually worthwhile outcome. As buyer, heaver, and carrier, I found it all very educational, but when Colin Clair sold us the second-division sections of his library from a top flat in Kennington I had to face that my allergies were not suited to my manoeuvring boxes of dusty volumes down innumerable staircases. It ruled out any thought of turning to a later-life sideline selling selected antiquarian books that I would probably want to keep anyway.

While building up the initial stock, we lent the empty premises to Bernard Price, who was glad of 'the peace of your bookshop in St Pancras' in which to write *The Story of English Furniture* for his BBC series. The loss of his ever-inquiring, wide-ranging mind to the curse of Alzheimer's seemed particularly sad to his many friends.

Margaret and Jennifer made an effective team. In 1968 I had published Madame de Staël's *Ten Years' Exile* with Margaret's introduction, enthusiastically welcomed in the *Observer*. With her wide knowledge of Continental literature, and of texts at the esoteric and seriously intellectual levels, she could both impress and charm the more highbrow customers, while Jennifer coped ably with the more predictable tastes of the majority seeking a good read, whether of modern novels or the more approachable classics. Except for a small case of paperbacks left against the outside wall for summer reading, there was no room for the really down-market, any more than for new books other than a few local histories and a selection of the less ponderous Centaur titles. The aim was middle-brow and above, and when Keele's day was called in 1985, it was through Sotheby's and Christie's that much of the closing stock was sold.

Although the profit margin from book sales was necessarily modest from such a small-scale operation, the venture did quite well overall. We boosted our income by letting the first floor flat, quaintly reached by an antique spiral staircase from the shop. Tenants included an altotenor in the cathedral choir; an assortment of stage hands at the Festival Theatre, all hopeful of rising to better things; and a large stonemason whose return each afternoon covered the books in a fine layer of sandstone, some of which he ground into vinyl and stair-carpet with his huge nailed boots. Best of all, the rise in the value of the freehold ensured that Keele's had not made the loss I had anticipated at the outset. But it was a relief – and not only to my nose's tendency to throw a fit at anything but pure oxygen – to have more time for the other plans that had had to be back-burnered.

Ever since SIUP had said they would take no more Centaur Classics beyond those already agreed, the fear grew that they might one day try to avoid receiving even the titles that had been passed in the spirit of our contract. Sure enough, through a rather unfortunate succession of petty ploys, creating an unhappy atmosphere of irritation and niggling accusation, SIUP dodged and weaved their way out of commitments that seemed clear enough to me from the correspondence, but which they indicated they would not honour unless forced to do so in law. Centaur's 1963, 1964, and 1965 catalogues had announced Scott's *Life of Dryden*, a selection from Camden's *Britannia*, the *Complete Poetical Works of Charles Cotton* (to be edited by Bonamy Dobrée), and G. W. Dasent's *Tales from the Norse*. To keep any kind of relationship on the rails, these had to be abandoned, along with the investment in time and resources that had gone into them. This did not come across as what publishing should be about, and the stress and time wastage involved in long-distance legal exchanges was a less manageable proposition for me as a small solo publisher than for an academic institution like SIUP. I realised it would be pointless to hawk around what would assuredly be seen as a cast-off; but it was a big blow that a series that had been so well thought of should have been so quickly and surely unnecessarily undermined.

But although the few years of collaboration with SIUP ended on a dying fall, I look back with pleasure at the best bits. Through inexperience and over-eagerness, I had responded to the genuine enthusiasm of a relatively small and accountant-led American university whose publishing arm was, like Centaur, still in its infancy. Had I had the patience, resources, and foresight to wait until one of the longer-established academic presses had recognised the series's potentiality, things might have turned out differently, but in my solo state I simply could not spare the time to do the kind of networking and travelling that would have been involved. As it was, by the end of 1967 only two more titles were yet to appear under the SIUP agreement. It had been good while it lasted, and the Classics had done the considerable service of giving Centaur Press a respectable and acclaimed identity. For that, at least, I am wholly grateful that I had that breakfast in the Vanderbilt.

8
'The Cause of Half Our Sorrows'

My worst minor blunder – though not to be minimised in terms of the resulting loss of time in dealing with its consequences – was to submit to being the literary executor of two writers: the Irish-Caribbean fantasy novelist M. P. Shiel, and the neo-romantic poet, editor and bibliographer John Gawsworth. Had writing been their only claim to moderate fame, my work in keeping their memory green would have been an insignificant chore. The problem was that they were also known as the first and second kings of Redonda, a small island in the West Indies whose romantic, if somewhat sinister, atmosphere prompted a whimsical invention that dates back to 1865 and became a literary legend that has been told often, usually inaccurately, and is a fitting extension of the fictional figments of the first king. Shiel, of whom more (necessarily only a little more) later, did not make much of the 'realm' he inherited as Felipe I. Juan I did.

Gawsworth, whose real name was Terence Ian Fitton Armstrong, was of lowland Scottish descent on his father's side, from which he also professed lineal connection with Ben Jonson and Lionel Johnson. His chosen *nom de plume* reflected the Jacobite link he claimed through his mother with Mary Fitton, supposedly Shakespeare's 'Dark Lady', who was born in the family home of Gawsworth, Cheshire.

I first met John in January 1949 when, intent on rescuing the Poetry Society from 'twentieth-century obscurity' in its Portman Square premises, he was wading through the 'dreadful legacy of promised acceptances' left by the *Poetry Review*'s previous editor, a blonde, buxom, combustible girl appropriately called Muriel Spark.

Minor poets who yearn for recognition are at the most vulnerable level of non-consummation, and the likely prey of women who – with the naivety of inexperience, or under the illusion that their own failed relationships are adequate qualification – defy all odds to make something out of patently unmalleable material. I would be a fat man if I had had a free meal for every depressed, tired, thin, chain-smoking woman I have known, whose mission had been to supply a struggling poet's background.

Not that Gawsworth's first wife, the dependable Barbara Kentish, a journalist with Fascist leanings, and stern of jaw, could have been blamed for supposing that their marriage in 1933 – if somewhat cerebral and spartan – had at least a sporting chance. Born in 1912, John had been single-minded and sharp as a thorn from pre-puberty in his relentless pursuit of literature. His *Ten Contemporaries, Apes, Japes and Hitlerism* (a study of Percy Wyndham Lewis), and *Lyrics to Kingcup*, had been published in 1932, the latter prompting John Masefield, the Poet Laureate, to describe him as 'one of the most beautiful and promising of our younger writers'. In the year of his marriage he published *Poems 1930–1932*, a retrospective volume whose precocity doubtless endeared him more to Barbara than to his struggling contemporaries, most of whom would have given their right arm to see their work in a printed leaflet, let alone a book. Already acclaimed for his knowledge of post-1890 literature, and remarkably adept at making rewarding friendships with famous writers and artists often considerably his senior, John has a sophistication and a selling 'nose' well ahead of his years. His vulpine features were not his greatest asset in his early days, but his infectious passion for literature forged rapid loyalties and earned him recognition as the originator and leader of the Neo-Georgian movement. He was made a Freeman of the City of London, an FRSL in 1938, and Benson Medallist in 1939.

While the downside of peaking too soon can be the magnet it creates for others' envy, more fundamentally serious in John's case was the implacable growth of poetry's Modernist school – a term that may conveniently embrace a multitude of 'tendencies', including the Movement, New Apocalypse, and Vers Libre in all or any of its often depressingly inept manifestations. T. S. Eliot, as a director of Faber and Faber, helped acceptance of 'difficult' poetry by his support not only of the likes of Auden, MacNeice, and Spender, but of rather too many of their imitators. It did nothing to stem the progress of the new wave that much of their output was seen by a dwindling few as inferior to that of even some second-eleven Georgians. An established publisher, prepared to back a forcefully promoted new tendency, will not lack for editors willing to welcome the new and speed its progress. The floodgates of Modernist poetry had been ajar since well before the war, and beleaguered Neo-Georgians became a handful of Pooh-sticks heading for the weir.

During the war, hunger for reading matter kept publishers as sleek and purring as restrictions on paper supplies allowed. The output of most younger writers was governed by the theatres of threat or conflict to which they were sent, and service personnel with literary leanings often found generous opportunities, frequently without hearing a shot fired in anger, to practise their skills. By contrast, civilians – the targets of shortages, rationing, restrictions, pressures to maximise production in field and factory, and the bombings that in one form or another were suffered or anticipated through the war years – were often more involved, under greater stress, and less inclined than the returned serviceman to look back later and wax nostalgic about their 'good war'. For many serving writers, the climate both during and immediately after their time in the forces enabled some small talents to strike undeservedly deep roots.

In general, Gawsworth's RAF postings had been favourable to his literary ambitions. The instinctive if usually short-lived comradeship of those drawn together by service overseas helped forge connections that lasted at least until they could be put to good use when gaining or renewing a foothold in civilian life. John returned to England with a considerable body of work under his belt. Three-quarters of the contents of his *Collected Poems* (1948) had been written during the war years, most of which he spent in Italy, the Middle East, and India. His election to the Salamander Society of Poets in Cairo marked the zenith of his acceptance as a poet, and of his skill in promoting what he had earlier produced. But his service years had done little to strengthen a weak character too easily tempted by liquor, and even before his *Collected* appeared his creative talent was in decline. His undoubted abilities as a bibliographer and editor became his mainstay. Lawrence Durrell wrote in 'Some Notes on My Friend John Gawsworth' (*Spirit of Place*, 1969):

> ... he was my first real Writer ... an ardent student of the nineties [who] looked forward rather hopefully to a Dowsonesque death ... His memory for a bibliography was simply amazing, and had he cared to be a bookseller he would now be the greatest one in England.

Sadly, John chose instead the less trammelled existence of a well-read book runner, and he combined this with dealings in his already considerable hoard of manuscripts, jottings, letters, drafts, and signed first editions begged or indefinitely 'borrowed' from those distinguished or otherwise saleable older writers who had been flattered and sometimes genuinely helped by the youthful pre-war Gawsworth. Even writers'

Noël Coward and Esmé Wynne in *I'll Leave It to You*, New Theatre, London 1920

Esmé Wynne-Tyson in 1929. Her fifth novel, *Incense and Sweet Cane*, was shortly to be published.

Son and father, Weybridge, 1946

J. D. Beresford, June 1939

Esmé, Trowbridge, 1946

Alec Beesley and Dodie Smith, California 1940s

17 Pond Street, Hampstead, 1948

LEFT Geoffrey Grigson, with trash facilities, 1965 RIGHT Phyllis Morris, 1966

By 1973 the loft in the new north wing supported several tons of books

The Gittingses moved from the cottage behind Christopher Fry's head (above)
into the barn below his East Dean garden

Microbiologist Catherine Roberts consults the Vicar of Fontwell, 1975

A needlemaker's cottage turned hairdressing salon (white front door, next to the butcher's) became our Keele's Bookshop in Chichester

Happiness is not just a good review. On *Curlew*, X121, 1978.

Jennifer and myself at Fontwell

wastepaper baskets had been a source of value-gaining ephemera. 'I am a dung-beetle,' he would admit, usually after emptying the bottle bought from the proceeds of the latest sale to Bertram Rota or one of the other West End dealers in manuscripts and high-value books.

But, as always, the publicans won. The income from this hand-to-mouth lifestyle could not save him from the courted Dowsonesque end that was to come in 1970. In these last two decades his addiction accelerated, coarsening his values, deadening his inspiration, impairing his judgements, and intensifying his attitudinising. His heroes were increasingly the strutters and dominators, the swashbuckling action-men of historical legend, rather than those with the vision, feeling, and ability to communicate at the level that had always been beyond his grasp. His Napoleonic posturings lost their novelty value. Gullible culture vultures visiting his increasingly squalid room in Paddington would be shown the crested drinking glass he kept on the mantelpiece. Putting his forefinger to the side of his by-now bulbous nose, he would throw a wobbly salute, wink, drop his hand to his left hip, draw with a flourish an imaginary (and sometimes real) sword, and point to the incised letter N below the crest of the glass: 'From one of his campaign chests, of course.' Even the dimmest devotees of the poetic style, if they knew the history of the Café Royal, were not fooled for long. Piccadilly's famous restaurant grew from a small café opened in Glasshouse Street in the early 1860s by Daniel Nicholas Thévenon, a failed Paris shopkeeper who came to London to escape his creditors. As his premises expanded, Daniel dropped his 'Thévenon', and by 1867 his business had added a Regent Street frontage and was known as the Café Royal. By the mid-1890s Daniel Nichols, as he was now called, controlled a substantial block a stone's throw from Piccadilly Circus. His restaurant's fame was due in large measure to its adoption by the literary and artistic set who patronised the Brasserie (or Domino Room, as it was better known from the 1890s until the whole building was replaced in the 1920s). Doubtless Nichols's successors budgeted for losing a percentage of the handsome 'Napoleonic' goblets.

But the 'Kayfe', as some of the famous clientele called it, underwent further major change a few years after the Second World War, and the preserved marble-topped tables and other remnants of the Domino Room passed unceremoniously into history, ousted, like the Brasserie's 'characters', by 'rationalisation'. This saddened me; I had a tenuous family connection – not biblical, I was told – in that my bohemian maternal grandmother's admirer Walter Wynne, the adopted son of the

Morant family of Brockenhurst, was a member of the 'Kayfe' circle that included Augustus John, Oscar Wilde, Aubrey Beardsley, Max Beerbohm, and the opportunistic T. W. H. Crosland, whose inscriptions in books I hold give weight to the impression that 'Uncle Walter' was loved more for his ability to patronise the arts than to practise them. Sent by the Morants to Jamaica to run the family estates, he became known as the Coffee King of the West Indies.

Gawsworth used the Café a good deal in its pre-Forte days, as to a lesser extent did I. In his essay on the Café Royal he wrote that

> In 1933, after lunch, I proposed to my first wife in the Brasserie. In 1939, at a luncheon upstairs given by the Royal Society of Literature, I received a successor of the medal George IV ordained when Sir Walter refused the Poet Laureateship, the estate of the poet of 'Land of Hope and Glory' paying for it. In 1948, before lunch, I proposed to my second wife in the foyer. Shades of 'Far off things and battles long ago'.

Whether Shiel was a patron is not, so far as I know, recorded. But from what I have written of John it may now be clearer to those not conversant with the story of the island of Redonda and its literary realm, why he was so eager to adopt Shiel's 'royal' mantle along with the more pragmatic role of being his literary executor. So keen was he to do so, indeed, that the matter was formalised at Shiel's home in Sussex eleven years before his death in 1947:

> Our Court, in Exile,
> L'Abri,
> New Road, Worthing Road,
> Horsham, Sussex

> We hereby proclaim that our most noble puissant Terence Fytton Armstrong, 'John Gawsworth', Prince of our Blood, Poet Laureate of our Kingdom, succeeds us as Monarch of our Island Kingdom of Rodundo (Redonda = Br.). Our sovereignty, upon our death, is his possession, to be conferred by him on his death unto such of his blood as he appoints.

> | | Given under our hand |
> |---|---|
> | *In Witness* | (signed) PHIPPS, R. |
> | WEDRIGO [EDGAR JEPSON] | 1st October 1936 |

How Matthew Phipps Shiel himself ascended the fantasy throne is better known than contemporaneously documented at the time. His father, Matthew Dowdy Shiell (Phipps dropped the second 'l'), created the legend in 1865. Shiell was a Methodist lay preacher and merchant who traded by schooner out of Montserrat, which at twelve miles to the south is Redonda's nearest neighbour. His son wrote of him: 'He had also the Irish foible of thinking highly of people descended from kings, and *had*, in truth, about him some species of kingship, aloofness, was called by all "the Governor ..."'

But Dowdy's rum-fed aspirations to Hibernian royal blood had faded with the years. Even if some quirky twist of fate had confirmed the link, continuity of the male line had not been ensured by a free-slave wife who had presented him with an unbroken run of eight dusky daughters. But on 21 July 1865, to his enormous delight, the miracle happened: Priscilla Ann gave birth to a boy.

Shortly after this joyous event, sailing northwards past the 300-metre-high island of Redonda, so named by Christopher Columbus when he sailed to westward of it in 1493, it came to him that the birth of Matthew Phipps could not be celebrated more suitably than by claiming the island on his behalf. This he did, not as a passing whim in an intoxicated moment, but with a planned intent that led to the boy being crowned King of Redonda on his fifteenth birthday. Phipps described the day as

> one of carousal, of a meeting of ships, and of people, to see the palm of the Rev. Dr. Semper, of Antigua, daub me with the balm of anointment; and this notion that I am somehow the King, King of Kings, and the Kaiser of imperial Caesar, was so inveterately suggested to me, that I became incapable of expelling it. But to believe fantasies is what causes half our sorrows, as not believing realities causes half ...

For those valuing the realities above the fantasies, the legend is tantalisingly incomplete and inconsistent. The American industrialist A. Reynolds Morse, Shiel's indefatigable bibliographer, plumped for Dr Semper as the cleric who officiated at the crowning, and at the time that Morse and I examined records in Antigua and Montserrat in April 1979, that seemed the reasonable assumption. Further research, however, has suggested that Bishop Mitchinson may have done the deed, as Shiel himself recorded in *Twentieth Century Authors* (1942).

Then, again, any certainty that Phipps was crowned on Redonda itself is not helped by his assertion that it was a 'rock-island of scarcely nine square miles', for its total length is barely three quarters of a mile, and its width about one third. A further uncertainty surrounds the number of kings who can claim to have reigned *in absentia* over that harsh thrust of precipitous volcanic rock, set like a grey humped whale in the blue sea. Gawsworth described himself as the island's third king, which suggests that Dowdy Shiell, in claiming it, regarded himself as its first. It is reasonable to suppose that he did, but there is no record of any formal gesture of appropriation. Perhaps the merchant in him was careful not to risk offending bureaucrats and estate owners on his patch.

Never much interested in the Redondan legend until it was wished upon me at Gawsworth's death, I cannot recall asking him to clarify such points, nor to comment on Phipps having referred, in 1901, in his essay 'About Myself', to his having nine sisters, only to revise this to eight in the version that later appeared in a collection of his shorter essays, *Science, Life and Literature*. So closely do the mists of fantasy shroud the statements and personal life of Shiel that the would-be precise biographer has a hard time of it, and can scarcely be blamed for finding the more available facts of John's more exposed lifestyle a less demanding task. Shiel's published work, which in the literary context is all that matters, can at least speak for itself, and Morse's painstaking endeavours have established many related matters; most importantly, those aspects of his life that were reflected in his writing, such as that his Spanish first wife, Carolina García Gómez, was the pattern for Laura, the heroine of his 1899 novel, *Cold Steel*. But uncertainties will remain. This does not matter. It is wholly appropriate that a fantasy writer should leave behind him a literary legend that is puzzling.

After his crowning, Shiel writes, 'I was translated to King's College, London ...' and later 'taught for a year what was called "mathematics" in a Derbyshire school'. Failing to develop any enthusiasm for coaxing the minds of the rising generation, he flirted with medicine at St Bartholomew's, but was rapidly turned from this alternative by the first operation he attended. With nothing left but literature, he persisted in this career, intriguing London's literati by his eccentricities of prose and person, his mulatto good looks, and his first marriage to 'Lina'. His success as a writer may be measured by those prepared to tackle over two dozen works of fiction written in a florid and verbose style that irritates some as much as it has captivated others. The elusiveness of his work may be judged from the fact that when his best-known novel, *The Purple Cloud*, was made into a film starring Harry Belafonte, Mel

Ferrer, and Inger Stevens twelve years after Shiel's death, its only connection with the book was a credit line to Shiel. But the outright deal that Gawsworth made for the rights was a useful addition to fees and royalties he received from reprints and translations of Shiel's novels and short stories.

While John did his best to keep Shiel's work in print in the early post-war years, the time was not right for serious revival of a writer whose main output spanned the years 1895–1937, and whose principal supporters were such writers of that period as H. G. Wells, Hugh Walpole ('A flaming genius'), Arnold Bennett, Arthur Machen ('He tells of a wilder wonderland than Poe dreamed of'), J. B. Priestley, and Rebecca West ('A writer of imperial imagination'). A full biography has yet to be written, but would need much research. The best we have is *Shiel in Diverse Hands*, a collection of essays compiled and privately printed in 1983 by Reynolds ('Ren') Morse, builder of the world's largest private collection of Shiel books and related material. No one has researched the life and works with more dedication and care, though since Ren's death in August 2000 the work is being continued by the able lawyer and publisher, John D. Squires. With the 1979 update of Ren's 1948 *The Works of M. P. Shiel* – bibliography with atti-tude – the intending biographer has much to get him started.

The sad pattern of Gawsworth's remaining years is more easily traced, and now that two novels touching on Redonda's kings and their literary settings have been written by a distinguished Spanish writer – available in many languages, and to be followed by a third volume – I shall be called to account if I fail to sketch in some of the salient facts.

John's marriage to Barbara Kentish had ended in divorce in 1948. They kept in touch, but I have little memory of her, rare meetings in Soho pubs not being the best occasions for arriving at in-depth assess-ments. John had been fond of her in his fashion. 'To Barbara' prefaces his *Collected Poems*:

> No more your grace distracts my sight,
> Luring my vision from its goal
> Far in the distance. Oh, delight
> Breaks like a wave within my soul!
> For you are here and always here:
> I cannot fashion now one line
> Which is not yours, so ever near
> Are you, one blood in me and mine.

Their parting was followed rapidly by marriage to Estelle Hayward, née Gilardeau, a pretty French divorcée. If any woman was going to help John overcome the ravages of premature acclaim and a galloping addiction, that woman – it was almost enviably thought – was Estelle. Practical, industrious, charming, a good cook and housekeeper, with earning skills (the heart-shaped black satin lavender cushions that she made for Harrods were startlingly sexy), Estelle *had* to have other than materialistic motives in taking on such a daunting challenge.

One of the reasons for Estelle's self-inflicted martyrdom was her faith in John's poetic talent. She responded readily to the best of his love poems, eager to detect the romantic soul lurking within the outwardly less appealing framework:

> Here I will build a citadel of love
> Impregnable against the hour's assault,
> So steadfast-rooted in felicity
> Its very blemishes possess not fault;
> So garrisoned, so bastioned and secure,
> That, placed in loneliness upon a height,
> No threatening may disturb its peace by day,
> No scaling foes encroach on it by night.
>
> Life shall dictate its form and Life its mould,
> Its towers and keep, its courts, its whole design,
> That, when 'tis builded, she for whom I wrought
> May cry, "Tis Love's own fortress – and 'tis mine!'

Perhaps Estelle's liking for nineteenth-century poetic forms prompted the hope that a Rimbaud, a Verlaine, or even a Baudelaire might some day rise above the alcoholic haze. It did not. No amount of regular meals and other creature comforts from the hands of a willing wife was going to compensate for the painful if unspoken suspicion that he would achieve no more than further work that was at a level below the best he had managed in earlier years. It was a beast of a realisation to live with.

Besides, the climate of the late 1940s was in many respects more unsettling than the war years themselves. Although Sidgwick and Jackson pluckily announced John's *Collected Poems* as the work of one 'who has always been identified with the post-World War One English lyric movement', that movement was in lean straits; by 1950 the heydays in which they had published Rupert Brooke, John Drinkwater and their ilk were beyond recall. John was fortunate that Sidgwick still had enough sense of auld lang syne to grant him a 'collected'. And he knew it. The book was reviewed, but mostly by friends and in small literary magazines. A leaflet was produced that quoted commendations by G. S. Fraser in the *New Statesman*, by Randall Swingler in *Our Time*, by Lawrence Durrell in *World Review*, by Roy Campbell, Richard Church, John Rowland, T. W. Ramsey, Kenneth Hare, Austin Clarke, and a handful of others, but nothing compelling in papers that carried weight in the cautious literary firmament of that hesitant era. The leading literary editors were not going to risk blotting their copybooks by wasting column inches on the work of a pre-war neo-Georgian who was a declared foe of the now established 'Faber' school and all that went with it.

Had John shown the sense and self-control to take advantage of Estelle's undoubted willingness to supply the comfort of a relationship with someone well-equipped to share the uncertainties and disappoint-ments lying ahead, he could at least have settled for being the leading spokesman for the English lyric movement, supplementing whatever modest earnings came from his writing by editing magazines and deal-ing in the books and manuscripts in which he had invested so much time and knowledge. The pleasant suburban house that he shared with Estelle in Golders Green was an adequate base, and after an earlier failed marriage she wanted affection and continuity. But John's drunken rages, rantings, abuse and threats wore her down, and by 1949 she was already feeling the strain of irrational recriminations, rampagings, and physical attacks. John, sober, could still be charming, amusing, intelligent, and kind. John, sloshed, was more often a pain, an irritation, and a crashing bore.

A portrait of John's state of being between 1948 and the mid-1950s has recently (2002) been written by his half-brother Mark Holloway, and published by The Redondan Cultural Foundation in Oxford. I know of no more readable a depiction of John's character, lifestyle, and shifting moods, nor a better snapshot of his second queen, for whom Mark held an unabashed admiration until his death in 2004.

For myself, the whole business of Redonda and its 'monarchic' connections was something of an embarrassment, from the day in June 1949 when, for the edification of the readers of London's *Evening News* and other media, John insisted on dubbing me a 'Knight Commander with the Order of the Star of Redonda' in celebration of his thirty-seventh birthday. I knew he meant well, and I tried to enter into the spirit of the ceremony, for which he wore Phipps's black velvet smoking jacket that was to disintegrate twenty years later in a cloud of dust and moths on the gravel drive of our Sussex house. He had rung to thank me for a present, and to say he was miserable, having wife trouble, and could find no alka-seltzer. Equipped with milk, bread, bicarbonate of soda, liver salts, and youthful susceptibility, I bought the analgesic and took a taxi to Wentworth Road to find the house stuffed with reporters and cameramen. The Queen was in the kitchen with an eye as black as night, annoyed less by her pain than by John having entertained their neighbours in the small hours by loudly and repeatedly damning her as a French whore. By then I had learned that this sort of thing was par for the course, but the ceremony in front of the brass urn containing, *inter alia*, the ashes of Shiel was something I could have done without. Maybe this tendency to keep out-back rather than out-front was connected with my being an only child who at five years old had made an unwelcome switch from his devoted if firm Victorian nurse to the sole care of an equally concerned but highly emotional, possessive, intelligent, and busy mother at about the same time that her husband had left home for what today might be termed space, but in 1930 was known as Another Woman. As Coward was to say years later on the Firefly verandah, 'Why you didn't turn out as gay as a hussar, my dear boy, I have never understood.' If I had, I might at least have found John's little dubbing more enjoyable.

Gawsworth, however, in time sensed my preference for merging with the wallpaper, so when he felt I should be pushed higher up his aristocratic ladder he addressed letters to me as Il Duca d'Immaculado (stet) often enough for me to cotton on. This unsought promotion, I supposed, was his well-meant and affordable way of thanking me for such services as recommending him for the editorship of a journal of philosophy and parapsychology called *Enquiry* (for which Muriel Spark also, but unsuccessfully, applied), and for arranging that Williams and Norgate should publish *Science, Life and Literature*, for which John, of course, edited Shiel's essays. Like most of his ennobled friends, I thanked him and forgot about it.

To return to Estelle. What happened to her, I do not know. An eminently practical Continental, her beauty fading, she probably studied her mirror one day, legged it back to France, and took up with someone more solvent, reliable, and I hope sober. She deserved something better.

Although John's third marriage, to Doreen ('Anna') Downie in October 1955, paid for by Richard Aldington, was never dissolved, it went the way of the others. Where drink (to use the euphemism) had served largely to drown his awareness of declining inspiration, it was by now becoming an end in itself. He never, I think, became totally alcohol-dependent in the sense that his body's chemistry had at all costs to be satisfied by yet another glass. He could stay sober if the motivation was sufficiently strong. Drink became the dominant compulsion, a rarely controlled response not only to the pain of living with the knowledge of his creative decline, but to the pain of living at all. Anna was ill-equipped to be Estelle's successor in the unrewarding task of 'doing something about John'. She might have saved herself much time and heartbreak by studying the quality and content of his later verse: sober or sloshed, he had irrevocably 'lost the plot'.

In those days there was still a seldom satisfied hankering for good traditional poetry. Many would have welcomed a worthy challenger to the moguls of modernism. But for all his flourishes and bravura, John was not the needed St George. Even at its best, his pleasant but derivative technique, and a heart that produced little more than light romantic sub-Dowsonian verses, was not enough. He lacked perception of the deeper yearnings and tragedies of the human condition and it was his special misfortune that his professionalism qualified him to know that he was never going to develop them. A self-directed critical faculty is a rarity among minor poets, as it is among many regarded as important by their peers. With less professional objectivity, John might have sustained himself more by hope than by booze. An ever-striving amateur with a big enough ego can get through life by blaming others' insensitivity, and by tireless anticipation of recognition in each day's post. John sensed from his thirties that he had reached his ceiling and could only glide to earth on the weakening thermals of readers' enthusiasm. Other means of survival had to be developed. Being a king offered some mileage.

Shiel had died in February 1947. On 29 June that year, in his Juan I crown, John published his first honours list. It was a somewhat unbalanced document, in that it consisted entirely of dukes, grand dukes, and an archduke. Not even some lout of an earl had slipped through. Among the forty-five elevations were Frank Swinnerton, Dylan Thomas, Eden Phillpotts, Arthur Ransome, Lawrence Durrell, and Henry Miller. The document was printed on eighteenth-century hand-made paper and is reproduced in full on the facing page. It was followed by two more, in 1949 and 1951. Included in the 1949 list were Roy Campbell, G. S. Fraser, Stephen Graham, Alfred Knopf, John Heath-Stubbs, Dorothy Sayers, and A. F. Tschiffely among the duchies, and twenty-three humble knights, including myself. In 1951, a further mix installed Fabian of the Yard (as Commissioner of Police for Redonda, needless to say), Leslie Pine (who acknowledged the honour on the letter heading of *Burke's Peerage*, of which he was the editor), Stephen Potter, J. B. Priestley, J. C. Trewin, and Rebecca West.

On 24 April 1947 John Connell's BBC Third Programme talk 'A Writers' Novelist' was published in the *Listener*, comparing Shiel's 'verbal exuberance and fantastication' to that of Baron Corvo, commending the best of his work as 'worth very serious attention', and forecasting – accurately – that he was in danger of becoming a cult.

Another and competent introduction to Shiel's writings was 'The Strange Realm of M. P. Shiel' by Julian Maclaren-Ross (incessant raconteur, Soho barfly, and Grand Duke of Ragusa in the Realm of Redonda), published some years later in the September 1964 number of *The London Magazine*, and drawing on Ren Morse's *The Works of M. P. Shiel*. Maclaren-Ross's unfinished but published *Memoirs of the Forties*, for which he had planned before his sudden death a section on Gawsworth – with whom, behaviourally, he had all too much in common – and the Redonda legend, is still a vade-mecum for those keen to glimpse more of that not very edifying period through the eyes of a pub habitué with few distorting illusions. However, the book's allegedly verbatim record of lengthy conversations with prominent literary figures begs a pinch of seasoning, especially as its author admits to not keeping a diary. His anecdotes, as someone delicately put it, turned slowly into art. But the memoirs are a lively read, though upstaged by Paul Willetts's more professional biography of Julian, *Fear and Loathing in Fitzrovia* (2003, a year after Penguin Books reissued his novel *Of Love and Hunger*).

The tedious aspect of the Soho literary scene of the '40s and '50s was that there was too much of a sad thing. Although I knew, if mostly superficially, many of its leading and ancillary characters, *en masse* they palled. The general assumption that life could not begin until everyone was plastered either drew you in or prompted a suspicion that if learning, earning, and communication were necessary for survival, the launching pad did not lie between Wardour Street and the Charing Cross Road, or indeed in Fitzrovia. Even the humourless and innocent

REALM OF REDONDA

Upon the Occasion of the Birthday of
H.M. KING JUAN I,
He is Graciously pleased,
In Recognition of their Services to His Royal Predecessor,
H.M. KING FELIPE I,
to Welcome into the Intellectual Aristocracy of His Realm
— with Succession to their Heirs Male —

TO
THE ARCH-DUCHY OF REDONDA
MACHEN, Arthur Llewelyn Jones,

TO
GRAND-DUCHIES OF NERA ROCCA

GOCHER, Kate,   MORSE, A. Reynolds,
GOLLANCZ, Victor,   SHANKS, Edward Buxton,
MILLER, Annamarie V.,   VAN VECHTEN, Carl.

TO
DUCHIES OF THE REALM

ARMSTRONG, Ethel Laura,   KING-FRETTS, Anne,   RICHARDS, Grant,
BELL, Neil,   MASON, A. E. W.,   ROBERTS, Walter,
CARTER, Frederick,   MEYERSTEIN, E. H. W., ROWLAND, John,
CHESSON, W. H.,   MYER, K. G.,   SWINNERTON, Frank
" CONNELL, John ",   NAYDLER, Merton,   THOMAS, Dylan,
DERLETH, August,   OWEN, Walter,   TYTHERIDGE, Alan,
DORO, Edward,   PHILLPOTTS, Eden,   WALKER, James,
FERGUSON, Malcolm M.,   POLDEN, DAVID C.,   WALLER, John,
FLETCHER, Iain,   " QUEEN, Ellery ",   WHEELER, John,
HENLE, James,   RANSOME, Arthur,   WIGGINS, G. H.

Further His Majesty is Graciously pleased
to Confirm the following Appointments, Admitted under His Patents as Regent
in the Reign of His Royal Predecessor, with Succession to their Heirs Male,
TO
BLAKESTON, Oswell, The Duchy of SANGRO,
DURRELL, Lawrence, The Duchy of CERVANTES PEQUENA,
JEPSON, Edgar, The Duchy of WEDRIGO,
JOHNSEN, Buffie, The Duchy of NERA CASTILIA,
LINDSAY, Philip, The Duchy of GUANO,
MILLER, Henry, The Duchy of THUANA,
RAMSEY, T. Weston, The Duchy of VALLADOLIDA,
ROTA, Cyril Bertram, The Duchy of SANCHO.

Given Under His Majesty's Hand, His Court-in-Exile, Kensington
The Twenty-ninth Day of June in the Year of Our Lord Jesus Christ
One Thousand Nine Hundred and Forty-seven.

Chamberlain.

anti-hero of *Square Peg*, Marcus Maelstrom, spent more time studying 'life' in NW3 than in Soho, the ragings and antics of the media-adored 'Angries' being more identifiable than the sodden aimlessness of has-been or wannabe writers and artists hammering their livers in the south-east corner of W1. Culturally, it could be said, postwar Soho was depressingly claustrophobic.

It may display a rather bourgeois turn of soul to say so, but the atmosphere of such alternative creative centres as Hampstead and Chelsea seemed less spirit-lowering. Even the much-anthologised Anna Wickham, who had known Gawsworth since 1935, and whom I met over coffee occasionally in a café between Pond Street and Parliament Hill in the 1940s, did not impart the unrelieved hopelessness that emanated from the sozzled of Soho. An undoubted bohemian, who nevertheless could remain a friend of D. H. Lawrence after complaining that his writings exuded 'a sort of miasma of menace towards women who detach any considerable portion of their energy from their purely sexual function', Anna had at least 'had a life', albeit one of much unhappiness, mental instability, and frustration, recently graphically confirmed by her American biographer Jennifer V. Jones. Louis Unter-meyer found her 'a magnificent gypsy of a woman who always entered a room as if she had just stamped across the moors'. Meeting her near her life's end, when she more resembled a lugubrious bag lady just decamped from a bush on the Heath, I was not surprised when her son James told me she had hanged herself at her seriously unkempt Parlia-ment Hill house on 30 April 1947. Over fifty years later Jim's wife assured me that Lawrence Durrell's tale that the increased price of ciga-rettes had been Anna's last straw was unconfirmed. The final tragedy, chronologically at least, was the loss of her book of clothing coupons – a sorrow that her normal appearance at that stage may have belied; but possibly the coupons were a symbol to someone who had been, in her time and in several directions, 'all woman'. Even before she died, the coupons had been found in the gutter. They were returned the day after her death.

If, one way or another, Anna left more to show for her life than the mega-egotist Julian, holding forth in his stolen corner of the Wheat-sheaf, branded by his teddy-bear coat, and so sometimes mistaken by journalists and culture groupies for the Establishment's true, if scruffier, baronet-poet John Waller, he could boast a fuller CV than most of the Fitzrovians; but the ceaseless flow of his unremittingly unilateral performance tended to daze rather than intrigue the casual observer. In the pubs and clubs centred on Frith, Greek and Charlotte Streets, 'characters' jostled for elbow room, and the cliché that 'we shall not see his like again' was unsustainable in clamorous postwar Soho. This surfeit of the extreme induced in some an antipathetic state of Sohoitis. But not in the Hon. Philip Inman, the twenty-year-old son of the one-time proprietor of Chapman and Hall, Lord Inman, then (1949) chairman of the Charing Cross Hospital, former chairman of the Board of Governors of the BBC, and Lord Privy Seal.

Like Marcus Maelstrom, Philip was knocked sideways by the ambience of Soho. When, at the suggestion of the literary agent Spencer Curtis Brown, we met in May 1949, he had been put nominally in charge of Williams and Norgate, originators of the Home University Library, a well-thought-of series that was taken over and expanded during the Second World War by the Oxford University Press. Philip's father hoped Williams and Norgate would give his son something to get his teeth into after a long sojourn in a Swiss sanitorium. By bringing M. P. Shiel on to the list, I had inescapably introduced Philip to Gawsworth. John, with his wild frenzies and often-expressed prediction of dying a poet's death worthy of his admired Ernest Dowson, soon helped to convince Philip that *la vie bohème* was at grasping distance. This made a further rod for my back because Philip already saw in me the Older Man With Experience, not only of publishing, writers, artists, and women, but also – especially as I was living in the Carlines' art-drenched Georgian house in Hampstead, where I wrote poetry that got published now and then in organs as wide apart as *John Bull* and Jon Silkin's *Stand* – of Life. As he had a strong imagination, an alarming vein of romanticism, a writing talent, and an imitative tendency that was positively hazardous, I felt increasingly obliged to encourage him into more promising social and literary pursuits than consorting with the hard-drinking set in the dingy dives where much was talked about, but little achieved. His parents were understandably worried about him, and seemed grateful that I was doing my best to extend my literary advising beyond the selection of new titles. Although he lived at home, mostly in his parents' solidly comfortable St James's Court flat off Buckingham Gate, they could do little to influence his daytime movements as a trainee publisher. A sizeable slab of my time was spent accompanying him on thinly justified visits to Soho, or, sometimes at the request of his firm's anxious manager Noel Ranns, who was very conscious of the Inmans' concern, scouring West One's south-east quadrant when he had slipped his leash and was needed back at the ranch.

Unhappily, Philip's constitution and susceptible temperament seemed to dictate decline. His impulsiveness and fixations got the better of him. Feeling 'betrayed' by my first marriage – a folly on my part that certainly gave no good reason for either envy or emulation – he was to follow me in my second by marrying a 'nice girl' who even bore the same Christian name. Their marriage did not last, though it produced a child, and by 1958 Jennifer had remarried and had a second baby on the way. In that year, Philip married Denise, twenty-six, French, and with remarkable facial resemblance to Joan, as seven-year-old Tilly was quick to point out. His early death in 1968 came not from absinthe or Juan I's preferred burgundy (in 1951 John had made him Redonda's only marquess), but from a glass of some caustic liquid that for an unexplained reason was on his desk. Whether it was a tragic error made in temper or despair, or the deliberate making-of-a-statement in an advanced condition of self-drama or intoxication – and any of these would have been in character – I have never learned. I suspect the truth was not established. His father had the power to suppress media interest, and by the time he died in 1979 it was, like many tragedies, at the most a minor matter to the rest of the world. As I was not blamed for playing an unintentional part in Philip's choice of direction, and had proved useful to Williams and Norgate, and as Philip – at least before my first marriage – had valued our friendship, his distraught parents kept in touch. But it was one of those truly 'What can I say?' situations that only time could deal with.

In 1949 the composer Leigh Henry wrote a rousing national hymn to the State of Redonda, 'O God Who Gave Our Island Soil'. Until the early 1950s this was all legitimate and good clean fun within the accepted parameters. By exploiting the fantasy's literary possibilities, John was able to invite wide publicity and boost his income. It helped to keep the memory of Shiel green, and to place new editions of some of his books. But this halcyon period was overplayed and short-lived. Increasingly impoverished by his addiction, John became ever more reliant on his kingly role. The legend was tailor-made for the tap room, and there were easy pickings to be had from journalists and hangers-on who found themselves in the company of a writer-monarch with Caribbean connections. Islands intrigue the human heart.

From there it was a short step to helping publicans to see the good sense in keeping happy such an excellent draw as an in-house king. 'Let's see if the king is in the Fitzroy' (or the Wheatsheaf, the Duke of York, the French, the Swiss, the Romilly, Les Caves, the Horseshoe, the

Cabaret, the Colony Room, or any of the other West End pubs and drinking clubs John frequented) was a phrase often heard in the streets of Soho. But the trick was overplayed. While an uncountable number of publicans wrote off a few drinks in the interests of increased trade, few were prepared to wipe a seriously full bar-slate clean for anything less than a dukedom. Soho dukes proliferated. The ennoblings were frequently confirmed in documents suitably inscribed in variable flow-eriness of hand and wording. Some were treasured and were to reappear years later.

Worse was to come. As his financial circumstances deteriorated, John realised that the sale – or at least the promise – of his realm itself was an even more negotiable asset. Shiel's prescient condition that John's successor to the throne be determined on his death, thwarting temptation to market the kingdom or abdicate for a mess of *potage de piquette*, was not allowed to sully this happy realisation. On 21 June 1958 John put an advertisement in the personal column of *The Times*:

> Caribbean kingship with Royal prerogatives. One Thousand Guineas. Box X.755

The response was enormous, not only from commoners drawn to the prospect of better things. One of the nobbier responses came from the twenty-three-year-old Count Bertil Bernadotte of Sweden. Perhaps feeling that the likelihood of succeeding his cousin Princess Margaretha of Sweden was remote, he paid (and lost) his £50 deposit.

John's plan might have come to something had he not already signed an irrevocable covenant four years earlier, undertaking that

> in consideration of Services to Our Person, upon our Death ... the succession of the said Realm of Redonda shall devolve to the said William Reginald Hipwell ... for life and at death to his son David Hipwell or to such male person as the said William Reginald shall have appointed ...

This did not go down well in some quarters. When the *Times* advertisement appeared, a letter from a City firm of solicitors left John in no doubt of the attitude taken by property entrepreneur Hipwell to his proposed transgression. In the event, both father and son predeceased him: David in 1964, and his father two years later. Whether some grandson or other blood relative will yet appear, waving the ancestor's covenant, is anyone's guess.

However, the Hipwells could have found themselves little better off had they outlived Gawsworth, for John's death revealed that several more irrevocable covenants were in existence. One claimant was Brendan Behan's brother and writer Dominic who, in 1984, following a radio programme in which I took part, rang the BBC to say that John abdicated in his favour in 1960, and that the BBC should have remembered the event because they had covered it. At least two other claimants were publicans, the most persistent producing a deed dating back to October 1966. Like all the other 'irrevocable' pieces of paper, it took no account of the inconvenient fact that Shiel had expressly laid down in writing that Gawsworth should confer the sovereignty on his (John's) death. One can see more than one reason why Shiel made this condition; not the least, I suspect, being his intention to tie down the volatile John to being his literary executor for as long as possible. Moreover, one of John's services to some of the older and impoverished writers in whose work and manuscripts he was so interested was to plead for their needs to the Royal Literary Fund, usually with sympathetic results. To add chaos to confusion, the 1966 taproom monarch-come-lately subsequently went on air to announce that he was giving Redonda to the nation, forgetting that the nation already thought it owned it. This capricious claimant then thought better of such ill-considered largesse and appointed a friend to carry forward the role of kingship, signing yet another irrevocable covenant to this effect. Membership of this gentleman's 'aristocracy' hinges not on the qualification of literary merit, nor even of literary interests, but on willingness to pay His Majesty a yearly subscription, currently available to all comers, I am reliably informed, for a modest £15. This glut of diverse claimants has reached the point where an open War of the Pretenders threatens to break out. The 1966 publican's successor has been driven to near apoplexy by a total impostor, resident in Antigua, who has not a jot of justification for claiming kingship, but is keenly aware of the cash advantages in sailing out of English Harbour in his elderly schooner with parties of tourists happy to commemorate their sail under the flag of King Bob by buying T-shirts and such edible goodies as Judy's Absolutely Hot Sauce 'By Appointment to King Robert the Bold'.

In the light of this maelstrom of covenants and kings, some of which have created their mostly pub-centred aristocracies, it is difficult to dismiss the view of Redonda's late Grand Chamberlain, Reynolds Morse (Grand-Duke of Nera Rocca since 1947), that the kingship cannot be divorced from the duties of Shiel's and Gawsworth's legally appointed literary executors, tempting though a workable alternative has been. But this is to move a little ahead of where I meant to be.

By the 1960s John's most idealistic friends were running short of ideas for easing his self-induced misfortunes. Even the profitable use of his biographical skills was frustrated by his having sold all manuscripts of much value. The older writers whose letters and first drafts he had acquired were mostly dead, and he lacked the energy and heart to scour the bookstalls and the many second-hand shops he had explored so profitably in the past. Where once he had badgered the Royal Literary Fund on behalf of his elderly impecunious friends, and done what he could to promote the work and memory of Shiel, he was now dependent himself on whatever small handouts and scarcely-earned funding might come his way; while his declining inner health was matched by increasing neglect of the exterior man. His efforts to keep Shiel's work alive had to take a back seat.

I remember he came for a meal at my Highgate flat in August 1954, awash with burgundy and carrying three bottles to show he intended to stay that way. By then the lone parent of three-year-old Tilly, my domestic antennae were fairly sensitive, so after giving him a black coffee strongly laced with salt, I drove him into a cold bath and, lacking more sophisticated equipment in those impoverished days, poured buckets of water over him while applying a stiff brush to his frame with a vigour not stretched since my male-nursing days. After that, and despite his complaints, a brisk walk on the Heath seemed to do wonders. His dinner, centred on a light omelette with salad, followed by an orange milk jelly prepared for Tilly's lunch next day, went down with gratifying alacrity and no liquid encouragement other than a glass of cold water. By now sober enough to admit that he didn't feel too bad at all after these excesses, he had a little rest while I packed his clothes in a box I had no wish to see returned. Nothing was fit for salvage. I gave him a vest, pants, shirt, socks, some adequate shoes, and the jacket of a green tweed suit whose trousers proved too narrow to reach above his thighs. His own trousers hardly complemented the rest of the ensemble but the whole passed muster in the circumstances. A little dazed, perhaps, he ambled unresentfully into the Kentish Town tube after assuring me that he would try to find a pair of trousers that did better justice to the jacket. Rather to my surprise, he rang the next day and invited himself to dinner again, bringing oranges, a melon, and a single bottle of hock. As near sober as ever seen, he gossiped cheerfully and amusingly about Bertram Rota, Frank Hollings, and other dealers who by then, he claimed, had bought nearly all his Shiel, Arthur Machen, and Havelock Ellis manuscripts.

In his final decade, the decline was inexorable. His last stable address was 35 Sutherland Place in Westbourne Grove, a house owned by Charles Wrey Gardiner, the eccentric landlord, poet, publisher, and editor whose *Poetry Quarterly* was the leading journal of the Neo-Romantic movement during the war and in the early 1950s. Wrey's anonymous *The Answer to Life Is No*, one of several autobiographies he mournfully churned out, paints a poignant picture of an elderly bohemian of the older school, entrapped by his commercial naiveté and kind-heartedness into letting run-down properties to unreliable literary and artistic tenants in less then salubrious districts. The book's last sentence reads:

> If only I could live without tenants, live a normal life in a room, in a house where there were no tenants, only the hour between writing poetry and going to work in the morning, a sane and happy human being.

Needing to sell, but lacking the callousness to put John out on the streets, let alone his fellow lodger the distinguished and near-blind poet John Heath-Stubbs, who occupied the first floor, Wrey sold the house for a price that reflected the disadvantage of sitting and penurious tenants. Less inhibited, the new landlord offered John a pittance to get out, which unfortunately he accepted. Heath-Stubbs held out for far longer and was eventually paid enough to buy the freehold of another flat in Paddington.

When Gawsworth burned his boats for the further temporary benefit of publicans, I helped him with his move rather than by continued financial hand-outs. On a fine day in June 1968 I towed up to London the six-foot trailer with built-up sides that over the years had earned its value many times over – not only by carting books new and old, but the children's donkeys, the tack and feed for a later pony, the sheep that kept the grass down in a paddock, gravel, sacks of potatoes, building materials, seaweed for the kitchen garden, manure (a good deal of that), and much else.

The trip to Paddington was not to clear John's room of furniture, for what little there was probably belonged to Wrey, but many stained and battered cardboard boxes of what can euphemistically be called his remaining archive: notebooks, typescripts, manuscript jottings, press cuttings, contracts, letters, fag-packet scribblings, Shiel's black velvet jacket – from which, even then, a flurry of moths ascended as I shook it gingerly in the street – and the brass urn containing its late owner's ashes. Already fortified round the corner after returning from a short convalescence in Kent, followed by a night in a police cell, John decided that he should leave Sutherland Place conspicuously, if not in style. Eleanor Brill, the last serious lady in his life, and two of their drinking companions, helped to heave and shove him to the precarious top of what appeared to be household rubbish leaving for the nearest dump. Only the trailer's high-boarded sides fended off another poet's obituary notices for a little longer. Fortunately, he wished only to be dropped at the Alma pub a few streets away, not brought back to Sussex where his possessions were to be stored. Lifting his half-empty bottle of burgundy to the populace of Westbourne Grove, Juan I of Redonda made the most of his last State Procession. From then on he was to spend the bulk of his days in pubs and most of his nights with Eleanor or on any floor that might be offered. Tales of his nights on park benches have been greatly exaggerated, as John Heath-Stubbs has wearily testified.

Three months later he visited us at Fontwell for what turned out to be the last time. He had been to Hove, calling on E. H. Visiak, whom he had knighted in 1949. Breaking his journey at Shoreham to ring me, he said he was missing the companionship of Shiel's ashes and had important matters to discuss. Even without my telling Jennifer that John's voice confirmed his normal condition, she was not overjoyed at the prospect of his being a house guest, so I booked him into the appropriately named Labour in Vain, a mile down the road in Eastergate. Sue, then eleven, had fewer reservations about the impending visit and showed interest in Shiel's urn for the first time. At her wish, I removed the lid. On a bed of mongrel ash lay a top set of John's teeth and the scribbled poem 'For a Centenary' by John Heath-Stubbs, written on the understanding that he became Redonda's Poet Laureate. It was not the only event that Sue was to remember. When I had collected John from Barnham station, Jennifer poured a large quantity of black coffee into him. It did little good. To get him moving, Sue and I took him to see her rabbits at the bottom of the garden. Staggering down the path, he waved his thick cane in warlike flourishes, sweeping the air above the rabbits and threatening to remove the ears of all vegetarians. I assured Sue that Uncle John was only pretending. She was only half-assured before Uncle John turned on me with Napoleonic curses and more flailing of his stick. To this day I am uncertain which of the threatened massacres upset Sue the most. On the way back to the house we introduced John to Dumbo, our morose donkey, whose genitals' failure to drop had deprived him of any hope of a meaningful relationship. It was love at first sight, but then Dumbo had never before been breathed on by anything like John. Perhaps they merely swooned in each other's halitosis.

The next morning I collected him before the pub was in business, and brought him home. Although the Labour in Vain's room had been booked on the condition that he be sold no more than one drink before bedtime, they had let him buy a quarter bottle 'for the road'. Offered nothing alcoholic by 10 a.m., he fell into his martyr act, moaning of deprivation and his lack of true friends. With frequent phone calls, post needing urgent attention, and a printer waiting to see me, I summoned enough hurt rage to stop John's performance. After being sick several times in the cloakroom, his plea to be allowed a small measure of whisky was indulged, and he was able to give me details of the whereabouts of some more manuscripts, his will, and matters relevant to his wish that I be his and Shiel's literary executor. This was only touched on lightly, and I didn't say yes and I didn't say no, hoping he would forget all about it. Unfortunately, he did not. After we had given him some absorbent elevenses, I put him on the London train at Arundel with copies of Bewick's *Memoirs* and John Nichols's *Literary Anecdotes of the Eighteenth Century*, both sobering titles in the Centaur Classics series, aware that they would doubtless be on Foyle's shelves by the late afternoon. As the train drew out, I slipped the quarter bottle into his decrepit bag alongside the urn, then waved goodbye until his carriage slid under the road bridge. My relief was tinged with a prophetic sadness.

Our next meeting was early in 1970 when John was in the Princess Beatrice Hospital in Earl's Court for exploratory tests. These left little doubt that he could not have long to live, but we were at least able to have a coherent talk about future arrangements for his literary estate. His manipulative Performing Monarch act forgotten, it was commoner John, aware of the running sand and focused on things that mattered. As always on such rare occasions, I was sadly aware of how things could have been ...

Perhaps the only bright spot in this final phase of his life was that two or three months later he left for Italy on a one-way ticket. There, without prior warning, he took up an old invitation from the Australian painter and writer Russell Foreman to stay with him and his wife in their villa at Borgunto, between Florence and Siena. There he collapsed

and was immediately taken in hand by Foreman's solicitous wife, a
Guy's-trained nurse. On 17 May John wrote to me:

Well, I have survived 16 days Ospedole, and, tho' utterly broke,
am determined to stay here indefinitely, as the way of life has
already set me on the mend and I feel ten years younger. I have
appointed you with [Ian] Fletcher [poet and English professor at
Reading] Literary Executors, with Russell Foreman ... executor in
a will ... in the keeping of British Consul in Florence. You and Ian
hold on to what papers you both hold for future arbitration
between yourselves; as to sale, disposal, publication, etc, after my
death, one third each of proceeds and of Shiel and my copyrights
to go to you both. I have temporarily (and ? provisionally) left the
other third to recompense any possible services I suffered in the
last 7 years at the hands of the *veuve* Brill [Mrs Eleanor Brill, the
last sad lady to try to establish a workable *ménage à deux* with
John].

I must have some money meanwhile to pay towards my keep
here in Italy. At the moment I am a guest and disliking my power-
lessness to contribute damnably.

I must stay here *indefinitely*, and recover not only my sanity but
health which I can see is not impossible, where I drink no spirits,
sleep long, do not vomit and am cared for as though I was human.
I would be absolutely mad to fly back to the squalor and hopelessness and hate that nearly did for me in England.

I have been plucking roses from Landor's grave in cheerful
sunshine – I don't feel like joining him yet! I am writing some
personal verses (there is a lady in the case who swears she is my
Impossible She – but as I am being speared with liver ampoules in
derriere I may step out of the ranks of Tuscany and surprise her
yet).

I am also making notes for an autobiography which will have to
be off the cuff – as I have no book of reference – only a pen and
paper and a clear head now. This, I'll swear, is the most cheerful
note you have ever had from me – but I mean all I say in it. You
can help if you can see some way of advancing some lira to the
Credito Italiano, Firenze Chief Office – for the account of 'T. I. F.
ARMSTRONG – JOHN GAWSWORTH'. I have instructed my Bank to
send any driblet there may be, and asked Fletcher (who, damn it,
is about to disappear to USA for some time) to send me the last

driblets from his Reading Barclays [some of John's friends had
contributed to a fund to tide him through some of his real, as
distinct from calculated, crises]. With whatever comes I shall
purchase lodging and food for a time here the while I gather
strength. I see I shall have to start from scratch – still there is sun
on this new chapter – though I'm naturally *solitario* in my soul. In
a calendar month (apart from one query re sending money which
he did not send, from Fletcher) I have not heard one word from
L'Albion Perfide. Tra-la – How I am loved! I spend this afternoon
with the Scots bard 'Adam Drinan' (Joseph Macleod, BBC
wartime announcer).

Love to all from your self-expatriated

GIOVANNI DI FIESOLE

Trying, not for the first time, to steer a middle course between
sympathy and refusal to supply counter-productive forms of aid, I
replied four days later:

My dear Giovanni,

I was most glad to get your letter. Your move to Italy shows a
much better sense of style. The apparently endless incarcerations
in the seamier west London hospitals were becoming a little more
than tedious and lacked that panache that is so essential in the
eyes of posterity and the University of Texas (from now on I shall
not only be stashing away your holograph letters, but also their
envelopes).

As to the honour of being one of your lit. execs, I feel the whole
think is a bit academic now that you are clearly set, I hope, for
another 40 years or so of uninhibited whoopee in the stimulating
climate of Upper Tuscany – an era that is likely to last as long as
the N.W.3 of Firenze can contain your ebullience. I only hope that
your Impossible She is in a position to gratify your New Bocca-
cian mood *within* the portals of the Villa Palmieri and no
nonsense. Failing this I shall look forward to your early requisi-
tion of the Villa Medici and an invitation such as shall befit your
Court one and all.

I do, seriously, agree, dear Lorenzo, that you should grab all the
time you can in new and such lovely surroundings. The Welfare
State and vile London have nothing to offer anyone. A few
cabbages might get something from it, but not kings. Get sunshine
into your bones and draw inspiration from an environment that

must surely lead your poetic frenzy to peaks way above the sleazy stimulus of our repellent capital.

Giovanni, I am sending no more dollops of cash just because you have switched from Kensington boozers to Florentian taverna. My offer to help towards the purchase of a freehold roof, whether that be in Earl's Court or Fiesole, remains (though I somewhat dread the thought of trying to negotiate such a thing at this distance), but I am *not* in any position to turn my few liquid assets into liquid waste.

As a source of ready cash, could your bibliographical knowledge be hired to a local (antiquarian) bookseller? There is a large firm, the Nuova Italia Bibliografica, with a Florence branch at 29 Piazza Indipendenza, who might merit a call, but I imagine the Foremans might know the ropes here.

Anyway, John, your letter was certainly on a different and more hopeful note that was most welcome, and if Albion has not been writing it could be because you haven't sent her your address. I saw the Times piece and hoped you would write with news.

Give Landor a pat on his headstone for me, and tell him Grigson's definitive hiccups along quite well considering. But I should stop swiping roses from his grave if I were you. The I-tiddly-I-ties feel rather strongly about that sort of thing, and while 'British Poet Found Stabbed on Landor's Grave' would be good for half a column in the Express, it's a messy way to go and very unfair on your executors.

Press on with that autobiography and those Second Italian Period verses, and have at the wine with that moderation that will emulate your new compatriots, command their respect, and preserve your liver for Christian Barnard or whatever matinée idol is grinning his way through the research departments when you have penned your last pregnant comment on the condition inhumane we laughingly call Life.

If I sent you a copy of Landor, could you flog it to the Nuova B. and persuade them that every tourist passing through should have one? Keep the proceeds of the flogged copy and take commission on all resulting sales. Let me know.

If you move on to Rome I might have the odd helpful introduction. (Depends on what you wish to be introduced *to*.)

What about Durrell? He should have some contacts in Italy, yes?

Please keep in touch. You are *not* forgotten and my unsympathetic responses are nothing like as numerous as the good wishes I have for you. (All right, so you can't drink good wishes.)

With that responsible and monstrously *dry* love you undervalue so mistakenly, Your beastly pal JON.

Not so much an answer to my letter as a slightly hurt progress report, John's response was sent on the eve of his return to England:

13 (of course) June 70. Just a line to say I'm leaving Italy for Inghilterra's good (I'd still like that Landor, though). Permanent (sic) address will be c/o Ham [the poet Hamish McLaren], 88 Lichfield Road, Cambridge, though I want to see my film at Shepherd's Bush and see Fletcher ere he goes. As usual the Eye-tiddle-E. Eyties have routed me wrong and I'm stuck here drinking *milk* for the next flight. The Consul has mislaid my will, but you'll get a copy as soon as he sends. I'm sad, sad, sad to return – but no money or letters got through to me – in 55 days I rec'd 6 missives! Hopeless! Sempre. GIOVANNI

Returned to England, courtesy of the British consul, he was quickly readmitted to the Princess Beatrice for further treatment of his haemorrhaging ulcers. As he told the *Times* Diary column (26 June 1970), 'I went there [Italy] to find spring, love and Italy and, I'll be damned, I found them all.' While in the Florence hospital he wrote eighty poems, 'of which probably four are any good', in tribute to his new 'impossible', La Gianna. 'I fell in love with her, and I'm broken-hearted.' He was able to look forward to the BBC2 showing on 9 July of a half-hour film, a tribute feature to him in which his friends Lawrence Durrell and Kate O'Brien took part. But the party was over. John's last letter to me, written at noon on 21 September, found him again on the Van den Bergh ward at the Princess Beatrice:

Ecoute, mon vieux. In a couple of hours I'm going in for a *major* op. The result – ? I have been here since 6 haemorrhages on Sept. 5 … I want to be cremated and *added* to Shiel whose ashes Estelle holds at 28 Addison Gardens; then the pair of us – 'in death they were not divided' – seek the asylum of Gawsworth church … I could do with the refreshment of a visit from you very soon, and would like you to bring that *Landor* with you … Did you see my Line Up half-hour on July 9th? It had definite pathos and Durrell was magnificently loyal. I have now 4 collections of hospital verse

... I am left some money by an aunt (Mrs Mabel Armstrong Bentham) in Canada, but there are 25 other legatees and Quebec law to sort out. As I may die this afternoon I can hardly look forward to the *bonne bouche* ecstatically; still, she was my godmother and fond of me in youth ... If the worst comes to the worst, old boy, please get the will from Florence ... I have just requested [an Eastbourne firm of solicitors] to act for me, as another aunt, Miss Elsie Armstrong [sister of Mabel], has left me something also, though probate is not through ... I'd got that far when I was led off for a shower and a blood sample. Here we go, back into action. Cheerio for now, as ever, Love to all the house,

JOHN

But it was cheerio for good. On 22 September I wrote to John and sent him the Landor *Poems*, then rang the hospital to be told by the ward's staff nurse that the operation was successful ('Ulcers as usual') and there was no likelihood of his dying. My previous visit having found him perky and clear-headed, I was reassured and went ahead with my plan to leave for France on 24 September. At 2.15 a.m. on 25 September, in a Versailles hotel bedroom, I read in *The Times* that John had been taken to the Brompton Hospital and died there on the 23rd. I never discovered if he had received my letter and the book.

When just turned seventeen he wrote 'A Plea for Life':

Life! Life! How I crave for it,
Long for it, pray for it.
Life! (In large letters I pray it be writ).
Life! With its bubbling laughter, its pleasure,
Life with its fellowship,
Cheer in good measure.
O God, that I soon
Its divine nectar sip.

What have I done
That I may not be worthy
To share in its joy, in its fire and its fun?
As cold steel to a lodestone
My heart is attracted;
No longer I count it as truly my own.
O, God, that I soon
Life's divine nectar sip.

Poor young Terry. In 1929 the romantic heart was firing on all cylinders and life was indeed beginning to offer those craved opportunities. Perhaps his wishes were granted too soon. But who can say? Maybe, impressed by the supposed glamour of a Dowsonesque end, and faithful to the muse 'in his fashion', he would have chosen the wrong nectar and the downward path, even had he been granted a convincing preview of other options. Arrogant pragmatism is certainly no more attractive.

The death of Gawsworth did not bring an end to the literary legend of Redonda and its kings, though it might have done if I had been less of an idiot.

When I submitted to John's decree that I should be his and Shiel's co-literary executor (a role I most certainly did not seek), it never occurred to me that being 'King of Redonda' should go with the chore. Such thought as I gave to it was that the Redonda story was best forgotten, or, at the most, was in need of a long rest in which to recover from the twenty years in which John's antics had overlaid its engaging literary and fantasy aspects, reducing it to a tabloid and pub giggle. However, he had made it clear in his will that his executors were expected to keep his and Shiel's literary reputations 'green', and if there was any good reason for asking me to be an executor, it was presumably because I was both a writer and a publisher, and he hoped that my business and practical qualifications – rather less apparent, I must admit, in my scholarly, kindly, amusing, well-meaning, but somewhat abstracted co-executor – would be slightly more adequate for the task. I can say only that I got on as best I could with pursuing opportunities to reissue Shiel's work, but it was eight years after John's death before Victor Gollancz asked for clearance to reissue *The Purple Cloud*, Shiel's best-known novel, followed in 1979 by *The Young Men Are Coming*.

It was at this point, with the aim of helping Gollancz to restimulate an interest in Shiel, that I foolishly let it be known that it had been John's wish that I be saddled with the thankless (I was yet to learn how thankless) role of being the next king. While my gesture was well meant, it turned out to be unwelcome to V.G.'s daughter Livia, who was then running the firm. She interpreted my attempt to help her firm's promotion as an intrusion, though my unilateral intervention had been no more than to admit to my role to Reynolds Morse who, in March 1978, had heard through the National Book League that I was Shiel's literary executor, and was surprisingly delighted to discover that he had also tracked down the current king. To this day I have felt twinges of guilt at how much, over the years, I must have dampened his enthusiasm by showing myself to be – and, indeed, being known as – the reluctant monarch, deficient in kingly ambition, and inclined to let sleeping islands lie. Not that he was that discouraged. My apprehensive reminders that I was a workaholic, single-handed, unclubby, travel-weary, apolitical, low-profile publisher-cum-writer, with a range of psychosomatic afflictions including positively life-crippling allergic rhinitis, so pestered by pretenders and journalists as to be verging on pulling the fastest abdication in history, cut no ice with Reynolds Morse. The man who was to create and stock the Salvador Dali Museum in Florida's St Petersburg, and become that artist's protector from the predators who invaded his last years, failed to take far stronger hints than 'no' from a tired and background-disadvantaged small publisher who preferred to emulate Ferdinand the Bull off a quiet lane in rural West Sussex.

Which is why, on Good Friday, 13 April 1979, I found myself some 1,000 feet above the shimmering Caribbean sea on the groin-contracting rim of an extinct volcano in a Force 5 trade wind, reading a proclamation to wheeling boobies and frigate birds, a rigidly-to-attention rasta who took the whole thing even more seriously than did Ren, and, sprawled on the rocks at my aching feet, the no longer youthful Caucasians with whom I had survived the horrendous and literally death-inviting ascent.

I had felt duty-bound to give in gracefully, and in retrospect must admit that the whole ridiculous exploit had some wonderful and unforgettable moments, even for an anchorite-*manqué* in his middle years. Determined that there should be a pre-centenary Shielian assault on Redonda's summit, Ren had flown me to Antigua, where he had booked me into the Admiral's Inn's 'royal' garden room overlooking English Harbour, the mecca of serious yachtsmen. We were joined by Richard A. Howard, Professor of Dendrology at Harvard University; Ben Wheeler, secretary of the Montserrat National Trust; Jack Murphy, curator of the Department of Geology at Denver's Museum of National History; Desmond Nicholson, archaeologist and historian, part-owner with his brother Rodney of their yacht-chartering business in English Harbour; Peter Hilaire from Antigua's Ministry of Economic Development; and Dick Liddle, skipper of our chartered yacht *Nor' Easter*, which I discovered belonged to Perry Knowlton, boss of my New York literary agency Curtis Brown.

In *The Quest for Redonda*, Ren Morse – who has died during the writing of this book – goes into more detail than I can give here of our bid to confirm the eternal child in every grown man. It proved, for some of us at least, that if all monarchies – like all forms of power, and the human condition itself – are pretentious nonsense, it is still possible for that nonsense to be agreeable, light-hearted, and bloodless. Not that the Antiguan government, whose politicians are seldom cited as prime exponents of a British sense of humour, were at all happy on hearing our reason for wishing to sail to what they regarded as one of Antigua's two dependencies. Hence, after Ren had wasted two costly days arguing with St John's bureaucracy, the well-fed presence on board of Peter Hilaire. The fact that he did not leave the yacht until it had returned to English Harbour rather short-changed his government's insistence that he join the expedition to ensure that no political hanky-panky was afoot. When, after our night anchored off the island, we clambered into the rubber dinghy to head for the foam-dashed rocks which offered the only conceivable landing point, requiring each of us to swim the last few yards in hope of being lifted by the swell on to a suitable boulder, Peter was not one of our party. On the eve of *Nor' Easter*'s departure from Antigua, he had insisted that his extremely nubile secretary accompany him. Not once seen to take as much as a line of shorthand, she doubtless had other duties in mind, as they disappeared below within seconds of our dinghy casting off for the rocks.

However, *noblesse oblige*. When, that evening, after surviving our almost vertical ascent (and, which was worse, the descent in full sun) through treacherous dusty scree and dislodged boulders, Juan II dished out dukedoms to his intrepid companions, it would have seemed churlish to exclude Peter. He asked to be known as the Duke of Waladli, an anglicisation of the missionary Father Breton's *Dictionnaire* entry for 'Oualadli' – the priest's understanding of the Amerindian name for 'Antigoa where the English live'. Some time later, a warm letter from Peter assured me that Good Friday 1979 had been the most memorable day of his life, though he did not list its highlights in any order of attraction.

For me, too, the week had been memorable. In 1961, when researching for the Crocker guide, the thought that eighteen years later I would be planting on the peak of a volcano a flag made by a queened wife out of a years'-old pair of my Marks and Spencer pyjamas was somewhat beyond my prophetic powers. A more detailed description of that absurd but eventful week must await another's enthusiasm. It is a story worth telling, but maybe only as part of a fuller account of Redonda's first two kings. Of their successor, Redonda's Reluctant Monarch, enough can be had from this book. In any case, he abdicated in 1997, and the realm along with its accompanying literary executorships are now in the hands of its fourth king – or fifth to those who take the view that Dowdy Shiell saw himself as the island's first.

Future pretenders to Redonda's nebulous throne beware. Almost every stage of being a king – never mind how low-profile – is fraught with problems. You cannot, these days, even bank on the rapturous adulation of the multitude, let alone the loyal subservience of your household. As for the respectful attention of the press, forget it. At every stage, your time is sought for all the wrong reasons. In the field of usurpers and claimants, Redonda can produce statistics leaving larger monarchies at the post. In the seventeen years that I inadequately filled the role of its reluctant ruler, uncountable days were wasted by those fascinated by the legend of Redonda, its literary and monarchical connections, and the perennial charm of an uninhabited Caribbean island. If the mega-bores were the pretenders, particularly those from the ranks of publicans, tosspots, and Fitzrovian drinking clubs, they were also a salutary warning of the lengths to which some will go to be associated with even the most intangible concepts if profit potential seems to be attached.

This potential was far more modest than some supposed, though it is a common misconception that if you appear on the media you must be receiving fat material rewards. Although I seldom sought chances to appear on television or elsewhere, I have sometimes succumbed if asked, usually where there was a book I had published or written that might benefit from the publicity. A few of these occasions were positively enjoyable, being handled sensitively and with professionalism. Invited to take part in a BBC 'Midweek' programme in October 1984, I found it an amusing event in those early days when Libby Purves's interviewees did not have to be as ratings-friendly as they are today. Sir George Solti's birthday was being recognised, and Libby's other guests were John Julius Norwich, Dulcie Gray (a Redondan duchess ever since her husband Michael Denison had been dubbed by Gawsworth on stage), and an unforgettable Captain Seddon who disabused Dulcie and me of any suspicion that *we* were Libby's comic turn of the week.

Seddon, of I know not what regiment, but ex-Gordonstoun, half-German (though as one-of-us as Nelson's Column), and carrying a revolting oilskin sailing bag, had arrived at Broadcasting House on his motorcycle, his clothing and skin suggesting prolonged exposure to traffic and not a lot of soap. An inventor, he brought with him samples of his battery-warmed clothing, an example of which was his uninviting leather waistcoat. Libby (who later graciously agreed, and deserved, to become a dame) very wisely declined his suggestion that she try on a pair of flying gauntlets he had brought to demonstrate.

But she made amends for her cowardice by asking some appropriate questions about my novel *So Say Banana Bird*, whose recent publication was the reason for my being invited on to the programme. Although the *Daily Telegraph* very acceptably called the book 'a superb account of one man sailing across the Atlantic', I was equally pleased by *Yachting Monthly*'s praise for its description 'of a well-known (but tactfully renamed) Caribbean island's life and politics which is hilarious, poignant and accurate', as this came nearer to recognising my attempt to convey something of the physical island of Redonda (also renamed); of our need to retreat from 'reality' into myth; and, for those sensitive to such a subtext, of the discovery by the book's anti-hero of meaning and purpose through 'a growing understanding of elements vital to a more feeling and viable relationship with the environment'. None of Libby's other guests was all that interested in discussing someone else's book, but Norwich was intrigued by the notion of royal succession through literary executorship. Even before the broadcast, the producer Pippa Burston told me that one of the throne's most persistent claimants had rung in after an early-morning announcement that I was taking part. He threatened to sue the Beeb if the 'impostor' was interviewed. 'A fruitcake?' Libby inquired at our preparatory meeting. 'Has things a bit out of proportion,' I conceded. After the broadcast, Pippa fielded three more calls from indignant pretenders, all of whom may well have possessed one of Gawsworth's irrevocable covenants.

It would have been all too easy to have exploited the Redonda legend, as some of the pretenders have been well aware. Even without my trying, the story has been covered – if seldom accurately – in almost every medium from travel guides to literary magazines, radio and television. But already exploring how best to shed Centaur Press, and to find time to return to the long-suppressed ambition to write more books, I – or, rather, that dratted 'throne' – was ripe for takeover. But the matter could not be rushed. My late mother imbued me from a tender age with the notion that when facing life's problems one should not, by and large, exercise 'human will', or 'outline', but wait to be 'shown'. A guideline, I must admit, that the passing years have often proved to be very sound.

I had lost hope of finding a likely candidate among my fellow Brits for a responsible successor to the Redondan throne and the literary executorships that went with it. There seemed scant likelihood of discovering someone with enough interest in, and respect for, those historical, contemporary and legendary aspects to restore the story of Redonda to its forgotten status as a pleasant fantasy worthy of preservation as a grace-note in the annals of literature. Once again, I let the matter slide.

The answer came several years later from a totally un-'outlined' direction. In 1992 I heard a radio interview with the already distinguished Spanish writer Javier Marías, whose Oxford novel *Todas las Almas*, translated by Margaret Jull Costa and published as *All Souls* by Harvill, was receiving rave notices and portrayed Gawsworth. Later, his *Tomorrow in the Battle Think on Me* took the 1996 Prix Femina Etranger and several other awards, and more recently he was publicly recommended by the prestigious German critic Marcel Reich-Renicki as a suitable candidate for the Nobel Prize. Of Marías's novel *A Heart So White*, which in 1997 received the £100,000 International IMPAC Dublin Literary Award, Reich-Renicki had said: 'It has been twenty years since a novel has moved me as much as this one ... It is a great and absolute masterpiece ... Javier Marías is one of the most grandiose authors alive. If I had to name a single contemporary author of his quality, it would be García Márquez.'

Although the broadcast prompted me to buy several copies of *All Souls*, I did not at that stage even consider the possibility of Marías being in the Redondan frame. And there the matter might have rested had I not learned that he was publishing a short story by Gawsworth in an anthology of fiction writers. Wearing my literary executor's hat, I was obliged to write to him in 1992 to point out that no request for permission to use copyright material under my control had been received. He responded instantly. Such had been my occasionally self-defeating determination to keep the reluctant royal pate below the parapet that Javier had had no knowledge of my executor role, let alone that I bore the burden of kingship. Winningly, however, he had by then bought a copy of *So Say Banana Bird*, in which aspects of the Redonda legend are more than hinted at.

If ever my ensuing correspondence with Javier should be published, the delicate manoeuvring that led him to accept the role of Redonda's fourth king might entertain students of mini-monarchies and the byways of literature. But it was not until September 1996, more than a year after I had sold through Sotheby's most of my Shiel-Gawsworth archive – much of which, unknown to me until after the sale, had been bought on the telephone from Spain by Javier – that the pieces began to fall into place, and I dropped the first hint of where my thoughts were turning. Even then, much had to be considered and discovered before I felt I should seek his interest in taking over Shiel's and Gawsworth's copyrights and the uneasy 'throne' that went with them. Besides which, I was not sure that a busy and successful Spanish novelist would be sensitive enough to the mercurial nuances of an English sense of humour to consider the offer in the spirit in which it might be made.

One huge plus about Javier taking on the king thing was that it would shift the 'seat of power' from tabloid Britain and its wearisome pretenders to a country – indeed, a continent – where writing, publishing, philosophy, imagination, and respect for time-honoured artistic standards seemed in somewhat healthier condition than in England.

Not everyone, of course, would regard the work of Shiel and Gawsworth as deserving any lofty position in the field of literature. But that was an added reason for finding a new king who might lift every aspect of the battered realm to a higher plane. I had tried to use my own term of office responsibly, but chronic overwork exerted a constant brake. What is more, I sympathised with those who hold that it is quite a good idea for a king to be something of a monarchist. That said, Javier himself had declared republican leanings, and with the way things are going in monarchic circles it may be that rule-with-reservation is a politically more correct and workable stance for the new millennium.

I became increasingly convinced that Javier could on several counts be the right successor. The transfer would not only move the action to another country, but he would be the first Spanish incumbent since Christopher Columbus claimed and named Redonda on behalf of Isabella I of Castile and Aragon. Moreover, he could even claim blood from a Cuban grandmother who moved from Havana to Spain in 1898. His literary credentials were impeccable, and he had already made though his books substantial contribution to keeping alive the memory of Redonda's first two literary kings. Above all, he was actively attracted by the legendary and literary aspects of the Redonda fantasy, was steeped in the writers and mores of that period, and shared my wish to protect the Zeitgeist of the legend, for which he saw the physical island as merely an intriguing and romantic symbol. Having more feeling for kingship in the philosophical and mystical sense, than for kingdoms with the pomp and ceremony that can go with even the smallest mini-monarchies, he was at one with me in favouring discreet and low-profile 'rule', and equally resistant to the all-too-easy option of letting the tabloids call the tunes. Fortunately, Javier was already an old hand at understanding the ways and wiles of the international press. 'I have been known as a writer for too long', he wrote, 'ever to be known as anything else but that.'

Recalling the persistent and humourless targeting of Morse, and later of myself, by claimants showing no genuine interest in the essentially literary and fantasy nature of the legend, I warned that pretenders could be even more tedious than journalists. Hoping it wouldn't decide him to remain a commoner, I told him that pretenders were 'a bearable thorn so long as one doesn't get drawn into discussion', and that I found the best response to be on the lines of:

> Redonda is a fantasy realm, a literary pleasantry, a legend whose longevity may be in inverse ratio to its exposure to the vulgar criteria of most monarchies. Those who have made the effort to explore its history fully, usually agree with this conclusion. Those who may nevertheless wish to claim the role of Redonda's king are of course free to do so, as fantasy cannot be circumscribed. Whether their claims will be recognised by posterity is a matter for conjecture. Meanwhile the physical island of Redonda continues to soar a thousand feet above the blue waters of the Caribbean sea, a home for the countless seabirds that are the symbols of its freedom from the pettiness and despoiling greed of the human species.

I need not have worried. 'The beautiful legend is to me mainly literary,' Javier wrote, 'and it should always be so.' His main concern was that journalists and pretenders might deprive him of the peace needed for his total commitment to writing. His reaction to the usurpers that are the plague of even the most minuscule realms was unequivocal:

> Never to pay any attention to any of them; never to worry about them; never to take any of them seriously; never to discuss, let alone dispute or contend with any of them; never to disavow their claims, as this would entail their consideration; accordingly, ever

to respect their freedom, as I respect my own to leave them alone and to ignore them, as that would seem the only 'kingly' thing to do.

His civilised ground rules failed to stem the devious and libellous railings of the dominant contender who, even before the free-for-all advent of the internet, had lost all sense of perspective, blithely circulating libels so easily shown to be lies that, like the dastardly 'King Bob', he should thank his lucky stars that Xavier I and his predecessor have not so far resorted to litigation.

But that is enough of pretenders and suchlike varlets. The only sound basis for determining the line of Redonda's kingship – should anyone have a serious inclination to pin down the lineaments of a fantasy – is to study the entire correspondence between the main claimant (none, as yet, has come forward with a better case), Reynolds Morse (in conjunction with Morse's third volume of his *Works of M. P. Shiel*), and myself. Only by adopting that marathon task will it be shown that there is no shorter route. Historians with nothing better to do, please note.

I was in two minds whether to include the Redonda story at all, but its ingredients are compatible, and Javier's books – particularly publication in 1998 of the first edition of *Negra espalda del tiempo* (Alfaguara, Madrid) and the several translations that followed – have made the legend and its literature so well known to his considerable following on the Continent, that no one else has more devotedly and responsibly taken the fantasy into the twenty-first century. Now that the English-language edition of *Negra (Dark Back of Time)* has been published in the USA by New Directions, and in England by Chatto and Windus, the need for my brief attempt at an authoritative overview seems at least timely.

Between Javier and myself there has been total accord on all important points. He may not fully share my view of the island's physical presence as a symbol of the remaining unexploited places that should be left in peace by our despoiling species, but I cannot see him countenancing the machinations of developers. As his work shows, he is primarily a people-centred writer, less drawn than am I to the charms of place. There are bound to be some differences of emphasis between a metropolitan intellectual Spaniard, and an eco-sensitive senescent Brit with a frustrated yearning to spend his terminal years in a writing hut on a Cornish headland.

A fantasy Redonda may be, but it is extraordinary how time hallows even the most make-believe legends. I was asked by the incomparable *Dictionary of National Biography* to write a biography of 'Gawsworth, John, King of Redonda'. I accepted the invitation, but with the reservation that I felt the kingship of Redonda to be a secondary qualification for inclusion, seeing that his entry in *Who's Who* and other sources centres rightly on his reputation as a poet, editor and bibliographer. The *DNB* graciously deferred to my quibble and left me to adjust the emphasis. After all, if they should ever seek a potted biography of myself, I would be peeved to learn from some astral plane that I was remembered not for my writing or publishing or ecological trail-blazing, but for being the reluctant fantasy monarch of a chunk of guano-spattered rock and a hotly-contested legend.

Redonda's future is now beyond my control – thank goodness and Marías. Asked by the artist Frané Lessac some years ago for an epigraph and foreword to her and Jan Jackson's delightful children's book *The Dragon of Redonda*, I suggested *Ride si sapis* (Laugh if you are wise) for the device. It might, of course, have been taken by the tabloids as an open invitation, but that is the problem with humour. Perhaps Xavier I will adopt a line I admired in one of his letters: 'Irony does not make things ludicrous, whereas seriousness may well do so.' But it is up to him to put it into the Latin.

9
Keeping It on the Road

Although a spell of kingship, however notional, may do something for the learning curve, the role of desk-bound commoner is infinitely preferable in the long term. But what with frustration over the limits to my publishing, given that I was determined to stay small; the lack of time and energy to give adequate attention to both publishing and writing; the approaching end of the Centaur Classics series; the realisation, heightened by the Hulton and Warburg episodes, that even disposing of Centaur might only be achieved either by abandoning it or continuing to run it on behalf of someone else; and finally, I suppose, that levelled-off feeling so many men seem to get in middle-age – with all these factors piling up toward the end of the decade it was, with hindsight, a pretty cloth-headed move to be launching two new series.

Considering that we were more financially secure than I had ever expected, I felt ungrateful and negative in lacking the drive to expand Centaur further, especially as things seemed to have gone well, on balance, without any real aptitude for business on my part. I could only attribute our survival to an appetite for work, doubtless inherited from both parents, and to a just adequate mix of flair and good fortune for picking books (many of them suggested by others) that on the whole made more money than they lost. My lifelong interest in books was more in their writing than in their publishing, and the most depressing signal that middle age was putting up was that time in which to give of my creative best was running out. The Nika and Fred show had hardened the suspicion that if enough was to be put aside to cope with the rainier days of old age, I must plug away at the publishing for a few more years. With the ever-increasing backlist to tend, this was going to give precious few opportunities for serious scribbling.

It would be pleasant to report that the new series, intended to fill the gap left by the curtailed Centaur Classics, took off like an eagle, proving that I had learned from my mistakes and been strengthened in my determination. Life, as it is said, is seldom like that.

The first five titles in 1969 were all published on 31 March. They were the last-but-one Centaur Classic to have been agreed with SIUP;

KEEPING IT ON THE ROAD

the first two titles in the new Travellers' Classics series; and the first two in the Regency Library.

Early in 1963 Grigson had suggested as a suitable Classic, *Omniana* (or *Horae Otiosiores*) by Robert Southey and Samuel Taylor Coleridge. Jack Cohen gave it his blessing and recommended that the 'number-one Southey and Coleridge man', Stephen Potter, immortaliser of the devious art of 'one-upmanship', or 'gamesmanship' as it is equally well known, should tackle the introduction. I had a slight doubt about this, as while Stephen, as editor of the Nonesuch Coleridge, was impeccably qualified (I had known him and his wife Heather Jenner, founder of the then famous marriage bureau of that name, since the 1950s, as they lived a stone's throw from Louis Golding in Hamilton Terrace), early old age had done nothing to destroy a reputation for being somewhat disorganised. Jack knew about this, so as our edition meant marrying to the 1812 Longman original, Coleridge's 1809–16 additions from Bohn's *Table Talk*, and inserting as footnotes his annotations to a copy of the 1812 in the British Museum, Jack asked his daughter-in-law Valerie to tackle this chore. She very obligingly did so, but without firm direction from Stephen it cannot have been a particularly welcome assignment. I forwarded her material to Stephen in April 1965, together with the 1812 two-volume set that I had borrowed from the London Library.

Dead silence followed. After being shown as forthcoming in the 1964 Centaur catalogue, it had been announced in the 1965, firmly but light-heartedly (Stephen having sent me a few lines of blurb), as coming that year. In the 1966 catalogue I regretted that no firm date could be given. That May I begged Stephen to send me his introduction, or at least a date for doing so, as I had received a terse card from the London Library, asking that the books, which had left their shelves fifteen months previously, be returned. At heart a delightful man, in whom old-school values fought a losing battle against his profitable commitment to one-upmanship, Stephen sent two apologetic cards in quick succession, then a letter to confirm that the books had gone back to the library. Three months later I reported receipt of a red-inked reminder from the librarian that *Omniana* had not turned up. Stephen swore blind that his secretary had delivered the books personally, and she confirmed this to me in writing. A month later the librarian regretted that the lost books would have to be charged to my account. Hearing this, Stephen sent me a copy of his letter to the London Library, undertaking to pay for their replacement. Jack felt I should let him do so. But there was still not a whiff of that introduction. In April 1967, with that year's catalogue again showing the *Omniana* as forthcoming, I wrote to Stephen in desperation, saying that with Val and Geoffrey long since paid for their work, and with booksellers' chasers for unfulfilled orders becoming more and more frantic, nothing had happened to take the project an inch further forward, and that we really must wind up the matter one way or another. I tried to word the letter's ending in terms that might ring some bell:

> As you have already made it clear in best bookmanship manner that our usual fee, although good enough for some of the highest paid scholars in the country, is peanuts to S.P., I shall quite understand if you would rather forget about the whole thing, but in this case please do let me have back Valerie Cohen's material. Then I can find some underpaid, grateful old hack, with two columns in *Who's Who* and fifteen Fellowships, who will produce the goods. But for pity's sake bring the matter conclusively to an end one way or the other, as I have but one life, one pair of hands, and one unduplicated set of nerves that already resemble a wire brush that has been scraping away at the hull of the Queen Elizabeth for years and years. Yours unployfully ...

For some reason best known to Providence, this – with a little push – seemed to do the trick. On 8 May, not having had a reply, I drove to London and called at Hamilton Terrace without warning, banking on Stephen not remembering my face since we had last met at Louis's. When he opened the door and regarded me blankly, I said I was sorry to be a little later than I had confirmed in my letter. As I had indeed written the letter, but deliberately not sent it, the perplexity that replaced the blankness was clearly not from the Potter bible. Not knowing who I was from Adam, he ushered me in apologetically and offered me cigarettes with the same fervour he might have shown had I just staggered from burning sands, moaning for water. To put him out of his misery, I produced the carbon copy of my unposted letter on the pretext that he might be able to match it with the original should it turn up on his laden desk, but really in order to spare him the indignity of having to ask who the hell I was. His relief was so great that not only did he hand over Val's material without any need to search for it, but he also – in the most matter-of-fact manner, and without explanation – gave me the London Library's *Omniana*. There are times when it is not politic to say anything. This was one of them.

I had just published Launay's *Dictionary of Contemporaries* and had brought a copy with me. He seemed pleased, and insisted on inscribing a copy of *One-Upmanship* 'from Stephen Potter (permanently one-down about writing for delightful editors)', and before I left he added his autobiographical *Steps to Immaturity*. This he inscribed 'To Jon for making my dreadful start into a delightful meeting'. He admired the camellia in my buttonhole. I had picked it from our garden to give to Heather, who was not there, and presumably at her office. This led to Stephen asking my advice about ground-cover plants for the 'dark end' of their garden, round which we walked. After a long talk about everything but Southey and Coleridge, he saw me to the door, which closed behind us as we stood on the step discussing squash, which he had decided to give up. He had no key on him, and there was no one in the house.

'It's all right,' he said, without conviction, 'there's a side window I can get through if I just pop over the neighbour's wall.'

I looked at the wall. It had clearly done good service for many years against the petty mafia of Marylebone, and Stephen's frame looked more suitable for giving up squash than for scaling serious walls. (Although still the right side of seventy, he was to die two years later.)

'Let me,' I said. 'I've quite a lot of walls at home.'

'No, no, wouldn't dream of it,' Stephen insisted. 'We'll knock them up next door. I'll manage.'

The neighbours were out, or perhaps lying low.

'There you are, then,' I said. 'Just give me a leg up.'

He looked anxious. 'There's a knack with that window. It really doesn't matter. Heather will be along soon, anyway.'

This struck me as unlikely if she was pairing people off in normal working hours, up west. But he was insistent, it wasn't actually raining, and I had other calls to make before getting back to Sussex. So I left him, a homeless man unwittingly robbed of the comforting chaos of his study, and I felt somehow guilty, even though the final act had not been of my making. A few days later I sent him the catalogue of a local garden nursery, marking the *Vinca major variegata* and the *Hypericum calycinum* as worth consideration. I added a copy of Lawrence's *The Symbolic Meaning*, appropriately inscribed, for good measure. In my letter I wrote:

Are you *sure* you didn't write an Introduction to *Omniana*? Among the stuff you gave me I have found the enclosed, which has all the aspects of an introduction. Am I being the victim of super-gamesmanship? Is the implication that Potter pens prefaces in his sleep, tapping some sub-conscious pocket of accumulated scholarship, sleep-writing reams of brilliance that are purged from the system and forgotten by daybreak? And did you get back into your house, or are you still on the pavement looking heart-breakingly rejected?

He replied by return, delighted by the catalogue, saying he would buy the Vinca, periwinkle and St John's wort from our nursery when he came down to see Andrew Young at Yapton, and have lunch with us. As a seeming afterthought, he said only of the introduction: 'I had quite forgotten I had started it.'

Although a beautiful friendship seemed to be burgeoning, it was clear that age and circumstance were against Stephen finishing the holograph draft of his introduction to an adequate standard, readable and enticing though it was. The one eventually used was written by Robert Gittings, the poet and biographer most likely to be remembered as 'the Keats and Hardy man'. An old squash, tennis and 'shop'-talking friend, Robert and his somewhat formidable wife Jo Manton – no mean biographer herself – lived for many years until the end of their days next door to Robert's lifelong friend Christopher Fry in East Dean, in a fold of the West Sussex Downs.

Finally, methodically, and with Stephen's rather thankful blessing, Robert sorted out Val's and Stephen's material and supplied an excellent scholarly piece. I later discovered that although Stephen's holograph pages had some sheets missing, he had also given me a complete version of his introduction in typescript. I did not tell him. It might not have increased what we would today call his self-esteem.

In that year *Omniana* was once more announced in the Centaur list, but with Robert's name as the writer of the introduction. Even then it had to be held over and re-announced in 1969 for March. But it had all been for not very much. Although Robert bravely justified the reissue by insisting on the excellence of Coleridge's later contributions, the otherwise friendly *TLS* reviewer doubted whether their easier availability merited the cost of such a handsome but commensurately high-priced indulgence. The commercial justification had, of course, been assessed on the probable readership for the reissue of a work so long out of print, but as it sold, in the Centaur edition, only about the same number of copies as *High Dive*, we had got it wrong. I hope the SIUP had a better experience with their edition, but by the time they would have been able to tell me it would not have been very tactful to ask.

The 1968 Centaur catalogue announced the coming of the Regency Library and Travellers' Classics series, though none had yet been put into the production line. Their listing was a kite-flying exercise to see what response might come from booksellers, libraries and institutions. There was enough of a flutter in the dovecotes to merit repeating the announcement in the 1969 list, this time showing Robert as the editor of the Regency Library (which had been his idea), and James (now Jan) Morris, suggested by Robert, as the editor of the Travellers' Classics. Only three of the advertised titles saw publication, some of those rejected being replaced by stronger alternatives; but interest in the general idea had been aroused. The main problem, as always, was finding an American publisher with enthusiasm to share the edition. Thanks to a further trip across the Atlantic, a Manhattan publisher with a good track record was found for one of the series sooner than expected.

In the 1960s, Frederick A. Praeger Inc. of New York, founded in 1950, were spreading their wings – perhaps, with hindsight, a touch too eagerly, for in the 1970s they were to become a division of one of the conglomerates then being spawned in the States, Holt, Rinehart and Winston, themselves a subsidiary of CBS. It was that happy and straightforward era when the nearest the UK had come to producing a serious conglomerate was Associated Book Publishers, the parent company of a respectable clutch of household names, in those days British from their Lobb brogues to their Trumper haircuts, and doubtless meaning to stay that way. In 1967 Praeger had asked to be sent reading proofs of *Dictionary of Symptoms* and *Dictionary of Contemporaries*, but I replied that both titles had already found their little grey homes in the West, the Philosophical Library having taken a timid 1,000 copies of the latter. In the light of the earlier proof of Praeger's interest in Centaur's existence, I sent a copy of the 1969 list, then wrote to suggest I called on them when coming to New York to see, among others, Sol Stein. At a cordial meeting with Praeger's Louis Barron, their highly regarded ambassador to London publishers (André Deutsch gave Lou the run of his Fulham house year after year), their interest in the Travellers' Classics was confirmed. The Regency Library did not fit their list, but it was a relief to have placed one of the series on a trip whose social content was in danger of overshadowing the business done. Under wifely instruction to 'relax a bit more this time, or you'll come back shattered', I had been drawn into the frenzied round of literary Manhattan, not to mention testing myself against squash-, racquets-, and real tennis-playing friends in the local club meccas. Christopher Campbell, treasurer of the Jesters and my main squash sparring partner back home, had laid on a game for me with one Charles Ufford at the Harvard Club. I knew nothing about him except that he was a member of the Jesters. We walked to the courts down the club's long corridor. Its walls were lined with brown wooden plaques, each confirming in gold lettering which player had won which cup in which year. On every board the ladder was headed by 'C. W. Ufford'.

'You?' I inquired casually. 'A relation?'

The modest shrug confirmed my worst fears. He had won the Metropolitan and reached the finals for the Nationals.

I made him sweat a bit, but I couldn't claim it had been a close-run thing. In the shower I said I was playing another of Chris's pals – like Charlie, a lawyer – the next day at The Racquet and Tennis Club. Hal Baker. Charlie grinned.

'You'll like Hal. Great guy. Could give me four inches.'

That made him a skyscraper.

The excess of physical and social zeal put me flat on my back with lumbago and bursitis for several days. The incarceration was not improved by the impossibility of lowering the dry, airless heat in my dingy Algonquin bedroom by struggling to open a window that had clearly never suffered such a liberty. By the end of the trip I was craving the supposed discomforts of home, where windows opened and draughts had healthy connotations.

Praeger's collaboration over the Travellers' Classics lasted, however, for all of four titles. Tobias Smollett's *Travels through France and Italy* and William Morris's *Icelandic Journals* were attractive productions, both wittily introduced by James, and well received; Joseph Baretti's *Journey from London to Genoa through England, Portugal, Spain and France*, introduced by Ian Robertson, followed in 1970, but although enthusiastically hailed by the *TLS*, its price reflected its size (demy quarto, 876 pages, two volumes bound as one, weighing in at over two kilograms) and not enough libraries and collectors felt deprived without it. Our sales fell short of 200 copies, and Praeger also reported a poor response.

The fourth title, T. B. H. Stenhouse's *Tell It All*, also known as *The Tyranny of Mormonism* or *An Englishwoman in Utah*, and published in September 1971 with only Fanny Stenhouse's own preface, had been suggested by Praeger themselves after seeing an enthusiastic letter by the novelist John Fowles in *Book World*. Written from his home in Lyme Regis, this read:

> In connection with Mr Mayfield's letter of June 7 about my interest in early Mormonism: the book I had in mind is actually Mrs T. B. H. Stenhouse's *Tell It All*, published by A. D. Worthing and Co. of Hartford, Conn, in 1878; and with a characteristically liberal introduction by Harriet Beecher Stowe. Its general tone would warm the hearts of today's militant feminists – indeed of all those who hate bigotry in any form. There is also an interesting eye-witness account of the goings-on behind the Mountain Meadows massacre of September, 1857. Some years ago I asked a young Mormon proselytizer who knocked on my door how he accounted for this blot on the Utah escutcheon. I wasn't very surprised to find that he had never even heard of it. Incidentally, if Mrs Stenhouse's autobiography hasn't been reprinted, it jolly well should be.

Despite this distinguished recommendation, and the *TLS* finding it a 'mystery' that 'her spirited account should not have been reprinted until now; it is an absorbing bit of social history as well as a vivid study of religious fanaticism', the Centaur edition did not sell even half the number of copies cleared by the Baretti. I hope that Praeger did better – if only because the collaboration with Lou and his delightful colleagues Lu Fenton, the sales manager, and Cherene, who had high hopes of their Fowles omen, had been so fair and friendly. But in November 1972 Lu had to write that 'Since we first agreed an initial four titles with you, our own program has changed drastically. We are ... completely out of this kind of publishing.' Although sorry that they had not, when worried about Baretti's slow sales, adopted my suggestion that the series be kept going by reducing the quantities ordered, I gathered that the call for quick turnover was once again governing editorial decisions. Six years later I was glad to be told by a Praeger executive at the London Book Fair that they were out of stock of all four titles.

The fifth and last Travellers' Classic was a new edition of William Beckford's *Recollections of an Excursion to the Monasteries of Alcobaça and Batalha*, with introduction and notes by Boyd Alexander. Sadly, although Praeger's Fred Kaplan had personally researched the market in the States, confirming an academic following and the interest of 'several young writers involved in this country's new "cultural revolution"' – and I would not have assured Alexander that we could go ahead, had Praeger not approved the project – the Beckford was not processed before the Baretti's sluggish sales contributed to the series being ditched. For us, the Beckford and the Morris made the difference between overall profit and loss for the Travellers' Classics, the Beckford being heralded as (1) '[his] finest work … a banquet of sense', (2) 'One of the most vivid and charming little accounts of a journey ever written', and (3) 'The finest of all his English writing has now become a classic', by, respectively, the *TLS*, *Church Times*, and *British Book News*.

Of the Regency Library, less worth saying can be said. The idea seemed sound, but the series failed to arouse much interest. Robert Gittings played his part with his usual conscientiousness. William Robson's *The Old Play-Goer* and Charles and Mary Cowden Clarke's *Recollections of Writers* were the first two titles, both introduced by Robert and published in 1969. They were followed in November 1970 by Mary Wollstonecraft's *Letters Written During a Short Residence in Sweden, Norway and Denmark*, competently and charmingly introduced by Edmund Blunden's divorced wife Sylva Norman; and by John Flint South's *Memorials*, again with Robert's preamble and the addition of an index. Although wrapped in a jolly Regency-striped standard dust-jacket, each title, apart from the indexed *Memorials*, was a naked reprint except for its added introduction. So, it is true to say, were the Travellers' Classics, but doubtless Smollett, Morris and Beckford had more going for them than the reminiscences of minor observers of marginally more major figures from a neglected period. Although reviews were meagre, the Wollstonecraft, as expected, sold most copies (a heady 235). Much better reviewed, the South petered out at 106. The Robson, hardly noticed by the papers, staggered up to 160, and the Cowden Clarke, the best reviewed of all, fell behind the Wollstonecraft by some twenty copies at the last count. Because of the standardised production quality of the four titles, only the South lost money if the bare manufacturing cost was taken as the yardstick of profit; the Robson broke even; the Cowden Clarke and the Wollstonecraft paid for Dumbo's hay for a year or two.

Robert Gittings's wife, Jo Manton, was at this time working on a full-scale biography of Mark Pattison's remarkable sister Dorothy. Her researches led her to sympathetic consideration of Pattison's background and character, and she suggested that a reissue of his 1862 *Memoirs* might be called for. 'Called for' seemed to be putting it a bit high, but more out of long friendship than expectation of riches I said we could put it out as a Centaur Classic, though with no hope of SIUP joining the party. It was published in September 1969 and nice things were said about it by Geoffrey Moorhouse in the *Guardian* ('A superb revelation of how Victorian society manufactured its quarrelsome, querulous dons'), by the *Church Times* ('One of the most justly famous of all autobiographical Victoriana'), and (eventually) by the *TLS* ('For anyone interested in university reform, in the history of Victorian Oxford, or in the Tractarians, this book is essential. It has its importance too for the student of the Victorian novel.') One might have hoped that such recommendations would have sold more than 187 copies, but they did not. The 1960s put paid to many predictions.

Centaur's last title in that uneven decade was published – as *Chimney Pots and Stacks* had been – as a Centaur Monograph, and I wondered whether we would get away with it, and why no one else had done it before (a speculation that must have created over the years an ocean of acidity in the stomachs of publishers). In the event, it was one of the more successful titles on the general side of the list. As with Fletcher's book, the idea came from an artefact, in this instance with a family connection.

My parents left Scotland in 1922 when my father was posted as assistant adjutant to the air base in Gosport. For the first year they rented first-floor rooms in The Crescent, Alverstoke, an attractive Regency terrace looking south across private gardens to the Isle of Wight. By the time I was born – in July 1924 – they had moved to Warwick House, one of the oldest properties in the hamlet of Brockhurst, some one and a half miles north of Alverstoke village on the road to Fareham.

In 1960 I drove Jennifer and the girls to see my birthplace, by then redesignated 212 Brockhurst Road. We found it was owned by the grandson of Mrs Seymour who had let the northern portion and her services to my parents when they moved from 9 The Crescent. Although my memories are faint, for we left Brockhurst in 1928 when my father was posted to Henlow in Bedfordshire, long-held photographs preserved a few threads of recollection. A clear one was of old terracotta kale pots, decorated with faint white slip work and almost certainly made by the famous Fareham pottery. They were still where I remembered them, nearly at the bottom of the long cottage garden in which I played, and I asked Mr Seymour if he would sell me any, though we had no kitchen garden in our Highgate flat. Perhaps because he and his wife lived on the first floor of the house, with use of garden, the rest being let as a café, complete with the ubiquitous Coca-Cola sign to flag in passing trade, he was not forthcoming. The pots were probably forcing his rhubarb, which was my own long-term aim.

As we were leaving, I noticed a very old letter-box set into the south gate-pillar. As the pavement-fronting garden wall had been rebuilt to a lower level, and the gates removed, the pillar looked vulnerable, so I took photographs as a record. As we drove back to Selsey, where we were holidaying, I tried to conjure up early memories, and the letter box began to be added to that nostalgic baggage that, as the years build up, most of us carry around. I thought of the innumerable letters that my mother must have posted in it (some, Jennifer speculated, announcing my arrival): to friends and family; to her agent, publishers, and editors; to my father, then a flight lieutenant, whom the RAF sent to Mesopotamia for eighteen months from February 1927. I wanted that letter box.

Six years later, in August 1966, I paid the Seymours £8 for their two remaining kale pots and the letter-box, the latter having been removed by the Post Office the previous autumn and sold to the Seymours for £1. On the 15th I wrote to the Records department of the GPO to ask if they could supply the age and provenance of the box. After sending them further information, I received a second letter, written on behalf of the departmental record officer by what I took to be a man of French-Italian parentage:

> First [he wrote], I must tell you how much I envy you your wall box. It appears to be a specimen of the first wall posting boxes ever made, dating from the period 1857–1859! I know of only one other example, this being the posting box at Challerton railway station.
>
> Secondly, I think your proposed book on posting boxes (featuring both pillar and wall boxes, perhaps?) would be a very exciting project. There is a great deal of interest in the subject, as I know from the scores of people who have written to me, and I would be pleased to show you what material is available.
>
> Yours sincerely,
> JEAN FARRUGIA

By then we had been five years in Sussex, and a few days later the 10.18 from Victoria pulled into Arundel station. A slight, bespectacled young woman alighted from it who looked anywhere between student age and twenty-two. This was Jean Farrugia – her married name. It was with some trepidation that I commissioned this slip of a girl to write a book whose high cost could only be justified if it was acknowledged as the definitive study of post boxes, needing not only to be written clearly and interestingly, but to be equipped with plentiful line drawings and half-tone plates, footnotes, a bibliography, a chronology, a good index, a compelling and authoritative introduction, and preferably a laudatory preface by a relevant 'name'.

For the latter, I had in mind Anthony Wedgwood Benn, as he had been Postmaster-General from 1964 to 1966 and, Jean told me, was sufficiently enamoured of postboxes to have been genuinely pleased to receive a VR specimen as a farewell gift when he relinquished his PMG status. He supplied the preface quickly and efficiently, and his name looked just right printed on the letter-box red of the dust jacket. Also just right was Jean's writing and putting together of *The Letter Box: A History of Post Office Pillar and Wall Boxes*, which was published in November 1969 and never looked back. Collaborating with Jean was a real pleasure. Her writing was excellent, her introduction first class, and her sense of order and organisation so admirable that I cannot think why she didn't succeed Tony as PMG. Of all the books I have published, I cannot recall one that came to fruition so painlessly. *The Letter Box* received few reviews, though a long one in the *Daily Telegraph* by F. J. Salfeld probably set the ball rolling, and the book has sold steadily and upwardly ever since to spotters and collectors the world over. Decommissioned wall-boxes were to change hands for three and four figures, those with their locks, keys and plates commanding substantial sums. Ten years later, 'Mandrake' in the *Sunday Telegraph* wrote an intrigued and intriguing piece about the Letter Box Study Group, of which Jean was by then president, and referred to her 'still definitive book'.

My 1858 box (I bought seven others subsequently), for which I obtained a copy of the minute written on 24 April that year to the Postmaster General from the Secretary to the Post Office, suggesting that a 'wall box be erected at Brockhurst as proposed by the Surveyor', is now a *pièce de résistance* in Kate and David James's Inkpen Postbox Museum near Taunton.

An end-of-the-decade restlessness was setting in. The reception given to the two new series invited the suspicion that churning out books just to maintain turnover was producing evidence of staleness. I admitted as much when Edmond Segrave invited another article for the *Bookseller*.

By then the Centaur imprint was fifteen years old, but had not really taken off until the first Centaur Classic appeared in 1960. In 'The Centaur in our Paddock' (2 August 1969) I gave a mildly facetious account of survival-to-date, of the weariness brought by a frenzied decade, and of some of the tribulations and blessings of independence.

But it was too soon to make a total switch from publishing into writing, given that an offer from some publisher-*manqué* was not a strong probability. Although many dream of becoming publishers, most fall at the first fence when they realise that it takes a mix of aptitudes that depend to a large extent on an instinct that cannot be proved sound or mistaken until substantial investments have been made. A chair or a turnip can be created and taken to market at very little cost. To produce a single copy of a new, marketable book takes thousands of pounds in production costs alone, never mind the know-how and structure needed to sell it through countless outlets worldwide, or to a specialist readership.

Reconciled to Centaur's continuing role in our lives, we were even considering buying or building a new house large enough to cope with the increasing storage and office needs, as well as living-in help and more space for entertaining and accommodating guests. Added to this was the possibility that my mother, despite her determination to continue living like a creative hermit, might need to spend her final years with us and an attendant nurse. After years of self-neglect, she was clearly not going to be around for long. However, despite reservations about merely enlarging the house we lived in, that was what we went for.

On a personal level, I needed to accommodate the urge to write a serious non-fiction book. Tilly, born in 1951, was well into her teens, and by the end of 1969 Sue was less than a year away from the first rung of that time of life that was being made hazardous and bewildering for her generation – not to mention its parents – by the postwar commercially-driven, media-hyped youth culture that no perceptive and caring parent could observe with equanimity. The 'swinging sixties', susceptible to the worst that was coming over from the States, were all too centred on London. Their ugly influence enticed an easily-besotted young to make choices beyond their wisdom, and to be 'with it' or feel out on a limb. Manipulated to believe that they were freely rebelling, and enjoying an autonomous sense of direction, many of the victims of this 'permissive society' grasped at the chimera of a lifestyle in which empty distractions and half-baked philosophies were made acceptable by the relentlessly orchestrated backdrop of youth culture and drugs in their many forms. This state of things, following the leaner and directionless 1950s, was understandably taken for granted by all but a minority of youthful doubters and drop-outs with disparate interpretations of the world's failings. So what is new? In every generation, when parents voice their fears, children see only a threat to their right to sample whatever goodies are on offer in what is assumed to be an adult, but basically safe, world. Only the wiliest fish learn that hooks have barbs. The long process of understanding what it means to be truly adult demands a depth of experience that, by definition, the young must lack. The misjudgements of my own youth taught me that, if little else; but most truisms are recognised too late.

From this bubbling cauldron of parental angst something, I felt, had to emerge that was more positive than sounding off against the many symptoms of society's decline, or making autocratic prohibitions that would get nowhere. As the educationists' and churches' agendas showed all too little constructive concern with more than the occasional symptom of corrupting influences being directed at the rising generation, the best I felt capable of doing was to hammer out some suggested guidelines aimed primarily at sixth-formers and their teachers. As, in the mood of the late 1960s, no commercial publisher was likely to be interested, I saw no credible option but to write *The Civilised Alternative*, and give it the Centaur imprint. I began it in January 1970, and it was published in 1972, sub-titled 'A Pattern for Protest', the front cover quoting a passage from the book:

> If we do not learn how to deflect the course of our violent, acquisitive society, we shall destroy not only our surroundings, but ourselves. Merely to 'drop out' is a negative gesture. We must be prepared to contribute towards a better pattern – a civilised alternative.

For all that my aim was to avoid a preachy, nagging tone, it is necessary to diagnose if prescription is to follow, and it soon looks false if one tries to dress up as merely tentative suggestions deep personal convictions that must either stand or fall. Those who distrust the first whiff of didacticism, even in the form of proposals for a happier and more workable world, usually hold weak or ambivalent values themselves, so it seemed best to write it 'as it came'. The book therefore, I assumed, risked being jeered into oblivion. Of all European countries in which to suggest a curriculum drawing on the wisdom of perennial philosophies, Great Britain was hardly the ideal choice. But choice was not on offer.

Contrary to expectation, a reasonable number of reviews were given, all either favourable or, at worst, not actually damning. The *TES* produced a response that was not so much antagonistic as uncomprehending. From the rest of the UK the reception was better than anticipated. In the *Sunday Times*, the influential columnist Maurice Wiggin found it 'full of luminous good sense', commending it to 'concerned young people, and old people concerned about young people'. C. P. Snow and Yehudi Menuhin recommended it, and in the *Observer* Philip Toynbee welcomed 'a trenchant and most heartening book, written by a man with a mind of his own who expresses both his anger and his hope with cogency and eloquence. He is strongly on the side of those of his juniors who believe there is something *radically* wrong with the modern industrial world.' But the most valued review was from Professor Duncan Williams whose own book *Trousered Apes*, a study in the influence of literature on contemporary society, had enjoyed bestsellerdom on publication in 1971, being nominated by four major newspapers for the Book of the Year Award. I wished I had been given the chance to publish it myself, or at least to have known about it in time to boost its importance in *The Civilised Alternative*, from which much of it might have been lifted word for word, even though Duncan was more pessimistic than I was to be about the young, and took a narrower view of 'permissiveness', seeing man's inhumanity to man as our only problem. However, his next book, *To Be or Not to Be*, which followed in 1974, being described as a companion volume, carried his thinking further and with more emphasis on prescription, stressing that only humane education in its fullest sense could save the day. In discussing his book in a long article in the *Daily Telegraph* of 22 June 1974, Williams warned that 'It is late, but not too late, for a *gradual* and *civilised* alternative to emerge.'

It was through reading *Trousered Apes* in 1972 that I first made contact with Duncan, and in writing to tell him that *The Civilised Alternative* was about to be published, I confirmed that it was through meeting some of Tilly's contemporaries that I had been encouraged to write the book. I felt there was a significant minority that might be responsive to more positive substitutes for the unsatisfying lifestyles that were being foisted on them. Duncan, too, had children, the oldest only twelve and still at the Dragon School in Oxford, where he lived and had earlier been at university (at Christ Church). 'As a university teacher', he wrote, 'I do see signs among the more thoughtful young of a reaction to the mindless slogan-chanting creatures who have recently dominated the media.'

If nothing else, publishing *The Civilised Alternative* was proving to be a learning-and-confirming experience. Duncan sent copies to Lord Dulverton's brother E. H. R. ('Bobby') Wills, who founded the Farmington Institute for Christian Studies in 1965, and to Sir Walter Coutts, former Governor-General of Uganda, who was taking over direction of the Farmington Trust Research Unit, endowed with a nice irony by the Wills tobacco family to re-introduce moral and ethical values into education. Wills seemed inclined to let others do the talking, but Walter Coutts shared Duncan's enthusiasm for the book, and we launched into what was to be a prolonged and congenial exchange. He confirmed that Wills wanted the Trust to do something more practical than pure research, which had not made much impact on the outside world, and made clear that

> it would certainly be part of the Trust's aims to try and sponsor some of the ideas which you have set out in your book if you wished to use our resources (admittedly somewhat limited) to develop the theories you have expressed. It might be possible for the Trust, for instance, to engage one or two people to write up particular themes with your assistance, and distribute such pamphlets or memoranda to schools, colleges of education, and other places where they could be expected to make an impact.

I put up some suggestions and in July (1972) spent a pleasant day in the Trust's Park Town offices in Oxford with Wills, Coutts, Duncan, and Sir Alister Hardy, the distinguished zoologist and staunch Darwinian. The latter's 1963–65 Gifford Lectures, published as *The Living Stream* and *The Divine Flame*, and his founding of the Religious Experience Research Unit at Oxford, had made examination of evolution theory and its relation to the spirit of man almost respectable.

All four men were charming and enthusiastic, although one sensed that familiar aura of academics trying to come to terms with the tedious demands of life's realities. Wally Coutts, however, was a feet-on-the-ground committee man, blessed by a vitally needed sense of humour, and splendidly unflappable. As well he might have been, having shouldered the cross of being chairman of Robert Maxwell's Pergamon Press and served as a university vice-chancellor at the time of the 'student

troubles' of the 1970s, besides proving himself an able colonial admin-
istrator in the last days of Britain's African Empire.

I had no occasion to go to the Trust's London office in Queen Anne's
Gate, but its Park Town offices spoke more of academe than of a hive of
businesslike endeavour. Shabby and masculine, its aged leather
armchair repaired with Sellotape, it was staffed by a young woman in
maroon boots with a pink knitted wool cap made, one suspected, by a
devoted mum in Boar's Hill. I produced a long letter received from
Yehudi Menuhin, approving of *The Civilised Alternative*, and they
asked the pink-capped girl to run off some copies, being keen to add to
their list of potential contributors to their work. Pamphlets and position papers, however, were outside my field, and I suggested a fairly
comprehensive outline for collaboration over a book-publishing arm to
Farmington's activities. Duncan and Wally seemed wholly in favour, the
former looking forward to working with me on the project when he
returned from his forthcoming winter stint at Marshall University, New
Virginia, to take up his post as the Trust's Director of Research. While
he was away, correspondence and meetings with Wally laid down some
of the framework, and it became clear that my added workload would
make necessary the employment of a helper.

On 8 October, however, under the headline 'Research men quit in
row over aims', the *Sunday Telegraph*'s education correspondent
Nicholas Bagnall published a report that did nothing to allay the suspicion that working in with the God-fearing for the general betterment of
mankind might set one's feet on a rather stony path:

> A ten-year £150,000 research project into moral education, based
> in Oxford, has run into difficulties because of disagreement
> between its director and the man who put up the money.
>
> Mr John Wilson, director of the Farmington Trust, resigned last
> week after seven years' work on the project. During that time he
> and his team of researchers produced ten books and nearly as
> many pamphlets.
>
> The benefactor is Mr Robert Wills, brother of Lord Dulverton.
> He is to continue the Trust under a different director, Sir Walter
> Coutts, former governor-general of Uganda, and with a new coun-
> cil which includes the headmasters of Rugby, Ampleforth, and
> Gresham's, Holt.
>
> Meanwhile the trust's former academic council and all the
> research workers have departed. The academics included Mr Alex

Peterson, head of Oxford University's Department of Education, Prof. Richard Hare, White's Professor of Moral Philosophy, Mrs Jean Floud, now principal of Newnham, and Dr Harold Loukes, Oxford reader in education.

Mr Peterson said: 'I left the trust when Mr Wills decided to give up fundamental research in moral education and to promote certain spiritual views instead.' Oxford University would not want to be associated with something more like a campaign than a research project, he said.

Disagreements between Mr Wills and the Farmington team began a year ago when Mr Wills produced a pamphlet of his own called 'The True Aims of Education'. The team felt they ought to have been consulted.

Mr Wilson said yesterday there were no ill feelings between him and Mr Wills. 'After all, it's his money,' he said. He is now continuing the work himself at Mr Peterson's department.

Mr Wills was not available at his Gloucestershire home yesterday.

The fact that Wally had not mentioned the brouhaha in any of his letters decided me to cut my losses and lie low. In March 1973 he sent me the final version of *The True Aims of Education*, by which time I had heard from Duncan that the Farmington Council 'seem resolutely determined to carry on with "research", though into what I do not know. It seems to me, anyway, that diagnosticians abound, but that there is no sense as yet of a need for prescription.'

While *The True Aims of Education* was an excellent presentation of the problems, it was not exactly inflammatory in its recommendations. It was, in fact, disappointingly short on calls for specific actions, which at a more secular level was presumably what the previous council were seeking. As for rooting for such revolutionary notions as closer ties with other-than-Christian faiths, evangelicalism rather than ecumenism seemed the more probable goal. The paper's tone prompted the vision of more comfortable talk-shops for elderly gentlemen, more witty exchanges over the port, and the eventual leisurely preparation of further short papers confirming aspects of a shared concern. It certainly gave no hint that anything so demanding and definitive as book-length contributions to the debate was in the offing.

This impression was strengthened in a letter from Wally received in

November 1974, by when the Farmington Institute for Christian Studies was firmly on course for awarding fellowships and bursaries to teachers of religious education in schools, colleges and universities. He wrote (and the capitals were his) that '... the Council of the Trust is getting much more positive about us collectively or individually saying that we have a RELIGIOUS belief and therefore, because we are not brown or black, that belief is CHRISTIAN'. As the general tone of his letter reflected his usual cordial self, I assumed that religious politics were stretching even his flexible tether, but that perhaps my timing had been unfortunate in sending him a proposal for 'A Partnership of Concern'. This was a manifesto I had launched, inviting a loose coalition of influential people aware of deteriorating values and 'willing to contribute in appropriate spheres to a wider recognition of humankind's moral and spiritual needs'. Minimal organisational structure was envisaged, but the response was so enthusiastic that it was more than I could do to realise its potentialities on my own, and (as is too often the case with idealistic ventures) no one suitable was prepared or able to take over the reins. At the time, however, it seemed something to which the Farmington Trust might have responded. The almost fierce confirmation of a corporate credo in Wally's letter helped to explain another rather strange response I had received from Alister Hardy, who seemed to fear that the POC manifesto could contain a hidden agenda of unwelcome flavour. He had not, however, even hinted at what that might be. It was all depressing ammunition for those who suspect that while religions survive wars will not cease.

Duncan, refreshingly (if dangerously) determined to be his own man, unhesitatingly became a signatory to the Partnership, as did a wide range of philosophical, scientific, environmental and other specialist and lay men and women given to lateral thinking and profound certainty that endless repetition of orthodox 'answers' could only perpetuate the world's problems. A compassionate but realistic eclecticism seemed essential. The signatories were themselves an eclectic cross-section of international freethinkers, from the philosopher and statesman Sir Sarvepalli Radhakrishnan and the Gandhian metaphysical ecologist Satish Kumar, to such more temporal laypersons and academics as Ruth Harrison, Stephen R. L. Clark, Philip Toynbee, Richard D. Ryder, Peter Singer, and Gerard Morgan-Grenville. Those, like Alister Hardy, who jumped to incorrect though understandable conclusions, were doubtless influenced by the sheer unpindownable mix of such signatories as Yehudi Menuhin, Philip Kapleau, David Ehrenfeld, Victor

Goddard, James Robertson, Michael Rubinstein, Trevor Huddleston and George Trevelyan.

I assumed I would not hear again from the Farmington Trust, but had underestimated Duncan's determination to give it a higher and more contributory profile. In July 1973 Trevor Huddleston, then Bishop Suffragan of Stepney, had published in *The Times* 'a prayer for an ethical think tank', having risen to Bernard Levin's challenge that 'our leading churchmen are so scared of being thought to have any view at all on moral matters that they ... have nothing to say'. Huddleston's prayer seemed to have been answered, for in April 1975 he invited me to give a paper at a two-day 'Compass' environmental conference in Oxford, sponsored by the Farmington Trust. Feeling it wiser to focus on practicalities rather than on philosophical and ethical matters in the home waters of such distinguished academic piranas, I made the subject of my paper 'Communication: a Petition'. It paved the way to later discussion of my suggestion that the Trust take over *Twentieth Century*, a recently folded literary magazine, converting it into a town-and-gown forum for those concerned by the drift into societal and environmental chaos. At that time – and I am not aware that the position has much changed – there was no such platform aimed at the middle-brow audience who saw the need for moral and humane education, and who might welcome readably presented reports of what was going on in this field in the academic sphere, and of what was, might, and should be happening in the larger world outside. Three other think-tank members gave papers. Sir Peter Medawar's did more to justify growing fears of the dangers in scientific complacency than to raise hope that research was likely to be restrained by such interruptive abstractions as ethical reservation. Hugh Montefiore, then Bishop Suffragan of Kingston-upon-Thames, gave a humanist's impression of secular man in full control of his spiritual appetites. Basil Mitchell, Nolloth Professor of the Philosophy of the Christian Religion at Oxford, drew matters a little closer to the subject supposedly in hand, but not so as to frighten any horses. Of the remaining thirteen members present, the contributions of two of the other clerics have been the most memorable: Trevor's, for his sincere and sensitive chairing of the proceedings; and Lord Ramsey's. Ramsey, whose Canterbury see had been filled the previous year by the Archbishop of York, despite high public estimation of Trevor as a worthy successor, joined us briefly toward the end of the second day, leaving himself no opportunity to draw any informed conclusions from what had taken place. Then, when papers were being shuffled as we prepared to disband, he peered round the table and made clear to Trevor that the innocuous proceedings should not be assumed to have the blessing of Canterbury. The reason for this concluding hatchet, which appeared to be a response come to beforehand, was difficult to understand from what had taken place. It would have been mollifying to be able to suppose that Ramsey had found insufficient drift toward the ecumenical, but that seemed an improbable explanation. Trevor was visibly bewildered and flustered by the abrupt warning. There was something saddeningly spiteful about what came across as a petty act of public humiliation; not only of Trevor, but of Duncan, whose intentions were also of the best, though I could appreciate that if apes can be considered as trousered, by implication they can also be cassocked and even splendidly enrobed. Which order of primate will be first to rise to Bernard's challenge remains to be seen.

In December that year Reg Davis-Poynter told me that Duncan had been ill, but I had no chance to talk to him until the following April, when he was again back from America. The Trust, sure enough, had gone Christian evangelical in a big way, and wanted nothing to do with Trevor's 'Compass' hopes. What part this incident played I do not know, but Duncan spent a few more difficult years, handicapped by manic-depression and money problems, taking almost anything offered that might make ends meet. He published more excellent pieces in academic and such specialist papers as the *Ecologist*, and a guest-column contribution to *The Times* showed that the clarity of his thought was undiminished. I did what I could to help with small assignments and introductions, but when I last saw him in 1979, at his home in Oxford, he was clearly losing heart. He had been bitterly disappointed by not being given the chair at Missouri that he had expected, and was about to go on a fund-raising world tour for OXFAM. He died suddenly, of a stroke, in March 1985, when dining with friends in Huntington, West Virginia, to celebrate the end of a successful lecture tour that I like to imagine he was hoping would be the start of an upward turn in his fortunes. He was another of those men I have known who were greater than the recognition an indifferent world allowed them. We ignore and suppress such people at equally high cost to ourselves.

From Trevor I heard no more after a rather sad letter following the 'Compass' conference. He was hoping to get 'the "*ad hoc*" committee off the ground very soon'. But when, years later, I tried to discover what had happened subsequently, the Lambeth Palace archivist was unable to come up with anything, and Robin Denniston's 1999 book *Trevor*

Huddleston, a Life cast no light on the matter. More trivial diary engagements are recorded therein than a two-day conference of distinguished scientists and academics, of which there is not as much as a footnote. But burials are a Church specialism. It was fitting, no doubt, that the last major appointment for the man who did so much for those who are 'brown or black' should have been that of the Archbishop of the Indian Ocean. Trevor did not die until 1998, but one felt it had happened sooner.

Digression has again taken liberties with chronology. The year was 1970, but starting to write *The Civilised Alternative* was a watershed, both personal and professional, and I hope that the reasons for introducing it out of sequence will become clear.

Apart from the Baretti, the South, and the Wollstonecraft, the year's publications were a mixed bunch. The first title, scheduled for 1969 but published in January 1970, was three dialogues propounding the argument endorsed by W. R. (Dean) Inge, that the only solution to the religious problems of the day was a new synthesis of Neo-Platonism and Christianity. *The Dialectics of Diotima*, introduced by Richard Church, was written, without ascription, by my mother, and although its form and content justified it qualitatively, it was a farewell gift-of-opportunity to someone not long for the world she had worked tirelessly to make a little more endurable for all creatures that struggle to survive in it.

Although the Publisher's Note to the book drew attention to the strange fact that Socrates, in those pederastic times, should have sat at the feet of a Mantinean woman on the subject of the philosophy of love, contemporary feminists overlooked the evidence that Diotima's teachings influenced Socrates' highest metaphysical conclusions, and not only those concerning love.

Speaking for the wider Christian audience, and with a gallant attempt at charitable objectivity, the *Church Times*'s critic thought it a pity that the book would not reach a wider readership, since, however strong their dissent, 'they would nevertheless also find themselves compelled to think – which, after all, is the object of the exercise called philosophy'.

A further impression of *The Myths of Plato* was followed two months later by a paperback edition of one of the two best-known of my mother's non-fiction books, *The Philosophy of Compassion*, first published in 1962 by Vincent Stuart Ltd. In his Foreword, G. P. Gooch

OM, CH, for fifty years editor of the *Contemporary Review*, wrote that 'the supreme merit of [*The Philosophy of Compassion*] is that it will compel its readers to ask themselves how much of their creed is dross, and how much is pure gold'.

Apart from the spring publication of William Kean Seymour's 'new and selected' poems, *The Cats of Rome* – the last book of poetry by a modern writer to be published under the Linden Press imprint, and his final book – 1970 closed with its most time-absorbing title, *Mrs Gaskell's Observation and Invention: a Study of her Non-Biographic Works*, offering a detailed commentary (and detailed was the word) on all Gaskell works except *The Life of Charlotte Brontë*. The dedication of its author, John Geoffrey Sharps, was as impressive as the fellowships and doctorates after his name. The only point at which his professionalism wobbled was in his understanding (by no means to be taken for granted in committed academics) of the need to be certain that the typescript sent to the printer is the book that is to be printed. *Mrs Gaskell*, with a Foreword by Professor A. Stanton Whitfield, made over 700 densely researched pages, carrying every known kind of *apparatus criticus*. Having received his galley proofs, Geoffrey – a delightful man whom none could wish to gainsay – proceeded to rewrite his book not once, but three times over. Had I been aware from the outset with what passion, and in what numbers, academics the world over had jumped on the Gaskell bandwagon, I would have stayed my hand, as perhaps more knowing publishers than I had already done. It exhausts me, as I write, just to thumb through the thick file of correspondence covering the seven years that it took to put the elusive monster between hard covers. When Geoffrey first wrote, in 1963, wanting to place his 'over 100,000 words' book, he hoped for a birth date of 1965, Mrs Gaskell's centenary year. I advertised it in the *TLS* as coming in October that year. Although already a good deal longer than expected, the galleys were printed on schedule, whereupon Geoffrey settled down happily to his first rewrite. Such squalid considerations as who was going to pay for the ruinous corrections were simply not entertained.

Our exchanges, nevertheless, were cordial, my stiffest letter in the early days confirming my concern that by 1966 he had 'virtually rewritten the book' after it was typeset and in galleys. In June the following year I warned that the printer was nearly off his head coping with the constant and often involved changes and additions. Threats that I 'would have to abandon the project unless you can finalise the matter within a reasonable and firmly promised time' fell on deaf ears. Sterner regret that 'this book has clearly become a sort of hobby for you, and I can see no reason for supposing that you will ever regard it as ready for press' was either ignored or simply failed to get through. In May 1968, in desperation, I wrote that 'I have had a phone call from the printer who has reached the end of his tether with your book. He points out, which I well know, that you have virtually rewritten it several times over, the enormous corrections and additions necessitating such extensive re-setting that he has in effect had the job of producing several books, each of some 600 pages.' After further constant reminders that any more trimming, polishing, stop-press additions, etc. could spell the ruin of one or both of us, I was at last able to send him page proofs in September 1969. Perhaps fortunately, my paper merchant simultaneously warned of a huge price increase for orders that could not be delivered by 1 January 1970. I made clear the horrific facts and the consequences of ignoring them. The penny at last dropped, and I was able to send dear, maddening Geoffrey a finished advance copy of his book in September 1970. It was published five years almost to the day after Mrs Gaskell's centenary. Geoffrey was delighted, but after such an extended cultural orgasm he seemed almost uninterested in the thing once it had been born. But the reviewers, thank heaven, were unanimously impressed. Geoffrey and I remained on friendly terms, but my years in service to Mrs G's memory were certainly a factor in my resolve to take on less onerous projects in the future. But then – as with marriage, parenthood, and much else in life – you don't really know what you are getting into until you are committed.

10

Some Passion Spent

So cloistered has life been as a one-man publishing band, buried since 1961 in relatively rural West Sussex, that I only recently came across Jeremy Lewis's delightful reminiscences *Kindred Spirits: Adrift in Literary London*. Identifying with so many of his reactions and priorities, I have enjoyed the book's humour, observation, and a healthy irreverence lacking in many forays into the literary jungle, which can take itself terribly seriously. I find Lewis's mindset-for-survival so often matching mine that, after the depression from recall that came from plunging back into the Gaskell years, his witty book has been the perfect antidote.

He writes, for instance, of his employment by André Deutsch, the Hungarian who founded and ran the publishing firm of that name from 1952 to 1985, a waspish account of which is given by André's formidable editor and co-founder Diana Athill in *Stet*, a book for bookwatchers that should be bought for its brilliant portraits of Jean Rhys and V. S. Naipaul, if for nothing more. Soon after starting work for André, Jeremy was asked to read and report at a single sitting on a typescript that André's staff unanimously adored for its self-conscious political correctness and dumbed-downness, but Jeremy detested. Called upstairs at the end of the day to give André his opinion, he had the guts or commonsense to be truthful. So far from losing his job for lack of compatible editorial sensitivity, he found that André shared, and was delighted by, his judgement. The anecdote puts in a nutshell one big reason why, if I was to make publishing my career, I knew I was destined to go it alone. I have never felt an iota of enthusiasm for the stresses of being an employer, least of all in a field where, even before you are faced by the task of selling it to the wider world, it is necessary to convince your employees of the product's merit if it is to receive their maximum support.

Reading back, I wonder if I have given a false impression of all work and no play. Though the one-man publisher may work harder and for more hours in the year than Incorporated Man, he can at least allot them according to whim, weather and opportunity. But despite any indication to the contrary, the sweet smell of hedonism had reached me early in life. As a toddler, a lighthouse flash from the Isle of Wight, my major ambition was to travel, as often and for as long as possible, on the Gosport/Portsmouth ferry, and thence – if the gods smiled – across choppier seas to the pier of Ryde. Unlike Jennifer, whose antecedents include a formidable array of admirals and generals, I know of no prominent sea-dogs or big guns in my own ancestry. Yet Jennifer is sick in a Force 2, whereas I – prompted originally by the Gosport ferry – took to helming small racing yachts in the English Channel. Not that I could afford the time to be more serious about it than to race an X-One-Design keel boat as a member of the Itchenor division in Chichester Harbour from 1968. But, variously crewed, though never by Jennifer, I raced in the Solent several times in the season, and from 1969 *Pepper*, bought from the belligerent accountant Henry Benson, then well on his relentless way to a peerage, was entered in most years for the Cowes Week Regatta. Henry had sold *Pepper* because he decided it must be the boat rather than himself that was responsible for not winning enough races. The process of proving to him that he had got it the wrong way round, both at Itchenor and in Cowes Weeks, made for a testing friendship, but anecdotes from those who encountered the competitive Henry on the water would make a book all to themselves.

Solent racing brought other early memories, one of the fainter being the six weeks in the spring of 1928 when my maternal grandparents rented a converted coastguard cottage for us at Seaview, shortly before my father returned from his eighteen months' service in the Southern Desert of Iraq. Forty years on, the 'different Englands' were still some way from merging indistinguishably, and to this day the Island remains in certain respects, unrepentantly and delightfully, seventy or more years in the past. Insular, perhaps; defensive; even a bit snobby. But all of a piece.

One of the enjoyable aspects of the publishing and writing world is that although, by and large, those you meet remain class-conscious, especially in the party-labelling way, this seldom comes across in judgemental guise. Class differences are still, thank goodness, an integral part of life's idiotic tapestry, and without them much writer's ink would be a lot thinner, as would the humour and enjoyment in mixing with one's own species. Though there is a general tendency to the left in the book world, I suspect much of it is connected more with poor financial returns and the rigidity of mind found at the extremes of the political spectrum, than with vowel sounds or the school you went to. People can be reassuringly samey.

Because I was making my living by publishing and writing, it was some while after we left London before the locals began to realise that, so far from being rantingly party-political, we could be relied upon only to vote for no one at all. This apolitical indifference was understandably looked down on, though it is a commoner tendency today.

Centaur's 1971 output certainly suggested I was keeping to my post-Gaskell resolution. The only additions to the Centaur Classics were paperbacks of the King, the Landor, and the Leland, which absorbed the flat sheets housed at the binders. The one general title, apart from the second impression of *Troilus and Criseyde*, and discounting Clyde Chantler's *The Ghana Story* published on a shared-costs basis under the Linden imprint, was a Centaur Monograph, *Our Grimy Heritage*, a 'fully illustrated study of the factory chimney in Britain' by Walter Pickles, a pleasant and appreciative Yorkshireman who lived in Garforth in a house called 'Dimple Dale'. However, sentiment and interest in factory chimney stacks was less than in Valentine Fletcher's domestic pots. Perhaps an emblem of servitude, inviting destruction, is a less hopeful subject for nostalgia than the symbol of Polly-put-the-kettle-on comfort conjured up by the nearer, friendlier, and even collectable cottage chimney pot. Sales were some fifty copies short of the 250 needed to break even.

1972 began with the last Centaur Classic, this being also the final title to be accepted by SIUP, who, twelve years later, were to write that 'our stock of Centaur Classics has reached low levels' – welcome confirmation of my faith in the series as a solid backlist investment, but far too late to save it. Less pleasing was the news from another quarter that Centaur Classics in the SIUP edition were being offered to university libraries and shops in the UK in a USA remainder firm's catalogue, which doubtless had a bearing on some of our own editions' sales having dried up. Stock being seriously low on a number of our titles, I was able to buy back some from SIUP, but they were themselves too low on most to be willing to part with them.

The Classics' swansong was John Aubrey's *Three Prose Works*. Edited by John Buchanan-Brown, it offered in a single and substantial volume the author's *Miscellanies*, the only book published in Aubrey's lifetime; the *Remaines of Gentilisme and Judaisme*, published for members of the Folklore Society in 1881; and, in *Observations*, unpublished material apparently ignored by his earlier editors. For those with a leaning toward Aubrey and his period, it was a considerable work of scholarship, welcomed by *TLS* and *THES* alike. Sales had not much exceeded 300 copies by the time Centaur passed into other hands, but it was never going to have the appeal of a Ford, or even an Allingham. But it was a worthy and worthwhile topping off for the Centaur Classics series, and is still a pleasant volume to handle, not least because it marks the last time I had to see such complex texts through the press.

In the same year I published a new and revised hardback edition, edited in the light of later scholarship, of the second of my mother's best-known non-fiction works, *Mithras: the Fellow in the Cap*, first published by Hutchinson in 1958 and reviewed respectfully then for its scholarship and the strength of its argument. Fourteen years on, the *Church Times* welcomed 'a deeply sympathetic study of the ancient pagan sun-worship over which Christianity ultimately triumphed'. Had its author not died three months before the new edition appeared, I suspect the *Church Times*'s reviewer would have been challenged over the term 'triumphed', but the rest of the reviews suggested growing receptivity to her thesis that, from the time of Paul, Christianity was infected with the Mithraic virtue, encouraging the growth of those persecuting and militaristic elements that have characterised the thinking of the Western churches ever since. *Mithras* was another contribution from one of the most perceptive feminist writers to have spoken against the influence of the extreme and devolutionary masculine values that have dominated both the religious and secular culture of the West.

With *Mithras* and *The Civilised Alternative* coming the same year as a sort of family double-act, my concern to move Centaur into a more purposive field hardened. My impression that the general climate of thought had moved further toward a more responsible regard for the total environment was strengthened by the invitation from Reg Davis-Poynter to write a book in amplification of two chapters in *The Civilised Alternative*. After leaving McGibbon and Kee in 1970, Reg had started his own firm, appointing as fellow directors Lord Goodman, Kingsley Amis, John Boulting, Nigel Lawson, Alan U. Schwartz, Baroness Wootton, and Sidney Gilliat. It was to Reg that I suggested Duncan Williams submit *To Be or Not to Be*, and this was published by him in 1974, a year before my *Food for a Future*, of which more later.

Although 1972 was my year of reappraisal, I could only plan and look out for books that would take Centaur in the direction of what might best be termed humane education. The fact was that I was burdened by what many may feel was an unnecessarily self-inflicted concern about the state of the world, and my place and obligations therein. I have tried to keep myself peripheral to this book about books, but some account is required of the experiences and soul-searching which informed that self-inflicted concern. Let me quote my response to a mailing from Javier Marías. By being directed at a third party, it may moderate any impression that I am launching a didactic attack on the reader. Jennifer can be thanked for demanding a shortened version of my initial draft:

My dear Javier,

Your challenging article arrived when *Finding the Words* has reached the stage where I have to explain what prompted the decision to focus the Centaur list more seriously on that area of environmental concern that sees the need for a wider view of our species' place and responsibility in the scheme of things (if 'scheme' is an appropriate term). I wondered how best to tackle the task, conscious that I might now lose those readers not much interested in motivations. Your piece sparked the thought of responding to it with an open letter. It expects no reply.

I suspect that semantics is up to its tricks again, and that you have not meant to imply that true satire can (undesirably) 'intrude upon literature and the arts in general', for the suggestion would strike some as no less dubious a view than that the greatest literature must be free of moral content. You and I would agree, I hope, that the most lasting literature has presented – however obliquely, delicately, and often satirically – the ethical perspective, and that it is often more satisfying for possessing that dimension. Of fiction, it has been said that all novels hold a moral, though some are more amorphous and sub-textual than others. Literature that merely gratifies a taste for voyeurism, or focuses solely on the downside of human behaviour, failing to depict our puny species wrestling with the demands of a code or a conscience, can be pretty thin stuff.

Even if you have read nothing but my letters, you may have realised that I have felt a lifelong concern over humanity's illimitable contribution to the suffering that is the dominant condition of most forms of sentient life, including our own. So constant are the reminders of that hell we have made that hardly a day in my adult life has passed without the need to cope with such promptings, and I often recall the lines from Schweitzer's *Memoir of*

LEFT M. P. Shiel RIGHT T. I. F. Armstrong ('John Gawsworth'), late 1930s

:FT Gawsworth marries Estelle Hayward in 1948 RIGHT A Paddington Canal dubbing, encouraged by John Waller and female supporters in the early 1950s

On 13 April 1979 the third and most reluctant King of Redonda tries to proclaim
with gravitas from his kingdom's precipitous peak

Javier Marías, the internationally acclaimed novelist and Redonda's fourth monarch, wrote that 'the beautiful legend is to me mainly literary, and it should always be so'.

John Gawsworth placing a wreath on the grave of Ernest Dowson at Ladywell Cemetery Lewisham, February 1950, watched by group of fellow poets

Eleanor Farjeon with goddaughter Sue and Jennifer, 1958

Wendy Hiller with Jennifer and Ronald Gow at Fontwell, 1977

Tea-break for Stanley Baxter, Dorothy Tutin and David Holt before *Marvellous Party*

Michael Byrom sets up his stall for a private viewing, Fontwell, 1964

With Sue, Jennifer and Tilly, 1986

ᴇFT Peter Singer and daughter Lee, Fontwell, 1979 RIGHT Richard D. Ryder, writer and campaigner, Gulf of St Lawrence, 1984

Philip Hoare researches for *Noël Coward*, Fontwell, 1992

LEFT Grandson Matthew taking stock to the garage RIGHT Derek Stanford, 1982

Open Gate's van collects the final load from Fontwell, April 2003

Childhood and Youth: 'As long as I can remember, I have suffered because of the great misery I saw in the world. I never really knew the artless, youthful joy of living, and I believe that many children feel this way, even when outwardly they seem to be wholly happy and without a single care.'

I have wondered to what extent Schweitzer was able or minded to move his daughter and grandchildren to live with the painful awareness of universal suffering. With respect to my own family, it has certainly been something I have tried to address responsibly. Unless we touch the hearts of children, we cannot move the hearts of men. How far should we go in turning their innocent joy into painful realisation of others' sorrow? The answer is blowing in the wind.

I am unsure of exactly when, in my case, this concern with the universality of suffering began, but my earliest memory of an incident that may have been the trigger was recorded in 'A Walk Across the Fields', the only autobiographical short story in my book *Sealskin Trousers*. Young children's perception of the pity of things so often emanates from the observed or reported ill-treatment of weaker creatures, and is as frequently crushed by the obtuseness, indifference, and fear-of-being-thought-peculiar of parents, peer group, and the heedless world at large.

An equally potent early influence may have been, in the 1930s, my mother's anger at the plight of coal-miners, for pit accidents were frequent and often horrific (she passionately advocated greater focus on opencast mining). It played a part in the formation of her own philosophy. One has only to look at the foreword to her 1936 *Prelude to Peace*, in which she proposed a teaching system under the title of the World-Brotherhood Educational Movement – a plan sympathetically received by forward-thinking educationalists, but soon to be swamped along with so much else by the dementia of nations committed to the 'solution' of the Second World War. (Published in the same year, and equally incapable of affecting the traditional acceptances that were again to push the combatants back into barbarism, was Aldous Huxley's *What Are You Going to Do about It?*, proposing that 'the great monopolistic powers' settle their grievances and claims round the conference table.)

At about ten years old, the wider thrust of my mother's ideals – more pragmatic than Utopian – were beyond me, but what 'stuck' was the fact that she was also distressed by the life-sentences to slavery, blindness, accident, and sometimes violent death, suffered by the mines' many pit ponies. To the child mind, as yet oblivious to adults' self-serving distinctions between species, it was equally upsetting to visualise already imprisoned song-birds being taken down the mines to give warning by their suffocation of the lethal gases that killed so many at the coalface. My mother's concern was what came to be called holistic: a response not merely to the human suffering in such outrages as the First World War and much industrial practice, but also to the often associated torment of other species relentlessly exploited by our own. The tens of thousands of horses killed, maimed, and left to die on the battle-fields of the First World War were a strong memory in the 1930s for those whose imaginations or experience could embrace the fates of 'mere' animals. My mother's less selective compassion prompted, I suspect, my awareness of the indivisibility of cruelty and suffering, though many years were to pass before I could perceive the full implications.

The Second World War was the catalyst I most clearly remember, as much from experience prior to its outbreak as for all that followed. That experience was the all-out drive by my public school, Brighton College, to make through its OTC 'officer material' of young minds already being subjected to the Government's hydra-headed propaganda machine.

On 26 August 1939 my mother and I left the Brighton flat to spend the remainder of my school holiday in the bungalow she and my grandmother had bought nine years earlier. Let when possible, it had brought a little income in the lean 1930s when my father's allowance to my mother had to be supplemented. They were not to divorce until after the war, and my mother's writing earnings were inadequate once my father had left us. The timber and asbestos property was on the east beach of Selsey, in West Sussex. Twelve miles to the west is Portsmouth, the naval base that was to be heavily damaged by German bombing, and seven miles north-east of Selsey is Tangmere, the village whose now disbanded airfield was to become, less than a year later, a key RAF station in the Battle of Britain.

For me as a child, Selsey spelt freedom. I detested my school-days to a degree only imaginable by similar square pegs, and to arrive on the flat Selsey Bill where, for the last time, I looked forward to a few weeks' swimming, cycling, and meeting old friends was simple heaven. While my mother unpacked, I pumped up the deflated tyres of my bicycle and pedalled into the village to call on one of those young friends, Katherine Hughes-Hallett. She was dying – I think of cancer or tuberculosis – and the sadness of seeing her immobile on her bed on that summer's day, her face as pale as the plaster of Paris that encased her thin body, was intensified two weeks later when, five days after we declared war, I met two boys from Brighton College eagerly discussing, without hatred or any muzzy concept of an 'enemy', their chances of getting into uniform before the 'show' was over. It was one of many incidents proving wars' inevitability; not because an unprompted majority wanted them, but because the young were so easily brainwashed. It brought painful understanding of how readily the young – far more afraid of being thought cowardly or poor team players than of the dim possibility of becoming casualties – could unquestioningly accept officialdom's bidding to kill whatever enemies might be identified; and that the easiest choice of all, as in so many situations through life, is to go along with the majority.

We have not discussed such matters, Javier, and you may never have been faced with the need for soul-searching in the climate of a nation committing itself to the warpath. It is an ugly and barbarous condition, however sanctioned by fine phrases and self-congratulatory motivations, and to this day it is a widely held assumption – usually made without regard to its link with the savage aftermath of the First World War – that the Second was a 'just war'; though have we ever known of any armed conflict between nations in which churchmen and politicians, on all sides, failed to justify mass murder by trotting out that most untenable of oxymorons?

It seemed particularly absurd that theologians – given that their bible is, after all, The Bible – should not have been deterred by such nakedly clear texts as that in John 16: 2, 3: '… the time cometh that whosoever killeth you will think that he doeth God service. And these things they will do unto you, because they have not known the Father, nor me.' But I soon learned that any trading of biblical texts on ethical matters is fatuous if argument defers to the assumption that 'everything in The Bible is true'.

You don't need telling, I suspect – even if you have not read a

page of *The Civilised Alternative* (and why should you!) – that I
have got no nearer to any of the established religions to claim
more than, at the most, a religious sense. From an early age – and
not, I think, prompted by my mother, whose upbringing had been
distinctly orthodox – I could not understand why the mystery of
creation should be so central to the Christian persuasion. Who or
what created the material universe seemed supremely unimportant. The notion of seeing an anthropomorphic being as the
creator of this appalling scheme of things struck me as embarrassingly arrogant and totally implausible. Some sort of devil might
possibly have been responsible, but for a god alleged to have been
good ... My religious sense contented itself, perhaps lazily, with
the assumption that it was enough to define god as good principle
or good force, and that the best our aberrant species could hope
for was gradually to evolve by 'worshipping' that principle in our
daily lives, regardless of such unprovable and unlikely destina-
tions as heaven, hell, or a life hereafter. If there was an omniscient
force around – man-shaped or otherwise – it was going to be one
ahead of me.

Whether or not you tune into this background stuff, you may
understand my relief when, in the early climate of the Second
World War, instinct and a developing power of deduction were
bolstered by two works, well known in their day, that confirmed
and influenced my adolescent thinking profoundly: *We Say 'No'*
by H. R. L. ('Dick') Sheppard, CH, DD, vicar of St Martin-in-the-
Fields in the 1920s, who transformed the Trafalgar Square church
into a centre of worship and social work renowned worldwide;
and Richard B. Gregg's *The Power of Non-Violence*, first
published in the same year (1935), appropriately dedicated to
Gandhi two years after that tenacious little man demonstrated to
the world's greatest empire the efficacy of passive resistance.
Today, thanks to our educators' priorities, even Gandhi is a
'Who?' name to most of the young, as must be Sheppard's dedica-
tees: Maude Royden, Arthur Ponsonby, George Lansbury,
Herbert Gray, Frank Crozier, and Donald Soper. Some of the
poets of the First World War have not been forgotten, but most of
their successors in the Second lacked the content and technique to
achieve immortality, proving again that 'finding the words' that
match the moment and the memory is not a soft option. But while
the acidities of Robert Graves's 'Base Details' and 'Blighters', and

Wilfred Owen's magnificent 'Dulce et Decorum Est', were but three of the war poems that impressed me, there were prose texts that did more to corroborate the convictions necessary to take a definitive stand against the majority view. Arthur Ponsonby MP's *Now Is the Time*, an appeal for peace dedicated 'to the millions who have fallen in war', published ten years earlier, and his revealing *Falsehood in Wartime* (published 1928, two years before he was made a peer), contributed powerfully – and far more than anything conveyed in the irrelevant years of my formal schooling. Through unsupervised reading I gained an education that at least instilled caution and awareness of the weasel words and wiles, the euphemisms and distortions, of those supposed experts and manipulative 'authorities' who in all ages have implanted fear, obedience, and unquestioning passivity, to mould a society that can be comfortably controlled for their own advancement and thirst for power. Superficially, at least, society today seems less naive about the blandishments and scams of politicians, professionals, and the military hierarchy, but recalling how many influential people appeared unwavering in their 1930s' pacifism until the first rallying exhortation sounded, I would not bank on their successors' convictions were a Third World War seriously on the cards. History is distorted from the moment it becomes the past. For 'children ardent for some desperate glory', Wilfred Owen's 'old lie', suitably attired for the climate of its day, will again come on parade. Although now into the twenty-first century, our fascination for *Boy's Own* military history – despite the graphic legacy of the foremost First World War poets and all that has happened since – remains depressing evidence of the continuing power of nostalgia founded on wilful supposition. That devolutionary mix embalms to this day such cherished misconceptions as that the pull of virtue and self-sacrifice drove men to mutual slaughter on the Somme, and that 'pro patria mori' is the noblest good. (Don't worry, Javier, I am not, nor ever have been, a closet Marxist, or of any other political affiliation; merely an observer with a distrust of 'labels' and of those who shelter behind them.)

The day before meeting the boys who were so excited by the all-too-easily acquired status that beckoned to them, another incident may have helped to steer my thinking. Selsey village being a mile away, via a rough road, the East Beach was served for vegetables and fruit by the weekly visit of a horse-drawn cart owned by the

Binsteads, a truly down-to-earth couple who grew much of their produce in nearby Sidlesham. He was a large, wild-eyed man. His wife, a tiny woman hardly more than half his height, provided such brains as governed their enterprise. Their moth-enticing horse was a subdued creature, probably 'rescued', for a not much better fate, from the knackers' yard. Arriving on my bicycle from some errand in the village, I found Binstead cursing and threatening the animal to make it move on. Well-known for his quick rages, he began to whip and punch the mare savagely on head and flank, making her whinny with pain and fear. Just what I said to him I cannot recall, but it was enough for him to redirect his fury, whereupon his wife, clearly long practised at dealing with such events, leapt between us and beat at his chest with all her might, yelling at him to 'leave the boy alone'.

Another incident, less to my credit, was when I cycled to Church Norton the following spring to identify birds on Pagham Harbour. I had taken with me a catapult, given to me some five years earlier, and had been aiming in a desultory fashion at inanimate targets such as fencing posts and telegraph poles. In the lane to the harbour was a tempting tree with a thorn bush growing beneath it. Somewhere in the vicinity a songbird was being audibly moved by sex or season. I loosed off a pebble at the tree, but it fell short and entered the bush. The song ceased. Hoping my fear was groundless, I looked into the bush, finding the limp body of a female linnet held by the fork of a branch. I drew it out, pricking a thumb on one of the thorns. A drop of my blood welled out, staining the linnet's breast feathers. By most standards, my shame and sorrow at the consequences of this thoughtless act may seem disproportionate, and I know that the bird's end in the claws of a hawk or a cat could have been more stressful. But I have needed no reminder of that day through all these years. It was somehow – absurdly, some may think – a microcosm of what was to be seen daily in a world yet again rejecting every value worth preserving, with every vile act to come being sanctified by the glib labels of 'duty', 'honour' and 'sacrifice'. In one's teens one can see – or only believe one sees – with a clarity and certainty so intense that in that moment almost anything would be preferable to the hollow sense of loneliness that it brings.

But this was the spring of 1940. On 19 September 1939 my mother and I had returned to Brighton – not to see me back to

school for the autumn term, but to arrange for the contents of our
now relinquished flat to be sent on to Selsey. The news that my
schooldays were behind me brought such joy that I hardly took in
the vague explanation that my release had come 'because Daddy
has gone back into the Air Force'. But it was true. Within a year of
returning from his eighteen months' service in Iraq, after which
we left Gosport for Henlow in 1928, he had gone off with a fellow
officer's wife in what, for those days, were fairly steamy circumstances. The King's Proctor being involved, the papers had picked
this up jubilantly, and my father thought it wise to revert to the
Retired List in 1929 and try his hand at business. In that May he
left us for a flat in Hampstead and joined Heinz, with whom he
gained managerial status at record speed despite no real experience outside the services. In 1930, by when his affair's first fine
careless rapture had lost its edge, we joined him in the flat. But too
much water had passed under the bridge, and my parents finally
parted in the summer of 1932. As my father was recalled to the
RAF on 3 September 1939, joining the HQ Staff of No. 74 Wing
in France, the further drop in income, and the risk factor in his
return to active service, made my school fees a luxury that I was
delighted to know he could not easily guarantee. From the
summer of 1939 I was therefore spared any formal education
apart from an ill-conceived correspondence course supplied on
coarse grey sheets by an Oxford 'college' employing teachers as
gone-in-the-hocks as the Binsteads' broken-down old mare. Much
as I would have liked to follow some of my contemporaries to
university, the incentive was insufficient to overcome my lacklus-
tre response to the depressing wad of indigestible facts that
arrived weekly. They might have been thought just the ticket by
Thomas Gradgrind, but to me they made Brighton College seem
like the cutting edge of progressive education. Even my mother's
attempts to enthuse me were unconvincing. As I was evidently not
going to develop the level of studious application needed to attract
invitations to affordable tutelage among the dreaming spires, it
seemed more realistic to put my future in the hands of the university of life. For better or for worse, I have stayed a member to this
day.

By chance, after the fall of France, from which he returned on a
collier from La Rochelle on 20 June 1940 to join the Staff of No.
11 Group at Uxbridge, my father was stationed during the Battle

of Britain at Tangmere, where he became Staff Officer in Charge of Administration under his old friend Air Vice-Marshal Leigh-Mallory. (Although promoted to group captain in August 1941, he was to be offered a tempting post with the NAAFI soon after, and retired in September after being recommended for an OBE. The fact that an earlier recommendation for a DSO and CBE had been ignored forced him to accept that the road to high rank and a knighthood had been closed by nothing more heinous than that 1928 indiscretion.)

Because of his proximity to Selsey, and unhandicapped by petrol restrictions, he was well placed to work on his son's unwelcome convictions. Although pleased by my aptitude for games, he was not reconciled to having a son who was unwilling to eat animals. Finding that by the summer of 1940 my thinking had moved no nearer to accepting the logic of ensuring peace by contributing to the inevitable legacy of total war, he was doubly motivated to persuade me of my folly, pointing out that the social and career penalties for stepping out of line in my diet would be as nothing to the odium and difficulties I would invite by not joining the armed services. I was already aware of the possible truth in these predictions, but he was unable to understand that I did not accept them as relevant. Needing no convincing that life was not a bed of roses for the majority of sentient beings, I tried to make him understand my belief that what he wanted of me could only increase the sum total of human misery and decline. We played some tennis now and then when he could spare an hour or two away from the airfield, and it may be that his time in France had been sufficient reminder of the insanity of the First World War to understand that my views, though wrong-headed in his eyes, were sincerely held and not without precedent. As a last shot, he made clear this his position as a senior officer with above-average connections could be useful to my advancement, should I see the error of my thinking before my call-up notice was served in late 1942. Stronger than his powers of persuasion, however, was our grandstand view from the bleak Selsey peninsula of a very lively sector of the air war over Southern England. By mid-June 1940 the Luftwaffe was inviting skirmishes along the east and south coasts, and Selsey's shoreline was being fortified with huge concrete blocks and barbed wire against the Germans' anticipated sea invasion.

On 11 July, the day after the Air Ministry's official date for the start of the Battle of Britain, with no forewarning other than an increase in the previous weeks of the air raid siren's undulating wail, a Heinkel 111, after taking part in a raid on Portsmouth docks, appeared as silently as a heron, skimming the flimsy roofs of the sea-front bungalows 100 yards to the east before crash-landing on a wide stretch of the shingle beach less than half a mile to the north. A jobbing gardener was helping us with the vegetables that day, and he and I ran through the sparsely occupied estate to where the Heinkel had come down. One or both engines were smoking, several Hurricanes having taken turns to gun it during its irreversible descent. The pilot was standing on the rough road, possibly in shock, and a few spectators began to gather. Pat and I did what we could to detect any sign of life in the plane, ready to back off if smoke gave way to flame; then someone behind us – perhaps a spectator able to speak to the pilot or the two apparently unharmed members of his crew – called out that there was no one left in the wreckage; later, however, the flight engineer was found dead in the fuselage. Army personnel arrived and took the pilot and his crew on to the verandah of one of the bungalows. The rear gunner, mortally wounded, was lying in the road, whispering 'Mutter, Mutter.' The knot of onlookers was growing, as people walked or cycled from the village, but watched in silence, keeping together as though there was still some threat to be feared. Neither they nor the plane's crew paid any attention to the dying man. Later, I felt badly about being one of their number, and knew I should at least have tried to find something to put between his body and the rough flint road. But the Heinkel was the first enemy plane to be brought down on the Bill, so for the onlookers, as for myself, there was probably a sense of unreality that diminished normal reaction. Everyone seemed to be waiting for something else to happen, which was the arrival of those appointed to take the crew into custody, and an ambulance to collect the dying man. He had managed to remove his left glove, lined with another made of linen, and was fumbling at a pocket of his flying-suit, perhaps for a photograph or some proof of identity. As I was close to him, I picked the glove up, which enabled me to murmur a few useless words that might be of some comfort. The glove had a name-tape sewn into the cuff: 'Müller, Willi'. I wondered if I should hand it in, but those who were guarding the crew wanted to keep the civilians at a distance from the verandah. Its occupants looked down at the small crowd, but still no one said a word except for the young man groaning in the road. I heard the next day that Willi Müller had died in the ambulance on the way to hospital, the Heinkel's exploding fuel tanks marking his departure. He was buried alongside the flight engineer in the churchyard of St Andrew in Tangmere, correctly acknowledged on the headstone, which confirmed he was twenty-one.

Many years later I entrusted his glove, still smelling of the mix of oil and leather, to the Tangmere Military Aviation Museum. They put it behind glass with some fragments from the site that I picked up two days later. I hesitated about lending the glove to the museum, aware that such places attract many englamoured by something they have not experienced, or nostalgic for the 'good war' that others have boasted of experiencing, or that they themselves, by definition, survived. Men's willingness to partici- pate in almost any action enjoying religious or political sanction cannot be discouraged by maudlin sentiment, but I took a chance on a proportion of younger visitors seeing the poignancy, and a more realistic symbolism, in the relic, and of their being more resistant than my own generation to the deceitful phrases that subvert the truth. Long before 1939 the country was being groomed for the coming of another war, and one of the weasel words from pulpits and hustings was that men were willing to 'give' their lives – a shameful misuse, I felt, of St John's 'Greater love hath no man than this, that a man lay down his life for his friends' – implying a benevolence seldom ascribed to and hon- oured in the military's odiously termed 'collateral damage'. The soldier's training prepares him primarily to take the lives of others, whether or not those others have also been trained to kill those guilty only of being young enough to be similarly deceived. The linnet in the bush did not give its life. I took it.

After 11 July there was sparse local 'activity' until early August, on the tenth of which month a friend little older than myself died from wounds received in a dog-fight over the Channel. Two days later began weeks of almost constant combats, many taking place at so great a height that the sun illuminated the planes' underbel- lies, and it was like looking up at a vast blue dome on which were pinned scores of silent silver moths – except that now and then one of them would break formation, having been crippled by the attack of some smaller 'moth', often difficult to identify from the ground. Frequently, one of the targeted, growing larger with descent, would turn black and then grey, shortly to be seen and heard for what it was, a diving or spiralling plane – sometimes discharging leisurely 'mushrooms' en route that would come down in the sea, or on the peninsula, or perhaps many miles away. That distant view of the harsh realities in the sky had for some the aura of a dream, or of something being seen in a cinema. My father's memories of the Somme confirmed that the more terrible the circumstances, the more that reconciling sense of unreality could take over, permitting commission of even the most barbaric acts, whether or not exhortation and alcohol had contributed to the blunting of fear and conscience. A few years on, having by then been a closer observer of war's realities, it was ironical to discover that I understood this capacity for distancing oneself from imminent danger better than did my three oldest male friends, who had spent their war years in the armed services without hearing a shot fired in anger. Not that all First World War participants enjoyed that strange psychological shield. Some went out of their minds, though if failing to do so convincingly by presenting acceptable clinical symptoms, they could face disgrace and execution as criminals incapable of perpetrating inhuman acts against strangers unknown. Maybe the term 'bravery' needs a more considered definition.

At this point in my letter to you, it is the first day of 2001, and on New Year's Eve the BBC's Radio 4 convened a panel of distinguished academics and religionists, one a Nobel prizewinner, to discuss conflict, technology, and the prospects for God and man. The consensus was that violence was the central problem for the new millennium. While this is hardly news to most of us, and while the chance to point to the related and equally important (indeed, fundamental) problem of human over-population was, as usual, missed, it is one of several signs of a growing awareness that our priorities need radical rethinking. Alain de Botton's recent book *The Consolations of Philosophy* (little connection, other than its title, with Centaur's Boethius!), while designed to reach, and not unduly tax, the mind of John Citizen, nevertheless regrets that 'academic philosophy has totally abandoned the original, Greek ambition of the subject: to make us wise'. (Boethius came on more strongly for virtue, but there are still many who would not accept the interdependence of those qualities.) 'Instead, it's far closer to a completely abstract subject like mathematics or linguistics. Academic philosophers have given up looking at the great questions, because they don't think they can ever answer them as strictly as they would like.' It's the truth, I'd say, but only half the truth. I don't know how it is in Spain, but over here and in the States academic philosophers – increasingly leaving the educational field to psychologists – ignore the 'great questions' and their answers, aware that such concerns are unfashionable and would not advance their careers in an increasingly science-dominated culture.

But that aside aside, ... because intensification of the raids on southern England was seen as the prelude to invasion, my father said we must leave the bungalow and move inland. In September 1940 we went to a guest house in Oxford for a month before renting a charmless villa in the straggling village of Long Hanborough, ten miles to the north-west. For the next two years I had good reason to neglect my correspondence course, as my mother's determination to avoid medical help for a common and curable condition had already rendered her a semi-invalid. As it was neither the time nor the place for finding permanent domestic help, even had it been affordable, I took on the house, garden, shopping and cooking for ourselves and J. D. Beresford, whose collaboration with Esmé was by then in full swing.

You may have little knowledge of 'JD', as he was known by the literary world of the 1920s, by which time he was regarded as one of the foremost serious novelists of his day. When my mother and I left Hove for a flat in Chesham Place, Brighton, in 1936, the Beresfords already lived opposite. I was then at preparatory school and had met JD's daughter Elizabeth, a jolly girl two years my junior, and in no time we installed lines – or, rather, strings – of communication between the top stories of our homes, attracting the amused tolerance of her three brothers, too old for such childish games.

My mother, then thirty-eight, and twenty-five years younger than JD, had published her first non-fiction book, *Prelude to Peace*, whose prewar appeal to Beresford marked the start of their friendship in 1937. JD was experiencing increasing difficulty in summoning the ideas and enthusiasm to sustain the output of his thoughtful and well-crafted novels. His advancing years were not alone responsible. Since giving up his work as literary adviser to Collins in 1923, after which the Beresfords lived for four itinerant years in France, home life with his wife Beatrice ('Trissie') was under considerable strain. Beresford's mind was inquiring, tolerant, and eclectic. Trissie was a rigid High Anglican, opposed to any questioning of religious orthodoxy. There was no disguising that Esmé's strong desire to develop spiritually and mentally attracted the equally questing and cerebral Beresford. They found a level of intellectual companionship that was understandably feared and resented by JD's wife.

When, in August 1939, JD moved out of Chesham Place into a flat by himself at 6 Chichester Terrace, it was not, as Trissie made out, 'to live with the woman opposite', but to escape his wife's vigorous scenes. These were nothing new, as for years Trissie had feared – not without reason – that the commercial appeal of her husband's novels was being reduced by his interest in speculative concepts out of step with the climate of the times. His quiet and non-confrontational nature was ill-attuned to cope with her outbursts, and by the eve of the Second World War he was near to breakdown. Ironically, neither then nor later was there a physical affair between him and Esmé – only what today might be termed a creative partnership. But Trissie painted her picture with such persistence that her three younger children were to believe otherwise for many years.

Tristram, the oldest child, and closest to his father, knew the facts and was later to find himself in similar domestic circumstances – a propinquity given little credence by those incapable of imagining the attractions of a mental or spiritual relationship over those of the primarily physical. Possibly only JD's closest friends, among whom were Walter de la Mare, Dorothy Richardson, Hugh Walpole, Naomi Royde-Smith, and Henry Williamson, would have had the perception to deduce the truth of the matter.

JD had been crippled by infantile paralysis in early childhood and relied on crutches for the rest of his life. Although his age and infirmity underlined the absurdity of Trissie's portrayal of a roaring affair, insult was added to her injury by Esmé's interest in the tenets of (*inter alia*) Christian Science, for Trissie's parents had themselves been drawn to Mrs Eddy's teachings. In his sensitive and unpublished study of his father, Tristram (who died in 1988) well understood the complex and sad dichotomies of our parents' situation. The misunderstandings and consequences in such cases are many, and even I, as a boy in my teens, had some reason to wish that Trissie's account had been truthful. Over the two years spent in dreary Long Hanborough, Esmé insisted that to observe the proprieties I should spend no nights away from home, and always be in by the supposedly indicative hour of 10 p.m. As there was little to do but housework, studying, writing, and enjoying the somewhat sparse companionship of the six hens whose eggs supplemented our wartime diet, this deadline was an only occasional hardship. Chess with JD, and his evening readings to my mother and myself of the works of P. G. Wodehouse (to which I had introduced him), alleviated boredom in the absence of a proscribed radio. For exercise I pedal-cycled to Oxford and in the countryside, sometimes up to a hundred miles in the day.

Excuse for this unsolicited reminiscence may be little more than its small indication of the effect of the Second World War on the mores of the twentieth century; though perhaps they were not that different from those inflicted by the First World War on JD's generation. He, after practising as an architect, began to write for publication in 1906, and in the years between his first novel, *Jacob Stahl* (1911), and his death in 1947, he published some sixty books. Most were novels, eleven of them collaborations with Esmé during the last nine years of his life; due to the terms of his contract, however, not all were published under joint names. Since the Second World War, only *The Hampdenshire Wonder* was reissued by Penguin, helped by the lift to his reputation brought by the 1940s' collaborations. His writing asked too much of the trivial tastes for which publishers were increasingly anxious to cater as the postwar world got into its stride. Unless there is a revival of the thinking-readers' novelists of JD's era, he may be remembered only by a slim section of exploratory students for the help and friendship he gave to such as Freeman Wills Croft, Sarah Gertrude Millin, Storm Jameson, Vita Sackville-West, Henry Williamson, Michael Arlen, Eleanor Farjeon, F. Scott Fitzgerald, Rose Macaulay, Katherine Tynan, and even Aleister Crowley, with whom JD sometimes played chess over tea in an ABC café: in his autobiography, almost completed before his death and forbidden publication by his wife despite the strong interest of Hutchinson and Lord Inman, JD gently recalls 'Beast 666' as 'quite a pleasant little man'. But if posterity shapes up as I suspect it will, it is more likely to remember JD only as the father of my first girl friend, creator of the doubtless more immortal Wombles of Wimbledon Common.

My early domesticity – which was to come in useful when taking up with the direly undomesticated female talent of postwar Britain – at least involved shopping trips by cycle into Oxford, where a touch-typing and shorthand course in Broad Street had some eventual value for a writer's future, and was handy for getting occasional tennis with friends at Balliol and Queen's. But at least the two distinctly isolated years enabled reflection and study, if virtually no opportunity for mental interchange with my peer group, male or female. My conviction grew that to join the armed services was simply not an option, however helped by parental string-pulling to join the right squadron. My father threatened to cut me off with a shilling if I persisted in my 'I say "no"' stance (an ultimatum that might have carried more weight had my only income not been sixpence a week from a mother whose allowance was the minimum her husband was allowed to get away with). I would not have enjoyed the prison sentence I was warned might come of my recalcitrance but it was preferable to the prospect of living with myself if I survived my period of service.

The reflective JD's wisdom and interest in my mental progress made a welcome substitute for the single-track concern of my father. He could sympathise with my inability to see no more justification, let alone heroism, in dropping bombs on men, women and children in German cities, or shooting other young men out of the skies, than in the actions of those who were doing precisely the same to ours. Having experienced two world conflicts and much else (he was born in 1873), JD had lifelong proof that countries who glamourise war do not prepare for peace; that militarism is by definition the problem, never the solution. Such reflection was totally irrelevant to my father, whose attempt to connect with my mental processes went no deeper than to express regret that I might waste my skill as a marksman, for I had been seen as a good shot at Brighton College and was lined up for the shooting team for the autumn term of 1939. Not that JD or my mother saw any need to pressure my thinking. With my own father back in uniform so soon after the 'war to end wars', the notion that any of the combatant countries could claim a 'finest hour' seemed shameful. It appeared to me that such small advances in civilised values as had been made after the First World War were being lost 'with interest' by the escalating barbarism of the present. The very nature of war had so changed that where combatant casualties in the First World War were some 90% of the total, and civilian 10%, in the Second those percentages were reversed. Unpalatable statistics for those days' romantics with misty visions of clashing armies, inspired leadership, danger, valour, martial tunes, and sacrifice ...

I hope all this runaway stuff hasn't bored you, Javier, but it may be my only chance to update the backdrop from the perspective of old age. But surely the 1930s' dictum 'Wars will not cease until men refuse to fight' has been vindicated rather than disproved by the years between.

On a more practical level was the problem of how best to serve one's community and oneself while contributing as little as possible to actions that would sow dragon's teeth. At the end of October 1942 my mother and JD moved to a guest house in the Wye Valley, relieving me of my domestic and chaperoning duties, and enabling me to join the connected market gardening community consisting largely of what might loosely be called broad-church Christian pacifists. I shan't expatiate on my relief at finding myself with very normal young people of a similar age and persuasion. On 22 December 1942 I was recognised and registered as a conscientious objector by a court ('tribunal') in Bristol, and in February I moved across the country to farm in the Thames Estuary, and later in Kent, before applying to join the Friends' Ambulance Unit abroad. Finding that the FAU was open only to older members of the Society of Friends, I started to work with the Friends' Relief Service in November 1944. The preceding years in Essex and Kent, when London and the Home Counties were bearing the brunt of the conventional air raids and the later V1s (flying-bombs, or 'doodlebugs'), which were followed by the 'if-you-hear-it-you're-alive' V2 rockets, gave ample opportunity for testing, and invariably deepening, conviction. The V1s, although their on-target effect was as horrific as any other 'successful' bomb, brought a ludicrous element that intensified awareness of the sheer madness of war. Pruning or cultivating in the Kent fields round Horsmonden (an area of starkest contrast to the depressing wastelands on the Essex side of the Thames Estuary) added another dimension of lunacy: to be toiling away, usually alone, while puttering doodlebugs passed overhead, often within catapult reach, aimed at London but all too likely to fall short or be shot down. The ear grew accustomed to the decibels indicating distance and direction …

Doing mostly dull, repetitive work, I lived in my own mind more than had usually been possible in Essex, and when I wasn't thinking of the girl I had known there, whom I loved with that unrepeatable intensity of late teenage awakening, my thinking centred on the war, on the values it prompted and destroyed, on one's own place and responsibility in the so-called scheme of things. Work on the land brings us closer than town life to the facts of life and death. It had not hardened me to the act of killing, *per se*, for as an act of mercy it must be defensible, and this human right could only logically be extended to any sentient creature to be spared undue pain. If squeamishness, or fear of consequences, deters mercy, inaction may be understandable, but hardly praiseworthy; but what is deplorable is unquestioning acceptance of another's 'solution' of pitting one evil against another, when we feel gut-certain that this can only aggravate and compound the wrong. I felt I could understand that great fear, or to be caught up in mass hysteria, may strain such conviction to breaking point, but I was increasingly certain that it revealed a tragic loss of commonsense to argue, for this reason, that no better solution should be envisaged, or no lesser sacrifice (such as of pride, territory or political control) be made to avert an evil so self-engendering and far-reaching in its destruction of lives and character as total war. Surveying the mess we are already making of the twenty-first century, I do not see we can avoid the need to evaluate the timeless wisdom of the 'Yogi' against the transient opportunism of the 'Commissar'. I am as convinced today as sixty years ago of an old *Black's Law Dictionary* maxim: 'Iniquissima pax est anteponenda justissimo bello' (The most unjust peace is to be preferred to the justest war).

Our unusual link is my only excuse for inflicting on you this unbridled retrospection, Javier; but I neither seek nor expect response, only your understanding of the influences to have affected my writing and publishing. So hold your hat on!

Just as my early reading of Graves, Gregg, Owen, Ponsonby and Sheppard helped make me aware of the futility of violence between nations, I was alerted through my personal experience during the Second World War that it has its roots in the wider savagery with which we treat the natural world. Only much later did I catch up with the writings of such as Victor Hugo, Montaigne, Gilbert Murray, Rousseau, Schopenhauer, Voltaire, and the cardinals Manning and Newman – powerful aids to recognising that the notion of kinship with all sentient creatures must, through positive education, be instilled in us all if we are ever to complete the greater task of behaving better toward each other.

I was pleased to learn that you had made the Redonda Prize-winning J. M. Coetzee a duke! He, like Milan Kundera and many of today's writers, has shown that the empathic concept is taking hold. The recently departed Isaac Bashevis Singer's short story 'The Letter Writer' contains, for me, perhaps the most powerful and double-edged passage I know in support of the above concept:

> In his thoughts, Herman spoke a eulogy for the mouse who had shared a portion of her life with him and who, because of him, had left this earth. 'What do they know – all these scholars, all these philosophers, all the leaders of the world – about such as you? They have convinced themselves that man, the worst transgressor of all the species, is the crown of creation. All other creatures were created merely to provide him with food, pelts, to be tormented, exterminated. In relation to them, all people are Nazis; for the animals it is an eternal Treblinka.'

One of my books owes its title to Albert Schweitzer's warning that 'until he extends the circle of his compassion to all living things, man will not himself find peace'. A profound truth, I believe, that could turn the tide of history more radically than any other. Among poets, it was Yeats who was one of my earliest influences with his moving line 'A pity beyond all telling is hid in the heart of love', though I did not fully perceive its universality until a serious threat to the future of my first daughter aroused a painfully strong protective reaction. I then realised the illogicality of reserving the deepest level of concern only for those dearest to us – or even for the entire human race – yet not merely denying it to most other forms of sentient life, but contributing actively, unnecessarily, if unthinkingly, to the fear and suffering of the infinitely greater number of creatures on whom our misguidedly nurtured species preys. It took me seven ground-breaking years 'finding the words' to put together *The Extended Circle*, but so far as I can judge, the time was not wasted.

When all is said and done, a decent regard for the well-being of weaker creatures can be justified merely – if one wishes – by the benefit it brings to our own. That, after all, is the crux of the ecological argument that is increasingly accepted as being inescapable. Personally, I would rather it came about through a change in the human heart than for reasons of self-interest, for the latter's virtue is only that of necessity, and I do my best to contribute my mite to the process without overtly thumping tubs, beating drums (heaven forbid), or hammering my friends into the ground like tent pegs. In fact, the recognition that our foremost need is for education based on humane principles, and that this realisation can claim historical and literary legitimacy, is not a thousand miles away from your own statement that 'in a way all literature is a translation, as in fact all speech is a translation too'.

Nevertheless – *mea culpa, un abrazo*, and – I hope – ever yours
JON

Javier's reply was, of course, courteous and non-committal, as befitted a fantasy monarch whose teaching years at Oxford had introduced him to its rich seam of eccentricity and unorthodoxy; such acquaintance soon teaches the futility of mere polemics. The ontological doubt that permeates his novels may well have been enough to quash any urge to analyse and debate. Life for many fiction writers is observation, not comment. But while I cannot wish upon him the day in which he might tune into realisation of the indivisible nature of sentient existence, wherein concern for all creatures' suffering cannot safely be circumscribed by race, colour, gender, boundaries, and species – for all suffer and are mortal – were that day to arrive, what a lodestar might even little Redonda become for the twenty-first century's ailing monarchies and its endangered citizens. And here, for myself, has been my justification for my publishing. One conviction that has grown steadily in the course of adding a few score of books – only a handful of my own – to the world's vast storehouse of largely ignored perceptions has been how hollow are the endless assurances that 'lessons have been learned'. Children may learn, but adults are virtually unteachable unless receptive to what is being said. Almost everything essential to our survival and characters has to be learned or sensed by the time we are seven, as the Jesuits know only too well. If there is to be a posterity left to judge us as having proved our adulthood, we have to be equipped in those early years to resist the pressures that would force us into the acquisitive and self-obsessed mould of our feckless Western 'civilisation', and would sell us the short-sighted belief that our concern need be only with the human predicament, and that we can afford to see our obligations to the environment as merely peripheral. Many can reason that this is so, and can predict where it must end, but as yet the pressure on the lawmakers, and on those who profit from chaos, has had all the effect of a butterfly stamping on a bull. Our numbers continue to rocket, and our greed makes ever more unsustainable demands on the environment; to write off the implications of such obvious facts as a lack of faith in the future merely postpones acceptance of the only answer – that it lies in our hands alone to understand and adopt, in the deepest spiritual, ecological, and practical sense, the meaning and demands of an international focus on humane education.

But back to those little local difficulties ...

11

Causes and Effects

Having decided to enlarge the house rather than rebuild it or buy another, from late in 1971 until the spring of 1975 we had the builders with us for as often as they condescended to be on site. The garage was rebuilt to give offices, workshop, a stable, and further storage above and below. Massive steel RSJs went into the first floor to bear the tons of books needing to be housed. (Some years later, the local blacksmith repaired a heavy Victorian weather vane for me that had crashed to the ground in a gale. He replaced the cock with a mythical vane in the shape of a centaur with drawn bow – an epigone of our publishing logo, copied from a ring found in the ruins of Ephesus – but the metamorphosis rides the Fontwell office block to this day.) Even more RSJs went into the big walk-in loft above the north wing that was built on to the east end of the house, for my ground-floor office in the 1966 extension needed to come into its own as the dining room it was designed to be, and the growth in files and library had been oppressive for some time. The new wing gave us a larger living room, also a bedroom, bathroom, and small kitchen, and we were able to let this almost self-contained portion of the house in later years, first to actors and producers doing the summer seasons at the Chichester Festival Theatre (with Ingrid Bergman expected for starters, we bought a king-size bed that henceforth was called The Bergman, and it saw out such delightful tenants and friends as Wendy Hiller, Donald Sinden, Angela Thorne, Ian Ogilvy, Penelope Wilton, and Kenneth Haigh); and later for longer periods to often less entertaining, but usually congenial, singles and couples whose infinitely varied private lives and not always private problems kept us fully in touch with most aspects of the real world we might be missing beyond the surrounding garden walls.

My mother, whose commonsense about her health and diet failed to match her recommendations for the cures of the world's malaise, pushed her frailty beyond all reasonable limits, but continued to hammer her typewriter until her condition made hospital the only option. She died there, after a last few weeks with us in Fontwell, on 17 January 1972, declining food and treatment, and pulling out any intrusive tubes until she lapsed into the coma that was merciful to all involved. The priest who offered her his services on the ward recalled the encounter until his own time came. Our parents were all to die in the 1970s, three of them in circumstances needing family support. Meanwhile, their grandchildren had begun to sniff the pastures of independence, and the small Chelsea flat that had become a must as a London office cum pied-à-terre was for some time a home for Tilly when she had changed from state to private teaching.

My own writing, with the media aftermath, was demanding more time than was there for the taking, but if 1972's Centaur output had been modest, 1973's was happily non-existent apart from a third edition of *Donkeys* and a fourth of *Teaching Without Tears*. But the need to invite business from friendly bookshops still took time, and in November 1973, for no particular reason I can recall, I listed all book-sellers who had ordered Centaur books since publication of the last (1971) catalogue. They came to approximately 1,000 different firms. In some businesses, I suspect, the chore of tending that number of customers would be the main responsibility of one person.

Although trips abroad, often with 'business content' (a phrase well known to the self-employeds' tax inspectors), had from 1955 to 1973 totalled no more than twenty-two, each meant that I returned to a backlog of daunting proportions, taking anything from a few weeks to three months to clear. Jennifer did what she could, especially forwarding orders to a distributor or, later, meeting the more important indents herself. Aspiring solo publishers with itchy feet, please note: self-employment in the book world is not for nine-to-five loners.

Not that I resented the burden of work. Stresses and irritations come in most walks of life, and while strict self-employment can mean free-dom-in-chains, for a certain temperament anything is better than being a cog in someone else's machine. Rereading 'The Centaur in Our Paddock', my response to the *Bookseller*'s 1969 invitation to give an account of Centaur's fifteen years of survival, I have found its reminders of the frustrations, uncertainties, and sheer slog of coping with every aspect of bringing a book into being – not to mention the need to live off the results – evocative enough to prompt a tightening in the stom-ach; but this was followed by an all-the-stronger wave of relief that I am now in the relatively calm waters that less sensitive friends dismis-sively see as my retirement.

In 1974 only one title was published. Its author, Catherine Roberts, a graduate of the University of California, was a professional microbiologist whose increasing dissatisfaction with the morally neutral attitude of the scientific establishment led her to abandon a successful career at the Carlsberg Laboratories in Denmark, where she worked for fifteen years after emigrating from her native California in 1946 (she returned in 1977). Dr Roberts devoted the rest of her life – she died in 1993 – to studying classical Greek and to writing and lecturing on the philosophical, ethical, and evolutionary implications of modern biological and medical research. Her first book, *The Scientific Conscience*, was originally published by the New York firm of George Braziller in 1967, being welcomed by Lewis Mumford as an important contribution to the broadening stream of criticism within science, represented by people as eminent as Michael Polanyi, Szent-Györgi, and René Dubos. In the UK, the *Observer* welcomed 'this very interesting and powerful book'; the *Ecologist* and *Aryan Path*, from their differing viewpoints, gave it intelligent and enthusiastic attention; but the most important of the few perceptive notices was by R. A. Crowson in *Nature*. It was not enough, however. By the late 1990s, yearly sales could be counted on one hand, and their total ran into hundreds rather than the thousands that the importance of the debate merited.

In April 1974 my father – his third and most long-suffering wife having left him in the care of his Irish maid in order to pursue a career that would give more rewarding rein to her undoubted talents – came to live in the now-completed wing for the last three years of his life. A fraught childhood had contributed to a depth of disillusionment that had made him no more happy than were the recipients of his failings. We were all the family he had left, bar a sister who was as jealous as her other siblings of his outward success. With our girls still coming and going, and my work not only bringing visitors to the house, but matters for discussion in which he could participate, we were probably his best shot for a future that could have been a good deal more lonely in the Surrey house that we were to persuade him was the least his wife deserved to inherit. He had suffered a horrendous driving accident a few years earlier, and this left him in the increasing grip of Parkinsonism, unable to pursue any of the sports he had enjoyed, and with nothing to do but brood on a long and varied career that had brought travel to most corners of the earth, but neither happiness nor the titular reward he could have expected had he kept a lower domestic profile. A sad end for a talented man whose only youthful failing in the eyes of his philandering and intemperate father was that he defended his gentle mother from her husband's bullying.

His presence in the wing across the drive partly accounted for no new titles being prepared for 1975. The hiatus may well have helped to recharge the batteries, however, and with Tilly getting married from the house that April, and *Food for a Future* being published in hardback by Davis-Poynter Ltd at the end of that month, there would have been little time to prepare additions to the Centaur stables.

I had begun the writing of that book in June 1973. My exchanges with Reg Davis-Poynter were as smooth as might be expected where both parties are publishers with long experience of dealing with authors, and few illusions about the problems of their trade, and Reg's professionalism encouraged the book's no-holds-barred advocacy of the perhaps inevitable, if eventual, abandonment of much animal food. It took two years from start to publication, and the publisher's press-briefing read:

> *Food for a Future: the ecological priority of a humane diet*
> Physiologically, man is not intended for a carnivorous (or omnivorous) diet – the retention in humans of the appendix and of teeth characteristics similar to those of fruit-eating anthropoids are sufficient obvious examples of this fact. Unfortunately, to most people a vegetable almost invariably means cabbage or carrot or some other shop-worn accompaniment to the daily meals of animal or bird. Yet the definition of a vegetable is both clear and wide: it means a plant, whether root, stalk, leaf, flower, fruit or seed. Almost everything we eat is derived either from vegetables or from animals, and even the bulk of the latter are largely vegetarian and therefore supplying us indirectly, wastefully, and at unnecessary cost, with what we would do better to consume at source.
>
> Jon Wynne-Tyson stresses the importance of a humane diet as part of an altogether more responsible way of life, emphasising that what we eat three or four times a day, and the immense proportion of the world's economy that is devoted to our stomachs, are possibly the most important aspects of our daily lives. But although the ecological arguments are formidable, we must also halt the truly terrible amount of suffering which we knowingly and unnecessarily inflict on other sentient creatures. Until man faces the enormity of his crimes against animals, he cannot logically be expected to show a consistent and lasting compassion toward his own kind.

In this new millennium it is not uncommon for scientists to discuss publicly the impact on human health of our exploitation and domestication of other species ever since early agriculture harnessed them to human use, and especially where populations have reached their critical density. But where, today, fewer are ignorant of the medical, nutritional, environmental, and humane reasons for why plant foods should be given prior place in the human diet, it was still somewhat revolutionary stuff for general circulation in the 1970s. The suffering of sentient non-human species prompted little concern outside the pages of magazines from a handful of campaigning organisations.

Since the end of the nineteenth century the most important corpus on the 'rights' of animals had come from the classical scholar, poet, naturalist, and humanitarian reformer, Henry Shakespear Stephens Salt (1851–1939). (In recent years there has been a shift from the concept of animals' *rights*, to an acceptance of our human *obligations* toward other forms of sentient beings.) His best-known book in the field of humane conservation, *Animals' Rights Considered in Relation to Social Progress*, first published in 1892, was forgotten from the mid-1920s until 1980. But it has been in print since then, and is better written and more to the point than many of the theses by students on today's academic ladder. The 1993 volume of the *Dictionary of National Biography*, edited by C. S. Nicholls, usefully expands Salt's entry in *Who's Who*, and George Hendrick's *Henry Salt* (University of Illinois Press, 1977) is a more reliable Life than Stephen Winsten's *Salt and His Circle*, 1951. Two books published in 1964 were the first to have significant impact after the Second World War. One was *All Heaven in a Rage* by the distinguished journalist E. S. Turner, which showed how 'the British race was persuaded, shamed and legislated into showing mercy to the brute creation'. The other was the very influential and widely publicised book on animal abuse, Ruth Harrison's *Animal Machines*. It centred on the cruelty, folly, and dangers of intensive farming. Although its author lacked an academic or scientific background her book was so powerfully and authoritatively written that even the hard-nosed newspapermen were moved, and helped to ensure that consciences were deeply aroused. Without antagonising those whose practices she opposed, Ruth worked through several animal welfare organisations and founded the Farm Animal Care Trust. She died in June 2000.

On 10 October 1965 the *Sunday Times* published Brigid Brophy's seminal article 'The Rights of Animals'. It covered the main areas of our ill-treatment of the animal kingdom, including vivisection and medical research. Despite her presidency of the National Anti-Vivisection Society, however, no obituary mentioned that, after six years' endurance of MS, Brigid could still write in her *Baroque 'n' Roll*: 'In the search for the cause of multiple sclerosis and other mysterious diseases, and for a means of curing them, it is vital that no animal, human or non-human, be tortured or killed.' I was pleased that *The Times* published my letter drawing attention to the passage.

In 1971 Brigid had contributed to *Animals, Men and Morals*, 'an enquiry into the maltreatment of non-humans', edited by Stanley and Rosalind Godlovitch and John Harris. It was a collection of essays, largely by young Oxford academics. Most of its contributors seem to have taken other paths subsequently, but those that stayed the course included Ruth Harrison, Maureen Duffy, and Richard D. Ryder. (The latter's *Victims of Science*, subtitled 'The use of animals in research', and the most authoritative study of the subject, written by a senior clinical psychologist at Warneford Hospital, Oxford, was to be published by Davis-Poynter Ltd in 1975, the same year as *Food for a Future*. It was extensively reviewed, and triggered a series of debates in Parliament which led, in time, to the reform of the law controlling animal experimentation with the passing of the new Act in 1986.) The 1971 essays' passage was eased by Peter Singer's 1973 notice in the *New York Review of Books*, and their main value was probably in imparting a whiff of academia-blessed respectability to the earlier interest aroused by Turner and Brophy.

In 1980, when the RSPCA was experiencing one of its lows, Brigid was to be a trenchant supporter of an informal group, chaired in its first and most effective six months by that formidable humanitarian John Alexander-Sinclair. Its purpose was to agree how best to resist a motion put forward at the February EGM, calling for expulsion from the Society of eleven progressive Council members. The Constitutional Group, as it was named after a preliminary meeting in the Athenaeum Club, brought together influential and determined advocates of putting animals into politics, including Lord Houghton, Richard D. Ryder, and Richard Adams. Most sessions were held in the Wig and Pen Club opposite the Law Courts in Fleet Street, the smallness and antiquity of the upstairs room adding, I thought, to the somewhat clandestine feeling of the proceedings. But the crisis being considered was more than a passing spat, and it was felt that it could be counter-productive to invite press attention to our efforts to encourage the Society toward a less complacent view of what they might achieve in the field of humane reform. By 1981, with the Group's contribution to that process completed, meetings were increasingly monopolised by RSPCA branch grievances and parochial side issues. This was not what the Group had been formed for, so as pressure groups go, it went. Anyone interested in the bumpy road of the RSPCA's progress since its foundation in 1824 should read *Animal Revolution*, Richard Ryder's outstanding overview of the people and measures that have helped to mitigate humanity's long record of barbarity. Studied in conjunction with Keith Thomas's impressive *Man and the Natural World*, whose focus is mainly on changing attitudes in England between 1500 and 1800, *Animal Revolution* is a vital text for a reliable grounding in the history of the humane movement.

In 1969 and 1971 two exceptional books by John Vyvyan were published by Michael Joseph. Combining to give a deeply felt historical survey of animal experimentation, *In Pity and In Anger* and *The Dark Face of Science* preceded, and provided counterpoint to, *Victims of Science*. But although Nigel Dennis reviewed *The Dark Face of Science* as Book of the Week in the *Sunday Telegraph*, Vyvyan was a scholar whose chronic ill-health precluded pursuit of formal academic standing and performance, and the general reception was less than these splendidly conceived and moving works deserved.

As yet, nothing of substance on the major theme of the place of animal foods in human nutrition had appeared since Salt's inevitably dated and forgotten studies. Chapters three and four of *The Civilised Alternative* had been written, as was the rest of the book, to reach the more thoughtful young of the 1970s, and laid particular emphasis on the need to accept our obligations to other sentient beings. But the problem with getting balanced press attention for books covering a broad spectrum of concerns is that the ideas seen as least popular with the majority are the most likely to be disregarded. It was indicative of how uncoordinated and in-turned was the animal rights movement of that day that even the specialist media, apart from the *Ecologist* and *Resurgence*, overlooked *The Civilised Alternative*.

I did not expect Reg Davis-Poynter to do much better with *Food for a Future* than I had done with *The Civilised Alternative*. I underestimated him. He knew – where I only knew of – a go-ahead Australian girl called Carmen Callil who, after training as a buyer in the heyday of Marks and Spencer and working briefly for several publishers, had in 1971 started her own firm as a book publicist in her flat off Chelsea's

King's Road, before founding Virago Books in 1972. Reg had employed Carmen to handle his firm's publicity, and in 1975 *Food for a Future* was entrusted to her colleague Harriet Spicer, who specialised in books of environmental interest. A few weeks ahead of publication I called to see Harriet for a strategy discussion in the Cheyne Place flat. It was soon apparent why Reg had asked this able partnership to promote his list.

While Harriet encouraged author-participation in her campaign planning, all follow-up to what we agreed was her responsibility. The book brought not only radio and television interviews (the most disappointing of the former being when Roger Cook questioned me on 'The World At One' without actually mentioning the title), but also a flattering spread of press notices. It was quite something for *The Times* of that era to devote a sixteen-inch column headed 'Man as herbivore' in terms suggesting recognition of a trail-blazing book whose argument could not seriously be questioned. I will push my luck by quoting only a few lines from the latter:

> He writes with a passionate conviction, but backs every statement with enough facts to satisfy the most hard-headed statistic-seeker. Perhaps his most subtle achievement is the slow revelation that the arguments *for* meat-eating are in fact those that are emotional and irrational.

Although my concern over our treatment of animals sees that 'emotion and irrationality' as governing all forms of maltreatment, the book's focus on human dietary habits pigeon-holed me under that concern in the years following. I suffered this restriction gladly, however, as our dietary use of animals is certainly the greatest of our inflictions on other creatures. The book's basic argument struck a chord with a media keen to be seen in tune with young people whose postwar education was encouraging broader awareness of how the world ticked, and a more socially and environmentally sensitive questioning of their elders' acceptance of the status quo. The good press brought opportunities for talks, debates, panels, and even a totally inaudible address from the outside pulpit of St James's, Piccadilly. The most agreeable forum, in the depths of Cornwall, was convened by the ebullient Teddy Goldsmith to debate the motion that 'An ecological society must be a vegetarian one'. Teddy chaired, and I had the support of Dr Alan Long, then research consultant to the Vegetarian Society, and Peter Roberts, the founder of Compassion in World Farming, now a widely respected educational and campaigning organisation. The opposing team was made up of Michael Allaby, the *Ecologist*'s associate editor; John Seymour, an early and passionate exponent of organic farming, and big in pigs; and Colin Blythe, consultant to Friends of the Earth. A transcript was published in the December 1976 issue of the *Ecologist*, including discussion contributions from Lawrence Hills, founder of the Henry Doubleday Research Association; Nicholas Hildyard; and others.

A measure of the anxiety felt by vested interests about the spread of humane concern for animals was seen in the Cambridge Union Society's debate in 1987 on the motion 'That this House would welcome the universal adoption of vegetarianism'. Alan Long and I were the invited supporters of the motion, and in opposition were Professor Colin Spedding of the University of Reading, and Chris Oberst, Director-General of the powerful Meat and Livestock Commission. 'Debate', alas, was hardly the operative word. Oberst blandly ignored the arguments for the motion other than to deny their validity – a technique, it may be remembered, that got the flat-earth lobby nowhere – and both he and Spedding abandoned even minimal reasoning for semi-abuse and petulant denial. Needless to say, the motion was defeated, but two students who came up to me afterwards were sufficiently embarrassed to apologise for such an appalling level of debate.

In 1976 *Food for a Future* went into its first paperback edition under the Abacus/Sphere Books imprint, and in 1979 I published a further revised paperback under that of Centaur. Another revision appeared in 1988, published by Thorson/HarperCollins, by when the *Guardian* was not alone in having welcomed it as a 'classic'.

Part of my work on the eventual 1988 UK edition was to add Thomas Huxley's incontrovertible table of comparative anatomy from his great work *Man's Place in Nature*. This identifies Man's physiological characteristics as being essentially identical to those of the frugivorous anthropoid ape, establishing Man as the primate species furthest removed from the carnivora. The resurrection of Huxley's table seemed long overdue.

If others have been right to say that *Food for a Future* did more than any other text to lessen our greatest single form of animal exploitation, I may not die happy, but certainly grateful to those who helped me to make that contribution to a climate of thought and behaviour from which we ourselves can only benefit.

In 1976 – apart from *Readings for Assembly*, which sold steadily until 1984, then declined until out of print ten years later – the only notable new title was *British Manuscript Diaries of the Nineteenth Century*, compiled by John Stuart Batts, an English professor at the University of Ottawa. A check-list of the considerable amount of nineteenth-century material that had come to light since William Matthews's *British Diaries: an Annotated Bibliography 1442–1942*, it was not a must-have for Everyman, but it met the needs of a few hundred libraries and doubtless continues to do so.

Apart from having a personal interest in distributing for Thomas Gibson Publishing a catalogue of the scrapbook drawings (1939–49) of Stanley Spencer, the little work involved justified its appearance during Centaur's tick-over years of 1973–78. 1977 was a sparse year, and 1978's excitements were two barely noticed titles, both involving distribution rather than full publishing responsibility. One of these, *On the Fifth Day*, originated in the States by Acropolis Books of Washington, was edited by Richard K. Morris and Michael W. Fox. It offered a collection of essays on animal rights and human ethics by prominent and mostly American academics, including Robert S. Brumbaugh, Roger Caras, F. S. C. Northrup, and the incomparable Ashley Montagu, who dealt briskly with the limitations of such popular determinists as Robert Ardrey and Konrad Lorenz. *The Times*, not previously given to noticing humane selections originating in Britain, praised the American product lavishly, for which one was truly, if a little wryly, thankful.

As a title, *The Ungainsayable Presence* was a trifle irritating for my taste, but I was delighted to give these sensitive poems the Centaur imprint in 1977. Sponsored by the Foundation Trust, they were published anonymously by J. D. Beresford's eldest son Tristram, although (or perhaps because) work of a different kind had appeared under his name. An intensely private, serious, and quietly influential man, Tristram was agricultural correspondent to the *Financial Times* for seventeen years and an equerry to the Duke of Edinburgh for eight. He chaired a major environmental conference in the 1950s. Although written in poetic form, the selection was offered as 'products of a state of consciousness ... not unfamiliar to those who devote themselves to meditation and other offices as a regular practice, both in community with others and alone'. Whether judged as poetry or meditative soliloquies, being 'written at a time and in a place set apart exclusively for quietness', they have been found most accessible when studied in similar circumstances.

The best source for in-depth details of humbler-sized firms surviving into the late 1970s is Audrey and Philip Ward's fact-packed *The Small Publisher*, still available from The Oleander Press, 16 Orchard Street, Cambridge, CB1 1JT. Certainly the general climate was not encouraging to a small solo publisher inclined to examine current trends and to be wary of bandwagons. But by the 1980s the most expensive period of middle life seemed over, and it became possible – if on a modest scale – to indulge in some one-off and single-issue project preferences. Just when the shift of emphasis began is difficult to identify, but 1979 seemed a turning point.

No Centaur catalogue was published between 1974 and 1979, as the anticipated income from the largely loss-inviting titles of that period did not justify the cost of printing and despatching more than an updating checklist to show price advances and availability. Also contributing to the hiatus was my determination – now that my father had died, the children had left home, and Keele's Bookshop was performing its compensatory function – to try to do something about the State of Fiction.

My own frustration dated back to my inability to exploit the potentialities of some of the fiction I published many years earlier. I felt that books as well received as Laurence Clark's *Kingdom Come*, and for that matter my own *Square Peg*, did not deserve so short a life. My current novel, *Anything Within Reason*, which I thought my best to date, had been rejected as unlikely to make a sufficiently fat profit, even though the editorial director at Secker and Warburg had told my agent that he 'loved it'. Most of the rejections of *Anything Within Reason* made clear that its best qualities were what principally influenced the profit-motivated thumbs down. It seemed a dismal reflection on the values with which we were approaching the millennium.

Then an article appeared in the *Sunday Times* bewailing the much increased cost of books, and the cuts in local government spending that were accelerating the serious decline in Britain's public library system, whose support had long been vital to new fiction. Insufficiently attentive to the runes, by 1977 I had researched and lobbied for long enough to distribute a briefing sheet that tried to impart a confident sheen to Centaur's hope of reaching

a neglected section of the fiction public by publishing novels that are readable without being facile; intelligent without being obscure; satirical rather than relentlessly 'broad' or witlessly abusive. If you are tired of the Cult of the Sordid; of violence and sensationalism parading as Social Relevance; of the confusion of aimlessness and introspection with sense and sensibility, and of human affection with mechanistic sex, then we may have something for you.

We are not against the experimental if intelligible, purposive and workmanlike. We are happy to be unfashionable without being old fashioned, and sympathise with readers failing to find novels portraying reasonably recognisable people experiencing conceivable reactions to at least imaginable events.

By the cosy, the humdrum, and the merely 'wholesome', however, we are less excited, believing that both the highs and the lows of human behaviour have their place in fiction, but that it is the why, the when and the how – the balance and purpose – of their portrayal that make for merit or meretriciousness. The cultural climate we help to create, not laws of suppression, decides tomorrow's world.

Proteus Books [the proposed title for the project] will encourage wit, style and the well wrought in fiction that at least entertains, and at best provokes thought and feeling. Merely to depress one's readers is to lose them, and if our novels sustain faith in the future as much as interest in the present, they will have served some purpose.

The god Proteus could take on all manner of shapes. Only when firmly held would he resume the true one and answer the questions of those concerned with futurity.

David Lodge, one of the briefing's recipients, wrote to me in January 1978 that 'The whole business of fiction publishing interests me greatly; and it is certainly true that the big commercial publishers are often blinkered in their tastes and weak in their judgments – *Changing Places*, for instance, was turned down by three publishers before Secker took it [his fifth], and it turned out to be easily the most successful of my novels.'

In May 1978 Ion Trewin, that most dedicated of bookmen, gave an 'Up to the Hour' talk on Radio Four about my plans. Inevitably, most of the submitted typescripts that resulted were non-starters, 99% of even midlist slush-piles being dross in most editors' experience. But by August I was able to report that we had one novel definitely lined up, and two that could be publishable if the authors did adequate work on them. On 7 September Ion's Literary Diary in *The Times*, under

'Cheering News for the Novel', announced that my plans to assuage some of the public library fiction readers' thirst for a good midlist read seemed to be progressing. A few days later I confirmed that his piece had already produced two calls and eighteen letters, the total for the broadcast being by then eight and a hundred and fifty respectively.

It all came to very little. *The Queen Sends for Mrs Chadwick*, David Sander's caustic send-up of the political scene during Mrs Thatcher's reign, was the first and only published result of long effort and Ion's valued support. It failed to tempt the paperback imprint it deserved, but if nothing more, it helped to keep the flag flying in 1979. Another submission, a well if unevenly written and amusing story with an Indian setting, was worked on by the author, Sara Banerji, at my suggestion, and presumably efficiently, as she was taken up by Gollancz and is now an established novelist.

Of the second also-ran I heard no more. I suspect its creator could not face the horror of a rewrite. The State of Fiction had not been greatly improved by my concern for its welfare, and by the trouble to which I had put third parties, and I could not summon the time and resources to continue the interminable struggle to convince literary editors that a small non-fiction publisher in deepest Sussex was going to share the fiction cake with the big battalions.

A month after *Mrs Chadwick* received her brief flash of literary lime-light, 1979's modest total of five titles was swelled by J. M. Frayn's thoroughly sound and unsensational *Subsistence Farming in Roman Italy*: a title that said precisely what it was about, and much more the kind of thing expected from Centaur. Dr Frayn's study was respectfully noticed by the *Classical Review*, *Greece and Rome*, *Current Archaeology*, and other distinguished journals that matter in this some-what esoteric area.

The Centaur paperback of *Food for a Future* was also published that year. The print run of 5,000 copies, by being topped up with bought-in overstock of the American edition, lasted until the further updated Thorson edition was published in 1988, by which time it was a relief to pass the buck back to publishers big enough to take it in their stride; for while many small bulk sales of the Centaur edition had gone to campaigning organisations such as Animal Aid, the Vegan Society, and the Vegetar-ian Society, the inevitable single-copy orders that the small publisher must expect were as costly as any other cheap paperback to process. Edi-tions whose necessarily modest size is why bigger publishers have not been tempted, and whose content, format and number of pages can command a hefty unit price, are the *sine qua non* for the small firm that wants to survive. The really small publisher of a quality list can handle only so many titles each year, and his turnover is unable to support a sales team capable of maximising his list's potential. There is no way around this, other than to cease to stay small, or to handle more popular books, in which case he will have to grow larger to cope with the demand.

Although environmental concerns have been dominant for many years, the market for the books they have spawned has not been commensurate. To jump still further ahead chronologically, as recently as 1996 the senior editor of Thorsons/HarperCollins complained that even the conglomerates were finding bookshops to be serving authors poorly in the environmental field, and that 'issue titles' were not being reprinted when stock was exhausted. Organisational links, she confirmed, remained vital even to conglomerate publishers in that area, but helpful though these are, issue organisations are usually small, underfunded, and with memberships who are more doers than readers. It was pleasing evidence of the growth of concern for the humane aspect of ecological sensitivity that *Food for a Future* had gone through four editions by 1990, and should still be in print had I been able to make time for a further updating.

After spending January and February 1980 in Antigua writing the second half of *Banana Bird*, another visit to the States was needed to tend the American edition of *Food for a Future* and arouse interest in *The Extended Circle*. My own writing had created a hiatus in Centaur's already reduced output from July 1979 until autumn 1980. Highlights ranged from visiting the frighteningly informed and most amusing anthropologist Ashley Montagu in Princeton to real tennis in New York's Racquet and Tennis Club. After a quick visit to the zoo in Central Park to see if it had improved (it had not), I left the States with a better memory of the park: its brick-enclosed merry-go-round on which smartly dressed senior New Yorkers – obeying, maybe, their shrinks' advice – gently rotated on colourful steeds to slow-time vintage tunes of the Victorian fairground.

Any laurel-reclining mood engendered by the success of *Food for a Future* was diminished by the fourth of the five titles I took on in 1979 – a work so far removed from my interests that those given to karmic judgements might say that the horrifically time-consuming complications that followed were my just desserts. Michael Packard – another solo, rather smaller, and local publisher – had been offered a licence to published a handsomely presented and lavishly illustrated record, in diary form, of all Royal Navy and allied ship engagements and major naval events from the age of Hawkins and Drake to the present day. The Navy was happy to take a quantity of the first edition for disposal through their own outlets, but this covered only such costs as it was calculated would leave the publisher in need of selling x number of copies in order to break even and begin to make a profit. The balance of the initial costs, and possible need for later up-front investment in new impressions, were somewhat beyond what Michael, with a young family and a relatively new business, could spare if he was to finance other projects likely to bring more immediate success. He was far enough committed to be chin deep in negotiation with administrative levels of the Senior Service; worryingly involved with a printer whose approaching insolvency was exacerbating his problem of tackling a job beyond his capacity and expertise; and dealing with a couple of editors with as much experience of putting books together as any other two long-serving RN officers accustomed to the comparative simplicities of controlling lower ranks. Mike and I agreed that two heads might stand a better chance than one, and that the book should carry the Centaur imprint.

A certain edge was given to these plans for *The Royal Navy Day by Day* by the fact that it was the brain-child of the First Sea Lord, Admiral of the Fleet Lord Lewin, who not unnaturally was interested in its progress, and not indifferent to being personally involved. While predictably not familiar with the limitations and hazards of publishing day by day, he was able to draw on his capacity for recognising problems common to most campaigns, and when it came to dealing with naval personnel who might be applying their telescopes to an inappropriate eye, he was in a unique position to ensure that incipient mountains were reduced to molehills. He was also able to lay on hospitality somewhat outside the normal range of small independent publishers. In May 1979, six days before the book's publication, I attended *The Royal Navy Day by Day*'s first launch party on HMS *President*. The First Sea Lord was there in his number fives with accompanying satellites, and when Michael had expressed our pleasure in being involved in the project, Lewin addressed the rather taut company with brisk competence. Keith Speed MP, then the Navy Minister, and the editors, Captain A. B. Sainsbury and R. E. A. ('Bushy') Shrubb, signed an advance copy of the book, Lewin adding his name to round things off.

After that there was not a lot to do, as the effect of a garbed-for-action First Sea Lord on supposedly at-ease underlings was somewhat akin to that of the Queen on her garden-party guests – everyone standing around hoping to be noticed, but rather dreading the prospect of it actually happening. Few of the press, made of sterner stuff, bothered to attend: London's foremost literary editors are a shade too world-weary to be turned on by shoals of top brass on put-out-to-grass hospitality craft with low-slung pipes well capable of scalping unwary heads. The media coverage, although not vast, proved to be enough to alert the nation's retired senior naval officers, and those numerous organisations with an eye to a handsomely presented volume suitable for passing-out and other prize-giving ceremonies.

On the following day a more enjoyable wives-too reception was held on HMS *Victory* at the invitation of the Commander-in-Chief, Naval Home Command, Admiral Sir Richard Clayton, who gave the book a splendid puff by brandishing it at the television cameras from the quarter-deck, with appropriate exhortations. He then lunched twelve of us in nearby Admiralty House, having shown himself to be an entertaining character with a quite T. E. Lawrentian enthusiasm for motorcycling holidays with friends who shared his passion. Most of the food stood stiffly in aspic, and each guest was accorded his or her individual steward. Jennifer, one of whose happiest memories is of a very spoiling holiday in Gibraltar where her uncle was captain of the dockyard, took it all in her stride. I, one of whose earliest memories was of rowing an admiral friend of my parents on the boating pond at Southsea ('starboard, boy, starboard'), distanced myself from the rather gruesome meal by pondering whether sales would ever be thought commensurate with the splendour of its launchings.

It was a vast relief when the book had nearly sold out, and Terence Lewin was rooting for an updated reissue. In April 1991 he invited Michael and me to a lunch party in the director's ballroom-sized office at the National Maritime Museum to discuss the matter with Tony Sainsbury and one or two others. The impressively orchestrated meal was centred on what, at first glance, seemed to be hairless tennis balls impaled by knitting needles. When my plate descended from the steward's tray, closer inspection suggested, vaguely, avian origin – quail, maybe, or some undeservedly juvenile partridge. For me, being no expert in such matters, the absence of wings or legs defied certainty. The long skewers driven through each smooth grey globe reminded me of the ferocious steel pins with which my Victorian nurse held in place her awesome and inseparable hat. For politeness's sake I managed to detach a small piece of what I guessed could be the diminutive breast of my anonymous victim. It was totally tasteless; possibly comparable with a tennis ball lacking the flavour of its rubber. Mike said later that I might have found a little more excitement in the stuffing, but I did not penetrate that far, concluding that this was one of those occasions when ritual is put before sensual gratification. I doubt if anyone noticed or cared that I stayed with the vegetables, and the lunch was not really about food anyway. Lewin had responded cordially and impeccably throughout our collaboration, his calls and letters usually coming from his home address in Suffolk, and I think he had appreciated our occasional talks when I felt he needed soothing explanation of how things worked in the uncharted waters of the book world. However, neither Michael nor I felt we could summon the time and nervous reserves to take on the all too likely headaches of dealing with a new printer, with MOD moneymen, and with background personnel not necessarily naval. Some of the latter had already proved less than capable of understanding the logistics of book production and promotion, and as their priority had understandably been to keep the Chief of the Defence Staff happy, it had at times been difficult to call up the tact and patience that the situation required. With this scenario anticipated, I had therefore – ahead of the meeting and with Michael's approval – drawn up and sent to Lewin some notes for discussion. The gist was that we felt he might be better served if he were to entrust the revised edition to a publisher more attuned to militaria. While this should have been so, I suspected he might have difficulty finding a publisher prepared to take over a book from another firm. At a suitable point in the meal, therefore, I encouraged discussion of other possible options, and gave Lewin a copy of *Publishing Your Own Book*, together with a list of publishers and distributors sympathetic to militaria and nautical works, urging him not to rush into a decision.

Lunch over, Lewin showed us the recently refurbished Queen's House, after which Michael had to leave and Lewin gave me a lift to the House of Lords. His subseqent letter, confirming that the meeting had been most helpful in clearing his thinking and that 'we will immediately go into the possibilities of an NMM DIY publication', crossed with mine. The latter read:

> I hope I made clear, and not tactlessly, one reason why I think it
> better not to offer Centaur's imprint for a totally revised edition. I

do feel that you personally – and quite understandably – might not
be happy that Centaur was doing everything possible for the new
edition. You might also have the same feeling if a larger firm took
it over. And on both counts you would be right. The book was
your brainchild and you are very close to it. I have reached a time
of life when I don't want an Admiral of the Fleet's guns turned on
me when the sales graph fails to satisfy expectations!

I added that if he went ahead I would gladly offer what consultative
help I could, without expecting any return, for I had warned that the
slim *Publishing Your Own Book* could not meet all the problems that
might arise. He replied very appreciatively. Our subsequent exchanges
concerned the last days of the first edition, and whether we should run
off another impression to ensure continuity of sales until his revision
was off the press. The book had been in print for over twelve years, and
had sold more copies in 1990 than in the previous year. An interim new
impression should therefore have made a useful profit, there being no
typesetting and design costs involved in a further 'as-is' impression, and
would have been within the terms of our agreement. But Lewin was
worried that provisional reissue of Mark I would steal the thunder of
Mark II; so we agreed to drop the idea. This entitled us to compensa-
tion for lost income, and obliged me to negotiate with the NMM's
publications' consultant, whose partial knowledge of book publishing,
and a determination to be seen in Greenwich as a tough negotiator,
forced me eventually to get back to Lewin and invite a spot of rank
pulling. To his credit, he could see our reasoning, and in due course a
less unsatisfactory fee for relinquishment of our publishing rights was
agreed and paid.

In 1992 he wrote that '*Royal Navy Day by Day* Mark II will be
launched on 2 December, published by Ian Allen under the NMM
imprint'. Perhaps because the intervention of the publications consultant had not created the best climate for consulting the publisher of
Mark I, my offered advice had not been sought, which caused me no
sorrow. A year later I rang him to ask if the NMM edition was still
available – the continued receipt of orders and inquiries for our long
out of print edition prompted the suspicion that all was not well. An
unhappy Lewin confirmed this to be so. About 1,000 copies, he
believed, were left, and were being 'sold off cheaply'. I thought, but did
not depress him further by saying, that this seemed a very premature
decision when he had acres of space in which to store stock of a title

that would almost certainly be absorbed ever a year or two. While he was critical of the distribution, from what had been observable over the years I suspected that in-house problems at the NMM may have contributed to the project's collapse.

Although Jennifer had been rather disappointed when further involvement with what promised to be a steady little earner had been declined, I felt it had been the right decision. It had been another of those trips on the learning curve, and quite enough to convince any cautious SIP that the art of survival depends on a nose for when enough is enough – which in seas studded with drifting mines and icebergs can sometimes mean putting into harbour when still only in a Force 5.

In 1977 I had been invited by Satish Kumar to guest-edit a food-and-vegetarianism issue of his magazine *Resurgence*. Among those I asked for contributions was Andrew Linzey, a young Anglican priest whose first book, *Animal Rights*, had been published the previous year by SCM Press when he was assistant curate at Charlton-in-Dover in Kent. He was also actively involved with the RSPCA. Thanks largely to its chairman, Richard D. Ryder, the RSPCA was in 1977 being pressured by its radical minority of council members into sponsoring a two-day symposium on the ethical aspects of man's relationship with animals, and this took place on 18 and 19 August at Trinity College, Cambridge. It was to be seen as a landmark event in the history of the movement, and Linzey had a part in the early stages of its organisation. In his letter accepting my invitation, he suggested I contribute to the symposium. This was attended by most of the key figures in that era of the movement, and the papers given by twenty-eight of those attending were published by Centaur Press in 1979 as a record of the proceedings of the symposium. Needless to say, most contributions were worked over by their authors before appearing in cold print. Peter Singer, unable to get over from Australia for the conference, supplied the preface to the book. As the RSPCA bought 1,000 copies of *Animals' Rights: a Symposium*, edited by David Paterson and Richard D. Ryder, it was possible to produce a well-turned-out volume which was widely reviewed and helped to immortalise Richard's term 'speciesism', a somewhat awkward mouthful that is now to be found in all the cutting-edge dictionaries. 'Speciesism' figured in Richard's short but powerful 'declaration' which attracted 150 signatories at the symposium, and was published in the proceedings.

The Rights of Animals
A Declaration Against Speciesism

Inasmuch as we believe that there is ample evidence that many other species are capable of feeling, we condemn totally the infliction of suffering upon our brother animals, and the curtailment of their enjoyment, unless it be necessary for their individual benefit.

We do not accept that a difference in species alone (any more than a difference in race) can justify wanton exploitation or oppression in the name of science or sport, or for food, commercial profit, or other human gain.

We believe in the evolutionary and moral kinship of all animals and we declare our belief that all sentient creatures have rights to life, liberty, and the quest for happiness.

We call for the protection of these rights.

This declaration was signed by some one hundred and fifty people at the time of the symposium at Trinity College, Cambridge, on August 19th, 1977. The signatories included the following:

Richard Adams, John Alexander-Sinclair, Rev. Jack Austin, Mary Rose Barrington, Brigid Brophy, Bill Brown, R. MacAlastair Brown, John Bryant, Susan Bryant, Dr Stephen R. L. Clark, Rev. Kevin Daley, Carol Dear, Anne Douglass, Clare Druce, Maureen Duffy, Robert Elliot, Dr Michael Fox, Ann Cottrell Free, Prof. R. G. Frey, André Gallois, Clifford Goodman, Judith Hampson, Clive Hollands, Susan Hough, Lord Houghton, Robin Howard, Helen Jones, Ronnie Lee, Rev. Andrew Linzey, Jack Lucas, Ian MacPhail, John Melville, Mary Midgley, Chris Murphy, David Paterson, Kerstin Petersson, John Pitt, Ruth Plant, Prof. Tom Regan, Jan Rennison, Richard D. Ryder (Chairman, RSPCA Council), Mike Seymour-Smith, Prof. Peter Singer, Violet Spalding, Dr Timothy Sprigge, Margery Sutcliffe, M. E. Tait, Angela Walder, Phyllis Walker, Barbara Walton, Caroline Wetton, Dave Wetton, Alan Whittaker, Rev. B. Wrighton, Jon Wynne-Tyson, Robert Young.

The media reception was in general excellent, although Richard Dawkins in the *New Statesman* was as faint in his praise as he may have felt his reputation demanded and the assistant editor of the *Shooting Times* saw fit to apologise 'that our reviewer (not on our staff) could not be more complimentary'. His brackets were appreciated.

The only review that I felt called for a serious response was by William H. Thorpe, Fellow of Jesus College, Cambridge, and Emeritus Professor of Animal Ethology at that university. Published in the Quaker journal *The Friend*, it displayed scientific humanism at its arrogant worst. In part irrelevant to the nature and purpose of the published proceedings, and disturbingly Cartesian in its uncomprehending and illogical coldness toward any curb on exploitation of other life forms than man, it struck me as so deeply inappropriate in a member of the Society of Friends that I sent a letter to the journal's editor. When it was published, I resigned my membership, feeling that in a supposedly spiritually-attuned Christian denomination there was not room for both of us. The gesture was not an empty one, as it caused considerable soul-searching within the Society, and in 1988, despite being no longer a member, I was invited to become a vice-president of Quaker Concern for Animal Welfare. The group was established as the Friends' Anti-Vivisection Association on the following resolution:

> That this meeting, recognising the supreme importance of justice and compassion over conditions of physical benefit, emphatically rejects the view that cruel experiments on animals can be justified by the anticipation of useful results to the human race, even where it proved, which does not appear to be the case, that such results are obtainable thereby.

It is sobering to consider that the resolution was adopted on 22 May 1891.

Although it has been argued – largely by those lacking sympathy for the notion that non-human creatures deserve compassion from our stronger, smarter, and allegedly more intelligent species – that animals cannot have rights because they lack any concept of duty, the assertion is a scholarly quibble. Nor does it say much for the equally questionable claim that the British are a nation of animal lovers that it took a nineteenth-century Frenchman to state his conviction

> that pity is a law like justice ... kindness is a duty like uprightness. That which is weak has the right to the kindness and pity of that which is strong. Animals are weak because they are less intelligent. Let us therefore be kind and compassionate towards them.

Victor Hugo's view was certainly shared by Henry Salt. Fifty years Hugo's junior, Salt had no problem at all with the concept of humane education. Reprinted five times until 1922, his *Animals' Rights* then

lay dormant until the Society for Animal Rights in Philadelphia produced a new edition. This was published in America, and in England
by the Centaur Press, in 1980. The reissue carried a preface by Peter
Singer, and copious appendices, both biographical and bibliographical,
compiled by Charles R. Magel, author of invaluable *Keyguide to
Information Sources in Animal Rights* (Mansell, UK; McFarland,
USA). Already heralded by Keith Thomas in the *New York Review of
Books* as 'A masterpiece; it remains one of the most lucid and persua-
sive of all books written in defense of animals', Salt's classic work
received few reviews in the UK for the 1980 edition. The nearest to a
blessing from influential orthodox papers was Brigid Brophy's review
in the *TLS*:

> Reissued, with trimmings, by the Centaur Press, which thereby
> keeps up its honourable record on this subject, and lives up to its
> species-reconciling name ... [*Animals' Rights*] appeals not to
> mercy (the other animals, Salt points out, are not criminals) but to
> justice, and the argument at its heart is an expansion of Jeremy
> Bentham's prophecy that, having 'begun by attending to the
> condition of the slaves', human beings will eventually extend the
> protection of the law 'to any sensitive being'.

Helen Jones, the dedicated woman who founded the (later International) Society for Animal Rights in 1959, and ran it until her self-
inflicted death in 1998, was rare among members of the movement in
not only realising the importance of books to the spread of radical
ideas, but in being prepared to work for their distribution at a time
when few such views were allowed to disturb the complacency of tradition and unthinking habit. In the States, the (I)SAR was already
promoting *Animals' Rights: a Symposium*, and the Centaur edition of
Food for a Future. Through Helen, and via another fervent Salt
admirer, John Ponting, from whom I bought a quantity of books and
papers from Salt's library, I was able to trace his second wife Catherine
(née Mandeville). In June 1981 Jennifer and I called on her in her rented
room in a small house in Brighton, a short distance from Henry's last
home. Ninety, nearly blind, of lowly origins, she was as bright, quick,
and almost as small, as a cockney sparrow. Prompt to correct my
assumption that she had been her husband's housekeeper before their
marriage in 1927 (she seemed a little offended by what she saw as the
implications of the suggestion), she confirmed that she had only gone
in during the day as his 'home help'. Though clearly devoted to her

memories of Henry, and forty years his junior, she saw him through unclouded wifely eyes; a trait that Salt's friend George Bernard Shaw had found amusing and endearing. When I explained why I wished to do what I could to widen public knowledge of Henry and his works, Catherine asked me to be his literary executor, but she was not over-impressed to learn that I had invited Lord (Fenner) Brockway to write an introduction to a new edition of Salt's *Seventy Years Among Savages*, seen as spicy in its day. 'Fenner', she said, 'was a frightful old bore. Not a patch on Mr Shaw.' I had to agree, but then I had not met Fenner until the garrulity of old age was firmly in charge. Of her late husband's Socialist principles, Catherine was cautiously sceptical. The son of an upper-crust colonel in the Royal Bengal Artillery, Salt became a King's Scholar at Eton and went on to Cambridge University in 1871, return-ing to Eton as a master for nine years after winning a first class in the Classical Tripos of 1875. He devoted the rest of his long life to writing many and distinguished books, including some splendid satirical verse, and to humanitarian causes encompassing all species, choosing a 'harmless' (vegetarian) and simple life in a cottage at Tilford, in Surrey. Henry's essential goodness seemed to have made him no enemies, save among bullies of weaker creatures, but fond of him though Catherine was, reverence was no part of the package.

On a later occasion, after recording an interview with Catherine, we asked her to choose the hotel where she would like to be given tea. Faced with a wide selection of the Metropole's sandwiches, she chose the turkey. The chandelier did not fall, and I suspect she would have made the same choice in Henry's day, in the unlikely event that he had agreed to abandon his spartan lifestyle to eat a little bread in such over-stated surroundings. Her fondest memories of Henry were of his musi-cal voice, his sense of humour, his happy disposition, and his love of flowers and country walks. His ethical socialism she saw as 'Just Henry'. She died in 1984, aged ninety-three.

There was special pleasure in being able, with Helen Jones's blessing, to pay Catherine some rather inflated royalties from the sales of *Animals' Rights*. I wish I had met her husband, but although my mother and I lived only a bus-ride away, I knew nothing about him when we left Brighton in 1939, the year he died, and I made no record of anything J.D. may have told me about him. My mother, who shared Henry's love of the countryside, was all too prone to haul me on to the Sussex Downs for healthy walks, and I have thought since of the slight possibility that we might have unknowingly passed Henry in the company of Shaw or Edward Carpenter in the Devil's Dyke or in the wild-flowered lanes of Poynings.

But I was able to make another small contribution to Henry's memory by writing a one-hour play, *A Pinch of Salt*, which I was invited to put on at the Cheltenham Festival of Literature in October 1989, where I also did a workshop with J. L. Carr on publishing one's own books. Some theatre friends had generously offered to give a reading from *The Extended Circle* (my 1985 'dictionary of humane thought', consisting of 'the voices of people who down the ages have thought about man's place in nature'), entrusting me to compere by linking the chosen passages. And after Michael Denison, Dulcie Gray, Angela Thorne, and Christopher Timothy had wowed the audience of near 400 they gave an unsurprisingly professional rendering of the play. In its crowded hour it traced Salt's life from schoolhood to death, its core being his sad first marriage in 1879 to Catherine ('Kate') Leigh Joynes, daughter of a fellow master at Eton. As George Hendrick records, Kate called herself an Urning. In his preface to Stephen Winsten's book, Bernard Shaw confirms that Carpenter taught Kate that Urnings were a chosen race, which cannot have helped her to find a harmonious balance in her marriage to the seemingly (and, if so, fortunately) low-sexed Henry, given that Kate's proclivities could not have fitted her to take much initiative. Her orientation was more than the trusting, gentle and unworldly Henry could take in his stride. But he bore up manfully and kept his thoughts on more productive matters.

The plan to reprint *Seventy Years Among Savages* foundered because the RSPCA withdrew their undertaking to share its distribution, and none could be arranged for the States, but the book was drawn on for the Salt anthology I was to publish in 1989. I could write much more of Salt, whose influence Gandhi was to acknowledge, and whose many other friends included W. H. Hudson, G. K. Chesterton, Ralph Hodgson, Olive Schreiner, Ramsay MacDonald, Ruskin, Meredith and Hardy. The widespread eulogies at his death seemed at odds with the bitter truth that few had shown the courage to endorse his unarguable precepts, let alone put them into practice.

There are so many friends and co-workers worldwide who have supported my endeavours over animal rights, but one in particular I must cite – North America's prolific Tom Regan, co-editor with Peter Singer in 1976 of *Animal Rights and Human Obligations*, later to publish a volume of essays, *All That Dwell Therein*, in which he contrasted his essentially 'rights' standpoint with that of Singer, whose utilitarian stance brought reservations from those responsive to E. F. Schumacher's view that 'it is impossible for any civilisation to survive without a faith in meanings and values transcending the utilitarianism of comfort and survival' (*A Guide for the Perplexed*). In 1983, Tom's major work, *The Case for Animal Rights*, was published.

More than any other two academic writers, Regan and Singer have kept the debate going at campus level for many years. In his preface to the latter work, Tom expressed his hope of having written a book

> that would command the attention of my professional peers in philosophy, one that had more philosophical substance than shadow, inviting the critical application of philosophy's highest standards, including rigor, clarity, justification, analysis and coherence. The dilemma faced, quite simply, was that a work that perks the attention of philosophers can put others to sleep, while one that keeps the non-philosopher interested runs the risk of philosophy's benign neglect.

I have no problem with recognising Tom's dilemma. But he found a comfortable balance, and his output has been enormous, not just numerous books, papers and articles, but even directing a film on religious attitudes to animals entitled *We Are All Noah*, and co-editing, with Andrew Linzey, *Song of Creation* – an anthology of professionally-written poetry inviting sympathy for the plight of other species without descending into mawkishness.

Centaur's growing focus on our obligations to other species did not imply any lessening concern for human suffering. On the contrary. My efforts on behalf of non-humans have been to help narrow the gulf between Western society's consideration for the human plight and our largely unthinking global exploitation of all other forms of sentient life. But if Mark Twain's dictum – 'Man is the only animal that blushes, or needs to' – passes you by, no diatribe from me will have much effect.

The shockingly successful destruction of the World Trade Centre on '9/11' has underlined the relevance of several trenchant studies of the state of Western society. In 1998 Niall Ferguson's *The Pity of War*, though not taking a positively pacifistic stance, graphically emphasised the weakness of armed might as a 'solution' to conflict between nations. In 1999, a Birkbeck Reader in History, Joanna Bourke, in her book *An Intimate History of Killing*, capped with overwhelming chapter-and-verse the peace-promoting works that influenced me in my youth.

Contemporaneously, both books were complemented by Jonathan Glover's moral history of the twentieth century, *Humanity*. In the twenty-first century, numerous texts have already made their contributions. Richard J. Evans's scholarly *The Coming of the Third Reich*, like its slighter predecessor Norman G. Finkelstein's *The Holocaust Industry*, does much to get recent history into perspective, attended by a number of studies of wars and human folly in general and particular. Few can be written off as the products of irresponsible journalists or weirdo revisionists, and most offer little hope of improvement in our species, or of a wider field of concern.

In their less strident way, however, academic and professional writers continue to help lift awareness of the need for broader and less anthropocentric systems of humane education. Few speak for greater sensitivity within the established Church, though Christianity might be thought to retain the potentiality for promoting that process. But while what serves me for a religious sense has no sectarian label, I acknowledge that whatever might be said for an enlightened humanism, our temporal society lost something of inestimable value in forgetting that affinities rather than hatreds must be cultivated if peaceful coexistence is to be achieved. 'Green' thinking offers some wise precepts, but man-centred pantheism is short on awe – and without awe, alas, there is no safeguard against the sly pull of self-interest.

A generation ago, Donald R. Griffin's *Questions of Animal Awareness* argued that non-human animals are conscious, thinking entities; a view which brought derision from those ignorant of Darwin's view that 'the love of all living creatures is the most noble attribute of man', and of his great work *The Expression of the Emotions in Man and Animals*. There was entrenched opposition to acknowledgement of other creatures' capacity for pain, sorrow, joy, astonishment, affection and loyalty, for recognition of their existence would have raised unthinkable implications and obligations. The mindset that two centuries earlier had swallowed Descartes' assertion that the screams of tortured beasts were of no more consequence than the squeaking of a rusty gate was still inviting the doldrums of credibility in which many scientists now find themselves.

Griffin's recent *Animal Minds: Beyond Cognition or Consciousness* (updating a 1992 text) could usefully be read alongside Frans de Waal's simultaneous *The Ape and the Sushi Master: Reflections of a Primatologist*; this argues a need to recognise that non-humans possess culture, developing – at whatever pace is appropriate to the species –

by accident, observation, experimentation, refinement of acquired skills, and in verbal and symbolised language, as we ourselves are assumed to have done, however imperfectly. I recommend making these works a trilogy by adding *The Great Ape Project: Equality and Humanity*, edited by Paola Cavalieri and Peter Singer, whose contributing scientists and philosophers have helped to bring reforming legislation in New Zealand, Australia, and the USA, by advocating the extension of the human ideal of equality to all the great apes. Our knowledge of them, at every scientific and observational level, shows there to be no sound, civilised argument than can tenably deny them that status. Singer's *Writings on an Ethical Life*, and Richard Ryder's *Painism*, are important later contributions, complementing the inspiring *Animal Minds and Human Morals* by Richard Sorabji, Professor of Ancient Philosophy at King's College, London, which shows a welcome focus on the tragic condition of both human and non-human creatures.

Students preferring the wisdom of the ancients to that of the post-Darwinians may know from *The Extended Circle* that from Pythagoras ('For as long as man continues to be the ruthless destroyer of lower living beings, he will never know health or peace') through Plutarch and many other major thinkers (even – as examples of enlightened religionists – the cardinals Manning and Newman: 'It is almost a definition of a gentleman to say he is one who never inflicts pain'), it has been unarguable that humanity must change course or perish – either by violence or by descent.

Is realisation that the fate of mankind is inextricably and causally linked with its behaviour toward the rest of sentient life beginning seriously to influence the agenda for this millennium? One should perhaps not ask questions at the end of chapters; but as the belief seems to be growing that extension of the 'circle' is vital to any meaningful survival, there could be reason for hope, if not for sitback optimism.

12

Taking Stock

The effective management of stock is crucial for all publishers, large or small. In the 30 May 1981 issue of the *Bookseller*, I published an article called 'Your Stock and Hard Times'.

As much of today's remaindering fever seems due to accountants' hysteria at the cost of warehousing stock, one small independent publisher's experience of backlist survival may be of interest.

Some 20 years ago I built a 25 by 20 foot timber boat shed within 200 yards of the sea on the south coast. Its walls' unplaned planks overlap with an accuracy that makes invading crawlies fall about laughing. Its roof is of asbestos corrugated sheeting that impedes neither wind nor rodents. Its cement floor has a damp-proof membrane, but a four-foot-deep inspection chamber is presently half full of water. The shed is in a paddock giving no shelter from sun, rain, or the Solent's salty mists.

In the late 1960s I began to store books there after a disastrous flood at our binders'. By 1970 the shed contained many thousands of books, most of them in single-wrapped packets stacked up to eight feet high without shelving or other visible means of support.

The shed is hot in the summer, cold in the winter, and in damp weather the paper round the packets is moist to the palm. Every few months I drive down and collect a few packets, which have been there for anything between eight and 12 years ... Have the pages become foxed? They have not. Are the laminated jackets stuck together? No. Are the art plates in good nick? They are. Is there mould on the cloth, cloth-type, and paper boards? There is not. Every packet opened offers mint-condition treasures from Centaur's backlist. Not everyone's idea of a light read, maybe; unreadable, perhaps; but mint.

I do not insure the stock because the cost would exceed the profit from selling perhaps 10 copies per title per year out of stock of several hundreds. But no such hazards as electricity or water are, or need to be, laid on. A big sea in the Channel did once sweep inland, but the shed's aura of concentrated culture proved more effective than Canute, and the waters stopped short. So far, mice have been equally respectful.

The rates on the shed, such as they are, are gladly paid by the good lady who keeps her horse in the paddock. The maintenance is a lick of creosote every five years and a coat of paint on the doors and the one window. Most light is overhead, through two perspex sheets ...

With publishers cutting back and expiring daily, and book-sellers being driven demented by the O.P. reports emanating from ditch-the-backlist policies, there may be some benefit from heeding the moral of this little tale, which is that books can survive almost anything but accountants.

Ten years on, a small rider was needed. Some of the older books containing art plates should have been double-wrapped by the binders, as a few copies in the outer reaches of the stacks were affected by changing humidity. But as the damage amounted to a fraction of the longest-stored titles – some probably doomed to be remaindered – the loss was negligible. Plastic is now the alternative to paper wrappings, and this seems to be wholly protective if not damaged.

In 1973 – which I know is somewhat short of where we should be in this oscillating chronology of Centaur's progress – storage of the stock was eased considerably by the newly-built block across the drive. A big plus was the ability to guard against fire or water damage by dividing the stock of each title between home, Selsey, and the London distribu-tors, at a percentage ratio of roughly 40/40/20 (Trade Counter under-standably wished to keep only a working stock that I could top up occasionally by car from Sussex). This arrangement also evaded ware-housing charges from the binders. When we added the north wing to the house, with a large loft above it, there was for a time space to spare, and I was even able to quarter risks by halving the stock held in the office block across the drive. But something akin to Parkinson's Law soon ensured that boxes of files, seldom used books from my library, and the domestic detritus inseparable from marriage and parenthood, filled the gaps in the bays.

By 1981 my major desk chore was still the compiling of *The Extended Circle*, involving much research and correspondence, and the only other serious commitment for that year was a further book by Frank Avray Wilson. Regretting my inability to do more for Frank's earlier book, I should not have given in to announcing his *Art as Revelation* in the 1979 catalogue, being aware that by 1977, fourteen years after Routledge had followed *Art into Life* with *Art as Understanding*, other small publishers had taken on further books by him, with no apparent success. But *Revelation* marked a stage in the development of an interesting painter and thinker, so I allowed myself to be influenced by the dubious superstition that sometimes things are meant to come in threes. Announced as a 'highly original analysis of the relationship between the arts and nature', the book was a courageous attempt to help retrieve for our modern industrial civilisation the largely neglected experience of a transcendental world.

Frank's parallel concern was with the relevance of contemporary science to this other dimension, and to share his excitement at recent evidence exploding the myth of scientific materialism, showing how physics in particular increasingly reveals the aesthetic of the natural world. A total turn-off for many, I fear, but challenging stuff for those alert to its relevance to the 'human predicament'. It must be conceded that Frank's talent as a communicator in words was less impressive than his powers of expression on canvas. In his farmhouse near Grasse, with its 180° view over the Mediterranean, displaying his striking paintings on its big white walls, he had given over an entire room to a magnificent mineral collection whose study under microscope opened up what for me was a whole new dimension of aesthetic experience. He himself was a skilful microphotographer of minerals, conjuring up a fabulous world that complemented his creativity as a painter.

Apart from distributing *The Wonderful World of Period Furniture*, a paperback guide to the recognition and restoration of antiques, already printed by its master-craftsman author Albert G. Hook FRSA, the only publication in 1981 was a slim excursion into prophetic faction.

Jenny: My Diary had been written by an astute and cosmopolitan journalist with the intriguing name of Yorick Blumenfeld, the son of a distinguished Dutch photographer, an anti-Nazi propagandist, and distantly related to Anne Frank. He was meeting the frustrations experienced by many who leave their acknowledged rut for the thorny path of fiction. Faced at the time with an assignment to accompany an earnest (and I suspect pretty) girl who was determined to take the civilising influence of puppets to the Sepik head-hunters of New Guinea, he was anxious that *Jenny* be published before he left for the uncertain rewards awaiting him in the East Indies.

Jennifer and I read *Jenny*, which was nothing if not short and to the point. Its theme – 'the horrific record of a young mother trapped in a World War III fall-out shelter' – seemed timely when the suppressed and less suppressed fears of the nuke nations were a major contributor to current neurosis. Having escaped one form of holocaust (the family were interned in a Vichy concentration camp in Morocco, but escaped to America), Yorick was disinclined to end up in another. Written in 'Jenny''s longhand, with minimal printed copyright details on an end page to lend credibility to its diary format, the book was certainly an original concept.

In Soho restaurants, in much correspondence, in Grantchester, where Yorick still lives with his brilliant sculptress wife Helaine, we hammered out a plan. It was Yorick's hope to find a major publisher as soon as a respected UK imprint, however small, had shown the faith to invest in *Jenny*. Centaur was happy to be the sprat that might catch the mackerel.

The Cambridge University Press had been lined up to print and bind the book, and in October 1981 we published it. I should have given more thought to its promotion in the climate of the time, for neither the theme nor its presentation registered with booksellers and literary editors chin-deep in the ever-rising tide of new books, and unlikely to suspect that a respectable but small imprint would have found something original that the blockbuster merchants had overlooked. Besides which, I had put out little fiction, and Yorick was not even known as a novelist.

The biggest response was from *Protect and Survive Monthly*, an earnest organ of the shelter industry, who ordered 100 copies in the apparent belief that the book offered hope of survival, rather than the precise opposite. They failed to pay for them, and a few months later were bankrupt. Otherwise a sprinkling of central London bookshops grudgingly placed small orders. It was all rather depressing, but we were not really surprised. We put our faith in the States.

In June 1982 Yorick wrote from New York that '*Jenny* will be published in the US by Little, Brown ... in the same format, but with a more American handwriting style! I shall also make some changes in content ... little details about the ozone layer, etc., that bothered me in the first edition.' American commercial considerations prevailed, however, and *Jenny* appeared in her original British handwriting. Meanwhile the Centaur edition staggered on. Upbeat moments were few and short-lived. Yorick, for instance, reported that *Jenny* was a cult book for the students of Cambridge. As they were photocopying the

Centaur edition for all they were worth, presumably from the only copy
that Heffers, the largest bookshop in Cambridge, had sold, the news
was better for our egos than for our coffers. Little, Brown reported
their print run as 20,000 copies, but a print run is not a sales total.
Usually.

On 27 October my phone rang. It was Peter Mayer's secretary. (Peter
was the high-profile chairman and chief executive of Penguin and had
taken over that great institution in the late 1970s.) He wanted to come
down the next day to Sussex with his UK sales director, Alan Wherry, to
give me lunch. Alan rang ten minutes later to set it up.

'You've done a fantastic job with *Jenny*,' he said.

I made suitably modest noises.

'I mean, three thousand four hundred copies sold,' he went on. 'I've
got a lot to learn from you.'

We had only *printed* between 2,000 and 2,500. I rang Yorick. He
said he hadn't told Peter the book had sold that number, and that it
must have come from Little, Brown, or from his New York agent Elaine
Markson. He said Peter had seen the Centaur *Jenny* almost by accident
when in Little, Brown's Boston office on other business. He read it on
the next plane back to London, and rang Boston from Heathrow to
make an offer, signing an agreement with Elaine Markson on 14
October.

At our lunch on the 28th, Peter and Alan were clearly excited by their
find. As it was too soon to have learned where that figure of 3,400 had
come from, and not wishing to dampen the enthusiasm, I murmured
that if Little, Brown were quoting the Centaur sales rather than their
own, it was a bit on the imaginative side. Later, when I had done some
more research, I rang Peter at his Chelsea home to say I was not happy
at the deal going through on wrong figures. But he brushed aside my
offer to let Penguin off the hook, assuring me that he was acting on his
own judgment of *Jenny*'s potentialities, and that Centaur's and Little,
Brown's figures were irrelevant.

Long before publication of the third edition on 10 March 1983, the
might of Penguin swung into action, and the media were jostling to be
ahead of the pack in rediscovering the discovery. The *Guardian* was
first off the mark on Christmas Eve, not having given a single line to the
Centaur edition. The *Bookseller* told 'The strange story of *Jenny*',
which I followed up with a letter published on 29 January. This
prompted Godfrey Smith of the *Sunday Times* to ring me, and a week
later he gave *Jenny* the lead story in his column. In early March the

Sunday Times published an extract, and in the *Bookseller* Eric Hiscock wrote:

> This remarkable diary makes most poignant, emotional reading. How odd it is that when *Jenny* was first published, in 1981, by Centaur Press, it moved only one reviewer (in a dead-and-gone organ, *Protect and Survive*) to comment. Now Little, Brown in America has issued it, and Penguin (three loud cheers for Peter Mayer) is giving it the full treatment with an enormous first printing.

For a heady month *Jenny* topped the *Sunday Times/Bookseller* list of hardback fiction bestsellers. But I suspect none of the three publishers did as well as the author, who at least received his royalties on the copies that were sold. Although their sales were massively more than Centaur's, neither Little, Brown (who were to report 12,000 copies returned by booksellers) nor Penguin (who received 15,000 returns, nearly half their printing) realised their expectations.

I never caught up with the press reactions to the American edition, though I heard that some of the reviewers were outraged that Yorick, a man, should write as if he were a woman. But the numerous UK notices, from most of the national dailies to specialist magazines and provincial newspapers, showed a wide range of reactions. The nationals, on the whole, damned by faint praise, as though to justify their lack of attention to the first edition. Although translation rights were bought by some fourteen countries (in which Centaur took no share), and *Jenny* was a bestseller in Germany as a Bertelsmann book club title, media interviews in the UK had little effect on the momentum, and serious talk of an HBO film being directed by Bryan Forbes, with Julie Christie in the role of Jenny, came to nothing. Maybe none of us faced the possibility that *Jenny* was being aimed at a fundamentally uninquiring, cautious, and head-burying public disinclined, by and large, to think much beyond its material comforts, and basking in the long-cherished assumption that a natural superiority would preserve the status quo.

We all survived the *Jenny* experience, but today it is a lot easier to get away with publishing an original and challenging book while staying in business. Where, in the early 1980s, I might have looked for a break-even-on-costs sales figure of 1,000 copies of an averagely-priced non-academic 'trade' title, today it is possible for a firm with minimal overheads to typeset in-house, deliver camera-ready copy to a suitable printer, and break even on 200 copies or even less. A cautious first print run to test the market can be followed by any number of later impressions at little higher unit cost.

A climate or technology that enables almost anything to be published may be a boon to writers and publishers, but it is a bane to literature. It floods the market with poor work. I saw another aspect of this downward drift when I served on the Southern Arts Association's literary panel from 1974 to 1978. Our meetings were held in pleasant Georgian premises in Winchester. Our roles were those of lords and ladies bountiful, appointed to dish out ratepayers' money to usually nebulous projects and half-baked ego-trips submitted by often very young or seriously amateur would-be writers and editors. By the end of my third year I had reached the limit of my hope and self-questioning, so put my doubts into a written submission to the secretary and the panel members. The only other panel member to support me openly was Richard Boston, editor from 1977 of an environmental magazine called *Vole*. Yet I felt that others were quite relieved that the point had been made, and some letters and calls supported that impression. It had been a revealing, if depressing, opportunity to take the pulse of the up, coming, and encouraged literary climate. Wearing my publisher's hat, it seemed appropriate to hold on as long as I did in the hope that things would improve. Evidence of whether this was sacrificing instinct to optimism surrounds us in all expressions of the arts, and I leave it at that. We live in a time when the self-esteem of the majority must be put before the qualitative judgements of the pernickety few.

In 1982 no new Centaur title was published. Merely keeping its backlist on the rails and compiling *The Extended Circle* left all too little time for the routine commitments of life. In 1983, by which time Richard D. Ryder's important *Victims of Science* was no longer available from Davis-Poynter Ltd, Centaur took on the trade distribution of a revised edition printed by the National Anti-Vivisection Society. Ever since, nearly thirty years earlier, a practising vivisector of considerable standing had told me, when sufficiently in his cups to have shed discretion, that he and his colleagues could get away with any experiment that took their fancy by skilful working of their applications to the Home Office, I had looked forward to the day when I might be associated with a reputable book that would put the record straight. No major publisher has backed an authoritative exposé that would at least pave the way to considering the reforms unquestionably needed if medicine's dismal and often misdirected record is to be improved.

Apart from *Punch in the Italian Puppet Theatre*, which showed that Michael Byrom's career as a Punch and Judy man must have been just the alchemy he needed to come to terms with the materialistic and self-absorbed society that had been such a challenge in his younger days, 1983 threw up nothing else worthy of mention. In 1984 we published only two titles: *So Say Banana Bird*, the first novel to be published under my own name; and *Baltic Countdown* by Peggie Benton, doughty wife of Kenneth, a diplomat who retired into crime-fiction writing. She married him, her second husband, in Vienna a few days before the Nazi *Anschluss*. They transferred together to Riga, the capital of Latvia, and their experiences through and after the war were a tale worth telling. For readers ignorant of the realities of foreign occupation it was a revealing read.

Of *So Say Banana Bird* I have said something already. I should probably have persisted in finding a known fiction publisher to take it on, but when an author knows the mechanics of producing a book, has better things to do than spend months (if not years) finding a home for an apparently first novel by a middle-aged publisher who should be sticking to publishing, and also has an old media friend keen on a joint publishing venture, the DIY path is tempting. The friend was Michael Storm, one-time story editor for Columbia Pictures, imaginative commercial artist (he originated the saucy letter V that has sprouted world wide on a vast range of animal-free products), and talented magazine editor. To put a little distance between Centaur and our plan, we called the new imprint Pythian Books, and Mike provided a striking dust-jacket for its first title, which was a line from a calypso lyric I had written for the book.

Once again, hope centred on the sprat-and-mackerel combination, producing the hardback that might tempt a bigger publisher to turn it into a paperback; that being where the serious returns were more likely to result. Despite being sabotaged at birth by a public relations appointee who had, let us say, overriding personal problems that militated against his launching anything but bottles at the end of a pier, the scheme nearly worked. Besides the reviews mentioned earlier, there was useful coverage from the *Financial Times*, *Contemporary Review* and other quarters; and from spreads in several national and overseas newspapers, the most effective being in the *Sunday Express* magazine section, which tied the book in with the story of Redonda, bringing invitations to appear on various TV shows. Enough, in short, to take sales of the 362-page novel well into four figures.

Banana Bird's paperback afterlife was a dismal non-event. It nearly happened, though. Having supplied the foreword to *The Dragon of Redonda*, it made sense to approach its publishers, Macmillan, who kept a strong presence in the Caribbean. *Banana Bird* was already selling there in hardback, and booksellers had shown a marked interest in a paperback. Macmillan's Caribbean manager Bill Lennox responded positively to my letter, stressing their suitability for handling the paperback, especially in Antigua and such nearer islands as Montserrat, St Kitts, Nevis and Barbuda. Soon afterwards he confirmed that they had been into costs and it only remained for his sales colleagues to discuss the book in the relevant West Indian markets, though they knew it was doing well in Antigua, its main (though disguised) locale. Their sole worry, that the hardback might compete with their paperback, was quashed by my remaindering the 800 still in stock.

This was a precipitate gesture, as Lennox wrote some weeks later that 'the distributors on whom we rely for the bulk of sales in the Caribbean do not feel that the market is great enough to justify a viable print run'. This made no sense, and inquiries brought the reason for this unexpected loss of enthusiasm. Besides its sailing and fantasy elements, *Banana Bird* – for those knowing enough of Caribbean politics to tune into the sub-text – gave a view of the corruption within and surrounding the Antiguan government that, following the dissolution of the Leeward Islands Federation in 1956, was controlled from 1960 by a constitution providing for a ministerial system. This, in one form or the other, continued through the granting of independence to Antigua and Barbuda in 1981 to the present day. In 1980, when I was completing *Banana Bird* in English Harbour, the political skulduggery bore no comparison to the corruption and scandal that received world coverage in 1990, implicating the prime minister Vere Bird and his sons Vere Jr and Lester. And herein lay the problem for my novel. Macmillan's distributors feared that the family would not be happy to see such a book making use of its name in the title.

I threw in the towel. Caribbean distribution being vital, any other publisher was going to be faced with the same response. Besides, Nick Austin, the experienced and scrupulous editorial director of Granada, had earlier seen the book and implied that its only serious fault was that it lay somewhere between lit. fic. and mass-market appeal. A fair point. But suspecting that self-publishing of some kind might be needed, I had written a novel that was deliberately self-indulgent and did not conform with the rigid rules beloved of category fiction. That said, it was probably enjoyed and might have done well in paperback, despite its somewhat unorthodox mould. With the growth of awareness of the Redondan legend since Javier Marías's books have reached millions in Europe and are now acclaimed in the States, it may be a candidate for revival. If not, 'win some, lose some', and the hell with it.

The only title for 1985 was *The Extended Circle*, an entirely in-house exercise, compiled by myself and published under the Centaur imprint in hardback and paperback in 1985, and reprinted in paperback in February 1986 with corrections. It was a special pleasure to be compiling a book that called on the best qualities of those who contributed to it. Spanning many centuries, most were beyond the personal acquaintance of an editor unconversant with the workings of an Ouija board, but of those still around I was particularly glad to be able to include Brigid Brophy, Kenneth (Lord) Clark, Maureen Duffy, Gavin Ewart, John Fowles, Robert Gittings, Jane Goodall, Lord Altrincham (John Grigg), Ruth Harrison, Elspeth Huxley, Philip Kapleau, Sir Peter Medawar, Yehudi Menuhin, Mary Midgley, Ashley Montagu, Jan Morris, Iris Murdoch, Isaac Bashevis Singer, Donald (Lord) Soper, Sir Keith Thomas, Sir George Trevelyan, E. S. Turner, Lord (Edward Henry) Willis, and most of those more holistic commentators and philosophers then less known to the general public. I was even able to dig up a couple of fitting passages from the Duke of Edinburgh, whereas I coaxed no response from his more, if selectively, environmentally sensitive older son.

Before publication, I subscribed the book to several branches of the SPCK bookshops, handing the buyers a dust-jacket proof before showing them the as yet unbound book. Most got no further than the early lines of the blurb: 'Its contributors have seen ... the connection between our behaviour toward each other, and our treatment of non-human creatures.' Rejection was instant in nearly every case, at times peremptory to the point of rudeness, or perhaps shock. My error dawned on me later. Among the named contributors on the jacket I had not thought to list a single saint, cardinal or curate, nor (perhaps more to the point) a bishop. It was as if I had offered them soft porn in plain covers.

Kenneth Clark died before *Extended* was first published, but when in 1988 his Trade Minister son Alan was conducting a behind-the-scenes campaign in Whitehall for Government action to restrict fur imports, I sent him the book with hope of a record of something he had said or written in support of Schweitzer's 'message'. He reported that he and his wife Jane 'read virtually the whole of it last weekend and were, in succession, moved, dejected and uplifted. It is a wonderful anthology, a veritable mine of quotation and wisdom.' His ebullient mix of political and private priorities may have accounted for his not getting round to sending me something, but he quoted Adolf Hitler's remark (recorded by Rauschning) that 'I do not understand how anyone who has visited a stockyard could ever eat meat again', and confirmed that 'it was this comment more than anything else which made me a vegetarian'. Which says something for Adolf for once.

By taking the less stressful path of publishing the first edition of the book myself, I was able to establish its format and retain control over the contents. If it was well received, I could seek a larger publisher to take on an extended edition in paperback, the student market being my primary target. It was a long shot, maybe, but in the end the encapsulated humanity of so wide a range of distinguished and perceptive contributors, from ancient days to the present, was too powerful a mix to be overlooked. Indeed, the reviews were numerous and almost wholly favourable. Head and shoulders above the rest was the review in *The Times* of 2 January, the day I had flown to Madeira to begin writing a play, leaving Jennifer in charge. Contributed by Jan Morris, the review was an inspiring feat of restrained passion, and since my task had been merely to select the clear thinking and just hearts of others, it may not be immodest to quote her view that the book was 'a dazzling register. Angry and sorrowful, but also full of beauty. The [book's] chief splendour is its absoluteness.'

When I returned two weeks later it was to find Jennifer waist-deep in the aftermath of Jan's *tour de force*. Within two days of her review appearing, the post and phone calls, and the consequent invoicing and despatching, had become incessant. Later, Jan sent a sheaf of letters she had received from people deeply moved by her compelling recommendation. The review seemed to be doing as good a job as the book itself.

I spent the next few days clearing the backlog, thankful that the Chichester-based publishers John Wiley were now helping with the despatches. But desk work was interrupted by having to give interviews, readings, lectures, and – in 1986 and 1988 – short guest-speaker talks in Channel Four's 'Comment' series, which reached more people than I had expected. A few review copies of *Extended* had been sent to the USA, and these helped to clinch a contract with Paragon House of

New York for American editions in hardback and 'in paper'. Both *Extended* and *Food for a Future* were given awards in the USA and UK, but as they carried no weight with the established literary circuits in either country, further details here would not impress.

In February 1989, Christopher Potter, senior editor under Nick Webb of Penguin's Sphere Books, was asked by Brigid Brophy to send me a copy of her book *Reads*. As Sphere, under their Abacus imprint, had already published the first paperback edition of *Food for a Future*, I asked Christopher to consider publishing a much enlarged edition of *Extended*. He seemed keen on this and invited me to lunch, at which he confirmed that on that very day Robert Maxwell had bought Sphere Books from Penguin. I took the news that my 'dictionary of humane thought' was now under the tender aegis of Maxwell with all the British grit I could muster. Which wasn't a lot. However, after a very pleasant collaboration, the 648-page paperback was published under Sphere's Cardinal imprint in May 1990. It had an attractive cover designed by Andrew Wyatt, and carried review quotes for the earlier editions, and a late puff coaxed from the amiable Jonathon Porritt.

But nothing in publishing stays still. As few will have forgotten, Robert Maxwell 'jumped yacht' in November 1991, and in the commotion that followed this internationally-savoured incident I was able, eighteen months after its publication, to take over the substantial tail end of Cardinal's edition at a cost of 20p per copy. Lacking any representation in these last years of running Centaur, I could only meet orders as word-of-mouth brought them in; but the stock ran out in 2004. Finding a publisher for a further enlarged edition has become a high priority.

By the middle 1980s, with the reception for *Extended* seeming a pointer to the road ahead, priorities became clearer. Although the energy-draining allergy and accompanying irritations had not lost me the gamble of relying on adequate health to see me through the income-producing decades, the feeling of achievement from a growing shelf of Centaur titles was no longer a spur to adding to them 'just because ...' The backlist was holding up pretty well, adequately topping up income from savings and the joyless role of minor landlord. It was hardly a hysterical success but it had kept the wolf at bay and (at that time at least) seemed to have ensured a reasonable buffer against the tribulations of an almost pensionless older age.

The priorities were to make a stronger return to my own writing, and

to focus more on new or reissued books in the field of humane education. But the aims could not be realised overnight. 1986's only move to
keep the flag flying was the first of several paperback editions of
Donkeys. In 1987 came *A Checklist* (of John Heath-Stubbs), compiled
by John E. Van Domelen and mainly for libraries, helpful to students of
the unstoppable Heath-Stubbs, Redonda's Poet Laureate, and now
almost the last living duke from the reign of Juan I.

In the same year came *The Incredible World's Parliament of Religions*, a curious, impatient, and prodigiously informed book by Clay
Lancaster. I had known Clay, a fierce correspondent with my mother,
since 1960. An American Buddhist, he was a specialist in the cultural
exchange between Asia and the West, and a prolific artist and writer
best known for his considerable achievement *The Japanese Influence in
America*. When we first met, in 1969, he was living in Brooklyn Heights
at the elegant Monroe Place apartment that housed his impressive
collection of art from South-East Asia. Curator of Prospect Park in the
mid-1960s, he wrote *Prospect Park Handbook* and *Old Brooklyn
Heights*, two of the more popular of his output of some thirty books
and booklets. When he died in Kentucky on Christmas Day 2000, he
was eighty-three, and the *New York Times*, in a long obituary notice,
regretted the passing of this 'historic preservation pioneer' – a fitting tag
for one concerned with the conservation of more than buildings and
landscapes. Much more could, and should, be written about Clay and
his association with the Millennium Guild's contribution to the humane
movement in the USA, and it is surprising that no one over there seems
to have been prompted to publish an account of the Guild, founded in
1911, and its leading promoters such as Henry Bailey Stevens, Roy
Walker, Henry L. Nunn, pioneer in humanitarian labour management,
and the Guild's indomitable founder, M. R. L. Freshel, George Bernard
Shaw's admired 'Emarel'.

Another novel – despite my best intentions – lent a little colour to this
rather sombre time-marking. In March that year I received a letter from
Kenneth Barnett, a demographer who, after a lifetime as a civil servant
in the Far East, was employed by the United Nations in Central Africa
and South Asia before retiring to Buckinghamshire in 1982, looking
(but only looking) more than his age of fifty-eight. He had been referred
to me by my childhood friend Austin Coates, son of the composer,
whose wife Phyllis Black had been given the part that Noël had written
for Esmé in *The Young Idea*. When Barnett was District Commissioner
for Hong Kong, Austin was his District Officer. They shared language

skills, Kenneth needing only four to six weeks in which to gain a working knowledge of a new tongue. He had mastered over twenty. A large, jovial man, he was also a scholar of local history, and a tremendous raconteur. Ten years earlier he had been bereaved of his Chinese wife with whom, he claimed, he continued almost telepathic communication. His suitability for the role of a senior administrative officer in government service was obvious. We were more doubtful, however, on receipt of his letter seeking consideration of his novel *The Long-Sighted People*, whether his fiction would prove saleable. It was a safe guess that it would be formidably intelligent, but that was not necessarily going to be in its favour at the more squalid level of attaining sales.

And intelligent it certainly was. So much so as to be unreadable by most mortals. I replied, with regret, that although the Pythian Books imprint was unquestionably open to a demographic satire, I could see little chance of such a demanding novel being sold on to the paperback firm that could offer our only hope of avoiding a thumping loss. I suggested a few established publishers whose size and aims might tempt them to be adequately impressed, but warning that, failing this solution, his best chance lay in self-publishing. He chose the latter course without even trying the alternative, so I put him in touch with John Sankey for the printing, and with Mike Storm for design of the dust-jacket. I wanted no other personal involvement, least of all in promoting the novel, for which I knew I could do nothing. But his skilful and charismatic letters wore me down, and we took on distribution, for better or for worse, under the Pythian imprint.

In June, Kenneth came to lunch to agree amendments to his foreword and the text of the jacket. He arrived in a rusting blue VW Beetle with a broken Malawi number plate and Chinese stickers. The jacket had had Mike floundering, but Ken (as he preferred it) was happy that 'the problem of how to depict the impossible – a moonbeam being focused through a so-far undiscovered type of precious stone' – was so cleverly solved. By Mike, not me. I had reached the stage of doubt where I feared that sales would be unaffected were the book to be wrapped in gold-leaf or a used nappy, but an exhaustive publicity programme was begun, for it was clear that the novel was probably Ken's last throw, and that he was longing to see it in print. Final proofs were passed in August, then Ken spent several weeks in hospital. Discharged, he was anxious to have advance copies of his book so that he could take them to Hong Kong in November, where he could work on two reputable Western bookshops and his friends.

It was not to be. On 26 October his barrister daughter rang to say that on the eve of her collecting the copies from John Sankey and taking them to Amersham, Ken had dropped dead while tending his garden bonfire. If anxious anticipation had had any connection with this sad piece of timing, perhaps it was a more merciful end than knowing what did (or didn't) follow. I rang Ken's son-in-law in Hong Kong as soon as his wife gave me the news, confirming that we would go ahead as planned, with no reduction in what promotion was possible, and that publication was still set for 15 February.

The best thing to happen was a full-page review from Ken's friend Derek Davies, editor of the influential *Far Eastern Economic Review*. He extolled the life and character of his friend, though he admitted to me later that he had assumed the book would have a Chinese setting. 'Its futuristic character denies it any special interest in China, I fear.' Nevertheless, his painstaking and intriguing review paved the way for stock to be held by the *South China Morning Post*'s bookshop in Hong Kong. However, the only UK review I knew about, resulting from a pleading letter to David Holloway, was a very fair mention in the *Daily Telegraph* by that good friend of small publishers, Martyn Goff. The day after Martyn's review appeared, Mike Storm died too – suddenly, at his typewriter. Our only 1988 title had lived up – or down – to expectation, and a little beyond. Sixty-one copies sold that year, six more in 1989, one in 1990. And that was that. In 1996, after exploring the few alternatives, of which remaindering was not one, I drove 832 copies in state to a waste-paper skip in Chichester, for the benefit of St Wilfrid's Hospice. I hope that Ken, with his fond wife's help, has continued to prove that even a dead author is not as dead as a dead novel.

I have referred already to *Publishing Your Own Book*. It deserves, perhaps, a few more lines of explanation, though it was (and remains) no more than a 32-page stapled booklet. Over the years I have been offered more publishable books than I could have handled, even had they fitted the Centaur list. Some of these I recommended for (and sometimes directly to) other publishers. But with perfectly adequate books of limited appeal that I knew stood little chance of finding a competent home, I had encouraged some authors to publish them themselves. Giving them an adequate picture of the pitfalls and procedures was time-consuming, so I decided to publish a succinct account of how to set about DIY publishing (already available manuals appeared too long-winded). This seemed borne out by the subsequent review in *British Book News*, who found in it 'more distilled wisdom and good sense than all its bulkier rivals'. Helped by other favourable reactions, the first edition of 1989 had to be updated and reprinted three years later. It was a title that sold readily if displayed. Of the few shops I covered myself, two who displayed it face up sold all ten copies by lunchtime. But kept on the bookseller's shelf, its lack of a title-displaying flat spine reduced sales drastically.

The main 1989 title, foolishly a hardback, was *The Savour of Salt*, edited by George and Willene Hendrick. But anthologies seem a difficult medium for small publishers. The book was pleasantly produced, with an in-period jacket, and it gave a good range of Salt's thinking. It deserved, as someone remarked, to be in every secondary school and university in the country, and its press underlined that accolade. But by late 1998, only 547 copies had been sold and not a single inquiry for paperback rights came from any quarter. It was a deeply disappointing outcome, but also a costly one, for in 1989 technology had yet to enable small publishers to break even on a short print run.

I made many more attempts to overcome the problems of my chosen path in publishing than this account suggests, though I suppose that the biggest underlying blockage was my long-suppressed wish to put writing before publishing. Like Diana Athill, I 'loathe responsibility and telling people what to do', which is why, for me, the solo path was the only way ahead. Also, again like her, I have always been hard put (as she puts in her autobiographical *Stet*) 'to understand how anyone can feel in their bones, as I can, that life is worth living when every day we see such alarming evidence that a lot of it is unacceptable; that idiocy and cruelty, far from being brought to heel by human ingenuity, are as rampant as ever'. I had to weigh my effectiveness as a publisher in the humane field against advancing age and a mounting fear of never finding time to tackle the books I still hoped to write. It was time to consider Centaur's future.

Married daughters were heavily taken up with families far too young to know whether they might want a career in publishing. With the Centaur Classics long dormant, most of the list would be of little interest to larger publishers with profit priorities, and I could not even offer a tax loss to oil some modest takeover. By now, moreover, the list fell into two such distinct categories – the classics/literary, and the humane education/environmental – that the chance of finding a buyer keen on both aspects was wafer thin. Nevertheless, I began to follow up such possibilities as chance and inquiry offered. It was a tedious chore.

Several interested parties were clearly exploring whether they wanted to be publishers at all; some, more focused, with minimal experience of publishing but a nose for carrion and hoping I might be desperate to sell, were the second biggest time wasters. Others, with sound enough lists already, but short of ideas and wanting stock for higher turnover at a bargain price for least effort, were out to promote the best of the backlist for a few years, then remainder such titles as they could not reissue as paperbacks. One larger firm had particular interest in reviving the Centaur Classics, and its managing director agreed to pay 30% of the stock's retail value. But instead of the contract confirming what had been agreed, I received a letter to say his board had put him under pressure to settle for 10%, not thirty. As they had no place for the environmental side of the list, and in those days I could have sold out to a remainder firm anyway, had I been seeking instant death at a silly price, negotiation ended there.

The greatest waste of time and outlay was the penalty for taking seriously the fervently expressed interest of a distinguished American medical consultant who, although wanting only the environmental list, was happy to pay the sum I was asking for the whole business. His wife, he said, would be running it, but it was he who did all the negotiating by letters, visits, and cordial transatlantic calls over the next two years, in which time every conceivable point seemed to have been discussed, agreed, and confirmed in writing. The only seed of doubt in my mind was that his wife had provided no input, and had shown not a spark of interest in the matter, either in correspondence or when they came to stay when everything seemed ready to be signed and sealed. But the deal was simple enough, and clearly agreed in our correspondence: they were to pay x for y. It was falling-off-a-log stuff, so transparently set out that nothing needed to be discussed further, least of all through lawyers. But aware that America the Free is not also America the Trustful, and that its lawyers are second to none at making their clients jumpy about any human transaction from cleaning one's teeth to taking the presidency, I agreed to the last-minute wish that some legally binding formalisation of our agreement be completed. Expecting a simple sheet confirming our perfectly straightforward arrangement, I was astonished to receive a fourteen-page 'Asset Purchase Agreement' of such fearsome complexity and seeming irrelevance that I forwarded it to Michael Rubinstein. Just retired, he passed it on to his successor who confirmed that the Florida lawyers had thrown in every imaginable ingredient in the hope of covering all conceivable and inconceivable contingencies, and that a much simplified version was preferable. Duly called for, it did not come. Nervous of the cost of asking the London solicitor to sort out the virtually unaltered verbosity, jargon and super-fluities, I studied the 'revision' myself. I was startled to discover that the deal now hinged on my handing over the copyright and all control in *The Extended Circle*. I knew that the book enjoyed cult status among the North American humane movement, but we had never even discussed such a stipulation, and I was completely opposed to handing on seven years' hard work, not to mention a book that had been welcomed as perhaps the most inspirational in its field. I cut my losses and pulled out.

In 1990 and 1991 nothing was published except – in 1990 – a limited edition of *Toreros*, a selection of John Gawsworth's poems made by Richard Aldington in 1961, with the addition of an introductory appreciation from Roy Campbell. Centaur's role was little more than that of distributor, for *Toreros* was financed and produced by Reynolds Morse and the Shiel authority John D. Squires.

After the poor sales following the good press for *The Savour of Salt*, I decided on one possibly last and more ambitious project to raise the list's humane education profile – a series, in uniform format and cover design, of reasonably-priced paperback reissues, mainly of early seminal works in that field. This time, I determined, there should be no doubt that the sixth form and university student was the principal target. The cover of each title carried the reproduction of a fourth-century ivory, 'Naming the Animals', and the 1992 catalogue announced that the Kinship Library titles would

> explore the deepest level of the environmental conscience and have particular significance for students, teachers, and those most responsibly engaged in furthering the welfare and rights of animals.
>
> The Kinship Library will present new books on the philosophy, politics and implications of those rights, and reissues of long unobtainable works of special merit, edited and introduced by modern scholars. The older reissues will be published as Kinship Classics.
>
> Editorial advisors to the Kinship Library: Maureen Duffy, Audrey Eyton, George Hendrick, Charles Magel, Jan Morris, Tom Regan, Richard D. Ryder, Peter Singer, John Stockwell.

Six titles were announced, the first four being published in September and October 1992. These were a reprint, with an added afterword from the author, of E. S. Turner's *All Heaven in a Rage*, first published and excellently received in 1964 (in the USA, 1965); Humphrey Primatt's *The Duty of Mercy*, subtitled 'and the Sin of Cruelty to Brute Animals', first published in 1776, now edited by Richard D. Ryder, with a preface by John Austin Baker, lately Bishop of Salisbury; Lewis Gompertz's *Moral Inquiries* ('on the Situation of Man and of Brutes'), 1824, with a foreword by Peter Singer; and the American J. Howard Moore's magnificent, but extraordinarily forgotten, work *The Universal Kinship*, introduced by Charles Magel, then Professor of Philosophy Emeritus, Moorhead State University, Minnesota. New books by modern philosophers and writers were also planned.

For the initial quartet, all possible advance publicity by catalogue (its cover reproducing the jacket design for the series) was embarked upon. Spare covers with individually typed letters preceded the despatch of some fifty review copies to literary editors, and numerous copies were sent direct to friends and sympathetic reviewers. Hardly any book-sellers could be expected to order for stock unless the books had been subscribed to them alongside more saleable general titles, so reviews in the few suitable journals were vital if the library and student markets were to be made aware that the series had been launched.

The *Independent* carried a review by the supportive Jan Morris of *The Duty of Mercy*, which was also noticed in *The Tablet* by Stratford Caldecott. Composite reviews of all four titles appeared in *Contemporary Review*, *New Statesman and Society*, *School Librarian*, and the *Journal of Applied Philosophy*. Otherwise, not a word except in magazines published by sympathetic organisations. The launch by a small and unsubsidised publisher of a responsible series aimed at an intelligent student level presented obvious opportunities for feature-article treatment. The hardening indifference toward a serious antidote to the damage done by the minority of activists, whose extreme forms of protest the press was only too happy to publicise as the norm, was disheartening to a degree. Bad journalism interprets the 'freedom of the press' as a right to ignore the influences that can help to restore the framework of a wiser and wider educational system. If we cannot agree on the urgent need to face this necessity, then the lemming millennium is firmly on course.

The writing on the wall had to be read and understood. All avenues had been stonewalled or ignored by seven out of the eight papers whose cooperation was most needed and expected for a scholarly series that any responsible and experienced editor could see was ground-breaking and deserving of a kick-start. It was dismal proof of how standards had fallen since the sixties, when a series such as the Centaur Classics – similarly conceived and produced, and different only in theme – had been proportionately and fairly dealt with by most of the critical sources that could have been reasonably anticipated. Censorship-by-neglect was clearly at work, and it was time to call it a day.

This decision was strengthened by the fact that in October 1991 I had done a coast-to-coast tour of the States, solely to talk to publishers and key figures in the humane movement, with a view to arranging for co-publication of the Kinship Library, or at least for distribution of the UK editions. It would, I knew, prove to be a decisive indicator of Centaur's future. It had its lighter moments, too, not least flying to Boston in the company of ninety-five Elvis Presley lookalikes on their yearly pilgrimage to Memphis. The amiable clone next to me had just been made redundant, and was blowing his final wage cheque on a third trip to the holy of holies. To emerge from the forward lavatory to a sea of identical male coiffures was eerie, not to say daunting. Those not reading shrieking tabloids were bulky men engrossed in inches-thick and doubtless relevant paperbacks whose covers hyped household names in big embossed gold letters. I did my best to concentrate on my thin and shabby copy of Gandhi's autobiography, cheaply printed on yellowing paper in Delhi, but part of my brain wrestled gloomily with where the decimal point would come in any percentage assessment of potential readers for the Kinship Library in the States.

In Washington I was introduced to a respectful audience as the 'elder statesman of the animal rights movement' – kindly meant, but somehow disconcerting. In San Diego I stayed with Charles Magel, academic luminary of the American humane movement (and a *good* four years older than myself); in Berkeley my hosts were Meg and John Stockwell, frantically overworked teachers from whose house John has for years published the inestimable journal of ethics, *Between the Species*, for the Schweitzer Center of the San Francisco Bay Institute. On my last night, in Boston, my hostess Evelyn Kimber's free-ranging rabbits skidded from one floor-polished room to another, and did their best to share her spare bed with me. I was sustained not only by great hospitality and friendliness, but with encouraging proof of enthusiasm for the Kinship Library; so much so that I got back to my desk feeling fitter than when I left it.

But little came of it all. The goodwill of individuals cuts no ice with commercial publishers seeing inadequate profit in catering to idealistic minorities, although offered co-editions that entirely relieve them of manufacturing costs. Even for the committed organisations, book publication at so relatively scholarly a level proved to be – in the UK no less than in America – too scary an alternative to selling impassioned T-shirts.

In the States only the ISAR, and Jay and Freya Dinshah's courageous non-profit organisation The American Vegan Society, were to take on distribution of the Kinship titles within the movement. Those who could most easily have afforded to do so were the quickest to make their excuses. Today the picture has somewhat improved, even in Britain. Organisations' sales catalogues, swollen with offers of environmentally-friendly clothing, footwear, cards, stationery, stickers, vegan chocolates, and wine in quantities that would have appalled the founding fathers of vegetarianism, are showing keener awareness that sustenance for the immaterial inner man can find buyers. Currently, VIVA!'s magazine *Life*, run by Juliet Gellatley and Tony Wardle, co-authors of the powerful exposé *The Silent Ark*, leads the field with an extensive and separately issued résumé of books, and Animal Aid's magazine *Outrage* is the UK's broadest platform for questioning the many cruelties to other species.

Although the decline in Centaur's turnover was not dramatic, infrequent additions to the general side of the list, and increased emphasis on subject matter still seen by most as 'niche', 'inspirational', or just plain uncommercial, gradually reduced it to a shadow of its former self. But the show had to go on, and discouragement was no stranger. At least my personal health was up to it, and I packed most of the orders myself from a purpose-made bench in the garage. By 1993 the arrangement with John Wiley for despatch of Centaur's larger parcels, and for their processing of occasional bulk orders beyond my packing capacity, had been switched to a smaller publisher more conveniently placed on our route into Chichester. Phillimore and Co. Ltd, another (though larger) niche publisher specialising in British local and family history, had moved in 1969 to Shopwyke Hall, a stately double-fronted Georgian house built in 1720. Phillimore's chairman and managing director, Philip Harris, a career publisher who lived to tell the tale of running one of Robert Maxwell's book companies for six months, converted the Hall's stables and outhouses into offices. By 1993 he and his wife

Louise had moved a few hundred yards north to the more picturesquely ancient Shopwyke Manor, with some of its timbers confirmed by the experts as circa 1130. Having fallen into farming hands, it underwent some modernisation in 1540. Louise's father did some more and the premises were all very in keeping for a publisher whose list carries a forty-volume translation of *Domesday Book*, and such complementary lightweights as *Arthurian Period Sources*. But if the Manor was slightly smaller than the Hall, the new offices, converted from a Sussex barn, were more spacious than those vacated, having a well-planned storage and packing area that was able to take in Centaur's modest contributions to turnover with a tolerant smile.

It would be pleasant to be able to record that I relinquished Centaur Press to some idealistic tycoon. I didn't. But although in the end Centaur found what was probably the best home I could reasonably expect in the circumstances, it all took time. After the Kinship Library pointers, a fair chunk of heart had been lost, and the only new title to be produced in 1993 under the Centaur imprint was the third and definitive edition of Henry Salt's *Life of Henry David Thoreau*, edited by George and Willene Hendrick in collaboration with Fritz Oehlschlaeger. Excellently produced by the University of Illinois Press, its long, scholarly, and impeccably topical introduction made extensive use of unpublished papers and Salt's own notes and correspondence. It seemed a prestigious and wholly acceptable title on which to finish. Neglected by reviewers, it sold appallingly – seventy copies by autumn 1998.

But it had been dawning on me that my own little problem with the media's declining interest in small publishers' value-based contributions to the educational process was but a part of the wider evidence of this country's galloping loss of pride, discrimination, and consequent identity. With a huge yearly rise in UK book publishers' output of new titles, press attention given to American books (a dismally reciprocated obeisance) was unquestionably eroding space already inadequate for the home product. In the 2000 edition of *The Writer's Handbook*, its editor Barry Turner trenchantly deplored the fact that the ever-widening gap between the UK and Europe was being more than filled by American encroachment, and that all too much of its culture was being bought on the sad principle that rubbish comes cheap; the first paragraph of 'Uncle Sam's Satellite' reads:

Americanisation continues apace. Almost everyone in the world

knows what is happening; even the Americans who, for understandable reasons, prefer to call it globalisation. Only the British
remain oblivious. Here, it just happens and no one seems to notice.
The media industry is a good example. In any other country it
would be a matter of interest, not to say concern, that of the
national press, the two foremost opinion leaders, *The Times* and
The Daily Telegraph, have North American paymasters, that of the
twelve top book publishing conglomerates, six are subject to
American dictates (HarperCollins, the publishing arm of Rupert
Murdoch's American-controlled News Corporation, is the largest
consumer book publisher in Britain by a margin of 30 per cent)
and that film and television are almost entirely subservient to
American interests. But not here. In Britain, while American
authors rule the bestseller lists (of the first 25 titles in the *Guardian*
list of the 100 top selling paperbacks, 15 are from American
authors), Hollywood fills the cinemas, American cop series and sit-
coms occupy television prime time, and newspapers give more
coverage to the States than to all other countries combined, we still
kid ourselves that we remain a nation apart, a cultural entity proud
of its independence. This is delusion on a grand scale.

But although declining support from the better end of the media
spectrum was certainly a big factor when considering for how long
Centaur could continue without a serious lift in output, I hope I have
not moaned unreasonably. The literary editor's lot has not become
easier. In particular, the relentless increase in new titles since 1954 has
not been adequately matched by the literary papers' allocation of
reviewing space, while reviewing standards have been increasingly
sacrificed to the cult of personality, and to a focus that all too obviously
panders to the circulation war.

In a way, after the Kinship Library disappointment the *TLS*'s further
passing over of an eminently deserving work was a relief. It confirmed
what I had done my best to harbour as no more than a suspicion. A
letter from Richard Gott, then literary editor of the *Guardian*, dispelled
any doubt. I had written:

Dear Mr Gott   16 August 1993
Life of Henry David Thoreau will be published on 15 October,
though in a small edition being imported from the States at high
unit cost and with a tiny quota of review copies.
   If you feel it would be of interest, please let me know. It may

seem mean or foolish to ask this, but we publish very unhypable books on a shoestring, and the *Guardian*'s total neglect of the first four titles in the Kinship Library series last autumn was a shattering blow because your paper was one of only three nationals we were relying upon to make the series known. All ignored them. So I am uncertain where the *Guardian* stands on green issues and whether Thoreau is a name to conjure with.

Gott replied that 'the Thoreau sounds a bit marginal, I'm afraid', and continued tellingly:

I'm sorry, too, that we didn't get round to noting your Kinship Library last autumn. The truth is, some parts of the *Guardian* are greener than others. In general, I think it is a mistake for small publishing houses to rely on the benevolence of literary editors.

In the then climate, I had to come to think so too. But what other sources of benevolence are midlist authors and publishers to look to?

So that, more or less, was that. Little was happening on the commercial front and in the field of IT to tempt a would-be independent small publisher of all-too-certain years to struggle on against – far less in attempted affinity with – the ever more time-consuming and nerve-straining complexities of what the wishful-thinking classes myopically define as progress. Justification for Luddite revolt was on all sides. In a hindsight piece in *The Times* in October 1996, Michael Sissons, joint chairman of the literary agency Peters Fraser & Dunlop, bewailed the decline of British publishing from its power and influence in the sixties, the disappearance of leading trade publishers down the maws of the conglomerates, and the increasing control permitted to salesmen and accountants. Publishing had become 'a demoralised industry which has lost its way ... Without exception, the conglomerates have been able to instil neither a sense of loyalty to the firm as a whole, nor stability and self-confidence within their staff ... The result has been disastrous.' He identified 'a handful of publishing houses which are demonstrably well run and well focused, the privately-owned Faber & Faber and John Murray, the new firms Fourth Estate and Orion Weidenfeld, among them'. But already the Orion Publishing Group has been acquired by Hachette, and Fourth Estate by HarperCollins in 2000; while John Murray has been taken over by Hodder Headline. Sissons perceptively concluded that a healthy publishing industry can survive with patience for the long term, respect for the editorial function that is its mainspring, and recognition that subsistence on a diet of best-sellers is a false trail to follow. While much that he wrote was of only marginal relevance to the smallest firms, for whom few literary agents have time, its generalities were undeniable, strengthening my determination to find a home for Centaur beneath some younger, independent, and more flexible wing.

But one other project had been nagging ever since David Farrer's faith in *Anything Within Reason* had been overruled by Secker & Warburg's salesmen. There had seemed to be no point in offering it elsewhere at a time when even established novelists were meeting resistance to midlist fiction. The novel's subtext, though in tune with forward-thinking younger people's concern with the need for more than cosmetic change in a world heading for the termitary, was still ahead of its time for the vehicle of current fiction. Nor was there any point in publishing it myself, either under a pen-name or my own. Second novels (and it would have been seen as such) were, historically, begging for abuse if their predecessors were praised, and for a small non-fiction publisher – of all people – to write and self-publish a second novel, satirical to boot, would in itself have been asking for trouble. So the book had been bottom-drawered in the improbable hope of better days to come, and my writing work went little beyond adding short stories to those being published in the UK and USA by academic and literary journals with a sympathy for – or at least not an arrogant indifference to – the plight of exploited non-humans. Although I have tried to avoid preachifying in fiction prompted by a hatred of human cruelty, and have been reviewed as having succeeded in doing so, I could not see how to make a late-life breakthrough into the jealously guarded province of supposedly serious fiction. In 2001, Ferdinand Mount contributed a witty and discerning article to the *Guardian* on gender differences in fiction. While rightly opposed to novels overtly preaching a moral line, or to be read as a tract against some social abuse, he sees that 'without a moral liveliness running throughout the book [a] truly satisfying novel will be somehow empty'. With a general preference for the work of women novelists, though not for all of them, he regards the more successful males of the species as 'honorary hermaphrodites':

> In all the modern writers I like, even the most caustic ones – especially the most caustic ones – this quality of moral sympathy comes as naturally as a shiver on a cold night. It isn't an effect that

they have striven for, and it isn't in the slightest bit sentimental. They simply take it for granted that this is how you write novels, just as George Eliot and Tolstoy took it for granted.

By contrast, in the case of M[odern] M[ale] N[ovelist], it seems as if this moral sympathy is gradually being bred out of them, so that in the most extreme cases their work feels almost autistic. Far from becoming increasingly sensitive and touchy-feely, the New Man seems to be running short of a female chromosome or two. All the hard work that went into making men understand that their lives would be infinitely richer if they encouraged the female side of their natures has had the opposite effect. I know Graham Greene said that every novelist needs to have an icicle in his heart – but he didn't say they needed the whole bloody fridge.

'Being more or less a man, and incurably given to writing novels', Mount is a welcome addition to the honourable company of hermaphrodites.

What might have been the best solution to the problem of my own unpublished fiction appeared in the person of Jane Inglis, a friend who had shown warming enthusiasm for the Kinship Library and, in her role as a teacher and school librarian, for *The Civilised Alternative*, *Food for a Future*, and *The Extended Circle*, which she welcomed as contributions to the hugely difficult – and inexplicably resisted – process of humane education. As a sideline to chronic workaholism, she had published a few books under the imprint of Oakroyd Press. When she read the typescript of *Anything Within Reason*, she was sufficiently rhapsodic to impress even a verging-on-seventy, disillusioned, struggle-weary publisher-reverted-to-author, fully aware of the creative writer's fragile assumption that a thirsting world cannot possibly be so obtuse as to overlook the quality of his own very special product. I had long admired her conviction, tenacity, and great ability to transfer her compassionate enthusiasms to her classes and her many friends, promoting the humane cause through frequent contributions to the *School Librarian*, and by work in a hospital secure unit, among children in Africa, and wherever she could help the less fortunate. She was one for whom the tag 'too good for this world', if often misapplied, was as close a fit as one could hope to find. Sadly, 'was' is the appropriate tense. In May 1994 Jane published *Anything Within Reason* – as a close collaboration, of course – and for good measure some of my published short stories were put together to appear simultaneously as *Sealskin*

Trousers. But even before that month was out, she faced physical problems that painfully and inexorably led to her death at the age of fifty-three, leaving a husband and two sons.

The search for Centaur's next home continued fitfully, bringing mounting awareness that book publishing, as I had been fortunate enough to know it, was recognised by a diminishing number of would-be entrants. Only two informed, hopeful, but brief discussions with the similar-minded took place. The first was with Martin Eve. Born two year ahead of me, he founded the Merlin Press two years after I started Centaur; sailed his boat to Holland and Scandinavia to call on their booksellers; self-published several books from his seafaring experiences to his political essays; and spoke my language and shared my priorities to a degree that prompted mutual consideration of a publishing link. But illness, which had not helped an earlier partnership with Norman Franklin, returned, and after a remission that enabled him to move to Suffolk and arrange for his firm's future, he died in October 1998, in the month I was able to finalise Centaur's future.

Before then, a hopeful exchange had been with William Rees-Mogg, to whom I had sent a copy of *Three Prose Works* on reading his article in the Boxing Day 1996 issue of *The Times*, in which he lamented the unavailability of Aubrey's *Miscellanies*. I kept no copy of the note accompanying the book, but it was to the effect that after a discouraging year seeking a suitable buyer for Centaur, I was entering the new one in the dismal knowledge that the existence of the *Miscellanies*-containing Centaur edition was not even known to him, and that he might as well have one of the under-appreciated copies before they passed into other and possibly less appreciative hands. Rees-Mogg's reply ended:

> I had no idea that the Centaur Press might be open to disposal. It is just possible that it might fit in with Pickering & Chatto, which I started in 1983. We publish a rather similar list but basically concentrating on direct sales to academic libraries. I enclose a current catalogue in case it would interest you. If you are wanting to dispose of the Centaur Press, it might be worth having a chat about it. It seems to me more likely that there would be a fit with another independent publisher rather than a conglomerate.

I responded enthusiastically, though until that day my cloistered rural life had denied me knowledge of his publishing connection. But a fellow director, it transpired, had plans for taking P. & C. in a rather different direction, and it was decided that the number of Centaur titles that would be saleable to their network was too small.

D[isposal]-day came with a scarcely-prompted suddenness that would have been no surprise to my departed mother with her faith in the efficacy of submission to a Higher Will. The editor and publisher Mark Cohen, Jack's son, a man as kindly and helpful as his father, wrote in March 1998 to say he had passed on the Centaur catalogue to a former colleague, Dan Leavey, whose distribution firm, BRAD, represented and warehoused a number of smaller publishers. At the London Book Fair, Dan had introduced Mark to the co-owner of Open Gate Press, Jeannie Cohen, who was seeking an opportunity to attain instant growth for her interesting small imprint. An Oxford classics graduate and teacher, Jeannie spent a day with us in Sussex on 17 April, soon proving that she had been worth waiting for. Intelligent and charming, she came across instantly as straightforward and uncluttered by the half-truths and devious nonsense so common to the negotiation process. Like me, she worked from home – fittingly, for someone of her academic bent, in West Hampstead's Achilles Road – not many stone throws from where Centaur was born forty-four years before on the far side of the Heath. She had a tolerant husband in software, but was running OGP on a shoestring, convinced as I had been of the need to finance its future from the profits of the present. What mainly persuaded me to accept the somewhat nominal sum for the transfer, however, was her interest in, and determination to continue, both the classical and humane education sides of the list. By my holding back from the sale the three-volume Ford's *Handbook for Travellers in Spain*, now distributed under the Pythian Books imprint along with some tail ends of titles that did not fit the OGP list, the value was adjusted to suit both parties; and as part of the deal I continued to hold the bulk of the Centaur stock that was surplus to BRAD's immediate needs, and would incur impossible charges if housed on their premises.

It was a very happy negotiation, and a quick one. Agreement was reached by 6 June, and with the splendid help of our five grandsons over my seventy-fourth birthday weekend in July, a great transfer of stock from stables and lofts to its pick-up point in the mercifully capacious garage was achieved without a broken packet or a damaged corner. Oliver, William, Matthew, Giles and Toby trolleyed boxes of books up the path from a stable in the kitchen garden, and carried packets of them from the main loft in the house. Victoria, our only granddaughter, too young to be a serious transporter of books, supervised the sumptuous tea and made felt the ordered and diplomatic presence of one clearly destined to introduce her brothers and cousins to the Power of Woman.

To celebrate the agreement with Open Gate, and wish them well, I asked Roger Smith, whose dust-jacket for *Sealskin Trousers* had been much admired, to draw for Jeannie a friendly if slightly apprehensive centaur in a paddock, approaching with hailing hand a wide-flung gate beyond which a view of Hampstead and a 'To the Heath' signpost helped convey a blend of gratitude and nervous anticipation.

It is quite a responsibility – to oneself as well as to others – to pass on a lifework, however modestly achieved. Would Open Gate take over the reins with success and satisfaction? Would the list's character be retained? Changed? Abandoned? It would be good to feel that its aims and image remained in the book reader's consciousness. I recall the Oxford academic's question to a colleague worried about the thrust and lucidity of a phrase proposed for his speech: 'Can you pat it on the wing?'

Patting centaurs can be another matter.

Envoi

Centaurs, mythology informs us, dwelt in the mountains of Arcadia. The general ruck of these creatures, given more to human than to equine failings, were a nasty bunch that did little to promote the idealised view of their harsh mountainous terrain as being a pastoral paradise of nymphs and shepherds. A few individual centaurs, it is claimed, showed signs of developing some of the more agreeable human traits, though not enough to merit the elevation of Chiron, allegedly the best of them, who ascended to the heavens when Zeus placed him among the stars of Sagittarius.

The later development of the species seems to have gone unrecorded, but the creature is seen by some, of evolutionary bent, as the symbol of humankind's ability to slough off the defects of its animal nature, and rise to better things. It was in the somewhat thin hope of pushing this process along a little that the Centaur Press imprint was created. Its contribution may have been a mere drop in the firmament, but – willy nilly – we leave this world a fractionally better or worse place for having passed through it, and if to hope that one's own drop has been more positive than negative is to invite the charge of political incorrectness, or worse, then so be it.

But it is sobering to note that in the last year of the old millennium, 116,415 books were published in the UK alone, nearly six times more than in the year I started Centaur Press. If the state of the world, or even the nation, had improved sixfold in those forty-six years, one could construct a cheerful hypothesis. As it is, the best explanation may be that the wrong books have been studied. In fact, I am sure of it. But it will be a crumb of some comfort, as one slips from one's perch, to know that a few of those Centaur titles have been acknowledged as having had a beneficial influence, even within my own lifetime, and I certainly have every reason to depart with gratitude for having been able to make a living by the congenial task of publishing works that on the whole have justified their existence. If only modest promptings to the civilising of civilisation, they did little harm, widened some horizons, and may even be remembered here and there.

After all, books – for both authors and their publishers – make a more revealing memorial than a headstone, and don't have to be read in the rain.

Index

Index

Where the Rainbow Ends, 132
Wherry, Alan, 276
White, J. Alan, 43
White, John Foster, 106
Who's Who, 35, 195, 249
Wickham, Anna, 172
Wig and Pen Club, 250
Wilde, Oscar, 162
Wilentz, Eli, 74
Wiley, John (distributors), 282, 292
Willetts, Paul, 170
Willey, Basil, 115
William Kimber (publishers), 47
Williams, Duncan, 210–16, 223
Williams and Norgate, 17–18, 20, 168,
  173–4
Williamson, Henry, 52, 237–8
Williamson, Hugh Ross, 101
Wills, E. H. R., 211–13
Wilson, Colin, 51–2
Wilson, Frank Avray, 32–3, 273–4
Wilton, Penelope, 245
Window, The (magazine), 29
Winterson Company, 62
Winsten, Stephen, 249, 268
Wodehouse, P. G., 238
Wolfenden Report, 29
Wollstonecroft, Mary, 204
Wombles of Wimbledon Common,
  239

Wonderful World of Period Furniture,
  274
Works of M. P. Shiel, The
  (bibliography), 165, 170, 194
World Trade Center, 269
Writer's Handbook, The, 293
Writings on an Ethical Life, 271
Wynne-Tyson, Caroline ('Tilly'), 17, 19,
  25–6, 48, 53–4, 72, 78, 83, 99,
  123, 174, 177, 208, 210
Wynne-Tyson, Esmé, 84, 132–47, 206,
  245, 267. As Esmé Wynne, 43
Wynne-Tyson, Jennifer Mary (née
  Tyson), 27, 53–4, 112, 115–16,
  121, 123, 221, 246, 260, 263, 266,
  282
Wynne-Tyson, Linden Charles, 133–4,
  206, 221, 231–2, 239, 247
Wynne-Tyson, Susan, 53, 78, 116, 179,
  208
Wynne, Walter, 161–2

X-One-Design, 221

Yacht Racing, 121
Young, Andrew, 200
Young Idea, The, 134, 284
Young Men Are Coming, The, 186

Zwemmer's Bookshop, 16, 38

By the same author

ACCOMMODATION WANTED

GRIN AND BEAR IT

BEHIND THE SMILING MOON (as Michel Fourest)

SQUARE PEG (as Jeremy Pitt)

DON'T LOOK AND YOU'LL FIND HER (as Jeremy Pitt)

THE CIVILISED ALTERNATIVE

FOOD FOR A FUTURE

SO SAY BANANA BIRD

THE EXTENDED CIRCLE

MARVELLOUS PARTY (a play)

PUBLISHING YOUR OWN BOOK

ANYTHING WITHIN REASON

SEALSKIN TROUSERS (short stories)